Emotion, Affective Practices, and the Past in the Present

Emotion, Affective Practices, and the Past in the Present is a response to debates in the humanities and social sciences about the use of emotion. This timely and unique book explores the ways emotion is embroiled and used in contemporary engagements with the past, particularly in contexts such as heritage sites, museums, commemorations, political rhetoric and ideology, debates over issues of social memory, and touristic uses of heritage sites.

Including contributions from academics and practitioners in a range of countries, the book reviews significant and conflicting academic debates on the nature and expression of affect and emotion. As a whole, the book makes an argument for a pragmatic understanding of affect and, in doing so, outlines Wetherell's concept of affective practice, a concept utilised in most of the chapters in this book. Since debates about affect and emotion can often be confusing and abstract, the book aims to clarify these debates and, through the use of case studies, draw out their implications for theory and practice within heritage and museum studies.

Emotion, Affective Practices, and the Past in the Present should be essential reading for students, academics, and professionals in the fields of heritage and museum studies. The book will also be of interest to those in other disciplines, such as social psychology, education, archaeology, tourism studies, cultural studies, media studies, anthropology, sociology, and history.

Laurajane Smith is Professor and Director of the Centre for Heritage and Museum Studies in the School of Archaeology and Anthropology at the Australian National University.

Margaret Wetherell is Professor of Social Psychology in the School of Psychology at the University of Auckland, New Zealand, and Emerita Professor in Social Sciences at the Open University, UK.

Gary Campbell is an independent researcher based in Canberra, Australia, and is affiliated with the Centre for Heritage and Museum Studies at the Australian National University.

Key Issues in Cultural Heritage
Series Editors: William Logan and Laurajane Smith

Also in the series:

Urban Heritage, Development and Sustainability
Sophia Labadi and William Logan

Managing Heritage in Africa
Webber Ndoro, Shadreck Chirikure and Janette Deacon

Intellectual Property, Cultural Property and Intangible Cultural Heritage
Christoph Antons and William Logan

Gender and Heritage
Wera Grahn and Ross Wilson

Cultural Heritage and the Future
Cornelius Holtorf and Anders Högberg

World Heritage and Sustainable Development
Peter Bille Larsen, Giovanni Boccardi and William Logan

Safeguarding Intangible Heritage
Natsuko Akagawa and Laurajane Smith

Emotion, Affective Practices, and the Past in the Present
Laurajane Smith, Margaret Wetherell and Gary Campbell

World Heritage and Sustainable Development
New Directions in World Heritage Management
Peter Bille Larsen and William Logan

For more information on the series, please visit www.routledge.com/Key-Issues-in-Cultural-Heritage/book-series/KICH

Emotion, Affective Practices, and the Past in the Present

Edited by Laurajane Smith,
Margaret Wetherell and
Gary Campbell

LONDON AND NEW YORK

First published 2018
by Routledge
2 Park Square, Milton Park, Abingdon, Oxon OX14 4RN

and by Routledge
711 Third Avenue, New York, NY 10017

Routledge is an imprint of the Taylor & Francis Group, an informa business

© 2018 selection and editorial matter, Laurajane Smith, Margaret Wetherell and
Gary Campbell; individual chapters, the contributors

The right of Laurajane Smith, Margaret Wetherell and Gary Campbell to be identified
as the authors of the editorial material, and of the authors for their individual chapters,
has been asserted in accordance with sections 77 and 78 of the Copyright, Designs
and Patents Act 1988.

All rights reserved. No part of this book may be reprinted or reproduced or utilised
in any form or by any electronic, mechanical, or other means, now known or
hereafter invented, including photocopying and recording, or in any information
storage or retrieval system, without permission in writing from the publishers.

Trademark notice: Product or corporate names may be trademarks or registered trademarks,
and are used only for identification and explanation without intent to infringe.

British Library Cataloguing-in-Publication Data
A catalogue record for this book is available from the British Library

Library of Congress Cataloging-in-Publication Data
A catalogue record has been requested for this book

ISBN: 978-0-815-37002-4 (hbk)
ISBN: 978-1-138-57929-3 (pbk)
ISBN: 978-1-351-25096-2 (ebk)

Typeset in Times New Roman
by Out of House Publishing

Contents

List of illustrations	viii
List of contributors	x
Series Editors' foreword	xviii

1 Introduction: Affective heritage practices 1
MARGARET WETHERELL, LAURAJANE SMITH AND
GARY CAMPBELL

PART I
Commemoration and remembering 23

**2 Labour of love and devotion? The search for the lost soldiers
of Russia** 25
JOHANNA DAHLIN

**3 Troubling heritage: intimate pasts and public memories at
Derry/Londonderry's 'Temple'** 39
MARGO SHEA

4 Commemoration, affective practice and the difficult histories of war 56
AMY MCKERNAN AND JULIE MCLEOD

**5 Constructing heritage through subjectivity: Museum of Broken
Relationships** 70
ŽELJKA MIKLOŠEVIĆ AND DARKO BABIĆ

6 The Battle of Orgreave (1984) 85
TOBY JULIFF

vi Contents

PART II
Belonging and exclusion 103

7 Apologising for past wrongs: emotion–reason rhetoric in
political discourse 105
MARTHA AUGOUSTINOS, BRIANNE HASTIE AND
PETA CALLAGHAN

8 Experiencing mixed emotions in the museum: empathy, affect,
and memory in visitors' responses to histories of migration 124
RHIANNON MASON, ARETI GALANI, KATHERINE LLOYD
AND JOANNE SAYNER

9 Coming undone: protocols of emotion in Canadian human
rights museology 149
JENNIFER CLAIRE ROBINSON

10 Touring the post-conflict city: negotiating affects during
Belfast's black cab mural tours 163
KATIE MARKHAM

11 Performing affection, constructing heritage? Civil and political
mobilisations around the Ottoman legacy in Bulgaria 179
IVO STRAHILOV AND SLAVKA KARAKUSHEVA

PART III
Learning, teaching and engaging 195

12 Understanding the emotional regimes of reconciliation in
engagements with 'difficult' heritage 197
MICHALINOS ZEMBYLAS

13 Affective practices of learning at the museum: children's
critical encounters with the past 213
DIANNE MULCAHY AND ANDREA WITCOMB

14 White guilt and shame: students' emotional reactions to
digital stories of race in a South African classroom 230
DANIELA GACHAGO, VIVIENNE BOZALEK
AND DICK NG'AMBI

Contents   vii

15 Settler–Indigenous relationships and the emotional regime
    of empathy in Australian history school textbooks in times
    of reconciliation   246
    ANGÉLIQUE STASTNY

16 'Head and heart' responses to Treaty education in Aotearoa
    New Zealand: feeling the timeline of colonisation   265
    INGRID HUYGENS

17 Raw emotion: the *Living Memory* module at three sites
    of practice   281
    CELMARA POCOCK, MARION STELL AND
    GERALDINE MATE

    Index   304

List of illustrations

2.1	Uncovering the *politruk*'s glasses	26
2.2	Searching and surveying in the Sinyavino area	30
2.3	Finding an icon	32
2.4	Showing the 'beautiful' soldier on the Sinyavino field	35
5.1	View of permanent display, Museum of Broken Relationships, Zagreb	73
5.2	My last 2006 checkbook with my name and my ex's name on it, Museum of Broken Relationships, Zagreb	73
5.3	A caterpillar 'Timunaki', museum object, Museum of Broken Relationships, Zagreb	74
5.4	A hamburger toy, Museum of Broken Relationships, Zagreb	74
5.5	My mother's suicide note, Museum of Broken Relationships, Zagreb	78
5.6	A list of 10 reasons to stay, museum object, Museum of Broken Relationships, Zagreb	78
8.1	Cinema section of display and interpretive panel featuring the story of Lena Vineberg	129
8.2	'Leaving home' suitcase interactive	130
13.1	Recreated cottages with laneway in the distance, Little Lon display in *The Melbourne Story*, Melbourne Museum Photographer: Ben Healley. Source: Museums Victoria	220
13.2	Interior of poorer cottage, Little Lon display in *The Melbourne Story*, Melbourne Museum Photographer: Ben Healley. Source: Museums Victoria	220
13.3	Interior of more aspirational cottage, Little Lon display in *The Melbourne Story*, Melbourne Museum Photographer: Ben Healley. Source: Museums Victoria	221
15.1	Occurrences of the most common themes used to describe Indigenous people across the textbooks	251
15.2	Occurrences of the most common themes used to describe Indigenous people in each textbook	252

15.3	Occurrences of the most common themes used to describe settlers across the textbooks	254
15.4	Occurrences of the most common themes used to describe settlers in each textbook	255
15.5	Authorship of sources on settler–Indigenous relationships in textbooks	256
15.6	Occurrences of empathetic practices of embodiment in textbooks according to their targeted 'embodied' individual	258

List of contributors

Martha Augoustinos is Professor of Psychology at the University of Adelaide, Australia. Martha has published widely in the field of social psychology and discourse, in particular on the nature of racial discourse in Australia. This has included an analysis of how Indigenous Australians are constructed in everyday conversation and political rhetoric. More recently this work has extended to discourse on asylum seekers and refugees. She is co-author of *Social Cognition: An Integrated Introduction* (3rd edn, Sage, 2014) with Iain Walker and Ngaire Donaghue and co-editor with Kate Reynolds of *Understanding Prejudice, Racism and Social Conflict* (Sage, 2001).

Darko Babić is Assistant Professor and acting Chair of the Sub-Department of Museology, Faculty of Humanities and Social Sciences (University of Zagreb, Croatia). He holds a PhD in Museum/Heritage Studies. After earning his MA (Ethnology and Information Sciences) he gained experience working as project manager on international projects, as an organiser of museum/heritage conferences, as an archivist and as assistant on national TV. He is active in contributing to the advancement of the museum/ heritage profession, serving as Chairman of ICOM Croatia and acting Chairman of ICOM-ICTOP, as well as being a member of the Supervisory Committee to the European Association for Heritage Interpretation. His research interests include topics related to museums/heritage and development, management and interpretation. He also has working experience on EU projects and as a freelance consultant for the museum/heritage sector including non-governmental organisations.

Vivienne Bozalek is a Professor of Social Work and the Director of Teaching and Learning at the University of the Western Cape, South Africa. She holds a PhD from Utrecht University. Her research interests and publications include the political ethics of care and social justice, posthumanism and feminist new materialisms, innovative pedagogical practices in higher education, and post-qualitative and participatory methodologies. She has co-edited four books: *Community, Self and Identity: Educating South African*

List of contributors   xi

Students for Citizenship with Brenda Leibowitz, Ronelle Carolissen and other colleagues; *Discerning Hope in Educational Practices* with Brenda Leibowitz, Ronelle Carolissen and Megan Boler; *Activity Theory, Authentic Learning and Emerging Technologies* with Jan Herrington, Joanne Hardman, Dick Ng'ambi and Denise Wood; and *Theorising Learning to Teach in Higher Education* with Brenda Leibowitz and Peter Kahn.

Peta Callaghan is a Research Fellow with the School of Psychology at the University of Adelaide, Australia. Peta's primary research interests include how ideological and political agendas set the tone for public discourse on controversial social matters. Peta's research work has included the critical analysis of public, scientific and political discourse on a number of contentious policy and social issues, such as climate change, disinvestment from publicly funded health technologies and race relations. Peta's current research aims to extend traditional academic thinking on prejudice by exploring the ways in which prejudice is constituted and practised in everyday settings.

Gary Campbell is an independent researcher based in Canberra, Australia and is affiliated with the Centre for Heritage and Museum Studies at the Australian National University. He has previously edited (with Laurajane Smith and Paul A. Shackel) *Heritage, Labour and the Working Classes* (Routledge, 2011) and has published papers in the heritage field on emotion and affect, de-industrialisation and working-class identity. He was active in the establishment of the Association of Critical Heritage Studies, having co-written its Manifesto.

Johanna Dahlin is a Postdoctoral Fellow at the Department of Culture Studies, Linköping University, Sweden. Her main research interests are heritage and memory work in a Russian context, and this more broadly translates into an interest in social movements, land and place. This is reflected in her current research concerned with how common resources are enclosed and privatised, focusing on the processes and relations involved in mineral extraction. While working in an interdisciplinary setting, her background is in social anthropology and she has a preference for ethnographic fieldwork as a way of uncovering the role of the past in the present.

Daniela Gachago is a senior lecturer in the Centre for Innovative Educational Technology at the Cape Peninsula University of Technology, South Africa. Her research interests lie in the use of emerging technologies to improve teaching and learning in HE. She holds a PhD in Education from the University of Cape Town, where she explored the role of emotions in transforming students' engagement across difference, and a Masters in Adult Education from the University of Botswana. She has published in local and international journals and is part of a range of inter-institutional research projects currently focusing on exploring socially just and decolonialising pedagogies in HE.

xii List of contributors

Areti Galani is a lecturer in Museum and Heritage Studies in the department of Media, Culture, Heritage, at Newcastle University, UK. She holds qualifications both in Museology and in Computing Science and has curated projects in Greece and the UK. Areti uses people-centred methodologies in the study and design of digital technologies for the cultural sector. She co-led the 'Rock Art on Mobile Phones' project (AHRC-funded), which used empathetic design to create three web apps for rock art sites in rural areas in the UK. Areti has also led the design of 'calm technology' digital interactive installations for Seven Stories and the Discovery Museum, UK. She is currently an investigator in the Horizon 2020-funded project CoHERE (2016–2019), which examines the role of heritage in the construction of European identity. Her research in CoHERE investigates the role of digital practice in fostering dialogue around heritage in the context of European identity/identities.

Brianne Hastie is an Adjunct Senior Lecturer with the School of Psychology, Social Work and Social Policy at the University of South Australia. Her research interests include prejudice and discrimination, social justice and discourse analysis.

Ingrid Huygens is a New Zealand-born child of Dutch parents with a longstanding interest in social and cultural issues. Her Master's thesis researched New Zealanders' reactions to Maori, Dutch and British accents. Trained as a community psychologist, she has worked in health, feminist, mental health and community development fields, and began work as a Pakeha Treaty educator in 1989. She has written many international papers and chapters, and is a co-author of *Tangata Tiriti – Treaty People* (2006) aimed at new migrants. She is currently a research leader at Waikato Institute of Technology, and continues to work as an educator around the country.

Toby Juliff is Lecturer in Critical and Theoretical Studies and coordinator of the Visual Arts Honours programme at The Victorian College of the Arts, University of Melbourne, Australia. He has published on contemporary British art, in particular on its use of heritage models (IJTA, 2013). Other published works consider sculpture and performance in the context of the contemporary monument. His current project examines the ethics of the re-presentation of art exhibitions of the past.

Slavka Karakusheva is a doctoral candidate in Cultural Anthropology at Sofia University St. Kliment Ohridski, Bulgaria. Her dissertation focuses on the role of social media in constructing identities and establishing transnational connections and networks among members of the Turkish community from Bulgaria settled on both sides of the Bulgarian–Turkish border. She is interested in nationalism, migration, anthropology of media, memory studies and cultural heritage.

Katherine Lloyd is a Lecturer in Museum Studies in the Humanities Advanced Technology and Information Institute (HATII) at the University of Glasgow, UK. She has held research and teaching positions at the International Centre for Cultural and Heritage Studies at Newcastle University, the University of Edinburgh and Heriot–Watt University, UK. She was a Research Associate on two EU-funded projects, Critical Heritages: performing and representing identities in Europe (CoHERE) and MeLa: European museums in an age of migrations. Her interests include heritage, identity, belonging, place, migration, co-production and digital participation. Her publications include *Museums, Migration and Identity in Europe* and *'Placing' Europe in the Museum: People(s), Places, Identities* (with Christopher Whitehead, Susannah Eckersley and Rhiannon Mason). She is a Facilitator of the UK Chapter of the Association of Critical Heritage Studies.

Amy McKernan is a lecturer and researcher in the International Baccalaureate programme at the Melbourne Graduate School of Education, the University of Melbourne, Australia. Since qualifying as a secondary history teacher, she has taught and lectured in the sociology of education at the University of Melbourne and undertaken research on learning in history museums. Her PhD research examined the ways in which several Australian museums represent and educate visitors about contested and confronting Australian histories of trauma, violence and injustice. Her research interests focus on the affective dimensions of learning and representation in museums, along with the ways in which museums can be mobilised to support learning for social inclusion and cultural recognition.

Julie McLeod is Professor at Melbourne Graduate School of Education, Australia and an Australian Research Council Future Fellow (2012–2016). She is Deputy Director of the Melbourne Social Equity Institute and a former editor of the international journal *Gender and Education*. She has taught widely across programmes in gender studies, sociology of education and qualitative research methods. Her research is in the history and sociology of education, with a focus on curriculum, youth, gender and inequality. Her books include *Rethinking Youth Wellbeing: Critical Perspectives*, co-edited with Katie Wright (Springer, 2015); *The Promise of the New and Genealogies of Education Reform*, co-edited with Katie Wright (Routledge, 2015); *Researching Social Change: Qualitative Approaches*, with Rachel Thomson (Sage, 2009); and *Making Modern Lives: Subjectivity, Schooling, and Social Change*, with Lyn Yates (SUNY Press, 2006).

Katie Markham is an ESRC-funded PhD student at the University of Leeds, UK where she is writing a thesis provisionally entitled 'Memory and Empathy in Post-Troubles Heritage'. Her research subjects the study of affect and culture to the critical gazes of postcolonial, critical race and queer theories, combining these with ethnographic methods to explore the limits of empathy in relation to post-conflict culture in Northern Ireland. Katie is a contributor to the *Irish Times* microsite 'Re-thinking the Hunger Strikes', and co-founder of the ESRC-funded Critical Race and Ethnicities Network.

Rhiannon Mason is Professor of Heritage and Cultural Studies in the department of Media, Culture, Heritage at Newcastle University, UK. Rhiannon's research and teaching interests encompass critical museology and heritage studies, cultural theory, identity in all its many forms, nationalism and migration. Her research focuses on understanding the role of heritage and memory institutions, practices and discourses in mediating public understandings of people's histories, cultures and identities. She was a co-investigator on the EU-funded project MeLa: European museums in an age of migrations (2014–2017) and is currently a co-investigator in the Horizon 2020-funded project Critical Heritages: performing and representing identities in Europe (CoHERE) (2016–2019), which examines the role of heritage in the construction of European identity.

Geraldine Mate is a Principal Curator in the Cultures and Histories Program at Queensland Museum, Australia. Her research interests encapsulate broad reflections on cultural landscapes in archaeology, the interpretation of industrial cultural heritage and labour history, considerations of social/industrial interplay in historical landscapes and the relationship between people and technology.

Željka Mikloševic is a postgraduate researcher at the Department of Information and Communication Sciences, Faculty of Humanities and Social Sciences, University of Zagreb, Croatia. She also teaches museum- and heritage-related courses within the Graduate Programme in Museology and Heritage Management. She obtained her MA in Art History, after which she worked for four years as curator at a local history museum, where she both managed an historical art collection and was in charge of educational programmes. She obtained her PhD in Museology from the University of Zagreb. Her research interests relate to museums' construction of discourses in and through different media (physical and digital) and visitors' meaning-making practices.

Dianne Mulcahy is a Senior Lecturer in the Melbourne Graduate School of Education at the University of Melbourne, Australia. Her published work in Education concerns the policy and practice of educators' professional formation and development. Her recent research activity has centred on capturing the complexity of children's learning within museums and 'innovative' learning environments in schools, with particular attention to the materiality of this learning, including its embodied and affective dynamics. Her publications include over 50 refereed journal articles and conference papers, three monographs and 12 book chapters.

List of contributors   xv

Dick Ng'ambi is an Associate Professor and a leading researcher in emerging technologies and digital practices in resource-constrained environments. He is the Stream Leader of the postgraduate programmes in Educational Technology and convener of the doctoral programme in the School of Education at the University of Cape Town (UCT), South Africa. He is also the founder and project director of the Educational Technology Inquiry Lab (ETILAB).

Celmara Pocock is a Senior Lecturer in Anthropology and Australian Indigenous Studies at the University of Southern Queensland, Australia and an Honorary Fellow at The University of Queensland. Her research interests encompass human relationships with the environment, heritage and museum studies, and heritage interpretation and tourism.

Jennifer Claire Robinson has, for the last decade, worked closely with community elders, artists, performers, curators, educators and researchers at several galleries and museums in areas ranging from collections management, archival research, education and public programming to curatorial projects. Jennifer is currently a PhD candidate in Visual Anthropology and Materiality and a Research Affiliate in the Residential and Indian Day School Art Research Program at the University of Victoria, Canada on the Coast Salish territories of Vancouver Island. Her current research focuses on how issues of rights and justice are researched, curated and programmed through Canadian cultural heritage institutions.

Joanne Sayner is Senior Lecturer in Cultural and Heritage Studies in the department of Media, Culture, Heritage at Newcastle University, UK. She specialises in memory studies and gender. She has published widely on the politics of remembering in contemporary Germany. Her most recent monograph is *Reframing Antifascism: Memory, Genre and the Life Writings of Greta Kuckhoff* (Palgrave, 2013). Her current projects include 'Silence, Memory and Empathy in Museums and at Historic Sites' and 'The Significance of the Centenary'.

Margo Shea is Visiting Fellow in the Collaborative for Southern Appalachian Studies, an initiative between Sewanee: The University of the South and Yale University, and is Assistant Professor of Public History at Salem State University, USA. Her scholarship examines the connections between place, memory and heritage and the theory and practice of public and oral history. She has implemented numerous community historical interpretation and public curation projects. Her scholarship examines the connections between place, memory and heritage and the theory and practice of public and oral history.

Laurajane Smith is professor and Director of the Centre of Heritage and Museum Studies, and Head of the School of Archaeology and Anthropology, at the Australian National University. She has authored

Uses of Heritage (Routledge, 2006) and *Archaeological Theory and the Politics of Cultural Heritage* (Routledge, 2004), and co-authored *Heritage, Communities and Archaeology*, with Emma Waterton (Bloomsbury, 2009). Her edited books include *Heritage, Labour and the Working Classes*, with Paul A. Shackel and Gary Campbell (2011); *Representing Enslavement and Abolition in Museums*, with Geoffrey Cubitt, Ross Wilson and Kalliopi Fouseki (2011); and *Intangible Heritage*, with Natsuko Akagawa (2009), all with Routledge. She is editor of the *International Journal of Heritage Studies* and co-general editor (with William Logan) of the Routledge series Key Issues in Cultural Heritage.

Angélique Stastny completed her PhD at the School of Social and Political Sciences at the University of Melbourne, Australia. Her areas of interest are settler colonialism, comparative politics, education and emotions. Her current PhD thesis explores the ways in which the historical and political relationships between settlers and Indigenous people are taught in schools in Australia and Kanaky/New Caledonia. She is affiliated to the ARC Centre of Excellence for the History of Emotions.

Marion Stell is an Honorary Research Fellow in the School of Historical and Philosophical Inquiry at The University of Queensland, Australia. She has developed the use of affective themes in museum interpretation and historical practice since 2000.

Ivo Strahilov is a doctoral candidate in Cultural Heritage at Sofia University St. Kliment Ohridski, Bulgaria. He has a background in political and cultural studies, and his research interests include contemporary uses of heritage, and intangible cultural heritage with an emphasis on masquerades and carnivals.

Margaret Wetherell is Professor of Social Psychology at the University of Auckland, New Zealand. Her main focus has been on developing discourse theory and methods for social research applied to topics such as men and masculinities, racism in settler societies and citizen identities. Her books include *Discourse and Social Psychology*, with Jonathan Potter (Sage, 1987); *Mapping the Language of Racism*, with Jonathan Potter (Columbia University Press, 1992); *Men in Perspective*, with Nigel Edley (Prentice Hall, 1995); *Discourse Theory and Practice* and *Discourse as Data*, with Stephanie Taylor and Simeon Yates (Sage, 2001); and *The Sage Handbook of Identities*, with Chandra Talpade Mohanty (Sage, 2010). Her recent work focuses on the problems posed by the study of emotion (*Affect and Emotion*, Sage, 2012). She is a former Chief Editor of the *British Journal of Social Psychology*, and from 2003 to 2008 was Director of the UK ESRC Identities and Social Action Programme.

Andrea Witcomb is Professor of Cultural Heritage and Museum Studies at Deakin University in Melbourne, Australia. Her research is attentive to the potential of museums and heritage sites to provide opportunities for cross-cultural encounters. Her work focuses on the interpretation of difficult histories. This leads her not only into a study of the politics of representation but also into an exploration of which curatorial exhibition strategies can enable a questioning of well-established narratives about the past and collective identities. Her books include *Reimagining the Museum: Beyond the Mausoleum* (Routledge, 2003); *South Pacific Museums: An Experiment in Culture*, with Chris Healy (Monash Epress, 2006; 2012); *From the Barracks to the Burrup: The National Trust in Western Australia*, with Kate Gregory (UNSW Press, 2010); and, with Kylie Message, *Museum Theory* as part of the International Handbooks of Museum Studies series edited by Sharon Macdonald and Helen Rees-Leahy (Wiley Blackwell, 2015).

Michalinos Zembylas is Professor of Educational Theory and Curriculum Studies at the Open University of Cyprus. He is Visiting Professor and Research Fellow at the Institute for Reconciliation and Social Justice, University of the Free State, South Africa, and Research Associate at Nelson Mandela University (NMU) – Chair, Critical Studies in Higher Education Transformation. He has written extensively on emotion and affect in relation to social justice pedagogies, intercultural and peace education, human rights education and citizenship education. His recent books include *Psychologized Language in Education: Denaturalizing a Regime of Truth*, with Z. Bekerman (Springer, 2017), and *Socially Just Pedagogies: Posthumanist, Feminist and Materialist Perspectives in Higher Education*, co-edited with V. Bozalek, R. Braidotti and T. Shefer (Bloomsbury, 2018). In 2016, he received the Distinguished Researcher Award in 'Social Sciences and Humanities' from the Cyprus Research Promotion Foundation.

Series Editors' foreword

The interdisciplinary field of Heritage Studies is now well established in many parts of the world. It differs from earlier scholarly and professional activities that focused narrowly on the architectural or archaeological preservation of monuments and sites. Such activities remain important, especially as modernisation and globalisation lead to new developments that threaten natural environments, archaeological sites, historic urban landscapes, traditional buildings and arts and crafts. But they are subsumed within the new field that sees 'heritage' as a social and political construct encompassing all those places, artefacts and cultural expressions inherited from the past which, because they are seen to reflect and validate our identity as nations, communities, families and even individuals, are worthy of some form of respect and protection.

Heritage results from a selection process, often government-initiated and supported by official regulation; it is not the same as history, although this, too, has its own elements of selectivity. Heritage can be used in positive ways to give a sense of community to disparate groups and individuals or to create jobs on the basis of cultural tourism. It can be actively used by governments and communities to foster respect for cultural and social diversity, and to challenge prejudice and misrecognition. But it can also be used by governments in less benign ways, to reshape public attitudes in line with undemocratic political agendas or even to rally people against their neighbours in civil and international wars, ethnic cleansing and genocide. In this way there is a real connection between heritage, social justice and human rights.

Heritage protection does not depend alone on top-down interventions by governments or the expert actions of heritage industry professionals, but must involve local communities and communities of interest. It is critical that the values and practices of communities, together with traditional management systems where such exist, are understood, respected and incorporated in management plans and policy documents so that communities feel a sense of 'ownership' of their heritage and take a leading role in sustaining it into the future.

This series of books canvasses the key issues dealt with in the new Heritage Studies. It seeks to identify key interdisciplinary debates within Heritage Studies and to explore how they impact not only on the practices of heritage management and conservation, but also on the processes of production, consumption and engagement with heritage in its many and varied forms.

William S. Logan
Laurajane Smith

Chapter 1

Introduction
Affective heritage practices

Margaret Wetherell, Laurajane Smith and Gary Campbell

Introduction

Although a consensus is emerging around the importance of emotion in constituting heritage, dilemmas about how to theorise and investigate affect are much less resolved. Emotion is everywhere – in the curl of a lip and a shrug of the shoulders at an exhibition of slavery, it is there in the will to commemorate and curate, in stifled sobs at remembrance ceremonies, in fired-up family genealogists, commitments to nationalism, the discomfort felt as tightly held assumptions are questioned, and in the sticky patina of fingerprints on popular glass cases in museums. Emotion is pervasive, but it is also difficult to think about, and in particular it is challenging to develop viable interdisciplinary perspectives that can recognise emotion's psychobiological groundings while exploring its social organisation. Emotion, feeling and affect are also difficult to define. Traditionally, affect is the more generic term, highlighting the embodied state and the initial registering of events in bodies and minds. Feeling refers to qualia and the subjective phenomenological experience, while emotion refers to the processing and packaging of affect in familiar cultural categories such as anger, grief, schadenfreude, etc. But even these conventional distinctions and definitions raise issues. They seem to suggest a kind of dubious chronology, for instance affect first and emotion second, or bodies first and the making of meaning second, when the initial registering and the generative processes of affect/emotion are always already embodied and semiotic. Affect and emotion are flowing, dynamic, recursive and profoundly contextual, challenging static and neat formulations.

It is perhaps enough to say that the contributors to this volume[1] are interested in phenomena that have some psychological presence, involving mild to strong degrees of turbulence in bodies and minds. We are all interested in the fact that emotion is action-oriented; it pushes people to do things. We value Margaret Archer's (2000, 2007) observation that emotions are part of commentaries on things that are important to us, a point also elaborated by Sayer (2005). Emotions are a form of evaluative judgement, inextricably linked to cognition, sometimes consciously so, or sometimes non-conscious and

2 Margaret Wetherell et al.

drawing on the neurological reinforcements of prior experience and learning (Marcus, Neuman and MacKuen 2000; see also Prinz 2004). Crucially for heritage studies and critical social research, emotion is also historically and culturally contingent, and bound up in power relations and politics. These formulations are strong starting places to begin thinking about what is it that emotion and affect actually do in heritage and museum contexts. How might an emphasis on emotion encourage new questions, or answer old ones in useful ways?

We suggest that attention to emotion and affect allows us to deepen our understanding of how people develop attachments and commitments to the past, things, beliefs, places, traditions and institutions. At the same time focusing on emotion can reveal the fractures and tensions that are both emotionally and discursively worked out as people reconsider and reassess their attachments to what was once common sense to them. Additionally, this focus can reveal the nuances of how people negotiate various forms of identity, sense of social and physical place, and feelings of wellbeing and discomfort. However, for a focus on emotion to achieve this, it is vital that the theorising of emotion be pragmatic, and at its core it must ask what it is that emotions do, and are used for; and we believe that this needs to start from a focus on performance and practice. To that end, we asked the authors in this volume to explore the ways that emotions are put to use when the past is mobilised as 'heritage' in the present.

Affective practice

Here we briefly overview the path that led us to privilege the notion of affective practice as a basis for critical social research. In part, this was a response to the problems we see with three current, popular formulations of emotion. One is the phenomenological emphasis on feelings per se; the second is the conventional Western set of assumptions about the psychology of emotion, which are often just taken for granted when heritage and museum studies researchers begin to notice affect; and the third is recent work in cultural studies which sets up affect as a kind of excess and formed intensity, a product of spaces and relations, hitting human bodies in an unmediated way.

The phenomenological approach, with its focus on subjectively experienced gradients and bursts of affects, is rich in detail and can be a stimulating starting point, and people's experiences in the course of a heritage encounter are often illuminating, strange and impressively articulated. But where should one go from here? As Bourdieu (1990) argues, the broad problem with social phenomenology is the difficulty in moving to a systematic and insightful reckoning of the conditions of possibility for social action. In this case, how is emotion assembled, what is required for feeling to arise, and how do we make sense of affective privilege and differential access? Rich detail can obscure collective patterning, context and location. The reach of the idiosyncratic remains unclear, as does how affect communicates, travels and potentially mobilises.

A second common standpoint in social research on emotion is to assume that traditional twentieth-century Western psychologies can be trusted to ground investigation. It is frequently naively taken for granted, for example, that emotion comes in discrete basic packets, templates or programmes, each with its own embodied signature or brain/body routine (grief, joy, anger etc.); that it is obvious these are human universals shared with animals and dating from early human history; that emotion, as distinct from cognition, can be treated as a spontaneous, automatic, authentic and unmediated response direct from the body/brain if not the heart; that emotions express rather than construct body states, goals and positions; and that there are fixed cause–effect relationships between defined environmental triggers and specific emotions so that the right stimulus will set off a particular emotion programme like anger, just as surely as pressing a key generates a software routine.

The problems with these assumptions for social research have been well rehearsed (e.g. Leys 2011; Wetherell 2012, 2015). Curiously, although it has rarely been explored by social researchers, contemporary mainstream thinking about emotion in experimental psychobiology develops an analysis which in many ways is highly amenable to critical social science (Barrett 2006, 2009; Russell 2003, 2009; Scherer 2009). The surprising lack of empirical evidence over a number of decades for the seemingly obvious, traditional 'basic emotions' view has led many psychobiologists to advocate psychological constructionism in its place. The embodied prod of sensation is now understood as a registration of the state of physiological core affect in terms of valence (positive or negative) and intensity (strong or weak). The process of 'reading' or registering core affect, however, simultaneously weaves together with meaning-making to produce dynamic flows of feelings, experiences and actions that are culturally recognisable (and communicable to oneself and others) as types of affect and emotion. As Klaus Scherer (2005: 314) describes, a burst of affect involves the synchronous recruitment of mental and somatic resources and, others would add, this recruitment is thus not the expression of an underlying basic emotion programme but a flexible, contextual, contingent and ongoing construction and assembling of bodily sensations, events, meanings and consequences. For heritage and museum studies researchers this disrupts any simple notion that an emotion expresses a natural and authentic reactive truth, that a heritage event will trigger a matching, singular, unequivocal emotion in its audience so that the event can be read to decode the emotion it must inevitably trigger, and the implicit assumption that emotions 'speak English' so that contemporary English-language emotion categories can be treated as basic universals for all peoples in all periods and places (Wierzbicka 1999).

The third strand of thinking about affect which we have not found so helpful (although it has been more so for some contributors to this volume) is the new emphasis on affect in cultural studies and cultural geography as a kind of unmediated intensity or excess. This is often traced back to Massumi's (2002) reading of Deleuze and Bergson, among others. Anderson (2009, see also 2006) articulates this view clearly in his work on affective atmospheres. In this account, for example, affect acts as a kind of extra-discursive excess mysteriously imbuing spaces and places – they acquire an atmosphere and affecting powers – which are then assumed to automatically organise and charge those who pass through this space. Anderson is interested in '… a class of experience that occurs *before* and *alongside* the formation of subjectivity, *across* human and non-human materialities, and *in-between* subject/object distinctions' (Anderson 2009: 78). Theorists in this particular 'turn to affect' explore processes of contagion, the viral and communal affect. Crowds and so-called crowd minds (Brennan 2004) become key exemplars, along with the ways in which lines of affect might be laid down or engineered in cities (Thrift 2004), so that the simple experience of city walking becomes an experience of being unavoidably assailed and hailed by affect. Thrift (2008) likens groups of humans to schools of fish, for example. He suggests that affect, channelled through automatic unconscious imitation and pheromones, travels rapidly from body to body, beyond discursive mediation, so that scenes begin to pulse with collective emotion.

Undoubtedly, these emphases have been productive in the ways they have drawn attention to the intersections of emotion, history and geography, and in particular the connections between the organisation of space and emotion potentials and available trajectories. They also usefully remind us that affect is a distributed phenomenon – not something that can be localised in the psychological individual alone, but demanding a level of analysis involving the episode, the broader articulation, the assemblage, historical contexts and previous affective patterns. But what is missing here is any account of the practical human work and meaning-making involved in this assemblage. Complex, feeling social actors become simple affect automatons. What becomes particularly mysterious in this account is any failure in affective transmission. Why, for example, do visitors to a museum exhibition of difficult history have such diverse responses, why do some members of a crowd resist its pull and affect? To understand this, we need to explore the ways in which participants are making meaning of the situation, patterns of identification and affiliation, and the role of previous histories of sense-making in setting up the resonances of any potentially affecting scene. These meaning-making activities, we suggest, massively exceed the role of any passive unconscious entraining of bodies and set the stage for imitation. They are crucial for understanding the constitution and recruitment of the past in the present.

What, then, does thinking about affect and emotion through the concept of practice offer as an alternative? Practice social theories have been around since the 1970s. They were devised to understand the core conundrums of human action, the re-instantiation and the new creation of social life, the regulated but

Introduction 5

only partially determined nature of human conduct, the problems involved in understanding the formation of social actors, what is internalized and what inheres. As Ortner (2006) notes, practice theories vary from the more deterministic (Bourdieu 1990) to the more agentic (Giddens 1979). Their relevance for questions around the social organisation of subjectivity, and specifically affect and emotion, is obvious (Wetherell 2008), but, for a variety of reasons to do with the disciplinary histories of psychology and social theory, are not often investigated. The time seems to have come, however, for re-invigorating social research on emotion through practice-based research, and a number of emerging cognate lines of inquiry can be found in critical social psychology (Brown and Stenner 2009; Cromby 2015; Walkerdine 2010; Wetherell 2012, 2013a, 2015), in sociology (Burkitt 2014; Reckwitz 2002, 2012), in history (Reddy 2001, 2009; Scheer 2012), and in geography (Everts and Wagner 2012; Laurier and Philo 2006). Despite a difference in meta-theory (Wetherell 2015), there are clear synergies too with Ahmed's (2004) important work on the cultural politics of emotion.

The notion of affective practice is not intended as a total theory of all affect and emotion. Rather it draws attention to a type of affect and emotion that is regular if not necessarily always routine, relatively predictably ordered and patterned (but with a could-be-otherwise quality), socially consequential and bound up with ongoing social relations. In other words, it concerns the kind of affect that is probably most to the fore in the investigations of heritage and museum studies scholars. Social researchers investigate social practices of grooming, cooking, sport, games and leisure, and explore communities of practice; in a similar vein we might attend to the organisation of affective practices such as righteous indignation on Twitter, communities of practice based on banter and their affects and subject positions, the affective practices which organise institutionalised emotional labour such as handling irate customers in call centres, or the ways in which those participating in a commemorative event move through the affecting possibilities set up by the music and speeches. Every social practice involves some kind of affect (even if that is just boredom and indifference, or just enough investment or fear to keep participants enacting); what marks out affective practice from general social practice, however, is that this is human activity where emotion is a specific and principal focus of the practice.

As Schatzki (2002) points out, a social practice is 'a nexus of doings and sayings'. As a consequence, we suggest that the kinds of discourse activities (formulating, accounting and narrating) that are the unavoidable and inevitable focus of most qualitative research offer a way in to important features of affective practices such as retrospective sense-making around emotion epsiodes, the cultural resources available to mediate affect, and the subject and identity positioning process, but also potentially, through more fine-grained qualitative work, to the stitching together of embodied states and meaning-making in flows of affect (Wetherell 2013b). Words are not ephemeral in affecting encounters, and qualitative research based on people's own accounts is not a pale second-hand substitute for 'actual emotion'. Rather, the qualitative researcher investigating affective practice approaches 'the practical relation to the world, the preoccupied active presence in the world through which the world imposes its presence, with its urgencies, its things to be done and said, things made to be said, which directly govern words and deeds without ever unfolding as a spectacle' (Bourdieu 1990: 51).

Bourdieu (1990) argued that what is instantiated in the social actor as a result of repeated social practice or coordinated regular activity is habitus or a set of durable and transposable dispositions. In this way social history (in the form of past practice) becomes corporeal, incorporated in new bodies and minds, and then objectified to form present and future social conditions. It is not clear how Bourdieu understood emotion – at times conceivably as a disposition in itself, perhaps as a kind of customized subjective habit, skill, value or preference (e.g. a facility in empathy), and at times as a kind of background universal psychological drive applied to dispositions (like energy or motivation) (see Crossley 2001; Probyn 2005). In many ways, too, his concept of habitus has begun to creak under the strain as the intersectionality, multiplicity and fragmentation of people's social positions has become more evident in recent years, along with the dynamism of social action. We can still recognise, however, that repeated affective practices have a dispositional potential and quality in the sense that they become canonical and entirely routine for individuals as a result of their personal history and for communities and social groups as a result of collective histories. Affective practices (and perhaps particularly those associated with engaging with the past in the present) wear what could be described as grooves or ruts in people's bodies and minds, just as walking particular routes over the grass year after year produces new paths.

As feminist researchers (Illouz 1997; Lawler 2005; Layton 2006; Reay 2004, 2005; Skeggs 2004) have pointed out, thinking about the acquisition of emotional styles and habits as dispositions and aspects of habitus allows the extension of Bourdieu's thinking about cultural capital, distinction and social value to aspects of self and subjectivity. The notion of emotional capital is complex because working out exactly who benefits is not straightforward, especially in the case of gendered emotion (Reay 2004); nonetheless, we can ask about the relationship among affective practices, power and privilege. What affective practices are valued by different groups, which are admired, which reviled? To adopt the terminology Raymond Williams (1977) proposed to make a similar point – what 'structures of feeling' are hegemonic, untroubled and taken for granted, which are subordinated, and what might be creatively emerging for new generations in new times?

Overall, it seems to us that developing analyses of affective practices is a hopeful move for critical social research. Our attention turns to the building of worlds, histories and feeling actors. We move outwards from

Introduction 7

the subjective, the phenomenological, the experiential and the psychological to the social organisation of heritage relations, episodes and the whole assemblage.

Utility of affective practice to critical heritage studies

Intuitively, heritage is easily understandable as emotionally constituted, linked as it is to the expression of a range of identities, to a sense of place and to wellbeing, while also often contributing to a range of social and cultural conflicts. However, the affective qualities of heritage have had little analytical traction within heritage and museum studies, often, as Smith and Campbell (2016) have argued, having been dismissed as problematic or treated with suspicion. Lowenthal (1985) argued early on in the development of heritage studies that heritage, as a particular form of engagement with the past, was nostalgic, sentimental and nationalistic, which was antithetical to the more measured, systematic and evidential approach of history. Moreover, early dominant criticism of heritage, that reacted strongly to Margaret Thatcher's return to 'Victorian values' and Ronald Reagan's championing of 1950s family morals, exclusively equated the populism of heritage with the emotive registers of conservative politics. This is despite both Samuel's (1994) and Hall's (1999) far more nuanced understanding of the diversity of strategic political uses of the past (see Gentry 2015 for a fuller discussion). The growth in local and regional museums and heritage centres that started to occur from the 1980s was equated to ersatz history that commercialised and commodified feelings of nostalgia to make the past 'the foreign country with the healthiest tourist trade of all' (Lowenthal 1985: 4). The growth of heritage tourism and other commercial uses of heritage in the 1970s and 1980s, alongside tourists themselves, were regarded as highly problematic phenomena in need of close and careful regulation.

The reaction within both museology and heritage studies to the perceived threats of politically conservative populism and tourism was to reinforce the legitimacy and moral duty of experts not only to act as stewards for the safeguarding of the physical 'fragility' of heritage resources, but also to guard against the erosion and 'Disneyfication' of the assumed innate historical values and meanings that heritage resources represented. In this process the public in turn was to be protected from feeling too keenly the rampant nostalgia and nationalism unleashed by the rise of interest in heritage. From the 1970s the international authority of the Authorised Heritage Discourse (AHD) that framed national and international policy and practice, which asserted the political neutrality and the impassivity of expertise, was redoubled through the increasing profile of both UNESCO and ICOMOS (Smith 2006). Within heritage and museological scholarship and practice, heritage as either sites/places or museum collections, in large part become a subject of unaffecting technical expertise. Through a focus on 'best practice' in terms of the development and implementation of conservation and management plans, the political uses of heritage were to be 'neutralised' or regulated (Smith 2004). Meanwhile, within museology, the educational role of museums was asserted as the core function of museum practice. It is important to note that professional neutrality and the flat affect of expert interpretations of the past that played down the more febrile emotional response are emotionally situated. Moreover, the assumed neutrality of expertise, especially in terms of nationalist politics, and the promotion of the quiet assumption of common sense were themselves fostering a political position. Within this process the 'taken-for-grantedness' of the nation, nationalism and expertise were of course legitimated. However, entirely lost within this technical and educational emphasis was any consideration of the affective qualities of heritage.

So obscured was the issue of emotion that the early work that began to self-consciously acknowledge the emotional nature of heritage was startling simply for the observation that heritage and museums were locations at which people consciously engaged in 'feeling' (see Poria, Butler and Airey 2003; Bagnall 2003). Since the turn of the century, attentive acknowledgement of emotion has been on the increase (see Smith and Campbell 2016 for an overview), and new ways of thinking about national heritage (Littler and Naidoo 2005), nostalgia (Cashman 2006; Pickering and Keightley 2006; Keightley and Pickering 2012; Campbell, Smith and Wetherell 2017) and pedagogy (Gregory and Witcomb 2007; Witcomb 2013) have started to emerge within heritage and museum studies.

However, latter engagement with affect and emotion has tended to draw on the idea of affect, discussed above, that developed in cultural studies and cultural geography and which focuses on the unmediated intensity or excess of the moment and the idea of affective 'atmospheres'. In particular, work has been influenced by Non-Representational Theory (NRT), which stresses the extra-discursive nature of affect and privileges affect as pre-cognitive and pre-discursive, a position initially championed by Waterton and Watson (2013). More recent work, while using this as a starting point, has refocused slightly to identify the 'more than representational' which tries to recognise the social elements of affect (see in particular Waterton 2014; Tolia-Kelly, Waterton and Watson 2016). However, this work has become mired in its inability to reconcile what are really incommensurable theoretical trends.

The idea of affective practice as laid out above, and as advanced by Wetherell (2012), has particular synergies with ideas of heritage as a form of social and cultural practice that have started to gain ground in heritage studies. The authorised account that heritage may be defined simply as sites, monuments and/or museological artefact collections has been extensively challenged not only within the academic literature, but also with the rise of the concept of 'intangible heritage' and its recognition by UNESCO through the 2003 Convention for the Safeguarding of the Intangible Cultural Heritage (ICHC).

Commencing with the work of Kirshenblatt-Gimblett (1998), heritage has been increasing addressed as a 'verb' (Harvey 2001: 327). As Kirshenblatt-Gimblett (1998) argued, heritage is very much a product of the present, and activities in and around heritage sites and museum collections are part of the performances of producing new cultural meanings and expressions for the present. Bella Dicks (2000) has similarly demonstrated that heritage may be usefully understood as a practice of inter-generational communication, a position also supported by more recent work by Kidron (2013) and Smith (2017). In addition, Smith (2006), drawing on Samuel (1994), has argued that heritage sites and museums are 'theatres of memory', since not only are they spaces and places that are actively utilised as cultural tools in the processes of remembering and commemorating, but also heritage is indeed what is done with such places rather than the places themselves. That is, heritage-making is explicitly done in and for the present to address contemporary political needs and aspirations, and it is something that is 'done' not simply by experts and professional bodies, but by nations, groups and individuals. Macdonald (2013) also argues that heritage is a process of what she calls 'past-presenting' in which the past is brought to the present to address contemporary cultural and social aspirations for the future. Significant to all of these arguments is the idea that the practices of heritage-making are firmly situated in the present and actively address the needs and aspirations of individuals and groups. Also significant is that, while emotion is often referenced, it has often not been actively incorporated in this re-theorising of heritage.

The concept of intangible heritage, which was initially championed by Japan and the Global South (Aikawa-Faure 2009), has also challenged previous assurances and common-sense assumptions about the materiality of heritage and also draws attention to the affective nature of the concept of heritage. Not to be conflated with the re-theorising of heritage as an overarching form of practice, the concept of intangible heritage defines heritage as a set of practices around specific cultural performances such as storytelling, music, craft, workplace knowledge, food and other phenomena. Intangible heritage has drawn attention to the dynamic and mutable nature of heritage meanings and values. Heritage values are now not simply cast as permanent fixtures of monuments and sites, but are understood as far more slippery and less subjectable to the exertion of control and regulation. Indeed, the degree of concern expressed in the early 2000s about the uncontrollable 'political' nature of intangible heritage speaks to the degree to which the AHD and its practitioners were made uncomfortable by their inability to control and define this phenomenon. Further, the degree of continuing concern over just how/ whether expertise can have a meaningful role in 'safeguarding' this heritage, which pivots on the concern that the mere engagement of currently dominant heritage expert practices will inevitably render intangible heritage 'frozen' in time and space (in effect monumentalised), is expressive of the degree to which dominant assumptions about the nature of heritage cannot address the energetic and affective.

Understanding heritage as a set of dynamic and affective practices opens up the theoretical scope for exploring the phenomenon of intangible heritage and engaging more fully with this on its own terms rather than through, as is currently done, a conceptualisation of heritage that still owes way too much to the Euro- and material-centric AHD. Secondly, it also adds to the theorising of heritage as practice by allowing a more nuanced engagement with the social and political consequences of heritage-making. A focus on practice requires a commitment to considering what it is that heritage *does* in society, for instance, how heritage upholds or challenges the way the past is brought to the present to legitimise or de-legitimise claims to identity, or particular claims for inclusion or exclusion, or upholds or challenges narratives of nation and citizenship, among other issues. A consideration of heritage as an affective practice requires an analysis of what particular affects and emotions *do*, not only in defining the heritage meanings constructed by practice, but also what their consequences are for contemporary aspirations and needs. Affect, and its discursive mediation, impacts on the cognitive processes and social and political judgements that people make, and the internal and external narratives they produce, to, as Archer (2007) argues, help people navigate day-to-day social interactions. The affective timbre of emotions, and the feelings that they underpin, work to help legitimise or not the ways in which remembering and forgetting are conducted and the meanings and narratives such reminiscences produce (Campbell 2006; Morton 2013). Heritage, as a practice of meaning-making, draws heavily on affect/emotion to legitimate the meanings and narratives that are produced and propagated. Heritage's emotional force is part and parcel of the power of heritage to stand in for and legitimate claims to inclusion or exclusion on the basis of identity, nation and citizenship. We asked the contributors to this volume to engage with the idea of heritage as an affective practice, and to consider the consequences of such a theorisation for understanding not only the nature of heritage but also the impact and effect that heritage has in and for the present.

Commemoration and remembering

In this section the affective qualities of the practices of commemoration and remembrance are documented and discussed, not only to reveal their emotive nature, but also to identify the flexible, contextual and contingent nature of affect and the way it is often actively managed and negotiated in social relations and collective practices of remembering. In the first chapter of this section (chapter 2), Dahlin investigates the post-Soviet-era practices of searching for the remains of Russian soldiers lost during World War II. As a form of affective heritage practice, she argues that the physical work of searching for and reburying the remains of soldiers actively forgotten by Soviet and post-Soviet authorities is an embodied act of remembering. This literal memory work is driven by a sense of patriotic duty and personal commitment to the memories of the dead and a desire to rework the memories of the war and what that might mean for contemporary understandings of Russian nationalism and citizenship. As a participant observer, Dahlin illustrates how the intercession of emotion is a primary focus of the practice of searching, and how the affective encounters with remains, mud and artefacts, and the physical discomfort of the work itself, are utilised by the community of searchers in negotiating and reworking the meaning of the war in the present. In this process affect is not only distributed and negotiated by the community of searchers, but also illustrates the ways in which patterns of identification and affiliation are brought into being and mediated to create attachments to the past and commitments to particular social values.

Continuing the consideration of the affective practices of engaging with histories of conflict and violence, Shea (chapter 3) considers the impact of the Temple art installation in Derry/Londonderry, Northern Ireland. The Temple, constructed of balsa wood in 2015, stood on the highest elevation in the city for one week, before it was purposely consumed within a bonfire. The intent was a cathartic practice of giving up distressing memories and the emotional burdens associated with the history of the Troubles. As Shea argues, the ways in which participants engaged with this commemorative space, and the practices it invited, were neither simple nor categorical and actively resisted binary positioning. The case illustrates the complexity and diversity of emotional attachments individuals and groups may make with the past. Moreover, it demonstrates the personal and social contextual and negotiated nature of affect and the way individual and collective mediation of emotion may work to renegotiate the meaning of the past for the present. A significant insight offered by Shea is that the contemporary social meaning constructed in affective commemorative practices may at once be complex, contradictory and ambiguous.

McKernan and McLeod (chapter 4) turn to the consideration of the ways in which affective encounters with the histories of trauma and violence were facilitated by two Australian exhibitions that commemorated the centenary of World War I. The chapter draws on critical readings of the exhibitions and interviews with curatorial and education staff at the Australian War Memorial's *Australia in the Great War* and Museum Victoria's *WWI: Love and Sorrow* to document the way the exhibitions attempt to construct affective responses. McKernan and McLeod reveal the ways in which the former exhibition reinforces established exclusionary narratives and discursive practices of war commemoration while illustrating the ways in which the latter exhibition works to destabilise and complicate received narratives and practices of remembrance. Acknowledging the growing attention to the use of emotion in museums for developing a critical pedagogy (Witcomb 2013), McKernan and McLeod make a plea for the self-conscious use of affective strategies within museological spaces to destabilise received narratives and to facilitate a more critically informed engagement with the past. Željka Miklošević and Darko Babić (chapter 5) also record the ways in which museums, in this case the Museum of Broken Relationships in Zagreb, may be understood to manage emotions. The authors consider not just the affective practices of exhibiting, and the ways in which emotions are managed within this process, but also the affective practices that frame the donation of objects and stories to the museum. They argue that it is the personal stories associated with the objects that engender the emotional impact of the museum's objects and illustrate, in opposition to much of the theorising of affect that focuses on its phenomenological nuances or treats it as an unmediated force, that context – in this case the personal and social circumstances outlined by the stories told around the objects – is what facilitates the affective responses to heritage objects.

In the final chapter of this section (chapter 6), Juliff looks at the 'participatory turn' in art and heritage re-enactment in the making of the documentary film *The Battle of Orgreave* (2001). The film, which featured a re-enactment of the 1984 battle between approximately 4,000 police and 5,000–6,000 striking British coal miners who had set up a picket and barricade outside the Orgreave British Steel coke plant in South Yorkshire, aimed to raise awareness and political recognition of the 1984–1985 Miners' Strike and its legacies. This chapter reminds us that commemorative affective practices, whatever their form, *do* things, in this case make claims for a form of recognition that acknowledges not just the inequities of past events but also the ongoing need for reparations and restorative justice.

Belonging and exclusion

A strong emphasis has traditionally been placed on the sense of belonging engendered by heritage, but heritage is always a simultaneous act of inclusion and exclusion. Exclusion may occur through the simple act of demarking what is or is not someone's heritage or though active attempts to forget or obscure diversity and difference by the very assertion of monolithic ideas of national or 'universal' heritage (Hall 1999; Ashworth, Graham and Tunbridge 2007; Naidoo 2016). This section focuses on the tensions and fractures revealed when analysis not only privileges affect and emotion but also seeks to understand how and why particular affective practices are valued and legitimised and others reviled and discounted. The power of emotions is illustrated though the ways in which they may be actively brought to bear on practices of inclusion and exclusion. This is illustrated by Martha Augoustinos, Brianne Hastie and Peta Callaghan's examination (chapter 7) of the contested nature of national narratives and the ideological struggles that ensue over competing versions of history. They examine how emotion was utilised within the then Australian Prime Minister Kevin Rudd's apology to Indigenous Australians for the history of forced removal of children practised by the Australian state and the then Leader of the Opposition Brendan Nelson's reply speech. The chapter illustrates the ways in which emotions are linked to appeals to reason in each speech to respectively justify or evade the apology. The authors reveal how each speech opens up or closes down the possibilities for reworking national and social identities and the national historical narrative that frames these expressions. In particular, the chapter reveals how an embodied sense of affect can be utilised by citizens to engage with or disavow the appeal to recognise and address the legacies of racism within Australian society.

Rhiannon Mason, Areti Galani, Katherine Lloyd and Joanne Sayner (chapter 8) explore how visitors to museums draw connections between historical representations of migration in the context of current public debates on immigration and refugees. Paralleling similar work by Dicks (2000, 2016) and Smith (2006, 2017), this chapter focuses on issues of empathy and draws on workshops with community members and visitors to explore how empathy underpins the complex and contradictory ways in which visitors respond to the exhibitions on migration. The complexity, and the sometimes contradictory nature, of responses parallels Shea's observations in chapter 3, and reinforces the importance of the personal and social narratives, particularly in this case associated with class and experiences of de-industrialisation, in framing the ways in which emotions come into play to mediate the meaning of the past in the present. As they illustrate, personal emotional responses to displays continually interact with broader community discourses of identity and place. Continuing the examination of empathy in museums, chapter 9, by Jennifer Claire Robinson, looks at the affective practices and emotional responses that occurred between heritage professionals and community partners during the development of contested history exhibitions in Canadian museums. She illustrates how emotional interplays between professionals and community stakeholders can lead to emotional vulnerability for both parties, and that, rather than guarding against such exposure, engaging with uncertainty may produce productive bonds of trust and empathy vital to the development of an inclusive museological practice.

Moving to black cab tours of Belfast's murals in chapter 10, Katie Markham develops the idea of 'affective synecdoche' that targets the 'micro-moment', and she argues that this idea addresses the spatial nature of emotional engagement during these tours. Drawing on a phenomenological concern for nuance, she illustrates the ways in which competing narratives of the Troubles are circulated and exchanged within the confines of the black cab tours and the ways in which the affective practices of touring, and the tourists themselves, become the focus of mediation of community belonging and exclusion.

In the final chapter of this section (chapter 11), Ivo Strahilov and Slavka Karakusheva take the reader back to a broader examination of the ways in which emotion is utilised in conflicting national narratives of belonging and exclusion. In this case, the chapter maps the way emotion is used to at once legitimise and de-legitimise the place of Ottoman history and Muslim claims

14   Margaret Wetherell *et al.*

to historic mosques in Bulgaria. Conflict is sparked when the Grand Mufti's Office, on behalf of Muslim Bulgarians, attempts to claim a mosque that has been proclaimed a national Bulgarian heritage site. Christian Bulgarians at once claim the mosque as part of their national heritage, while simultaneously disavowing Ottoman involvement in the creation of the Bulgarian state and redefining Muslim Bulgarians as 'foreigners'. Emotion is used to justify and authorise the holding of two contradictory positions by the state and Bulgarian Christians. The chapter also illustrates how conflict is then circumscribed as the mosque in question is redefined as an archaeological museum, thus denying the political context of the site while attempting to 'rationalise' and thus depress its affective context. Ultimately, the chapter illustrates how both emotionally intense and 'flat' affective practices work to reinforce continuing patterns of identification and affiliation.

Learning, teaching and engaging

A key and early area of debate on emotion in heritage centres on the role of affect and emotion in the pedagogical aims of museums and heritage interpretation (Gregory and Witcomb 2007; Witcomb 2013; Trofanenko 2014). This section explores a wide range of issues centred on the communication of heritage issues and the ways in which emotion is central to cognition and the implications of this for a critical and affective heritage practice within museological and other spaces of learning. While there is some debate about the extent to which museums and heritage sites are indeed primarily used by their visitors for educational purposes,[2] education remains a significant pillar of heritage and museological practice. The aim here is to consider how such practice may become more effective through a critical engagement with affect and emotion. The section starts with a consideration by Michalinos Zembylas (chapter 12) of the emotional regimes, or the 'structures of feeling' (Williams 1977), that can be utilised when engaging pedagogically with difficult histories. He draws on work in history education to map the emotional engagement of museum visitors to difficult knowledge in the context of a reconciliation process. In doing so, Zembylas outlines the various affective pedagogical options available to facilitate engagement, including separation, harmonisation and multiperspectivity, and the work that they do to challenge or reproduce existing structures of feeling. He argues for the importance of developing critical analytical positions that aim to understand the complex and ambivalent nature invoked by contested history that avoids getting caught within certain unproductive emotional regimes. This debate is continued in chapter 13, wherein Dianne Mulcahy and Andrea Witcomb draw on a number of mixed innovative qualitative methods that include data from body cameras worn by school children while visiting the Museum of Victoria. They demonstrate the embodied nature of affect and find that the idea of affective practice has utility in identifying the continuities and repetitions that follow the 'grooves and ruts' in peoples' minds, but also conceptually helps identify the ways in which continuities can be challenged and established practices and understandings unsettled and reconsidered.

Turning to the South African classroom, Daniela Gachago, Vivienne Bozalek and Dick Ng'ambi (chapter 14) reflect on student responses to a digital storytelling project that engaged with difficult knowledges about the legacies of apartheid. Drawing out the implications for museum education and practice, the chapter demonstrates that emotions are both relational and performative, and that emotions such as white guilt and shame are mediated by race, class, gender and age. Power and privilege are an important context for understanding not only the embodied expression of emotion, but also how it is transformed into, and frames the limitations of, certain privileged affective practices. They illustrate how passive empathy towards historical experiences of difference that allows students to become stuck within affective moments facilitates a disengagement with power relations and the wider socio-economic and cultural contexts that drive those experiences. The chapter argues for the pedagogical utility of emotional reflexivity in engendering an active empathy that takes on responsibilities for the plights of others. Continuing the discussion of empathy and learning, Angélique Stastny (chapter 15) examines how empathy is mobilised in school history textbooks with the aim of promoting reconciliatory practices between Indigenous and non-Indigenous Australians. As with the previous chapter, Stastny illustrates the racialised expressions of shallow forms of empathy that work to impede recognition, responsibility and social change. Conversely, Ingrid Huygens (chapter 16) discusses how sincere forms of empathy facilitated reflection and insightful re-evaluation in Pākehā and other non-Māori learners engaged in educational workshops about the Treaty of Waitangi in Aotearoa New Zealand. Huygens, drawing out implications for museum and heritage learning, argues that indifference is a colonial affective practice and that empathy was key to facilitating the emotional journeys of the coloniser that remain vital in the practices of decolonisation. This reinforces the point made by Robinson (chapter 9), namely that acknowledging and engaging in the emotional complexities and ambiguities reflected in sincere expressions of empathy is central to destabilising the established understandings called for by other chapters in this section.

Celmara Pocock, Marion Stell and Geraldine Mate (chapter 17) offer another emotionally engaged method for facilitating the development of counter-narratives. They document the use of a video recording module at three heritage and museum settings in which people were asked to record their personal stories that were in some way linked to the heritage location. Further, the storytellers were asked to select a particular emotion (such as fear, hope, joy etc.) from a proffered list that would feature in the story or around which they would frame the storytelling. The chapter argues for the utility of such spaces in interpretive contexts wherein visitors may utilise their emotional engagement with their own stories and experience to reflect on the broader issues and contexts of the heritage on display. Moreover, they argue that this practice requires individuals to make an emotive linking between the past and contemporary circumstances by actively including individuals in the affective practice of heritage storytelling. This inclusion is not simply through the retelling of individual histories, but through the performing of emotional attachments and identifications with the wider narratives on display.

Conclusion

The chapters in this book illustrate the complexity, the ambiguity and, at times, the contradictory nature of affective responses to, and uses of, heritage. They illustrate that affect does not have to be intense to have a consequence, but that flat forms of emotion, such as indifference and disregard – or indeed the nonetheless emotional claims to rational emotional neutrality – also have powerful and abiding social and political consequences. The contextual, performative and discursive mediation of affect is richly identified throughout the volume in ways that draw attention to the analytical dangers of becoming focused on the unmediated intensity or excess of the moment of affect. Such a focus tends to strip away or obscure the social and political context that drives the moment and the consequences it has. Indeed, as several authors in this volume have demonstrated, such an analytical focus may itself be understood as part of the affective practices of privilege as cultural theorists, thus analytically engaged, exempt themselves from the force of affect. The idea of affective practice, defined as an activity where emotion is a principal focus, draws forceful attention to the patterns in the various ways affect and emotion come into play in social relations. This in turn requires an analytical consideration of not simply the social contexts, but also the consequences of emotionally driven and mediated practices. This idea has synergy with the theorisation of heritage as itself a form of social practice; heritage, linked as it is to expressions of identity and place, is itself a form of affective practice. Two categories of affective heritage practices are identified throughout the volume, namely those that work to uphold received and comfortable expressions of identity and belonging/exclusion and those that aim to destabilise and assert competing heritage narratives of identity and belonging.

We asked at the start how might an emphasis on emotion lead to new questions in heritage studies, or answer old questions in new ways? We contend that understanding the patterns and consequences of affective heritage practices opens up new ways to challenge authorised and exclusionary accounts of heritage, and the dominance of the authorised heritage discourse and the depoliticising technical and nationally focused heritage practices it frames. Identifying the well-trodden routes and paths of certain affective heritage practices and understanding the ways in which emotions constitute and recruit the past in the present provides analytical insight for intervention and challenge. One of the key insights that develops across many of the chapters of the volume is the utility of engaging with emotional uncertainty and ambiguity. As many chapters illustrate, it was at the nexus of emotional ambiguity that new alliances and attachments were made. This ambiguity and complexity, we contend, has historically led to a reluctance within heritage studies to engage with its emotional characteristics and consequences – despite the fact that historically heritage has been used to make problematic emotional connections to ideas of national, ethnic and class privilege. However, it is in the complexities and ambiguities of emotional responses to heritage that new and socially productive analysis may be had. Further, engaging with the role of emotion and affect as a part of the processes and practices of heritage meaning-making will facilitate critical accounts that have implications for the ongoing development of policy and practice.

Notes

1 This volume grew out of a shared interest in engaging with and developing Margaret Wetherell's idea of affective practice within the broad area of heritage studies. While we had hoped for contributions from a wide range of disciplinary and geographical backgrounds, various disciplines and regions of the globe remain unrepresented in this volume. We make no claims to geographical or disciplinary representation, but the volume offers a snapshot of current work addressing the themes associated with the affective practices of bringing the past to the present.
2 A body of research has begun to question the idea of learning and linear transmission of messages that tends to dominate much museological and heritage interpretation practices and to illustrate the range of ways visitors use such places (see, for example, Dicks 2000, 2016; Smith 2006, 2015, 2017; Pekarik and Schreiber 2012; Coghlan 2017; Dudley 2017).

References

Aikawa-Faure, N., 2009. From the proclamation of masterpieces to the *Convention for the Safeguarding of Intangible Heritage*. In L. Smith and N. Akagawa, eds. *Intangible Heritage*. London: Routledge, 13–44.

Ahmed, S., 2004. *The Cultural Politics of Emotion*. New York: Routledge.

Anderson, B., 2006. Becoming and being hopeful: Towards a theory of affect. *Environment & Planning D: Society and Space*, 24, 733–752.

Anderson, B., 2009. Affective atmospheres. *Emotion, Space & Society*, 2, 77–81.

Archer, M. S., 2000. *Being Human: The Problem of Agency*. Cambridge: Cambridge University Press.

Archer, M. S., 2007. *Making Our Way through the World: Human Reflexivity and Social Mobility*. Cambridge: Cambridge University Press.

Ashworth, G. J., Graham, B. J. and Tunbridge, J. E., 2007. *Pluralising Pasts: Heritage, Identity and Place in Multicultural Societies*. London: Pluto Press.

Bagnall, G., 2003. Performance and performativity at heritage sites. *Museum & Society*, 1(2), 87–103.

Barrett, L. F., 2006. Are emotions natural kinds? *Perspectives on Psychological Science*, 1, 28–58.

Barrett, L. F., 2009. Variety is the spice of life: A psychological construction approach to understanding variability in emotion. *Cognition & Emotion*, 23(7), 1284–1306.

Bourdieu, P., 1990. *The Logic of Practice*. Trans. Richard Nice. Cambridge: Polity.

Brennan, T., 2004. *The Transmission of Affect*. Ithaca: Cornell University Press.

Brown, S. D. and Stenner, P., 2009. *Psychology without Foundations*. London: Sage.

Burkitt, I., 2014. *Emotions and Social Relations*. London: Sage.

Campbell, G., Smith, L. and Wetherell, M., eds., 2017. Nostalgia and heritage: Potentials, mobilities and effects. Special issue. *International Journal of Heritage Studies*, 23(7).

Campbell, S., 2006. Our faithfulness to the past: Reconstructing memory value. *Philosophical Psychology*, 19(3), 361–380.

Cashman, R., 2006. Critical nostalgia and material culture in Northern Ireland. *Journal of American Folklore*, 119(427), 137–160.

Coghlan, R., 2017. 'My voice counts because I'm handsome.' Democratising the museum: The power of museum participation. *International Journal of Heritage Studies*, 1–15, doi.org/10.1080/13527258.2017.1320772.

Cromby, J., 2015. *Feeling Bodies: Embodying Affect*. Basingstoke: Palgrave.

Crossley, N., 2001. *The Social Body: Habit, Identity and Desire*. London: Sage.

Dicks, B., 2000. *Heritage, Place and Community*. Cardiff: University of Wales Press.

Dicks, B., 2016. The habitus of heritage: A discussion of Bourdieu's ideas for visitor studies in heritage and museums. *Museum & Society*, 14(1), 52–64.

Dudley, L., 2017. 'I think I know a little bit about that anyway, so it's okay': Museum visitor strategies for disengaging with confronting mental health material. *Museum & Society*, 15(2), 193–216.

Everts, J. and Wagner, L., 2012. Guest editorial: Practising emotions. *Emotion, Space & Society*, 5, 174–176.

Gentry, K., 2015. 'The pathos of conservation' – Raphael Samuel and the politics of heritage. *International Journal of Heritage Studies*, 21(6), 561–576.

Giddens, A., 1979. *Central Problems in Social Theory: Action, Structure and Contradiction in Social Analysis*. Berkeley: University of California Press.

Gregory, K. and Witcomb, A., 2007. Beyond nostalgia: The role of affect in generating historical understanding at heritage sites. In S. J. Knell, S. Macleod and S. Watson, eds. *Museum Revolutions: How Museums Change and Are Changed*. London: Routledge, 263–275.

Hall, S., 1999. Whose heritage? Un-settling 'the heritage', Re-imaging the post-nation. *Third Text*, 13(49), 3–13.

Harvey, D. C., 2001. Heritage pasts and heritage presents: Temporality, meaning and the scope of heritage studies. *International Journal of Heritage Studies*, 7(4), 319–338.

Illouz, E., 1997. Who will care for the caretaker's daughter? Towards a sociology of happiness in the era of reflexive modernity. *Theory, Culture & Society*, 14(4), 31–66.

Keightley, E. and Pickering, M., 2012. *The Mnemonic Imagination: Remembering as Creative Practice*. Basingstoke: Palgrave Macmillan.

Kidron, C.A., 2013. Being there together: Dark family tourism and the emotive experience of co-presence in the Holocaust past. *Annals of Tourism Research*, 41, 175–194.

Kirshenblatt-Gimblett, B., 1998. *Destination Culture: Tourism, Museums and Heritage.* Berkeley: University of California Press.

Laurier, E. and Philo, C., 2006. Possible geographies: A passing encounter in a café. *Area*, 38(1), 353–363.

Lawler, S., 2005. Disgusted subjects: The making of middle-class identities. *The Sociological Review*, 3(3), 429–446.

Layton, L., 2006. That place gives me the heebie jeebies. In L. Layton, N. C. Hollander and S. Gutwill, eds. *Psychoanalysis, Class and Politics: Encounters in the Clinical Setting*. London: Routledge, 51–64.

Leys, R., 2011. The turn to affect: A critique. *Critical Inquiry*, 37(3), 434–472.

Lowenthal, D. 1985. *The Past Is a Foreign Country*. Cambridge: Cambridge University Press.

Littler, J. and Naidoo R., eds., 2005. *The Politics of Heritage: The Legacies of 'Race'*. London: Routledge.

Macdonald, S., 2013. *Memorylands*. London: Routledge.

Marcus, G. E., Neuman, W. R. and MacKuen, M., 2000. *Affective Intelligence and Political Judgment*. Chicago: University of Chicago Press.

Massumi, B., 2002. *Parables for the Virtual: Movements, Affect, Sensation*. Durham: Duke University Press.

Morton, A., 2013. *Emotion and Imagination*. Cambridge: Polity.

Naidoo, R., 2016. All that we are – heritage inside out and upside down. *International Journal of Heritage Studies*, 22(7), 504–514.

Ortner, S. B., 2006. *Anthropology and Social Theory: Culture, Power and the Acting Subject*. Durham: Duke University Press.

Pekarik, A. and Schreiber, J., 2012. The power of expectation: A research note. *Curator: The Museums Journal*, 55(4), 487–496.

Pickering, M. and Keightley. E., 2006. The modalities of nostalgia. *Current Sociology* 54(6), 919–941

Poria, Y., Butler, R. and Airey, D., 2003. The core of heritage tourism. *Annals of Tourism Research*, 30(1), 238–254.

Prinz, J., 2004. *Gut Reactions: A Perceptual Theory of Emotion*. Oxford: Oxford University Press.

Probyn, E., 2005. *Blush: Faces of Shame*. Minneapolis: University of Minnesota Press.

Reay, D., 2004. Gendering Bourdieu's concept of capitals? Emotional capital, women and social class. In L. Adkins and B. Skeggs, eds. *Feminism after Bourdieu*. Oxford: Blackwell, 57–74.

Reay, D., 2005. Beyond consciousness? The psychic landscape of social class. *Sociology*, 39, 911–928.

Reckwitz, A., 2002. Toward a theory of social practices: A development in culturalist theorizing. *European Journal of Social Theory*, 5(2), 243–263.

Reckwitz, A., 2012. Affective spaces: A praxeological outlook. *Rethinking History*, 16(2), 241–258.

Reddy, W., 2001. *The Navigation of Feelings: A Framework for the History of Emotions*. Cambridge: Cambridge University Press.

Reddy, W., 2009. Saying something new: Practice theory and cognitive neuroscience. *Arcadia: International Journal for Literary Studies*, 44, 8–23.

Russell, J. A., 2003. Core affect and the psychological construction of emotion. *Psychological Review*, 110(1), 145–172.

Russell, J. A., 2009. Emotion, core affect and psychological construction. *Cognition & Emotion*, 23(7), 1259–1283.

Samuel, R., 1994. *Theatres of Memory. Volume 1: Past and Present in Contemporary Culture*. London: Verso.

Sayer, A., 2005. Class, moral worth and recognition. *Sociology*, 39(5), 947–963.

Schatzki, T., 2002. *The Site of the Social: A Philosophical Account of the Constitution of Social Life and Change*. University Park: Pennsylvania State University Press.

Scheer, M., 2012. Are emotions a kind of practice (and is that why they have a history?). A Bourdieuan approach to understanding emotion. *History & Theory*, 51(2), 193–200.

Scherer, K. R., 2005. Unconscious processes in emotion: The bulk of the iceberg. In L. F. Barrett, P. M. Niedenthal and P. Winkielman, eds. *Emotion and Consciousness*. New York: The Guilford Press, 312–334.

Scherer, K. R., 2009. The dynamic architecture of emotion: Evidence for the component process model. *Cognition & Emotion*, 23(7), 1307–1351.

Skeggs, B., 2004. Exchange, value and affect: Bourdieu and 'the self'. In L. Adkins and B. Skeggs, eds. *Feminism after Bourdieu*. Oxford: Blackwell, 75–96.

Smith, L., 2004. *Archaeological Theory and the Politics of Cultural Heritage*. London: Routledge.

Smith, L., 2006. *Uses of Heritage*. London: Routledge.

Smith, L., 2015. Theorising museum and heritage visiting. In A. Witcomb and K. Message, eds. *The International Handbooks of Museum Studies. Volume 1: Museum Theory*. Chichester: Wiley Blackwell, 459–484.

Smith, L., 2017. 'We are … we are everything': The politics of recognition and misrecognition at immigration museums. *Museum & Society*, 15(1): 69–86.

Smith, L. and Campbell, G., 2016. The elephant in the room: Heritage, affect and emotion. In W. Logan, M. Nic Craith and U. Kockel, eds. *A Companion to Heritage Studies*. Oxford: Wiley Blackwell, 443–460.

Thrift, N., 2004. Intensities of feeling: Towards a spatial politics of affect. *Geografiska Annaler*, 86B(1), 57–78.

Thrift, N., 2008. *Non-Representational Theory: Space, Politics and Affect*. London: Routledge.

Tolia-Kelly, D. P., Waterton, E. and Watson, S., eds. 2016. *Heritage, Affect and Emotion: Politics, Practices and Infrastructures*. London: Routledge.

Trofanenko, B. M., 2014. Affective emotions: The pedagogical challenges of knowing war. *Review of Education, Pedagogy and Cultural Studies*, 36(1), 22–39.

Walkerdine, V., 2010. Communal belongingness and affect: An exploration of trauma in an ex-industrial community. *Body & Society*, 16(1), 91–116.

Waterton, E., 2014. A more-than-representational understanding of heritage? The 'past' and the politics of affect. *Geography Compass*, 8(11), 823–833.

Waterton, E. and Watson, S., 2013. Framing theory: Towards a critical imagination in heritage studies. *International Journal of Heritage Studies*, 19(6), 546–561

Wetherell, M., 2008. Subjectivity or psycho-discursive practices: Investigating complex intersectional identities. *Subjectivity*, 22(1), 73–81.

Wetherell, M., 2012. *Affect and Emotion: A New Social Science Understanding*. London: Sage.

Wetherell, M., 2013a. Feeling rules, atmospheres and affective practice: Some reflections on the analysis of emotional episodes. In C. Maxwell and P. Aggleton, eds. *Privilege, Agency and Affect: Understanding the Production and Effects of Action*. Basingstoke: Palgrave Macmillan, 221–239.

Wetherell, M., 2013b. Affect and discourse – what's the problem? From affect as excess to affective/discursive practice. *Subjectivity*, 6(4), 349–368.

Wetherell, M., 2015. Trends in the turn to affect: A social psychological critique. *Body & Society*, 21(2), 139–166.

Wierzbicka, A., 1999. *Emotions across Languages and Cultures: Diversity and Universals*. Cambridge: Cambridge University Press.

Williams, R., 1977. *Marxism and Literature*. Oxford: Oxford University Press.

Witcomb, A., 2013. Understanding the role of affect in producing a critical pedagogy for history museums. *Museum Management and Curatorship*, 28(3), 255–271.

Part I

Commemoration and remembering

Chapter 2

Labour of love and devotion?

The search for the lost soldiers of Russia

Johanna Dahlin

Let me begin this text in the woods and bogs of the Sinyavino heights east of St Petersburg, Russia. From 1941 to 1944 fierce battles raged here and helmets, splinters and barbed wire are still visible. Trenches pierce the forest and the sun is reflected in the small war-made lakes the landscape is dotted with. What is not as visible is that the ground is also filled with the remains of the soldiers who fought here. I want to start here, in the mud a day in September a few years ago. It is my third day at the same spot, in the same pit and, to be honest, I am getting bored. Digging is slow. The remains I am uncovering are in very poor condition and I have to be very careful. There are at least two soldiers in the pit. But this morning, in contrast to previous days, I have company. A. has just returned from working in the city and decides to help me. He starts digging where I have not yet, and suddenly he encounters a pair of glasses (figure 2.1). I inspect them, both fascinated and slightly annoyed he would come here and find the most interesting things. 'It must be a *politruk* [political commissar]' A. decides, explaining that glasses are a rare find.

'If it is a *politruk* he will definitely have a pencil too', he announces, and proceeds to find a decomposed pencil and an eraser. We also find the remains of what appears to have been a purse containing 25 kopecks. In contrast to the two soldiers I previously dug up out of the pit – a crumpled mug seems to have been their sole collective property – this is quite a find in all its modesty. The lenses in the glasses are intact, but the frames are loose and broken. It is unusual to find glasses, A. once more explains. They made him expect something more: at least a medallion, the Soviet equivalent of an ID tag. I shrug; medallions might be more common than glasses, but it is quite rare to find them as well.

These events unfold as I am in the middle of fieldwork for my doctoral dissertation, following the work of a search unit looking for the remains of soldiers who died in the battle for Leningrad 1941–1944. While the Sinyavino area is 'dense' in terms of war remains, it is not unique. On battlefields across the former Soviet Union there are soldiers lying as they fell or rudimentarily covered in dirt in so-called sanitary burials, often carried out by the Germans,

Figure 2.1 Uncovering the *politruk*'s glasses: photo by the author

who threw bodies into trenches as they advanced. The Russia-wide voluntary search movement carries out search work through relatively autonomous units in all areas of the country that saw direct fighting. During the years the movement has been in operation, its members have found the remains of nearly half a million soldiers.[1] Speaking about the war in the present tense on the battlefields, this movement is trying to bring closure to the war long after its end. The work is not only symbolic, but also highly emotional. It touches on questions of life and death, right and wrong, belonging and community. The work of the search brigades is memory work in a very concrete way, literally hard work, digging and searching in woods and bogs.

The battlefield has been transformed from a theatre of war into a 'theatre of memory' (Samuel 1994). The area, with its visible traces of combat, is in itself a witness of the past, a link to the war, as well as a setting for present action. As Laurajane Smith has pointed out in a different context, 'country' is important in itself, but it also provides background and setting, gravitas and sense of occasion, and, not least, this is where knowledge is received and passed on, where memories are shared (Smith 2006: 42). Just being in this landscape is cherished by *poiskoviki*, as the search unit's members are called, but place is also central to learning and teaching about the war, and about the search. To use Pierre Nora's (1996) terms, the battlefields can be seen as *lieux de mémoir*; there is a large memorial and cemetery at the Sinyavino heights where funerals and commemorative ceremonies are held, listed as formal heritage (or 'cultural inheritance' which is the more literal Russian term), although late-Soviet plans for a large memorial complex and visitor centre were never realised. The woods and bogs are also dotted with many smaller memorials, and the searches also have traits of what Nora termed *milieux de mémoir*, where ongoing interaction and work create a very lively memory culture, of which the landscape is an intrinsic part. These two aspects feed into one another, where the living memory is externalised in memorials, documenting both the search work and the war, and the memorials form significant landmarks in the search geography. The search work is a form of 'past presencing' (Macdonald 2013) where the past is not only remembered, but directly engaged with, brought into the present in order to finish an unfinished business.

In this chapter, I will investigate the search for lost soldiers as an affective practice, which, following Margaret Wetherell, I understand as embodied meaning-making. I will try to show how discourse and physical work are entangled, and how emotion and affect play roles in the actual work and when the work is displayed, talked about, discussed or otherwise presented. Wetherell says that affect is sometimes taken to mean every aspect of emotion, and sometimes only the physical reactions such as blushes or sobs. She also notes that the term 'affect' in everyday language has more general connotations, 'being affected', which points to modes of influence, movement and change (Wetherell 2012: 4). I will use affect as a broad term, and will argue that affect and emotion are key components in how the search movement relates and makes sense of the past, thus following the argument put forward by Smith and Campbell that 'affect and emotion are essential constitutive elements of heritage making' (Smith and Campbell 2016: 3). Making is a central term here, where both heritage and meaning are continually made in a process of ongoing work, action and interaction. Although the area in itself, the woods and bogs of Sinyavino Heights, is important, it is so not only because of what happened there in the past, but also because of what goes on there now (Smith 2006). And in these contemporary processes, affect and emotion play a key role.

Adopting a participant research position, my fieldwork made me engage not only with the human subjects, but also with the landscape and the material remains of war. I cannot engage with affect without considering my own embodied meaning-making working on this project. The incident retold above took place close to where I, two years previously, had my first encounter with this search for fallen soldiers. I was deeply affected when I found my first soldier. I had never handled human remains before, and the emotional impact it had on me was in many ways crucial in shaping my doctoral research. Getting to know the Russian search movement was both an intellectual and an emotional process. And this involvement has given me a relation to and sense of

28 Johanna Dahlin

belonging with a heritage which can be seen as 'not mine'. I have engaged with that heritage in similar ways to the people I studied, although our frames of interpretation are quite different.

In a discussion of visitor engagement at heritage sites, Smith and Campbell especially consider empathy as important, and they also stress that visitation of these particular sites creates a sense of place which helps facilitate emotional authenticity. The emotional response was part of the reflections on the meaning of the history on display (Smith and Campbell 2016: 6). They further identify 'deep empathy' as a key to critical meaning-making (Smith and Campbell 2016: 11). While there is certainly an empathic aspect to the search work, I would rather speak of three 'key senses' in the affective meaning-making of the search unit. These are sense of place, sense of community (or *sense of svoi*, as I will outline later) and sense of connection. I prefer to use the term connection rather than empathy in order to stress not only feeling for someone, but also feeling connected to this person or event, thus highlighting how certain practices can create a link between an object and oneself. These senses all contribute to bringing the past into the present, to making it alive.

The war and the search for lost soldiers

From September 1941 to January 1944, Leningrad, as St Petersburg was then known, was subjected to a siege by German and Finnish troops. As the Red Army tried to break through the German lines to establish a land connection to the besieged city, it largely concentrated its efforts on the Sinyavino area, where the land held by the Germans was at its narrowest.

While figures are notoriously unreliable, it is assumed that no fewer than 25 million Soviet citizens lost their lives during the war;[2] there are hardly any families that did not lose a member. The prominence of the war memory in contemporary Russia is an important background for the search movement. The war enjoys high official status and is highly visible in public life, not least in spring when Victory Day is celebrated on 9 May, leading some commentators to talk about a cult of the war, or comparing it to a religion (Tumarkin 1994; Merridale 1999; Dahlin 2012).

While many of those killed during the war were civilians, the search work is focused on military deaths that in many cases went unrecorded. Many soldiers were not issued with or did not carry their ID medallions, and it is only a small percentage of the found soldiers that can be identified. However, identification can have great significance. To be missing in action was almost equalled to deserting (Merridale 2005; Dahlin 2012), a crime for which relatives could be punished. The symbolism and moral redress associated with an identified soldier can thus be enormous.

Three times a year the search unit discussed in this chapter carries out *vakhty pamyati* (which roughly translates to 'on duty for memory') search expeditions lasting for two weeks each. In addition to the practical work, the expeditions can be seen to have traits of both ritual and pilgrimage. Camp life is both physically and mentally distant from the participants' normal urban life. Far removed from the war in time, the search unit's predominantly young members nonetheless all have a connection to those times through the traces the war left on society and families. Some have relatives who went missing in this area, several have a burning interest in military history, others simply enjoy the outdoors, and extended expeditions create a close-knit community within the group. I have followed this group since 2009. It is based at a St Petersburg university from which it receives some support, such as modest premises on campus, but the work is done on a voluntary basis. The search unit is led by a history professor, and the members are mainly, but not exclusively, former or current students at the university.

The goal of the activity is to find, identify and bury soldiers, but also to spread knowledge of the war. To this end, members of the group for instance visit schools, and a regular part of the annual activity is to arrange tours of the battlefields. In the following sections I first discuss the search work and its potential for affective meaning-making, before considering the tours and the narrative constructed in presenting the war and the work of the search unit.

The work of the search unit

The search for lost soldiers is perhaps first and foremost hard work. A lot of people dedicate much time to digging and searching in woods and bogs. The work creates skills and practices, as well as a *sense of community* within the group. I have previously analysed the search unit as a community of practice (Lave and Wenger 1991) where shared work and learning create a strong sense of community (Dahlin 2012).

There is a discursive side of belonging, where two key terms, *svoi* and *nash*, speak the unit's members into a community with the group, the overall movement and their country – and not least with the fallen soldiers. Various 'we' are created. An important prerequisite for the community is the shared experience and work. Anthropologist Margaret Paxson (2005) has elaborated on the use of the pronoun *svoi* in the context of social memory in the rural Russian north. She claims the creation and reproduction of *senses of svoi* are a crucial part of the social memory practices outlined in her study. *Svoi* (which can appear in many forms as it is declined according to gender, number and case) is a reflexive possessive pronoun to which English has no direct equivalent. *Svoi* can be used by all persons. You would, for instance, say 'I'm reading *svoi* book' and not 'my book', unless you wanted to stress that the book is yours. But *svoi* is also used to express belonging, and this is the sense of the word that Paxson draws upon. 'Pashtetka, svoi!' is the usual way of telling the search unit's dog Pashtetka to stop barking at people approaching the camp. 'Svoi' – they are a part of this group, they belong here. Paxson argues that to create a svoi-formation means pulling the other into your own sphere (Paxson 2005: 78). A *sense of svoi* indicates both community and belonging.

While its grammatical uses are a bit different, the pronoun *nash* (our) can also have strong connotations of belonging. A person can be 'nash chelovek', literally our human but meaning one of us, and the Red Army is most often called just 'nashi'. *Nash* is also used to characterise goods produced in Russia, or to describe Soviet things found on the battlefields. The most idiomatic way of asking whether whatever object you just found is Soviet is to ask 'eto nash?' – is it ours? Since this expression assumes that the thing and the asker belong to the same community, I was always a bit uneasy about using it and would normally say 'Soviet' instead of 'ours', thus necessarily not only creating a distance between myself and the object, but also distancing myself from the people.

The search work and the time spent in the woods and bogs and scenes of battle create affinity and intimacy with places (figure 2.2). *Poiskoviki* have to learn to interpret landscape and terrain types. Experienced searchers know these areas like the backs of their hands. They can describe places with a remarkable accuracy, pinpointing sites down to the nearest tussock, even during conversations in the city. They remember what they found, and where they found it. The *sense of place* is important in the execution of the work, and it is also key in reconnecting with the past and lost soldiers. It is the basis for imagining the war and what the soldiers went through, and this is a

Figure 2.2 Searching and surveying in the Sinyavino area: photo by the author

prominent part of the battlefield tour that I will discuss later. Place and found objects, as well as historical documents, are used to piece together a detailed image of the past.

Place is also ascribed a sense of agency. Places can 'draw' you, and 'search intuition' is valued and viewed as a skill. Places can also be eerie and make you uneasy. The affect some specific places create is sometimes discussed among the search unit's members. Although they are not very prominent in the day-to-day discourse of the unit, there is an abundance of ghost stories associated with the battlefields. The souls of the soldiers are quite often alluded to, and the dead are ascribed agency. 'They are hiding' is a common remark if you do not find anything. 'Whenever I walk here, I have the sense that someone is walking behind me', the group's leader tells the audience at one particular spot during a ski tour. Affect of this kind can make a place frightening, but eerie feelings also trigger an emotional response that can increase the sense of connection.

Vakhty pamyati expeditions includes long days of hard physical work, search work as well as chores related to the upkeep of the camp, such as fetching wood or water. It is a matter of washing in icy cold water, line ups by the flag, as well as communal meals and socialising by the campfire. You should try to stay reasonably dry and warm; keeping clean is, however, almost impossible. After a few hours of digging you are covered in mud from head to toe. 'Sinyavino manicure' is a common joke to describe dirty hands and cracked nails. To some this is a very real problem. G., who works at a restaurant, is worried dirty nails could get her sacked, and she uses a toothbrush to carefully scrub her nails every night to get them as clean as possible.

Working on a battlefield, *poiskoviki* have to learn to be careful. You cannot drive the shovel full force into the ground, as unexploded ordnance may be detonated by impact: 'Use the probe and dig carefully.' Every day, all present need to sign a waiver saying they will adhere to the PTB – the safety instructions. If you want to light a fire, you need to make sure that there is nothing that can detonate near or underneath it. *Poiskoviki* have no right to handle ammunition. Instead, you should call the MChS (Ministry of Extraordinary Situations) and the police. One person in each district is responsible for such matters, and the searchers get to know them pretty well. Despite the warnings from the MChS, it can be an unpleasant experience to be close to a controlled detonation. I especially remember one summer night, and I do not think I have ever heard a scarier sound than the pressure wave after the detonation, which moved through the forest with a muffled rustling. The blast itself was bad enough, but the pressure wave ...; there was something almost ghostly about it whining in the night. As I was sitting around the campfire and heard the explosion's eerie aftermath, I for a short moment had an intense sensation of having gotten a closer understanding of how it was to sit here during the war. Work and events

Figure 2.3 Finding an icon: photo by the author

create a sense of place and a sense of connection with the past, bringing the past into the present.

The search stands outside everyday life in and outside mainstream society. Within the unit, there is an abundance of jokes referring to themselves as *sumasshedshie* (lunatics). 'Not even my mother understands why I'm doing this', says A., and several other members of the unit testify about similar reactions from relatives. *Zabolet'*, to become ill, or *zarazit'*, to infect, are other words used to jokingly describe themselves and their relation to the search. The viral metaphors describe the search as having a physical effect, affecting your very being. But this is also something people enjoy doing; when in the city, they long for the battlefields, for the forest, for the bogs. While official discourse stresses the search work as a duty, the unofficial stories stresses enjoyment. This is not contradictory. There is no inherent contradiction between a strong sense of patriotic duty and enjoying a day in the woods, a long *perekur* (literally smoking break but also taken by non-smokers) or the friendship of the unit (figure 2.3).

The usually quite light mood that prevails should not be mistaken for a lack of seriousness. Bones might be commonplace, but there are strong norms on how these should be handled. The excavated soldiers are frequently referred to as relatives, as *blizkie* or close ones. At the funerals, the search unit members in many ways take the roles absent relatives otherwise would.

In an album called 'The Price of Victory' on a social network site, A. has posted pictures from the search, including unusually explicit photos of human remains. He received criticism for the unpleasant content, and published the following defence:

> This album will keep being filled. These people gave us the dearest gift – their lives. Everyone has forgotten them. Their remains are decaying in forests and bogs. We need not fear bones, but forgetfulness and indifference. I think that they died for me personally [...] therefore I relate to every soldier I have excavated, as to my closest friend. Let us be worthy of their memory.

A strong sense of having understood something that most people have not is frequently expressed. The glamorous image of the war displayed at the public Victory Day celebrations is contrasted with the horrible images unfolding in the woods and bogs. As in the album discussed above, the objective of the unit's official dissemination is not only to spread knowledge of the war, but also to deepen the official picture with poignant examples of the very high cost of that victory.

Guiding the war

Three general tours of the battlefields are arranged each year by the search unit (and other tours are arranged for special occasions or visiting groups), two in winter, on skis, and the third on 1 May. The tours are paid for by the university and are mainly targeted at its students, but open to the general public. Connecting place to knowledge, increasing awareness of the past, the war and sacrifice, the tours have a strong element of commemoration. The tours go over areas in which the search unit works, telling the stories of the Leningrad and Volkhov fronts. In this section I will focus on the annual 1 May tour, and any direct quotes are from a recording of the 2010 tour made by one of the participants. The leader of the search unit is the one giving the tour, and he always assigns great importance to this event. I will use two stops on the tour to illustrate how the narrative appeals to emotion and aims to create a sense of place and a sense of connection with the past.

The guide meets the group at Nevsky Pyatachok (Neva Bridgehead), one of the most famous, or infamous, battlefields of the eastern front. It is located on the elevated left (eastern) bank of the Neva, projecting into enemy territory. It lends itself to excursions since it is a small, confined and relatively accessible space. It was taken, lost and retaken by the Red Army at great cost. Ultimately, it did not prove of any greater strategic significance, since the siege was broken further north. The small physical space of Nevsky Pyatachok can be seen as a concentration of the horrors of war. Leading the group down to the river Neva, the guide tells the following story:

> This territory along the riverbank was considered rear [not front], and the soldiers jokingly referred to it as *prospekt* [broad, straight street],

34 Johanna Dahlin

which they called 'run faster'. Here right by the river they built so-called *zemlyanki* [dugouts]. When the water recedes, and it will in summer, you can walk along here and you might think you're dreaming. It is full of splinters, parts of shoes and gas masks, spades and bones, bones, bones. [The water was significantly lower in 1941.]

Pointing over the wide river, he says that you see here the distance that you had to cross. It may not seem difficult, he says, but there is a strong current here and the place was under constant fire. Crossing the river was the most dangerous moment, only about half of those who took off from the other side made it over. The current towards Leningrad, he says, pointing in the direction along which the river flows, carried away those who died.

The guide also tells the audience about the conditions the soldiers lived in. The soldiers were hungry, because the Red Army had not managed to secure food supplies across the Neva. He asks the audience to imagine what it was like on the site in autumn 1941: the fighting was going on uninterrupted, around the clock for days on end. The village that existed here had already been obliterated. The land on Nevsky Pyatachok is red sand. 'When you are searching here you get the feeling that it's blood.' The sandy nature of the land also meant that trenches were quickly eroded by the tremors caused by exploding shells. In the morning, he says, you could stand in a trench that reached up to the chest, and in the evening the trench was down to your knees. The soldiers used their dead comrades, either stacked horizontally as a wall or made to stand up as if they were alive, to shore up the walls of their trenches. So some people were killed one, two, three, and more times.

After stopping at some more places on Nevsky Pyatachok, the excursion heads some 10 kilometres east to the Sinyavino field, an area where the search unit worked very intensively in the years leading up to 2010. A large poultry farm complex now covers the field, and what was not found then is now lost. With the change of location, the focus shifts from the course of the war to the search work. The guide leads the group out onto the field to a pit where some members of the group, myself included, have spent the day excavating a soldier. We have been in telephone contact with the tour guide. The soldier is unusually well preserved, 'beautiful', as they say – and it was decided that this was something to see. They proceeded to uncover him *po arkheologicheski* – slowly and carefully.

The guide shows the terrain and points out how *nashi* attacked from the bogs, whereas the Germans had the benefit of higher ground. He then invites the students to have a look at the soldier (figure 2.4). The students peer curiously and apprehensively down into the pit:

> See, here's a soldier. See, here is one, and here is the other. Do you see? You can go around to the other side. They have not taken him up yet, but you can see how he lies here. He's in front of you. Do you see the boots?

Figure 2.4 Showing the 'beautiful' soldier on the Sinyavino field: photo by the author

Here he lies. Who knows, maybe it is one of your grandfathers, father or great grandfather? I think that war to some extent touched all of us. By God, let us hope that he has something on him. By something I mean a medallion, I will show you one later.

L., who was the one who found the soldier, outlines his features in the pit. There were two soldiers, and he shows how the other had lain before he was excavated. The tour guide is expressing a hope that they should find something to identify him with. But the soldier was 'naked' except for boots and belt. And this, apparently, is what everyone expected. Soldiers in combat rarely carried anything by which they could be identified, and this soldier probably died in 1943 when medallions had already been discontinued.

The discovery of the soldier is used both to demonstrate the group's skills and to establish a sense of community with the fallen. By evoking the image of kinship, the guide alludes to the stories of the missing that most likely exist in several of the participants' families, and by saying 'because I think that the war touched us all' he ties in the diverse experiences of war that all present have brought with them. The soldier there in the pit becomes a symbol in which all these stories are concentrated. The relationship need not actually be there, but through fictive kinship metaphors a larger community is evoked that includes both the present and the past.

What the tour participants are shown is a 'deathscape', or the remains of one. They are looking at traces of tragedy. It is the death, disaster and horror that are the focus of the story and the landscape. During the tour, the guide constantly interacts with space. He uses the physicality of place to conjure an image of what is not there, pointing to terrain features to indicate the strategic relevance of elevation and create an image of what the war was like, and at several points inviting the audience to imagine it. He also repeatedly points out how the place was different during the war years. The absences highlighted by the tour can be seen to be crucial in inviting the participants' imagination to bring the past into the present (cf. Gregory and Witcomb 2007: 65).

Place becomes a link, and great significance is attached to it happening right here, although little may remain. The place acts as a concentrator of meaning, the basis upon which to create an imagination of how things were. The war is referred to in the present tense (not only on this tour), and the guide tells the participants that 'now we have visited the war'. Past and place merge (cf. Kverndokk 2007). When bringing participants to the battlefield, the guide takes the role of witness, and invites the participants to re-witness the past. Although not in direct opposition to the official narrative, this is an invitation to remember it differently. Memory is in this way reconstructive (Campbell 2006: 373), and the tour hopes to change the role the war memory has in the lives of the participants.

The guiding is quite focused on the conditions of the common soldier; it emphasises an everyday existence where matters of life and death – especially death – were very present. At times quite a vivid account of life in the trenches is created, asking the audience to imagine what it was like. The cost of war is a main theme, but the war is not politicised. The guide does briefly address the question of whether some lives could have been saved, but there is very little commentary on the political context of the war. In a work discussing the Anzac legacy in Australia, it is claimed that expression of strong emotion 'is a way to avoid discussion and circumvent debate. Most significantly, such reactions de-politicize war commemoration by reducing the event to an emotional story of sacrifice and service' (Damousi 2010: 96). Going on to claim that sentimentality and nostalgia are the dominant modes for young Australians to relate to Anzac Day, Damousi deprecates the scarce knowledge of, or focus on, the reasons why the soldiers were made to suffer in the first place. But the very formulation of affective practice as embodied meaning-making contradicts any separation of emotion and rationality (cf. Wetherell 2012: 13; Smith and Campbell 2016: 8). The emotional meaning-making need not serve *one* political purpose, it can be mobilised for pacifist as well as militarist ends.

Within the search movement, there is a political edge directed at current politicians and the perceived hypocrisy in official Russian commemoration of the war. However, the narrative shares the conviction that the Great Patriotic War is the most defining moment of Russian history. While not glamorous, it stresses the heroism of soldiers enduring inhuman conditions, contributing to the sacralisation of war and reinforcing it as the prime master narrative of contemporary Russia.

Conclusion

Let us go back to the mud where we started, with the decomposed bone fragments I was slowly unearthing. The search work gives 'firsthand' experience of war and loss. Although removed in time, *poiskoviki* are interacting with the same space, and handle the material remains of war. It is a very tangible memory. Uncovering 'naked' soldiers gives a very direct view of the material shortcomings in the Red Army. The physical experience of the localities, of discomforts such as rain and cold, mosquitoes and adders, adds a sense of connection to the war history. Being touched by the place, feeling it, creates a connection between past and present. Seeing affect as embodied meaning-making means sense and sensibility are intertwined. The emotional qualities of the search work are integral to making sense of the war. Being touched, or affected, by the search experience is part of developing the senses I outlined earlier: sense of community, sense of place, sense of connection.

The search movement is dealing with a great tragedy. Its work is about coming to terms with not only the human loss, but also the fact that the remains have remained unburied for so long. The indifference of the Soviet and post-Soviet authorities, allowing the remains to decay unburied and uncared for, is a difficult issue to grasp, not least since the fully-fledged cult of the Great Patriotic War developed in the Soviet Union during a period in which the remains were ignored. This official forgetting did not, however, obliterate the memory of the missing, and, as the Soviet Union crumbled, the issue resurfaced. Now, the search movement is creating its own memorials (as are, I should perhaps add, many others). While memory is very alive within the movement, it is also considered frail. Memory must be not only communicated but also given material form in order for it to be protected, but this also 'freezes it', and peels off layers of meaning that are part of the search unit's memory culture.

In Russian war commemoration, a vow to remember, is often expressed and framed as a patriotic duty. Within the search movement, this sense of duty is interpreted as a call to action. Remembrance is not words alone; memory is literal work. Duty is simultaneously a rhetorical and a discursive figure, a call to action and an emotion that motivates continuous work. However, quite different emotions are also at play when the actual work is carried out: pleasure and satisfaction, friendship and community. Duty is not the sole reason for people giving so much of their free time; to many, this is a labour of love.

Notes

1 This is according to the old homepage of the organisation, www.sporf.ru/, which is more informative than the new http://rf-poisk.ru/.
2 For a discussion on how to count Soviet losses, see for instance Harrison (2003).

References

Campbell, S., 2006. Our faithfulness to the past: Reconstructing memory value. *Philosophical Psychology*, 19(3), 361–380.

Dahlin, J., 2012. *Kriget är inte över förrän den sista soldaten är begraven: Minnesarbete och gemenskap kring andra världskriget i St Petersburg med omnejd*. PhD Thesis. Linköping University.

Damousi, J., 2010. Why do we get so emotional about Anzac? In M. Lake and H. Reynolds, eds. *What's Wrong with Anzac? The Militarisation of Australian History*. Sydney: UNSW Press.

Gregory, K. and Witcomb, A., 2007. Beyond nostalgia: The role of affect in generating historical understanding at heritage site. In S. Knell, S. MacLeod and S. Watson, eds. *Museum Revolutions: How Museums Change and Are Changed*. London: Routledge.

Harrison, M., 2003. Counting Soviet deaths in the Great Patriotic War: Comment. *Europe–Asia Studies*, 55(6), 939–944.

Kverndokk, K., 2007. *Pilegrim, turist og elev: Norske skoleturer til døds-og konsentrasjonsleirer*. PhD Thesis. Linköping University.

Lave, J. and Wenger, E. 1991. *Situated Learning: Legitimate Peripheral Participation*. Cambridge: Cambridge University Press.

Macdonald, S., 2013. *Memorylands: Heritage and Identity in Europe Today*. Routledge: London.

Merridale, C., 1999. War, death, and remembrance in Soviet Russia. In J. Winter and E. Sivan, eds. *War and Remembrance in the Twentieth Century*. Cambridge: Cambridge University Press, 61–83.

Merridale, C., 2005. *Ivan's War: The Red Army 1939–45*. London: Faber and Faber.

Nora, P., 1996. General introduction: Between memory and history. In P. Nora and L. Kritzman, eds. *Realms of Memory: The Construction of the French Past. Volume I: Conflicts and Divisions*. New York: Columbia University Press.

Paxson, M., 2005. *Solovyovo: The Story of Memory in a Russian Village*. Bloomington and Indianapolis: Indiana University Press.

Samuel, R., 1994. *Theatres of Memory*. London: Verso.

Smith, L., 2006. *Uses of Heritage*. London and New York: Routledge.

Smith, L. and Campbell, G., 2016. The elephant in the room: Heritage, affect and emotion. In W. Logan, M. Nic Craith, and U. Kockel, eds. *A Companion to Heritage Studies*. Oxford: Wiley Blackwell, 1–26.

Tumarkin, N. 1994. *The Living and The Dead: The Rise and Fall of the Cult of World War II in Russia*. New York: Basic Books.

Wetherell, M., 2012. *Affect and Emotion: A New Social Science Understanding*. London: Sage.

Chapter 3

Troubling heritage

Intimate pasts and public memories at Derry/Londonderry's 'Temple'

Margo Shea

Introduction

High on the east bank of the River Foyle, literally at 'the Top of the Hill' at the highest elevation in the city limits of Derry/Londonderry, Northern Ireland, a temple stood briefly. At 72 feet high, it towered over its surroundings, a thin spire mirroring the city's cathedral steeples on the river's opposite bank. The sign at its entrance instructed 'Leave a memory behind, let go of the past and look to the future.' Memories relinquished would not remain – at least not in their material forms. 'Temple' was made to be ephemeral, built to be consumed in flames on the night of the vernal equinox, one week after a team of local and international volunteer builders had completed its construction in March 2015.

Sponsored and organised by London-based Artichoke Trust, which specialises in helping artists engage communities to stage large-scale installations located in unpredictable spaces, Temple was two years in the planning. Led by American artist David Best, known for his 'build and blaze' temples to loss and catharsis associated with Nevada's annual Burning Man festival, a volunteer crew from Northern Ireland and around the world assembled the intricate balsa wood construction in six weeks. Aspirations for the project were as imposing as its form. In David Best's words, Temple had 'to be so beautiful that you [would] give up the thing that has been troubling you [for] your whole life' (Anon. 2015a). In terms of visitor engagement, those aspirations were largely met. Over 60,000 people visited the site, which was open to the public for one week before it was set ablaze, leaving messages and mementoes or simply experiencing Temple. About 15,000 people witnessed the burn. Derry/Londonderry is a city of 100,000; even factoring in regional visitation, these numbers are significant. The nature of this engagement deserves attention because very little research has been done that investigates memory work and heritage practices in relation to the well-documented continued emotional burdens of the Troubles on people in Northern Ireland. Through this chapter, I suggest that memorial processes that intend to address, obliquely or explicitly, the pervasive effects of post-traumatic stress disorder (PTSD) in Northern Ireland must develop new approaches to facilitate remembrance that is simultaneously private and public, intimate and shared.

This chapter is a scholarly reading of the Temple project that explores the ephemeral memorial process as a case study to discuss the ways in which both heritage practices and emotions are necessarily spatialised, contingent, embodied, relational and performative. Temple's contributions to post-conflict place-making and 'dealing with the past' in Derry/Londonderry can be more fully understood if the affective practices exhibited through this participatory public art project are linked more explicitly to the study of heritage practices and processes in post-conflict Northern Ireland. Through its form, composition, location and crowd-sourced construction and interpretation, Temple structured, quite literally, an open-ended process of meaning-making. When people physically 'entered into' the project space, I propose here that they co-created a shared place in which private loss and pain could be acknowledged and shared obliquely in ways that were communal without being confrontational. Further, I suggest that, while Temple has broadly been recognised as a successful project, the reasons for engagement and participation have been somewhat underdetermined. In practice, then, Temple was neither a repository for Troubles-related memories nor a container for quotidian suffering. Rather, the memorial process it enacted invited participants to acknowledge the intertwined composition of their emotional inheritances.

A Temple to loss: Heritage and affect in post-conflict Northern Ireland

Conceived and planned explicitly as a post-conflict community memory project that would explode divisive traditions, Temple was built both out of specific conceptions of heritage in Northern Ireland and out of a desire to destabilise those conceptions. I suggest that the collaborative, crowd-sourced and processual nature of the project, its spatial positioning and its echoes of familiar ritual allowed it to transcend, while still containing, remembered histories and emotional injuries of the Troubles. By inviting creation of an ephemeral intimate public, I posit that the sharing of personal and private memories promoted healing in part because of the impossibility of separating individual responses to grief, anxiety and trauma from the broader cultural legacies of the Troubles. Temple was effective, I argue, because it made space for reckoning with historical legacies of violent conflict that wove together public and private memory in subtle, significant ways.

In accord with the premise that heritage scholars must not treat affect as the result or byproduct of interpretative and curatorial processes, this chapter endeavours instead to engage with 'the agency, context and above all, consequences of the affective moment' in relation to Temple (Smith and Campbell 2016: 455). It draws on scholarship of affect to suggest that the outcomes of the project were different from, indeed more complex than, what the organisers had intended because Temple resonated with and through a set of affective practices that simultaneously shaped and emerged from a wide range of emotions, framed here as active, embodied and never fixed. In the words of Sara Ahmed (2004: 26), emotions 'do things, and they align individuals with communities – or bodily space with social space – through the very intensity of their attachments'. Following Ahmed, emotions factor in relationships between the individual and the collective, as Northern Irish people negotiate private and public memories of the past in relation to understandings of the present and visions for the future.

In its design and intent as a post-conflict project, the hilltop site, symbolism of bonfires and architectural mirroring with the city's cathedrals echoed events and experiences associated with the conflict and the peace process and also connected the project subtly to broader histories of Ireland and Northern Ireland. In interviews, news articles and invitations to participate, I postulate here that Temple organisers worked under the assumption that the injuries of the Troubles would adhere to these familiar representations and references – that the emotions raised by and through Temple would echo, challenge, implicate – but always imbricate with the ideologies that had trellised the conflict.

Paradoxically, this premise may have liberated participants to contribute expressions of memory of deeply private and personal experiences they might not necessarily associate with the Troubles. If, following Cvetkovich (2012: 2), 'everyday feelings' are often linked to political or public feelings, those filaments of loss and burden weave through and around the histories of civil conflict in Northern Ireland, particularly in the ways citizens have learned to carry and cope with depression, anxiety and trauma both individually and as part of divided publics. Making multivalence both a design and a process goal may have been intended to allow conflicting memories to share space, but in the end it may have done more; I suggest it made possible a shared reckoning with emotions that defy easy and neat boundaries between public and private losses. In this sense, engagements with Temple linked the emotional burdens of private, ordinary experiences to longer and larger traumas that were more specifically and directly associated with the decades of civil conflict in Northern Ireland. By enacting an embodied memorial process that was negotiated and experienced spatially, kinesthetically, relationally and communally, I posit that participants in the memory process could be released from the responsibility of carrying Troubles memories. Paradoxically, the private griefs they relinquished in the fire cannot be divorced from the larger and longer histories of conflict.

Like others engaged in memory projects in Northern Ireland, Helen Marriage, director of Artichoke Trust, entered the "project space" (Cahn 2014) by conceptualising heritage problematically and staging Temple as an intervention. Heritage has largely been viewed instrumentally 'as a set of cultural productions that articulate parallel, oppositional narratives about the past' (Shea 2010: 290). In the years following the 1998 Good Friday Agreement, heritage in Northern Ireland has been increasingly conceptualised as troublesome itself, as a set of cultural productions that articulate parallel, oppositional narratives about the past. Working within this framework, many scholars of heritage have highlighted the ways the past has been wielded as an ideological tool to justify the present by those on either side of the conflict (McIntosh 1999; Crooke 2005; McCarthy 2005). This discourse gave credence to the assumption that heritage and memory work serve primarily to calcify difference and to provide safe cocoons for separateness in Northern Ireland, nurturing polarities instead of facilitating convergences.

As a result, the goal of many post-conflict heritage projects, including Temple, has been to create opportunities for more inclusive memory work that reframes the purposes of heritage and topples the longstanding parallel-narratives framework. Drawing from urban design theories on public space and the heterotopian possibilities of place-making, the Temple project thus emerged out of the notion that art and culture can be 'productively disruptive', creating new forms through which to destabilise heritage practices and the ideologies they purportedly bolster and amplify (Artichoke Trust n.d.).

I assert in this chapter that Temple was in keeping with an emergent thread that sees heritage as a potential tool for reshaping post-conflict society in Northern Ireland instead of as a weapon wielded by those with competing interests and identities. In this view, heritage practices act as conduits for an engaged and participatory public at peace with its differences. By moving away from divided and mutually exclusive heritage processes built out of divided and divisive ideologies that shape identity, new kinds of public engagements with the past, present and future become possible. Temple was part of a genre of projects intended to facilitate citizens' efforts to engage in memory work that transcends dual narratives and begins to make space for broader, more complicated engagements with the past (Marriage 2015). Marking a transition, indeed a transformation, from performing 'ideology as heritage' to 'emotion as heritage', I propose here that Temple relied on discourses of emotion, emphasised ritual and used deeply symbolic spatial understandings and place-identities to connect citizens to the project. As such, Temple is an object lesson in the productive unpredictabilities of multivocal heritage processes, where participation and meaning-making do not point to any *one* thing, but rather illuminate myriad histories and narratives and their undeniable interrelatedness.

Spatialising Temple

Temple's location was important to its role in a post-conflict constellation of memory and identity projects. Place and the spatialisation of memory are critical to the synergies between heritage and affective practices.

Like memory, place is highly contingent and thus unfixed, always in the process of being revised and reshaped. Landscapes thus resonate as palimpsests of experiences, memories, beliefs and emotional and affective responses.

I propose that, in its location, Temple operated at the nexus of multivalent spatial resonances and engaged diverse heritages in Derry/Londonderry's long history. The structure echoed sites, events and themes that connect both to Catholic nationalist and to Protestant unionist memorial narratives. At the same time, its location operated in dialogue with key post-conflict public spaces and gestured to the proximal hillsides of County Donegal, several miles away in the Republic of Ireland.

Historians recount that the site at Ebrington saw King James II's troops encamped during the Siege of Derry in 1689. They probably first saw the city from the Top of the Hill, where Temple stood. In the folkloric mythologies that have emerged, supporters of William of Orange famously withstood the siege trapped inside the walled city of Londonderry as James' troops besieged them after a winning streak across Ireland (McBride 1997). The Williamites stood their ground, ultimately surviving to secure an Orange victory in 1690 at the Battle of the Boyne. While European histories tend merely to mention in passing the siege in the tale of the Glorious Revolution, for the Protestants of Ulster it loomed large as an historically pivotal event. The walls of Derry became symbolic of their struggle for religious and political self-determination. As Macdonagh explains, for Protestant unionists,

> the siege of Derry of 1689 is their original and most powerful myth. They see themselves in that, and since then, as an embattled and enduring people. Their historical self-vision is one of an endless repetition of repelled assaults, without hope of absolute finality or of fundamental change in their relationship to their surrounding and surrounded neighbours.
>
> (Macdonagh 1983:14)

British Crown forces established barracks at the Ebrington from the mid-eighteenth century, mostly housing locally recruited regiments. It served as a place of colonial spectacle, a parade ground, in the mid-nineteenth century. From 1939 to 1970, it was a navy base and, when the Troubles began, British soldiers made their barracks at Ebrington, vacating in 2003 as Operation Banner wound down. For most of its history, then, the site was understood through a sectarian lens; for some it was an official and legitimating site of Northern Ireland's belonging in the United Kingdom, while for others it situated and symbolised the power of the colonial other.

The River Foyle, which runs between the Ebrington site on its eastern banks, or Waterside, and the historic municipal building the Guildhall on the 'cityside', was long seen as a symbolic dividing line between Catholic nationalists and Protestant unionists. Thus, the opening of the Ebrington site in 2012 as public space connecting the city centre to the Waterside was an important departure for Derry and, by extension, for Northern Ireland. It not only changed the historic lens through which the space had long been viewed, but also created an important public space, of which the city of Derry and Northern Ireland itself has historically had few. As a concert venue, a staging ground for major city events and an open space for walking or sitting with friends, the site introduced unprecedented possibilities for public life. Further, this was not simply symbolic. In order to make the Ebrington site accessible, it was connected by the Peace Bridge to create pedestrian access from the heart of the Waterside to the city centre. The bridge, designed by Wilkinson Eyre Architects and open for foot and cycle traffic in 2011, has opened up the city, reduced spatial divisions, and created new possibilities for how people, particularly young people, move through and around the city. Literally and figuratively, it has bridged historic schisms.

In its forms and purposes, Temple was situated in post-conflict Northern Ireland as part of a larger spatial discourse, whereby geographies of conflict and separateness between Protestant and Catholic, unionist and nationalist, have entered into flux. This includes security architecture, flags, painted curbs, murals and other markings of both territory and religious–cultural, ideological affiliations. The siting of Temple functioned within a larger spatial discourse by helping to break down binaries in public space between private and public, 'ours' and 'theirs', 'Waterside' and 'cityside'. Further, its close proximity to successful post-conflict public spaces in the city such as the Peace Bridge and the Ebrington site likely affirmed collapsing geographic divides. Temple was spatialised within a familiar framework, inviting responses to the project and its purpose that fell within the same registers of feeling as accompanied other successful post-conflict spatial projects. As such, it appeared to take inspiration from urbanists who imagine the ways urban space is constantly created and recreated through individual and collective practices. Space thus becomes fluid and multivocal as meanings are layered and relational dynamics affect social and political life (Tornaghi and Knierbein 2014).

Temple's design included a tall spire that mirrored the spires of Derry's two cathedrals – the Church of Ireland's venerable St Columb's Cathedral and the Catholic Diocese of Derry and Raphoe's St Eugene's Cathedral. As ephemeral as it was, a third spire in the skyline – unattached to any religious tradition – may have sanctified the project and claimed its purpose to be credible, even sacred. I propose that it also suggested that the project itself was to be entered into with seriousness and intentionality.

Temple's referents extended beyond Peace Bridge, Ebrington Square and local sacred spaces. It reached across the border, embracing the landscapes, histories and legends of nearby Donegal, located in the Irish Republic. The hills of Donegal have long been celebrated in song and story as emblematic of Irish and Celtic identity (Dorian, MacSuibhne and Dickson 2001; Shea 2010). As a parallel to Ebrington, during the colonial period, Donegal was seen as illegible and unconquerable space, the last corner of Ireland to capitulate to colonisation. The Top of the Hill site of Temple connects Derry to Donegal through continuity of landscape. Additionally, for many

Catholic nationalists in Derry, the Grianan fortress, a 'northern Tara' only a few miles from the city centre, built centuries before the Christian era, connects the city both to Donegal and to traditional Irish identities (Deane 1998). The Grianan fort is also implicated in histories of colonialism and resistance. Tradition has it that the loyal troops of Ulster's last great chieftain, Hugh O'Neill, slumber within caves beneath the old fort. They will awaken when the time comes to conquer 'the Saxon' and to free Ireland once and for all.

Fire and its multiple meanings

The connection to Donegal went beyond imaginative geographies. Spatialised references to Derry's rural hinterland, I suggest, related to the very notion of fire and the premise that Temple would be built to burn. Helen Marriage identified Northern Ireland's bonfire tradition as a key factor in bringing David Best and his work to Derry/Londonderry after spending some time in Derry. 'One of the things that came up constantly was the issue of bonfires' (Marriage 2015). Marriage was referring to the highly localised tradition of lighting bonfires to mark religious and political events annually; these became sectarianised in the early twentieth century and implicated in conflict in the decades leading up to, during and since the Troubles. For Protestants, there were fires to commemorate July 12th, the Relief of Derry in August and Lundy Day in December. Catholics built bonfires to observe Lady Day, or the feast of the Assumption of Mary in August. These, Seamus Deane (1971) has argued, were a heritage practice of sorts – artefacts of the ancient bonfires lit to signal calls of distress in Gaelic Ireland and to celebrate festivals like Lúnasa, the harvest festival of light.

Temple was designed specifically to respond to the bonfire tradition in Northern Ireland. Said Marriage, 'we wanted to bring people into the same physical space and share something that would normally divide them' (Bennhold 2015). While Catholic and nationalist bonfires in Derry never reached the same heights of community organisation or cultural and ideological resonance as they did in Belfast, both Protestants and Catholics, unionists and nationalists, in Derry/Londonderry understand and identify the bonfire tradition as an artefact of the conflict that continues. At the heart of urban bonfires, there has always been an articulation of community and cultural identity as well as an inclination to impose physical boundaries that segregate neighbourhoods and proclaim territory. Artichoke brought Temple to Derry/Londonderry to take the long-held tradition of bonfire burning and 'turn it on its head, reinventing the tradition as a shared space ... with a very different set of values' (Marriage 2015).

As Marriage put it, conversations about this history gave the artists at Artichoke the idea to marry the bonfire tradition in the North with the Celtic notion of burning as cleansing and link it to ancient Celtic observances of the Spring Equinox. 'Perhaps we could bring David [Best] with the values that are associated with peace, love, reconciliation, meditation, a kind of spiritual renewal ... people could bring offerings, mementoes, messages and try to ditch some stuff of the past that they need to let go in order to move on' (Marriage 2015).

The possibilities of the project for inviting the public simultaneously to engage and expel their memories and experiences revolved around the Troubles. Temple was envisioned as a cathartic release of memories deemed unproductive to healing and peace. The organisers hoped that it would help those 'encumbered by the past' to release that which 'is ingrained, in what our parents and our grandparents said or did' (Marriage 2015).

Initially, artist David Best also conceived Temple as a memory initiative that reflected the Northern Ireland conflict, though his perspective was somewhat different. Upon his arrival in Derry, he framed it as a way of healing in post-conflict society, a means of creating unity and marking a celebration of the fact that the Troubles are over. 'What I was building was a piece of celebration, that the people of Ireland have come to grips with the Troubles – and this is a place for them to celebrate their accomplishments' (Best 2015).

What they brought to Temple: Affect and engagement with a multiplicity of histories

As I have argued above, the site, situation and symbolism of Temple were initially intended to foster and facilitate memory work about the Troubles. As an ephemeral public art project, Temple organisers didn't build an archival or documentary component into the plan. However, the documentary Marriage directed, *Temple: A Radical Arts Project in Derry–Londonderry*, recorded many participants' responses. Further, journalists of all stripes spent time at the installation and interviewed those engaged in the memorial process. I have utilised these documentary traces as well as interviews with participants and observers to explore the affective responses to Temple.

Some of those who came did bring memories and mementoes from the Troubles to Temple. Former member of the Provisional IRA and longtime peace and reconciliation activist 'Big' John McCourt was filmed holding up a photo of Jim Wray:

> Seconds after that photograph, after thinking he'd actually run past me, I looked on the ground and he was lying, on the corner on the curb, half on and half off of it, shot through the spine. And I watched the soldier walk over to put another round in his back. And I'm the last guy out of Glenfada Park on Bloody Sunday. Maybe it's time to put this down, not to forget about it, but just put it down. And I am going to take that opportunity now.
>
> (Marriage 2015)

As a counterpoint to McCourt's story of his own physical vulnerability and personal memories of witness to the inhumanity of a British soldier during Bloody Sunday, one of the most public and famous events of the Troubles, city resident Gerry Temple recalled an abiding memory of a particularly painful experience during the Troubles:

> I have struggled all my life with the memory of seeing a soldier shot dead in Derry. It's a nightmare that has haunted me my entire life. One of the memories I had was of a girl dancing with joy after the death of the soldier ... Dave [Best] suggested I use 'Temple' to try and move past it. So I wrote a message and put it into the structure to be burned with all the other messages. My message simply read 'bye dancing girl – no more nightmares'.
>
> (Marriage 2015)

The correspondences between the two stories deserve attention. Both memories involve violent death in the midst of the Troubles. I suggest that both men express trauma and vulnerability here, though differently. For McCourt, his body was under threat in the event remembered. Identifying with Wray, his memory of victimisation corresponded more broadly to a nationalist and republican discourse of abusive power, invasion and injustice. The body became, in this discourse, part of extensive spaces of vulnerability. On the other hand, Temple's remembered experience, as he articulated it here, emphasised both the death by shooting of someone who was there to protect him and a woman dancing in response. Mr Temple cited recurrent nightmares, a longstanding traumatic response he could not control in response to an event over which, similarly, he had no control. While McCourt came to Temple to release a sense of violation and fear, Gerry Temple came to the site with a memory of control that had been lost.

In many ways, Temple's objective was to create space for stories like McCourt's and Temple's. As Best explained by way of example, 'Maybe somebody who did something like, say, putting a bomb in somebody's house and was sorry, might leave something in the Temple to be set alight – it will help them get a form of closure' (Moriarty 2015). The project, seen from this perspective, highlighted the shared cost of the Troubles from those on different sides of the conflict. It aimed to create a space where many people in Northern Ireland could lay to rest traumatic memories. If trauma is to be understood, as Jervis (2015: 6) claims, as the 'repetition of the past as crippling present', then the project may also have allowed a traumatised society to pause the cycles of grief.

The prospect of letting go and achieving catharsis, of bringing deeply personal memories to a public space, echoes and engages some of the most potent positions developed by scholars of the social and political experiences and implications of emotion and affect. Particularly, Sara Ahmed's (2004) insistence that we pay attention to the body and Lauren Berlant's ideas of both sentimentality and intimate publics (Berlant and Prosser 2011) suggest the ways Temple may have allowed people to co-create a shared space for emotional experiences of heritage, even when the experiences were deeply divided. The sharing of the affective space, I posit, counterbalanced divisive memories.

In Ahmed's work, the relationships between emotions, bodies and civic and cultural life are examined carefully (Riedner 2006). Ahmed (2004) considers the body a conduit along which emotions travel back and forth from self to world. Registers of feelings are not private, she claims, nor do they emanate from within ourselves. Rather, emotions 'create the very effect of the surfaces or boundaries of bodies and worlds'. These processes are central to the 'production of the ordinary' (Ahmed 2004: 118). In fact, it is the very fluidity of our emotions that gives them staying power. Framed through this lens, sectarian identities in Northern Ireland have taken root in the interstices of individual, social and collective memory – performed, enacted, spatialised and embodied.

In this frame, memories that express vulnerability, fear and confusion from nationalists and unionists alike are based on longstanding circuits in which narratives of injury created coherence and cohesion within identity groups and generated animosity between them. The ordinary and familiar nature of these narratives made them persuasive and pervasive over decades, as a broad register of emotional experiences simultaneously echoed and amplified the feelings that wove through and could not be separated from divisive ideologies. Whether British soldiers performing state violence or soldiers being targeted by paramilitaries in front of an audience of joyful enemies, examples from Temple participants, these narratives, and the 'sticky' figures they trellis (Ahmed 2004: 120), have been particularly effective when they did not have to contend with each other directly.

At Temple, the long-held habit on both sides of the conflict in Northern Ireland of privileging the 'fetishisation of the wound' was made to lose potency, I suggest, by complicating a parallel circulation of emotions that had accompanied parallel and oppositional memorial narratives. Proximity reframed narratives of memory. Again, Ahmed (2004) helps us read the experience through the lens of affect. Borders between self and others, she claims, operate effectively through the 'slide' between signs that are used to categorise objects and figures. Distance reinforces and reifies fear and draws on 'hate' to establish unities and coherence among groups (Ahmed 2004: 118).

In this way, Temple worked in exactly the way organisers had hoped that it would. Surrounded by thousands of images, messages and objects, each of which carried emotional weight, the claim to injury as something uniquely associated with one identity or another, one event or another, one neighbourhood or another, lost any coherent footing.

Berlant's conception of sentimentality helps us to understand Temple as an intervention in longstanding, multigenerational dispositions of affect in relation to the Northern Ireland conflict. Temple produced what Berlant calls sentimentality:

> a mode of relationality in which people take emotions to express something authentic about themselves that they think the world should welcome and respect; a mode constituted by affective and emotional intelligibility and a kind of generosity, recognition, and solidarity among strangers.
>
> (quoted in McCabe 2011)

Here, sentimentality itself was performative; it brought into being, briefly, an intimate public drawn from a broad range of Northern Irish citizens. I propose that Temple produced an ephemeral community around memory, inheritances, dispossession, loss and reflection. As William Scampton, a steward for the event who spent more than 50 hours at the Temple installation, put it,

> they came in their thousands, bringing their hopes and fears, their pain of loss, items of sacred memory and turmoil, images of those dear to them combined with messages by their thousands scribed and scribbled on every available surface for fellow citizens to read.
>
> (Scampton 2015)

If, as Berlant (2008) explains, intimate publics are experimental project spaces where we might endeavour towards alternative versions of the past, present or future, then the multivocality and de-centredness of individual and sectarian memories, along with the experience of physically being together in a space of shared cultural production around the past, drew important connections between ordinary affects, political feelings and formal and intimate publics. This made Temple significant in its own right. I would assert that the project worked; it did what it was intended to do.

However, the actual affective resonances of Temple, I want to suggest, were overdetermined. Personal memories that fell outside the bounds of the Troubles far outweighed memories of the conflict brought to the site. By some estimates, there were 40,000 names inscribed on the Temple, 'etched into its wood or pinned to its structures on handwritten notes, some with flowers and photos' (Anon. 2015b). Along with objects, messages and a range of visual narratives, visitors carried a complex set of intimate emotional inheritances, burdens, traumas and desires to the site. For example, the parents of 27-year-old police officer Philippa Reynolds came to Temple to honour the memory of their daughter, who was killed on duty in 2013 when her vehicle was hit by the driver of a stolen 4×4. The Reynolds brought a piece of crafted wood on which they had written 'daughter, friend, colleague' (Deeney, 2015). Through these remembrances of quotidian loss and pain, relations between Temple and other experiences, histories and memories defied existing heritage categories.

Intimate pasts and public memories

I want to suggest that sharing intimate, personal and private memories would be likely to promote post-conflict healing in part because it is impossible to separate individual responses to grief, loss and trauma from the broader cultural legacies of the Troubles. Over decades of violent conflict, trauma and depression led citizens to develop coping and defence mechanisms for anxiety, insecurity, isolation, loss and fear. In these ways, public and private emotional experiences wove together in subtle and significant ways. As a welcoming, inclusive space girded with all of the symbolism of history and the intention of post-conflict peacemaking, Temple created a place where the lines between private and public pasts and memories blurred.

From early on in the building process, volunteers and visitors took on and articulated an array of deeply personal emotional goals that nonetheless found connections in a broader public, evidenced by the tens of thousands of names, pictures, objects and notes brought to the space (Scampton 2015). If, as Kathleen Stewart theorises, ordinary affects are feelings that begin and end in public spaces and public discourses, but also 'the stuff that seemingly intimate lives are made of ... the varied, surging capacities ... that give everyday life the quality of continued motion of relations, scenes, contingencies and emergencies', then Temple was an experiment that married ordinary affects with exceptional histories:

> They work not through 'meanings' *per se* but in the way that they pick up density and texture as they move through bodies, dreams, dramas and social worldings of all kinds. Their significance lies in the intensities they build and in what thoughts and feelings they make possible.
>
> (Stewart 2007: 5)

Following Stewart, the process of exploring ordinary affects was a critical intervention in Northern Irish heritage practice precisely because it was enacted as a memorial process that permitted ordinary affects to co-sign with extraordinary emotional burdens and inheritances. 'Ordinary' pain and grief wove through the more extreme instances of hurt and trauma associated with civil conflict that were memorialised before they were incinerated. They became, for a short time, one stream.

One volunteer, Belfast resident and breast cancer survivor Caroline Murphy, explained that 'The Temple is about dealing with your losses, things that you've been carrying, baggage that's been holding you back. The Temple is very much a place where, if you're ready, if you want to, you can take representations of those things ... it is a beautiful, safe place where hopefully people from Derry and wider environs can leave things that are holding them back' (Artichoke Trust 2016). Scampton conveyed the sense of ordinary affects when he wrote that Temple was a place for 'people to bring "their burdens, their hopes, their sorrows and their tears"' ... and fostered understanding 'that we are all making our way through life, for better, for worse, as best we can' (Scampton 2015). By the end of the build itself, as people came to visit, even David Best had reframed Temple, choosing an expansive interpretation, tied but not limited to the Troubles. He said, on BBC *Front Row*, 'the degree of loss goes from rape and murder to someone losing their dog. There's a whole lot of losses in people's lives' (Best 2015).

One message read 'Happy birthday, daddy, watching over us all.' Another referenced miscarriage or stillbirth, 'Baby Kath, we look forward to meeting you one day.' There were notes about domestic violence, loss and suicide. Those who came with mementoes to the Temple included a woman who had survived breast cancer, parents of a car crash victim and a mother whose son had committed suicide eight months earlier. An 89-year-old came to spend time remembering his wife who had died of cancer – they had been married for 40 years (Anon. 2015c). Observers noted that many visitors to Temple made affective investments in what they saw, read and heard, entering into one another's stories and thus co-creating an alternative narrative. As Scampton (2015) explained, 'one could not but be drawn by the messages and mementoes, the tears shed as people left behind their objects, their images, their photographs or left a message that meant so much to them and spoke of their innermost thoughts and emotions'.

Through Temple, we see the possibilities for heritage practices and memory work to respond to public depression, a form of collective immobilisation that will not respond to old patterns of being and doing. As Cvetkovich (2012) observes, that 'form of being stuck, both literal and metaphorical, requires new ways of living or, more concretely, moving'. In Northern Ireland, of course, this is particularly poignant. With antidepressants prescribed at two and a half times the rate in England, the Northern Irish are more commonly medicated to address anxiety and depression than people in almost any other region in the world (Anon. 2014). A 2007 study found that about 10% of 3,000 Northern Irish residents who responded to a completely random telephone poll met the criteria for a PTSD diagnosis (Muldoon and Downes, 2007), and recent research indicates that Northern Ireland's population had the highest rates of PTSD out of 28 countries surveyed by the World Mental Health Survey Initiative (Ferry *et al.* 2014). When one takes into account issues of class and regional intensities (the Troubles affected urban and border areas particularly), the rate of PTSD in particularly badly affected regions is probably 25% or higher.

Depression is a byproduct of trauma, and, as I have argued elsewhere, one cannot disentangle individual experiences of depression in Northern Ireland from broad, pervasive cultural and political inheritances (Fay *et al.* 1999;

Shea 2010, 2015). However, even more strikingly, struggles to express loss and grief in other areas of one's life were deeply affected by generations of conflict. Further, the legacies of the Troubles have had pervasive and long-lasting emotional and relational consequences.

Public conflict shaped personal coping mechanisms in a variety of ways. Social isolation, secrecy, suspicion and uncertainty as well as the performance of cultures of violence and accusation fostered a range of private everyday responses, including deflection, compartmentalisation and withdrawal, to name but a few (Shea 2010, 2015). In the *Cost of the Troubles Survey,* these emotional responses to the civil conflict and its legacies were studied. It was found that over 70% of respondents had experienced the inability to speak freely due to safety issues, while 63% had experienced feeling wary in the presence of those from a different community. In addition, 39% had had the experience of changing routes, routines and habits because of a sense of threat, and 40% of respondents felt that they had personally been blamed for the Troubles (Morrisey, Smyth and Fay 1999). These effects, the study illustrated, spilled out into everyday life. For example, 60% of respondents experienced wariness about sharing details of their lives with others or expressing an opinion, and 30% expressed generalised bitterness. In addition, 64% claimed to experience the feeling of powerlessness and 44% felt that the effects of the Troubles included 'shattering the illusion that the world was a safe place', while 43% reported feeling either very jumpy or that that they had to be on 'guard all the time' (Morrisey *et al.* 1999: 73–74). This research supports my argument that the traumatic inheritances of the Troubles have as much to do with how people carry *all* of their tribulations as they do with how they have shouldered pain associated with the conflict itself.

The distinction between ordinary traumas and trauma associated with a generation of violent conflict is also tied, I posit, to distinctions between public and private. The weft and weave of structural, interpersonal and personal violence are difficult to disjoin. This shapes and defines the ways they produce affect. 'Often what counts as national or public trauma is that which is more visible and catastrophic, that which is newsworthy and sensational, as opposed to the small dramas that … draw attention to how structural forms of violence are so frequently lived [and] how their invisibility or normalization is another part of their oppressiveness' (Cvetkovich 2007). The post-conflict moment is a vulnerable one. Periods of structural transition can create an imaginary impasse, whereby we live on while not knowing what to do, and develop accounts and practices of how to live as we do so (Berlant and Prosser 2011). This concept is expressed by Scampton (2015) as he reflected on the experience of Temple, 'It became a reliquary or repository of personal hurt, loss and memory for so many hoping that the burn would remove such from them and at the same time illuminate a way forward for those unsure of the path ahead.'

Conclusion

In the face of complex legacies of civil violence, affective practices refuse to be contained within binary frameworks like before/after, war/peace, public/private and us/them and insist on the traces that link ordinary and everyday experiences to histories of conflict. Bodies interrupt discourses as well as participate in them. Visitors, bystanders and participants in heritage practices may confirm, deny or, in this case, simply complicate the goals of heritage in the present. Temple's aim was to explore and expunge emotional burdens associated with a history and heritage shaped by conflict and violence. But it did more; the project made possible a shared reckoning with emotions that defy easy and neat boundaries and refuse to be contained within binary frameworks like before/after, war/peace, public/private and us/them. Through their emotional engagements, participants with Temple insisted on the integrity of traces that have linked ordinary and everyday experiences to their histories of conflict. Doing this together in a shared space was possible, I suggest, because Temple was designed and situated to shoulder some of the historical burdens that have been part and parcel of Northern Irish society for centuries.

Temple's overdetermined post-conflict framework freed people to respond outside familiar tropes of post-conflict memory and to move beyond familiar memorial frames of reference bounded by the Troubles. For a week, this created an intimate public, a space of identification that created, enacted and legitimised a complex range of emotional attachments. Examining the ways those who built it, and the thousands who visited, experienced Temple allows us to think seriously about emotion as something other than that which accompanies ideology or offers up its antidote – particularly in relation to contentious and difficult history. In turn, the incalculable complexity that accompanies a reckoning with personal, political, social and cultural inheritances yields to a more diverse and engaged public heritage that transcends ideology, situates injury as myriad and collective and encourages compassion towards self and others.

References

Ahmed, S., 2004. The *Cultural Politics of Emotion*. Hoboken: Routledge.

Anon., 2014. Northern Ireland 'one of world's highest rates for anti-depressants'. *BBC News*, 16 November. www.bbc.com/news/uk-northern-ireland-30073669 [Accessed 16 November 2014].

Anon., 2015a. How We Built Temple. Available from www.culturenorthernireland. org/features/visual-arts/how-we-built-temple#sthash.TWoCgwWE.dpuf [Accessed 14 December 2015].

Anon., 2015b. Hand-crafted 'Temple' in memory of dead burns in Derry. *Irish Times*, 22 March. Available from www.irishtimes.com/news/ireland/irish-news/hand-crafted-temple-in-memory-of-dead-burns-in-derry-1.2148823 [Accessed 1 June 2016].

54 Margo Shea

Anon., 2015c. A bonfire of the tragedies. *Belfast Telegraph*, 21 March. Available from www.belfasttelegraph.co.uk/news/northern-ireland/a-bonfire-of-the-tragedies-31084904.html [Accessed 13 June 2016].

Artichoke Trust, n.d. 'Power of Cultural Disruption'. Available from www.artichoke.uk.com/talks/the_power_of_cultural_disruption/ [Accessed 14 December 2015].

Artichoke Trust, 2016. *Temple Stories*. Available from www.youtube.com/watch?v=jILWVSWVfLs [Accessed 12 August 2017].

Best, D., 2015. *Front Row*, www.bbc.co.uk/programmes/b0543yjt [Accessed 3 January 2016].

Bennhold, K., 2015. Healing fire in Londonderry: The Temple was built to burn. *New York Times*. Available from www.nytimes.com/2015/03/28/world/europe/using-flames-to-soothe-a-northern-ireland-city-scarred-by-fire.html [Accessed 27 March 2015].

Berlant, L., 2008. *The Female Complaint: The Unfinished Business of Sentimentality in American Culture*. Durham: Duke University Press.

Berlant, L. and Prosser, J., 2011. Life writing and intimate publics: A conversation with Laurent Berlant. *Biography*, 34(1), 180–187.

Cahn, Elizabeth, 2014. *Project Space(s) in the Design Professions: An Intersectional Feminist Study of the Women's School of Planning and Architecture (1974–1981)*. Doctoral Dissertations May 2014–current. 160. http://scholarworks.umass.edu/dissertations_2/160.

Crooke, E., 2005. The construction of community identity through heritage in Northern Ireland. In M. McCarthy, ed. *Ireland's Heritages: Critical Perspectives on Memory and Identity*. Hoboken: Routledge.

Cvetkovich, A., 2007. Public feelings. *South Atlantic Quarterly*, 106(3), 459–468.

Cvetkovich, A., 2012. *Depression: A Public Feeling*. Durham: Duke University Press.

Deane, S., 1971. Why Bogside? *Honest Ulsterman*, 27, 1–8.

Deane, S., 1998. *Reading in the Dark*. New York: Vintage.

Deeney, D., 2015. Grieving parents of police officer Philippa Reynolds pay special tribute at art project. *Belfast Telegraph*. Available from www.belfasttelegraph.co.uk/news/northern-ireland/grieving-parents-of-police-officer-philippa-reynolds-pay-special-tribute-at-art-project-31080726.html [Accessed 20 March 2015].

Dorian, H., MacSuibhne, B. and Dickson, D., 2001. *The Outer Edge of Ulster: A Memoir of Social Life in Nineteenth-Century Ulster*. Notre Dame: University of Notre Dame Press.

Fay, M. T., Morrissey, M., Smyth M. and Wong, T., 1999. *The Cost of the Troubles Study. Report on the Northern Ireland Survey: The Experience and Impact of the Troubles*. Derry/Londonderry: INCORE.

Ferry, F., Bunting, B., Murphy, S., O'Neill, S., Stein, D. and Koenen, K., 2014. Traumatic events and their relative PTSD burden in Northern Ireland: A consideration of the impact of the 'troubles'. *Social Psychiatry and Psychiatric Epidemiology*, 49(3), 435–446.

Jervis, J., 2015. *Sympathetic Sentiments: Affect, Emotion and Spectacle in the Modern World*. New York: Bloomsbury.

MacDonagh, O., 1983. *States of Mind: A Study of Anglo-Irish Conflict, 1780–1980*. Boston: Allen and Unwin.

Marriage, H., 2015. *Temple: A Radical Arts Project in Derry–Londonderry*. Available from http://templederry-londonderry.com/about [Accessed 11 February 2016].

McBride, I., 1997. *The Siege of Derry in Ulster Protestant Mythology*. Dublin: Four Courts Press.

McCabe, E., 2011. Depressive realism: An interview with Lauren Berlant. *Realism*, (5). Available from www.hypocritereader.com/5/depressive-realism [Accessed 3 February 2018].

McCarthy, M., 2005. Explorations of Ireland's Heritages. In M. McCarthy, ed. *Ireland's Heritages: Critical Perspectives on Memory and Identity*. Hoboken: Routledge.

McIntosh, G., 1999. *The Force of Culture: Unionist Identities in Twentieth-Century Ireland*. Cork: Cork University Press.

Moriarty, G., 2015 Derry prepares for symbolic burning man fire ceremony. *Irish Times*. Available from www.irishtimes.com/news/ireland/irish-news/derry-prepares-for-symbolic-burning-man-fire-ceremony-1.2135911 [Accessed 11 December 2015].

Muldoon, O, and Downes, C., 2007. Social identification and post-traumatic stress symptoms in post-conflict Northern Ireland. *The British Journal of Psychiatry*, 191(2), 146–149.

Riedner, R., 2006. Review of *The Cultural Politics of Emotion* by Sarah Ahmed. *JAC: Journal of Composition Theory*, 26(3–4), 700–706.

Scampton, W., 2015. Telephone interview, 12 June.

Shea, M., 2010. Whatever you say, say something: remembering for the future in Northern Ireland. *International Journal of Heritage Studies*, 16(4), 289–304.

Shea, M., 2015. There were streets: Urban renewal and the early Troubles in London/Derry, Northern Ireland. In F. Samuels, F. and D. Wendel, eds. *Spatializing Politics: How We Know Politics through Space*. Cambridge: Harvard University Press.

Smith, L. and Campbell, G., 2016. The elephant in the room: Heritage, affect, and emotion. In W. Logan, M. Nic Craith and U. Kockel, eds. *A Companion to Heritage Studies*. Oxford: Wiley Blackwell.

Stewart, K., 2007. *Ordinary Affects*. Durham: Duke University Press.

Tornaghi, C. and Knierbein, S., eds. 2014. *Public Space and Relational Perspectives: New Challenges for Architecture*. Hoboken: Routledge.

Chapter 4

Commemoration, affective practice and the difficult histories of war

Amy McKernan and Julie McLeod

Introduction

War commemoration occupies a significant place in public history in Australia, forming a highly visible part of the representation and performance of national identity. Traditions surrounding the two national holidays associated with war – Anzac Day (25 April) and Remembrance Day (11 November) – flood the national media every year, with particularly powerful imagery and discourse attached to Anzac Day, the anniversary of the ill-fated Gallipoli campaign of World War I, when Australian soldiers were said to have 'been tried for the first time, and ... not been found wanting' (Ashmead-Bartlett 1915:5). Children are typically included in these practices of remembering, marching with returned servicemen and women, visiting memorials, and entering essay prizes and competitions about the 'Anzac spirit'. Children are not born knowing, of course, how to participate in war commemoration, and, although the images, actions and discourses associated with remembering war in Australia are so established as to seem ancient, even natural, they are nevertheless relatively recent 'invented traditions' (Hobsbawm 1983; Twomey 2013). The affective practice of commemoration in Australia now feels, in the words of Margaret Wetherell (2012:142), like 'a pre-existing given', and yet it is 'actively created and needs work to sustain'.

This chapter examines two recently developed Australian museum exhibitions and their role in inducting visitors into affective practices of war commemoration and remembering; it draws on analysis of each of the exhibitions examined as well as interviews with key curatorial and education staff at the two institutions. To develop this argument, we frame the museum through the theoretical lens of the heterotopia (Foucault 1966, 2008 [1967]). We argue that representations of war history offer valuable insights into the ways exhibitions work with emotion and affect to teach visitors particular ways of engaging with and understanding the past, and that different approaches speak to the political and social purposes for museum learning. As we show, museum curators work with the affective potential of objects to construct encounters with the contentious and confronting history of war, and to reinforce or undermine established discourses and practices of war commemoration. The exhibitions *WWI: Love and Sorrow* at Museum Victoria and *Australia in the Great War* at the Australian War Memorial (AWM), which are the focus of this chapter, were developed as part of the centenary of the First World War in 2014, attracting government funding to support their creation. The two museums responded to the challenge of interpreting war history for the general public differently; the AWM reinforced discourses of national identity, victory, bravery and resilience, whereas Museum Victoria examined the often long-lasting and devastating impacts of war on bodies and minds, with little sense of, or attention to, the triumphant narrative of victory. Both exhibitions explore the 'darker' side of war history, dealing with violence, conflict and trauma; however, these difficult histories are put to work to invoke sometimes contradictory affective practices. Before exploring these exhibitions, we explain the key conceptual resources drawn upon in the analysis.

Affective practice and the heterotopia

Heterotopias are 'other' spaces, according to Foucault (2008 [1967]), or spaces of difference that stand in 'an ambivalent, though mostly oppositional, relation to a society's mainstream' (Saldanha 2008: 2081). As such, they provide a space at once separate and integral to society; as heterotopias, museums provide the chance to 'visit' a construction of a reality that is positioned to be 'outside' the society of which it is nonetheless a part. The museums explored in this chapter, for example, are located within metropolitan centres – their physical location reflecting their centrality to the communities they represent. Yet, at the same time, it is as if we exit the reality of everyday life in order to view another type of life represented in museum displays. The concept of heterotopia is inherently fluid and often 'disturbing' (Sohn 2008); in methodological discussions it is commonly described in contradictory ways, perhaps because its strengths as a concept lie not in its potential to provide clarity but in its capacity to trouble or challenge taken-for-granted social relations and dynamics. Ultimately, however, the notion of heterotopia resists clear definition (Sohn 2008), which can be advantageous in recognising the complexity and even contradictory dimensions of the museum's role as a 'space of difference'. Understood as an 'other' space, both separate from and situated within society, we argue, the museum can act to both reinforce and undermine dominant historical narratives and discourses. One of the ways in which *Australia in the Great War* and *WWI: Love and Sorrow* work to achieve these things is through engaging affectively with visitors and in particular through framing and reframing in complex ways what might be referred to as 'traditional' Australian commemorative practices relating to the First World War.

Tamboukou (2004:400) writes of heterotopias 'in relation to a specific cultural, social and historical context', suggesting that some spaces exist as heterotopias only at certain times or in certain places, with the same building or institution ceasing to be heterotopian when its place in society becomes less problematic. Tamboukou uses the example of women's colleges, the heterotopian character of which emerged in the context of the turn of the nineteenth century, when 'they challenged the gendered totalizing domination of the male educational space and created alternative educational emplacements for women' (Tamboukou 2004:400). Heterotopias, then, at once challenge hegemonies and open spaces in which alternatives can be built and explored. For museums, this heterotopian function is often desirable, as demonstrated by ideas associated with the 'New Museum', in which a significant aim has been to challenge unjust social structures by representing 'better' or 'fairer' alternatives in exhibitions (Andermann and Arnold-de Simine, 2012). Moreover, in some instances, the promotion of multiple perspectives in museums can create 'safe' spaces for 'dangerous' ideas, to paraphrase Elaine Heumann Gurian's (2006) well-known arguments about museums. This partly renders dissent a less transgressive act in heterotopian museums where this is a more overt focus; where contested perspectives are displayed and historical interpretations are represented as perspective-based and tentative, there is also space for visitors to feel that their own views are acknowledged and respected.

Although they can create spaces that offer alternatives to dominant discourses in society, museum-heterotopias can also reinforce hegemonies, and even close off avenues that might allow visitors to critique dominating ideas. As Heynen (2008:322) observes, heterotopias 'can easily be presented as marginal spaces where social experimentations are going on, aiming at the empowerment and emancipation of oppressed and minority groups; they can as easily be presented as instruments that support the existing mechanisms of exclusion and domination, thus helping to foreclose any real possibility for change'. It would be misleading, therefore, to suggest that a view of heterotopias as challenging hegemony and creating alternatives is unproblematic. Heterotopias are not immune to or ever completely separate from the structures and norms of the societies in which they exist and of which they are essentially a product. In Tamboukou's example, 'heterogeneous and sometimes radical discourses coexisted with fears of breaking social taboos, as well as with traditional practices of educational discipline and control' (Tamboukou 2004:410). In museum representations of war in Australia, powerful affective practices of commemoration can be employed that provoke visitors to respond in ways that reinforce beliefs about the nation, provoking feelings of pride rather than scaffolding critical historical understanding of the complexities of war. We cannot leave our social worlds at the entrance to the museum, nor can the museum eschew its own history as an institution of power and authority and also often a perpetrator of historical injustice.

Today's museums employ a vast array of strategies to impart particular messages and to encourage museum visitors to think and feel in particular ways. The effect and mobilisation of affect and emotion are increasingly a focus in the design of museum exhibitions and programmes (see for example Gregory and Witcomb 2007; Trofanenko 2011; 2014; Witcomb 2013; Mulcahy 2016); associated research has explored, for example, the place of affect and emotion in representing and teaching histories of trauma and violence (Zembylas 2007; Bekerman and Zembylas 2011). Wetherell (2012) identifies two major directions in affect research: the first emerging from psychological notions emphasising emotions, sometimes focusing exclusively on physical manifestations of these; and the second describing affect more broadly as 'force' and 'intensity', drawing non-human actors into understandings of affecting and being affected. As Wetherell suggests, adhering to one or the other of these ways of understanding affect is not necessarily the most productive way forward. Both of these approaches view affect as distinct and separate from discourse and cognition – essentially responding to the exclusion of feeling and experience in language- or discourse-centred research by excluding those elements in turn. As Leys (2011:450–451) describes, this is representative of the 'turn' to affect, where attention is shifted 'from considerations of meaning or "ideology" or indeed representation to the subject's subpersonal material-affective responses, where, it is claimed, political and other influences do their real work'. Analyses of affect as divorced from discourse and cognition rely upon the notion that embodied affect comes before meaning-making in an 'initial bodily hit'; however, as Wetherell (2012:355) suggests, 'Any initial bodily hit ... is always already occurring within an ongoing stream of meaning-making or semiosis.' In the context of our analysis, this is an especially pertinent point, as any affective moments in the museum must also be considered in the context of existing and sedimented historical narratives and discourses of Anzac that are likely to influence the ways in which Australian visitors experience the exhibitions.

In part we explore whether, as Trofanenko (2014:25) argues, the 'nod to emotions/affect has realigned the essence of museums once thought of solely as authoritative sites for gaining knowledge directly from displayed objects and organized narratives framing an exhibition'. Accordingly, we argue that the growing emphasis on feeling and affect in the design of exhibitions is linked to the museum's heterotopian role – that is, they are examined as strategies employed to encourage visitors to feel in particular ways to support specific interpretations of the past. This works, however, in multiple ways, shaping visitor perception to suit the aims and culture of the institution or the exhibition. In some cases, these affective strategies can destabilise assumptions and established narratives, creating spaces for visitors to think differently and for themselves; they can equally close down the opportunities for transgression and promote very specific notions about the past and its significance in the present. Affect can be considered one of the means by which a museum can function as heterotopian in disrupting and challenging dominant discourses and structures of the society in which it exists. Andrea Witcomb (2013:267), for example, examines a range of exhibitions overtly employing affect which all carry an 'ability to not close off narrative', requiring 'that visitors engage imaginatively in the space between themselves and the objects or the spatial and aesthetic structure of the displays'. Additionally, we argue that, although attention to affect is a characteristic of many transgressive and social justice-focused exhibitions, it can also be used to silence and limit critical reflection on the historical narratives that are represented.

Our analysis engages with these conceptual debates to investigate the ways in which museum exhibitions reach and teach visitors through affective practices of commemoration. We draw in part on interviews with curatorial and education staff at the two institutions, but predominantly focus on the opportunities for informal learning that are evident in the two exhibitions. We seek to better understand the work of museums in mobilising and constructing affects, although we do not pretend that visitors' affective and emotional responses are always predictable. As Falk and Dierking (1992) have argued, learning in the museum takes place within and is mediated by personal, social and physical contexts. We sought therefore to explore the decisions and design intentions of museums and to understand the ways in which exhibitions are constructed to affect visitors, embedding this analysis within broader understandings of the social and political contexts for museum work about the First World War in Australia. The analysis involved 'reading' the museum, paying close attention to representations and displays that focused on troubling events and/or troubling emotions, but also looking for 'silences' informed by our knowledge of the contentiousness of Australian public histories of the First World War.

Australia in the Great War

The Australian War Memorial is the figurehead for what many historians refer to as the 'Anzac myth', the ideal of the courageous, honourable, good-humoured and resilient Australian soldier that circulates powerfully through media, politics and public history. Australia's national war memorial is an imposing building that opened in 1941 in the country's capital city, Canberra. Its location says much about the centrality of Anzac to politicians' ideas about the nation – the new Parliament House, constructed during the 1980s, is situated opposite the Memorial, the two landmarks facing one another along the length of Anzac Parade. This emphasis on Anzac commemoration – it is forever in our federal politicians' line of sight – has been the target for considerable discomfort from historians, who are in part concerned with the privileging of the image of a white, male soldier in national identity and collective memory as well as the extensive erasure achieved by the myth, including the role of women and the forgetting of frontier wars against Indigenous people (see for example Lake, Reynolds and McKenna 2010; Reynolds 2013). The Anzac myth has come to stand as a kind of foundation story for Australia, a bedrock for national identity. In doing so, however, it has effectively erased from view significant events prior to the First World War in colonised Australia as well as another national story, that of New Zealand. This forgetting is striking given Anzac's literal meaning as an acronym for the Australian and New Zealand Army Corps. In both of the exhibitions discussed here, and in the circulation of the Anzac legend more popularly, New Zealand soldiers – both Māori and Pākehā – are minimally, if at all, included in Anzac stories within Australia.

The Memorial's newly redeveloped First World War exhibition, *Australia in the Great War*, does little to contradict the sense of triumph and resilience embodied in the Anzac mythology. Rather, the galleries employ tried and true discourses and images to evoke and reinforce the narrative of the brave Australian soldier, with objects and text used to produce powerful affects that are, for many Australians, fuelled by familiarity with public First World War narratives and longstanding affective practices of commemoration. The First World War galleries were redeveloped between 2013 and 2014 at a cost of around $32 million dollars.[1] The exhibition *Australia in the Great War* is manifestly expensive, an impressive overview of the history of Australia's involvement in the First World War. It is, undeniably, a very informative and useful exhibition for those wishing to know about key battles, weapons and the experiences of soldiers at the front. It does not, however, present any significant invitation to critically engage with ideas of heroism and victory in war.

Immediately visible upon entering *Australia in the Great War* is one of the landing boats from the Gallipoli campaign, an object with a powerful capacity to produce an affective response in Australian visitors. These boats are ubiquitous in representations of the campaign – most school students will have seen images of the boats in historical sources and have read descriptions of soldiers boarding the vessels between ships and shore. That this is an original boat used in the landing at Gallipoli allows the display to tap into two powerful sources of affect: first through the Gallipoli mythology; and then through the encounter with historical 'authenticity', a real object with provenance to the moment of interest in the past. Some of the affective power of this moment emerges before we enter the room, however, with the impressive stone façade of the building bearing down on us from the moment we approach and then, once inside, the muffled sound of this crypt-like building weighing us into solemnity. We are well-primed to participate in commemorative practices, already experiencing the bundle of affects with which we are familiar from years of Anzac parades, the 'Last Post' played on the bugle, and phrases like 'lest we forget'. Australians are well-practised at experiencing a mixture of sadness, regret and pride in the face of war sacrifice. To that end, our affective practice of commemoration has begun even before we encounter the first object.

Australia in the Great War works within a framework of all that is characteristic of First World War commemoration in Australia to achieve an emotionally rich and informative exhibition that provides enormous scope for sensing and feeling the past and its place in the present. Contributing significantly to our experience is the collection of dioramas, beautifully crafted depictions of significant battles accompanied by appropriate sounds evoking the drama of the battlefield. These are likely to be familiar scenes to many visitors – recognition of the chaos of a battle, the agonised gestures of wounded men, the lifelessness of ruined bodies and the heroism of the charge – drawing in the viewer with filmic qualities. War is often likened to sport, or sport to war, and in Australia these connections are highly visible in the ever-popular Anzac Day football game. Scenes of battle, like those depicted in the Memorial's dioramas, can invoke an affective charge not unlike that which accompanies a football game. We are invited to be drawn into the scene, be moved by its sense of drama and excitement, while experiencing a jolt at the recognition of loss and violence spread out before us. The dioramas achieve a great deal in this space to 'reconstruct' the past for us. Their tangibility is partly what makes them powerful; they are a step more 'real' than a painting, three-dimensional and – although we are understandably barred from doing so – with the sense that we could move within them, become part of the landscape.

Elsewhere in the exhibition, an extensive range of objects is used to explore different events, themes, and experiences of the First World War, and to prompt different affective responses in visitors. Weapons are likely to appeal to many boys – an underlying message – and are displayed to achieve the full effect of their dark impressiveness. One floor-to-ceiling-high cabinet has a red background and reveals an array of First World War technology: guns, of course, but also armour, trench-raiding weapons, grenades, shells and shell fragments, flamethrowers and gas masks. Weapons are of course highly evocative objects. This display, with its red background, the height of the case and the fact that we are almost overwhelmed by the objects before us as we stand there, asks the visitor to engage in an affective experience of war that is characterised by fear and danger; here, we are invited to remember something of the violence of war, although this knowledge is immediately entangled with the sense of heroism and honour that has been carried along with the viewer since entering the building. The effect is more likely to be an understanding of the importance of the Anzacs' sacrifice, a feeling of being protected from the weapons nearby those who fought. Feelings of gratitude and pride are likely to be evoked, rather than ones that encourage pausing to consider the horror of the objects and the devastating effects such weapons might have had upon others.

This is an area expected to be of interest to visitors – a great deal of information is provided through electronic captions for those who wish to know more about the objects on display. One of the achievements of this exhibition is precisely that it includes an enormous amount of information about Australia's involvement in the First World War; while a detailed narrative is

Commemoration 63

accessible at the 'surface' of the exhibition, by looking and reading what is visible, a whole other layer of material can be found in electronic text and image displays and in interactive features like a map of Gallipoli projected onto a wall, which allows visitors to manipulate, zoom in and out, and highlight the history of the landscape. To actually 'complete' the exhibition could take days.

The apparent extensiveness of this exhibition belies its silences though, and there are facets of Australia's First World War history that are not included here, or included only in quite limited ways. Where histories challenge the ideal of the Anzac soldier as brave, good-humoured and resilient, they are generally either presented as anomalies or shaped to fit the myth. War trauma is an obvious example – one display includes an electric-shock machine, noting the existence of shell shock as a 'hitherto unknown condition' that was 'caused by the strain and trauma of industrialized warfare'. This is a problematically oversimplified representation of significant psychological injury, and the display also exemplifies some of the problems that emerge from depicting the past as distant and divorced from the present. Psychological injuries in war remain common and are not fully understood – although the text panel on shell shock in *Australia in the Great War* suggests otherwise – and this aspect of First World War history presents a valuable opportunity to build understanding for soldiers returning from present-day conflicts with similar injuries and conditions. Essentially, we argue that many of the tensions or dilemmas suggested in this section of the display emerge from what is not there.

What is also largely invisible in the exhibition is a sense of diversity amongst the Australian soldiers. While some attempt has been made to include the stories of Aboriginal soldiers, there is little attention to the complexity of the social contexts these soldiers found themselves grappling with both during and after the war. Questions of class and sexuality are notably absent. We could argue that women are represented as marginal, although we would probably be met with the response that they *were* marginal to the action of the battlefields, which is what is focused upon in this exhibition. All this highlights the enormous amount of silencing work this exhibition does through its focus on the Anzac myth, as it was forged and played out in battles throughout Europe. It is undoubtedly challenging for the Memorial's curatorial staff to manage the multiple demands and expectations of audiences. In our discussion here, though, we are more concerned with examining the design and aspirations of exhibitions rather than elaborating in detail what alternatives could or should be achieved. Heterotopias are characterised by a capacity to disrupt established discourses and hegemonies (Tamboukou 2004), but *Australia in the Great War* directs this energy towards short-circuiting the arguments of historians for a more inclusive, more critical engagement with the history of Australia's involvement in the First World War. Rather than employ affect to provoke understanding of the terrible exclusions and harms

WWI: Love and Sorrow

Museum Victoria is an institution viewed within and without as having a 'social conscience'; interviews with curators and educators reflected their keen awareness of the potential of their museums to contribute to social justice and inclusion in the state of Victoria. *Love and Sorrow* opened in 2014 and focuses on the impacts of war on minds and bodies, individuals and families, reflecting a deliberate shift away from museum representations of war that focus on broader stories of battle and strategy and wider social histories of life on the home front. As curator Deborah Tout-Smith reflected in 2013 in an unpublished interview, exhibition staff 'felt that an exhibition that focused on injury, distress, violence, and long-term recovery was something that an Australian museum hadn't done before'. The resulting exhibition presents an experience of war that is confronting and emotional, with the stories of eight people – service people and their families – underpinning the representation of some of the most difficult experiences of war, including trauma, mental illness, and facial and other injuries. As Australian war historian Michael McKernan noted in his review of the exhibition, *Love and Sorrow* 'openly and deliberately works on the emotions of its visitors to proclaim its strong and powerful message: war is an unmitigated and abhorrent disaster and we need always to be conscious of its enduring impacts across subsequent generations' (McKernan 2015).

In part, *Love and Sorrow* invites visitors into an increasingly familiar practice in museums – one in which we encounter the 'untold stories' and engage in discourses of acknowledgement and remembering the unremembered. Some war stories and images are established triggers for the affective practices of commemoration, but there are many ways of understanding war that are not often seen in public commemoration in Australia. Kerry Neale, an interview participant from the AWM who drew on knowledge of facial injury she gained during her PhD research to consult on *Love and Sorrow*, observed that 'we've become a little more comfortable with' certain types of war injury, with amputees, for example, becoming 'iconic of the cost of war' (Neale 2014). Images of amputees allow us to access a comfortably familiar feeling of commemoration where we feel a mixture of pity and pride, a sense of a very real sacrifice – in this case, of a limb – and of what we imagine to be the courageous soldiers' return to a full life following the war. *Love and Sorrow* deliberately challenges any belief we may hold about soldiers' resilience and their capacity to live out the rest of their lives in contentment. In doing so, it precludes the possibility of uncomplicated national pride emerging from the understandings of war offered in this exhibition.

The stories of facial injury and reconstructive surgery are examples of histories that have rarely been displayed in public spaces. *Love and Sorrow*'s section on facial injury is confronting, with difficult-to-view portraits of men in various stages of recovery from serious wounds. The story of Bill Kearsey, one of the eight individuals whose story can be followed throughout the exhibition, is much more nuanced than tales of war heroes usually are in museums; it details the joys and sorrows of his post-war life and the trauma of the approximately 29 operations he had. The depth of information relating to Kearsey's story is made possible by limiting the focus for the exhibition to a smaller number of personal stories. The information we have about Kearsey provides a foundation for a very different affective engagement from that achieved in the AWM. In *Love and Sorrow*, we are allowed an intimacy with the people who are featured, and thus we can enter into an affective practice that is based upon connection to another person rather than to the nation. There is nothing truly 'generic' about Kearsey's story; although it can be (and is) used as a springboard to discuss the broader histories of facial injury, visitors are mostly encouraged to connect with this history through the person who experienced it.

A connection to the people in this exhibition is supported through the use of a range of strategies, including a focus on the use of personal objects, letters and photographs. Some of these objects are similar to those used in the AWM. However, while objects are more likely to be grouped by type or time period in *Australia in the Great War*, in *Love and Sorrow* they are more usually grouped by theme or individual. In our view, encountering more than one object from the same person or family supports a deeper reading of text throughout the exhibition by provoking a stronger sense of connection, just as text helps to make meaning of objects. Visitors also encounter considerable details of soldiers' lives, and the lives of their families, after the war, and these stories are employed to highlight particular personal and social issues they faced, including long-term mental illness. This type of detail serves to construct a kind of intimacy with real people and families – a 'that could be me or my family' feeling. In recent years, representations of Indigenous Australian soldiers have begun to appear in Australian museums. However, even these are not usually allowed to detract from the narrative of mateship, resilience and triumph that is the Anzac myth. Perhaps unsurprisingly, given Museum Victoria's dedication to working with and supporting the fight for racial equality in the state, *Love and Sorrow*'s story of the Murray brothers – Aboriginal soldiers who enlisted in the First World War – does not avoid reference to the discrimination and injustice Aboriginal soldiers faced on their return from war, noting that Herbert Murray was refused a war pension, a common experience for Aboriginal soldiers (see for example, AIATSIS n.d.; Hall 1997).

As noted earlier, Museum Victoria staff members hold a firm belief in a social role for their museum, and are particularly dedicated to working for social justice agendas across a range of measures of disadvantage. In *Love and Sorrow*, this drive to teach for social change seeks to challenge established narratives of triumph and victory, and to undermine any notion that soldiers can return from war unscathed. As an institution, Museum Victoria is self-consciously heterotopian, overtly aware of its capacity to act as a 'space of difference'. As Lord (2006:7) has argued of the museum, the real 'difference' lies not in the different objects, times and places represented, but in the 'experience of the gap between things and the conceptual and cultural orders in which they are interpreted'. In the case of *Love and Sorrow*, dissonance is created for the visitor by shifting objects and images that are an established part of the Anzac myth into a new narrative, one largely characterised by pain and struggle, death and trauma. The exhibition uses letters, images of soldiers and nurses and their families, and other personal objects we have seen before in exhibitions about war, but places them in a different narrative from the one we have come to expect. It also adds to the images and discourses we associate with Australia's experiences of the First World War – casts of injured men's faces, for example, as well as objects used in the treatment of sexually transmitted diseases – revealing aspects of the history that present a considerable challenge to popular ideas about the triumphant soldier returning from battle. In support of Tamboukou's (2004) discussion of the temporal specificity of heterotopias, one of the factors that allows *Love and Sorrow* to have such a capacity for acting as a space of difference is the wide popularity of the Anzac myth in Australia. This gives *Love and Sorrow* a capacity 'to teach', to provoke and guide visitors towards understanding historical and contemporary events in a new light. And, we argue, this unsettling is connected to a larger orientation to seeing museums as cultural agencies promoting social change. The exhibition's exhortation to know differently about war is absolutely deliberate, and strongly supported by the construction of new opportunities for affective engagement.

Love and Sorrow is not intended to be entirely bleak or to present a hopeless vision of life during and after war – there are moments of respite from the pain and suffering we observe. There are, however, no stories presenting a tale befitting the courageous, resilient soldier of Anzac legends. No one emerges from the war unscathed. As Tout-Smith reflected in her interview, 'of the stories that we follow through, every one of them is injured or killed … there's no one who sort of comes out of the war experience without being hurt by the war. So it's a fairly grim story I have to say.' Curators hoped the exhibition would be considered 'ground-breaking' in its attention to 'really difficult and confronting and potentially very upsetting' history according to Tout-Smith, and indeed we argue that the museum has succeeded in this aim. It is possible that Museum Victoria has been influenced by the burgeoning scholarly attention to trauma in discourses of Anzac in Australia, which pays heed to the 'deeply personal' facets of war and brings to light more individual stories of trauma (Twomey 2013:107). Yet these personal stories are also constructed, as we have shown, to foster insight into histories of the broader social impact of war and its political contexts. This is a depiction of Australia's involvement in the First World War that invites the visitor into an emotional encounter characterised by sadness and a view onto the absolute and, crucially, lasting horror of war.

Concluding comments

Most representations of First World War history in Australia tap into problematic ideas about the bravery and resilience of soldiers, their noble sacrifice and heroism, and the triumph of war victory. These ideas are problematic because, even where they contain elements of truth, they fail to present a complex, multifaceted version of the past that allows for multiple perspectives and interpretations. They also effectively silence the voices of those who had different experiences. The fact that 'Anzac' is presented as almost synonymous with 'Australian' in popular discourse renders the impact of this kind of exhibition even greater; first we are told a narrative of history that neglects the stories of difference that are part of it, and then we are told that it is this story that represents us as a nation, notwithstanding the erasure of the role of New Zealand soldiers and New Zealand's own national story in this process. Visitors are presented with a version of 'the nation' that is predominantly Anglo-European and white, serving to undermine – or negate – the significance of the history and culture of Australia's first peoples to the national identity and collective memory. *Australia in the Great War*, while a beautifully constructed, coherent and in many ways historically accurate exhibition, does a great deal of this type of silencing and erasure. In this exhibition, the visitor is asked to emotionally invest in this erasure – when participating in affective practices of Anzac commemoration, the white visitor can become entangled in a narrative of the nation-self that is not available to others.

Perhaps most effectively, the exhibition achieves this through the successful deployment of an arsenal of powerfully affective objects and artworks, all housed in a building that tugs at us with its sense of mausoleum and monument. The Memorial is after all a place of commemoration, and the cool grey stone of its walls imbues its halls with a solemnity that primes us to receive the messages of sacrifice and honour that are promoted through the extensive displays. The incredible charge of the affective practices of commemoration that are employed in this museum is difficult to resist, and likely to leave visitors with few openings to think differently. Affective practices here are engaged to silence and erase as much as to inform and evoke.

Love and Sorrow presents quite different facets of war and promotes what is ultimately a more confronting narrative of suffering and loss. This exhibition works much more towards constructing a heterotopian museum in the sense that Tamboukou describes, where hegemonies are challenged and spaces opened for alternatives to grow or be built and explored. The ideal of the resilient and good-humoured Anzac is not obliterated, but it is significantly added to and complicated – these Anzacs are sometimes brave and sometimes demonstrate an incredible capacity to survive, but they are more often hurt, afraid and irrevocably damaged by their experiences, as human beings are by violence. *Love and Sorrow* prises open a space for difference; its emphasis on individual stories negates any suggestion that we can assume a collective experience of war. Both of these exhibitions are powerfully evocative representations of war that employ the affective potential of objects and images to move visitors into particular ways of understanding the past. In the case of *Australia in the Great War*, the narrative produced silences and erases; in the case of *Love and Sorrow*, it opens. Attending to how emotions are engaged in exhibitions, and how they guide (consciously and unconsciously) the anticipation of audience reception, helps us to understand how these exhibitions have different effects and are integral to the contested collective and biographical affective practices of commemoration of war.

Note

1 'New First World War Galleries' *Australian War Memorial*, www.awm.gov.au/1914-1918/first-world-war-galleries [Accessed March 20 2016].

References

Australian Institute of Aboriginal and Torres Strait Islander Studies (AIATSIS), n.d. Why did they join? Available from http://aiatsis.gov.au/collections/collections-online/digitised-collections/indigenous-australians-war/why-did-they-join [Accessed 25 August 2016].

Andermann, J. and Arnold-de Simine, S., 2012. Introduction: Memory, community and the New Museum. *Theory, Culture and Society*, 29(1), 3–13.

Ashmead-Bartlett, E., 1915. Battle of Gaba Tepe. *Hobart Mercury*, 12 May, p. 5. http://nla.gov.au/nla.news-article10412577 [Accessed 25 August 2016].

Bekerman, Z. and Zembylas, M., 2011. *Teaching Contested Narratives: Identity, Memory and Reconciliation in Peace Education and Beyond*. Cambridge: Cambridge University Press.

Falk, J. H. and Dierking, L. D., 1992. *The Museum Experience*. Washington: Whalesback Books.

Foucault, M., 1966. *The Order of Things*. London and New York: Routledge.

Foucault, M., 2008 [1967]. Of other spaces. In M. Dehaene and L. De Cauter, eds. *Heterotopia and the City: Public Space in a Postcivil Society*. Hoboken: Routledge, 14–30.

Gregory, K. and Witcomb, A., 2007. Beyond nostalgia: The role of affect in generating historical understanding at heritage sites. In S. J. Knell, S. MacLeod and S. Watson, eds. *Museum Revolutions: How Museums Change and Are Changed*. London and New York: Routledge, 263–275.

Hall, R., 1997. *The Black Diggers: Aboriginal and Torres Strait Islanders in the Second World War*. Canberra: Aboriginal Studies Press.

Heumann Gurian, E., 2006. *Civilizing the Museum: The Collected Writings of Elaine Heumann Gurian.* London and New York: Routledge.

Heynen, H., 2008. Heterotopia unfolded? In M. Dehaene and L. De Cauter, eds. Heterotopia and the City: Public Space in a Postcivil Society. Hoboken: Routledge, 311–323.

Hobsbawm, E., 1983. Introduction: Inventing traditions. In E. Hobsbawm and T. Ranger, eds. *The Invention of Tradition.* Cambridge: Cambridge University Press, 1–14.

Lake, M., Reynolds, H. and McKenna, M., eds., 2010. *What's Wrong with ANZAC? The Militarisation of Australian History.* Sydney: UNSW Press.

Leys, R., 2011. The turn to affect: a critique. *Critical Inquiry*, 37(3), 434–472.

Lord, B., 2006. Foucault's museums: Difference, representation, and genealogy. *Museum & Society*, 4(1), 1–14.

McKernan, M., 2015. *WWI: Love & sorrow. reCollections: Journal of the National Museum of Australia*, 10(1). Available from https://recollections.nma.gov.au/issues/volume_10_number_1/exhibition_reviews/wwi_love_and_sorrow [Accessed 1 February 2018].

Mulcahy, D., 2016. 'Sticky' learning: Assembling bodies, objects and affects at the museum and beyond. In J. Coffey, S. Budgeon and H. Cahill, eds. *Learning Bodies.* Singapore: Springer, 207–222.

Neale, K., 2014. Poor devils without noses and jaws: Facial wounds of the Great War. Canberra: Honest History. Available from http://honesthistory.net.au/wp/wp-content/uploads/Neale_Honest-History-MHC-paper.pdf [Accessed 26 August 2016].

Reynolds, H., 2013. *Forgotten War.* Sydney: Newsouth.

Sohn, H., 2008. Heterotopia: Anamnesis of a medical term. In M. Dehaene and L. De Cauter, eds. *Heterotopia and the City: Public Space in a Postcivil Society.* Hoboken: Routledge, 41–50.

Saldanha, A., 2008. Heterotopia and structuralism. *Environment and Planning A*, 40, 2080–2096.

Tamboukou, M., 2004. Educational heterotopias and the self. *Pedagogy, Culture and Society*, 12(3), 399–414.

Trofanenko, B., 2014. Affective emotions: The pedagogical challenges of knowing war. *Review of Education, Pedagogy, and Cultural Studies*, 36(1), 22–39.

Trofanenko, B. M., 2011. On difficult history displayed: The pedagogical challenges of interminable learning. *Museum Management and Curatorship*, 26(5), 481–495.

Twomey, C., 2013. Trauma and the reinvigoration of Anzac. *History Australia*, 10(3), 85–108.

Wetherell, M., 2012. *Affect and Emotion: A New Social Science Understanding.* London: Sage.

Witcomb, A., 2013. Understanding the role of affect in producing a critical pedagogy for history museums. *Museum Management and Curatorship*, 28(3), 255–271.

Zembylas, M., 2007. *Five Pedagogies, a Thousand Possibilities: Struggling for Hope and Transformation in Education.* Rotterdam: Sense.

Chapter 5

Constructing heritage through subjectivity

Museum of Broken Relationships

Željka Miklošević and Darko Babić

Introduction

Working in museums today does not seem to be an easy task, especially for those who have not yet developed mechanisms for adapting to the constantly changing socio-cultural, political and economic circumstances of the post-modern, post-industrial era. Transformed views on culture and heritage in general, the growing importance of digital networking, marketisation of culture, mass tourism, democratisation of voices and the like 'escape the horizons of curatorial control' (Fyfe 2006: 40) and transform the authoritative status of museums. Although many museums still try to resist these changes, new developments and transformations still find their way into museum practices. Heumann Gurian's (2010) distinction between classical and inclusive museums is apparent today, as there are different levels and types of inclusivity that are being explored in a growing number of museums. These might include everyday experiences and important issues that people regularly face in their lives around the globe, ranging from cultural disenfranchisement, natural disasters, migration problems and atrocities during war to more peaceful endeavours to engage local communities. The influence of these museums and heritage projects is considerable, 'because they experiment with multiple strategies of interactivity, interesting administrative techniques and controversial subject matters that push the boundaries of the field as a whole' (Heumann Gurian 2010: xiii). These institutions, or whatever administrative status they have, also challenge the epistemological foundation of the conventional museum as a producer of objective knowledge (Cameron 2010).

This chapter focuses on the Museum of Broken Relationships in Zagreb (referred to hereafter as MBR), which, if discussed in professional circles, would probably evoke different opinions about whether it really 'deserves' to be called a museum. It is a private enterprise whose status remains undefined within the Croatian museum-based legal framework because of its 'deviation' from the norm. Its collection is formed exclusively from donated objects that are related to broken relationships and exhibited with stories about break-ups written solely by the donors. We will try to develop in this chapter arguments

Constructing heritage through subjectivity 71

demonstrating that this museum has been built on a fluid concept of heritage. This fluidity supports and sustains the efforts of the museum's creators to achieve social impact through the affective practices of all of the parties involved in its activities – donors of museum objects, the museum creators and curator, and visitors. Their personal contributions to the affective topic of broken relationships are what brings to life a feeling and awareness of the collective, both cultural and social.

Affect in museums and heritage sites

In her account of the challenges twenty-first-century museums face, Barbara Kirshenblatt-Gimblett stressed the need for museums to rethink 'what they are as a medium and their role in society' (Kirshenblatt-Gimblett 2010: 1) amid wider social changes. She also drew attention to new relationships between information and experience, display and mise-en-scène, things and stories, thinking and feeling, identity and identification, which have marked a paradigmatic shift in museum communication. The second pair of elements – display and mise-en-scène – can be said to form part of the affective technologies of display that have contributed in one way or another to the affective work of museums and heritage sites. These technologies have also been explored in relation to difficult social topics presented in museum environments. An emotional approach to interpretation, shaped through design and other material modes of address, facilitates visitors' engagement with a topic, which, in turn, leads to a 'transformative moment of learning' through reflexive critical understanding (Bonnell and Simon 2007: 81). The production of emotional responses in visitors also forms the basis of pedagogical practices for better cross-cultural understanding (Witcomb 2013) and historical understanding that needs to evade romanticised nostalgia for the past (Gregory and Witcomb 2007). Knowing about and understanding history and the consequences of historical events are today widely discussed, and are some of the most controversial topics in the museum and heritage sector (Logan and Reeves 2009; Macdonald 2009).

In addition to topics of socio-cultural importance that often touch on political and ideological concerns, emotional engagement has been successfully employed in those areas of the heritage sector that produce types of cultural and historical learning more aligned with entertainment (Bagnall 2003). The goals and outcomes of emotional engagement with heritage take a range of forms. This chapter presents another sort of emotional engagement made possible by the MBR. The imaginative process of discursive knowledge construction in museums, resulting in classification according to the nature of their contents, criteria for grouping objects on display and multiple taxonomies of individual exhibits (Jordanova 1989), rests here merely on affect. A range of different emotions, taken as a universal human feature, forms the rationale of the museum and permeates all its activities. Furthermore, basic human emotions, largely freed from personal cultural and historical meanings, help create bonds and feelings of identity and belonging among its visitors.

Museum of Broken Relationships

Unlike most museums which collect and research material culture that connects in different ways to the socio-cultural life of people, the MBR collects and showcases artefacts that are contextualised solely by personal accounts of people's relationships and their break-ups. A former couple, Olinka Vištica and Dražen Grubišić, whose time together left them with relationship mementoes that neither of them wanted to keep, led to the concept of the MBR. The things shared at the moment of the break-up became a burden of the past. Still, reluctant to just throw them away, they made those relationship leftovers the basis of a temporary exhibition, a sort of community art project, which was shown in 2006 in Glyptotheque Zagreb as part of the 41st Zagreb Salon. On that occasion, they invited people to donate material traces of their own past relationships to collectively create the exhibition/artwork. The success of the Zagreb exhibition encouraged Olinka and Dražen to continue organising similar events throughout the world. What started as an art installation, and continued to assume the form of temporary travelling exhibitions, was transformed in 2010 into a museum with an exhibition space (figure 5.1) and auxiliary facilities such as a shop and café. In addition to the two concept creators and owners, the museum now has a fully employed curator, Ivana Družetić.

The museum's collection has been formed solely by donations, without any introduction of collecting criteria either by the two museum creators or by the curator. Anybody can become a donor by sending to or leaving at the museum an artefact and a text relating to it that tells a story about his or her broken relationship. These two elements – artefact and text – are inseparable elements that together form *composite* museum objects. Each museum object has a label that includes a title, the name of a city and/or country and the date of the break-up. Even though the museum creators originally envisaged that donors would provide only one year, i.e. the year of the break-up, most donors put two years, or the number of months/years, to mark the duration of their relationships (figure 5.2). There are no instructions on how texts should be written; they need only contain said information – donors/authors can freely decide on the structure, language, style, tone etc.

Although most the artefacts are mass-produced things, the explanations with which they are exhibited make them unambiguous and provide them with an authorial imprint and an artistic aura, even though there are no names which specifically attest to the authorship. Originality arises from the combination of the artefact and the highly personal and subjective texts.

Personal accounts that, in fact, create exhibits at the MBR are just one manifestation of the culture of subjectivity and personal narration that

Constructing heritage through subjectivity 73

Figure 5.1 View of permanent display, Museum of Broken Relationships, Zagreb

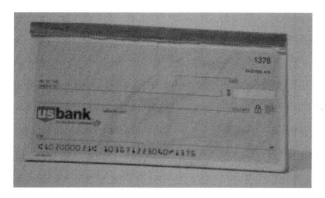

Figure 5.2 My last 2006 checkbook with my name and my ex's name on it, Museum of Broken Relationships, Zagreb

characterises contemporary society (Langellier 1999). Telling stories about significant events in our lives is something that people do daily, especially in the company of friends. It is the quotidian narration and shared experiences that keep us together, consoled and not alone. Personal narration, which is nowadays proliferating especially prominently on social media, feeds the voyeuristic tendencies of people and a therapeutic culture (Langellier 1999) that

Figure 5.3 A caterpillar 'Timunaki', museum object, Museum of Broken Relationships, Zagreb

Figure 5.4 A hamburger toy, Museum of Broken Relationships, Zagreb

Constructing heritage through subjectivity 75

grows exponentially with the number of volumes on popular psychology. It is no surprise that the MBR, a museum that deals in the individual, subjective personal and, most of all, emotional, is visited by almost 90,000 people annually.

Since they are animated by emotions, the stories, which are displayed in a written form, read more like short pieces of literature whose style of writing can significantly influence the way they affect readers/visitors. The way stories are narrated, with all the details that suggest certain things, whether implicitly or explicitly, is what evokes our affective response to a situation (Hogan, 2003: 5). The artefact is in a way re-created through its accompanying text because the story assigns it specific meanings by situating it in a context – biographical, historical, geographical, cultural etc. Texts also reveal multiple ways in which artefacts relate to a break-up (figures 5.2–5.6).

The story and the artefact act together as a product of emotional exteriorisation, and they can together be considered creative endeavours in their own right, as well as being part of a bigger creation, that is, the museum. These *composite* museum objects, whose creation was motivated by a past emotional event or sequence of events and a creative, almost literary urge to pour feelings into words, establish a basic form of affect that impacts on the concept creators, or 'museum curators', and visitors alike. Unfortunately, the anonymity of donors prevented us from finding out more about their reasons, motivations and need to participate in this museum.

Methodology

In this chapter, and following the view of affect as a mixture of the bodily and the discursive (Wetherell 2012; Schorch 2014), we will examine the relationship between the affective practices of the concept creators, or 'museum curators', and museum visitors through the museum (or exhibition) medium. It is our belief that all these agents involved in museum communication contribute to the affective flow instigated by donated objects, and that their individual mix of emotions and thoughts, based on the individual biographical stories of the donors, plays a major role in the production of a form of universal collectivity.

As Margaret Wetherell points out, affect is not only the ineffable reaction that we can feel in our body; it is also 'practical, communicative and organised' (Wetherell 2012: 13). In fact, these two components, body and discourse, are brought together into a relationship of mutual influence and together compose affective practice. As Wetherell states,

> In affective practice, bits of the body [...] get patterned together with feelings and thoughts, interaction patterns and relationships, narratives and interpretative repertoires, social relations, personal histories, and ways of life.
>
> (Wetherell 2012: 13–14)

In trying to define components in the flow of affect within the communication process at this museum, we chose a purely discursive research methodology, hoping it would provide certain insights into curators' and visitors' experiences. Structured interviews were first conducted with the curators Olinka Vištica and Ivana Družetić, who were asked to give accounts of the museum's developmental stages, from its inception to the present day. We were particularly interested in their everyday activities related to the museum functions of collecting and communicating, or, in other words, their curation strategies. Visitors to the museum were surveyed over the course of two months (December 2015 and January 2016), and 108 people participated in answering a questionnaire that contained both closed and open-ended questions, the answers to which were noted down verbatim. The first part of the questionnaire was more market research, to help us develop a demographic profile of visitors. The second part of the questionnaire aimed to explore the emotional relations of visitors to the museum by asking them what thoughts and feelings had been evoked by the exhibition, what objects/ stories had made the biggest impression and why. Unfortunately the data obtained from visitors' answers to these questions were not as extensive as we had expected. This was due to the use of English as a *lingua franca*, both by us as researchers and by non-native English-speaking visitors who were not fluent enough to express nuanced emotional states.[1] Additionally, some visitors were reluctant to talk about their emotions and often gave generic, pleonastic and circular descriptions, such as 'sad because the stories were sad'. Others wanted to write everything down by themselves after taking some time to think about it, which we agreed to and let them do. We ended up with 57 responses that could be subjected to discourse analysis. This made us aware of the need to take the analysed data more as an indication than as substantial proof, and to cross-reference the data with responses to a multiple-choice question that addressed several overall types of experience of the museum that pilot research had alerted us to. Another topic we were interested in was the visitors' opinions of this museum in comparison with other, more 'conventional' types of museums, which we explored through their accounts of what they thought was the same/different, better/worse and why.

Museum creators' affective practice – from individual to social through curation

One of the main characteristics of this museum is its form, which Olinka recognises as an amalgam of different features: 'It's not art because it is not our own creation but a participative project; it is a museum because it is called museum but has no legally grounded institutional status, it collects anthropological material which is not anthropologically researched.' This mixture of different functions of the MBR resulted from Olinka and Dražen's need to

Constructing heritage through subjectivity 77

overcome their break-up through a joint initiative – a project that could help them deal with their emotional states. It was first envisaged as a metaphorical place that might take up all the remnants of their relationship that could not be easily forgotten, a place that could transform their inner emotional battle into something else. The idea of a museum, as Olinka claims, 'stemmed from a human need in a particular situation. It was not a rational decision to start up something new and innovative.' The intrinsic need, a sort of corporeal urge, was responsible for the conceptual creation of the museum that celebrates its tenth anniversary in 2016. 'Today', Olinka continues, 'in spite of the somewhat pessimistic name of the museum, the goal is to create a feeling in the museum community about others through a unique human characteristic, something we all share.'

Creativity is emphasised both in the museum space and in individual objects, most of all the stories. Using language creatively, through play and *open-endedness*, is, according to Olinka, a more appropriate way to experience people's lives than through definite statements, 'since our lives are blurry mixtures of different elements, feelings, achievements, different sorts of backgrounds etc.'. A major creative role of language is in its affective impact that governs the process of selection for display. Objects/stories that are selected to be showcased have the strongest impact, which can move visitors and with which they can engage. 'It is purely subjective', says Ivana Družetić, whose choices have defined the present permanent exhibition. 'When I reach for an artefact and read the story, I immediately know that is something people should see because it touches you, or makes you laugh …' Sometimes artefacts are very appealing, but it is primarily the story, the emotional message, that determines whether certain objects will be placed on illuminated stands or wall cases in the exhibition space. With a growing number of donations, curious links between objects (stories and artefacts) start appearing, such as the story about the diet book *I Can Make You Thin* that a woman received as a gift from her boyfriend and a pair of jeans that a girl wore before she lost weight. These two stories, coming from different parts of the world, put together, are both ironic and funny in their own right, but they also show how, no matter where you live, the issue of weight is present. Certain social preoccupations come to the fore from all these subjective stories – 'when they [stories] start mutually communicating […] that's what's most exciting in the entire process', says Olinka. It is also how topics or themes are formed. Though the museological procedure of object grouping has been followed here, it is grounded in anthropological connotations and poetic expressions. The resulting theme titles, such as Coming of Age, Private Battles – Global Wars and Once Upon a Time … Happily Ever After, Tomorrow is Another Day, add another subjective interpretive layer to the display. This is what Olinka calls open-endedness in terms of the fluidity and volatility of interpretations framed by these themes. This open-endedness also characterises the growth of the collection, because people interpret the

Figure 5.5 My mother's suicide note, Museum of Broken Relationships, Zagreb

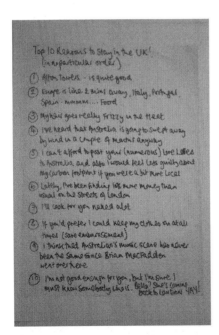

Figure 5.6 A list of 10 reasons to stay, museum object, Museum of Broken Relationships, Zagreb

Constructing heritage through subjectivity 79

concept of broken relationships differently. Although a large majority of donations tell stories of break-ups of romantic relationships, the present exhibition proves that broken relationships can be of a different nature, such as the death of a parent or the abandonment of children. Previous exhibitions showcased objects that respectively symbolised a break-up with religion and a prime minister. Emotionally more difficult and sombre stories (figure 5.5) are often evened out with stories that produce humorous effects and positive feelings (figure 5.6) 'so that visitors are not submerged in sadness', Olinka explains.

Visitors' affective practices – engaging with the self and with others

The data obtained from the survey show that the largest number of visitors to the MBR came from two age groups. One spans the age range 19–30 (60.2%), while the other includes people between the ages of 30 and 55 (32.4%). Among the visitors surveyed, there were almost equal numbers of males and females. Croatian citizens accounted for 29% of visitors, 55% of visitors came from other European countries, while the remaining 16% came from other regions (for example, 6% from the USA and 3% from Australia). For a very high number of the visitors surveyed (94%), it was their first visit to the museum.

Emotional engagement and the way the visitors use the museum to negotiate their emotions depends on the sort of relationships they form with the exhibits and their consequent emotional states. The analysis of the data points to a continuum of possible relationships with stories/other people and their gradual transitions, starting from affected self-reflexivity to a distanced, abstract relationship with the stories/authors and meta-emotional states.

The most common type of relationship is *Self-Reflexivity* or instances of visitors engaging in conversations with themselves, having interior monologues and reflecting on their own experience, which was instigated by one or more of the stories they had read. They thought about either their former or their present relationship with a partner or a family member. For example, 'I was thinking about my husband and what would have happened if something like this had happened to us. I feel happy I don't belong to this group of people.' This sort of emotional state can be interpreted as the relief coming from the realisation that the suffering of other people is equal to or greater than one's own. On the other hand, there is also the relief that comes from belonging, which is illustrated by the words of a female visitor: 'I feel good, consoled, I'd say, because there are other people like me (laughter).' For some, the affective impact was less strong: 'It was a sort of time-travel for me. I have my own stories and personal objects that I can donate, but I feel balanced. It was a nice experience.'

Empathy is another dominant point on the continuum, and it proved to be the second-most-important overall experience of the museum as reported in the answers to the multiple-choice questions. One of the most interesting reactions was that of a male visitor with a really gloomy facial expression, who stated 'Man, I need a drink! These stories were so depressing. I feel all sad now.' He did not have any personal stories to tell, but felt sorry for the people whose stories he had read. This was often the case when the last stories were those about parents leaving children or the mother's suicide letter (figure 5.5), where there was not identification, just compassion.

A step towards emotional abstraction and personal detachment is what we have termed *Seeing a Bigger Picture*, which is represented by thoughts and feelings about human relationships and emotions in general, or about the inevitability of life running its course, for all of us, in one way or another. For example, 'The guiding thought I had was that our lives are strong, peculiar, happy and unhappy at the same time ... I feel calm because everything comes to an end but life goes on.' or 'I felt some positive melancholy, it all about the transience and the quality of life.'

The last point on the continuum representing a sort of emotional distance is evidenced by what we called *Evaluating Other People's Emotion*. This category reveals disassociation from active personal involvement such as meta-emotional engagement in the form of judgement of other people's emotions: 'I went around thinking "all this is so pathetic!".' What seems to be the most cognitive and intellectual response was a visitor's cultural analysis of emotions in certain texts: 'I noticed different approaches and different perceptions of love ... different cultural background influencing the stories – the Balkans – fatalistic, the UK/Paris – a bit bitter, the US – it was like that and that.'

These attitudes are reflected in the answers that show the visitors' general view of the museum and the way it influenced them. For 37% of the interviewees, the main value of the visit was bringing them closer to the emotions of others, whereas 36% of them considered the museum helpful in making them remember and deal with personal feelings about their own relationships. Around 19% of visitors saw the museum as a good and innovative idea, while 8% of visitors found the most interesting part of the museum to be learning experiences about the culture of others, in terms of glimpses into the cultural contexts of the people who wrote the stories.

Looking at the survey results that address museological issues, the answers show that over 86% of visitors thought that the MBR offered different experiences from those offered in other museums, only 5% said the MBR was similar to other museums, and the remaining 9% were reluctant to make any judgement. Visitors' experiences shaped by the MBR were coded in relation to the most common elements of museum communication – who does the talking and about what, how topics are mediated, and experience. Five themes arose from the data, the two most salient of which are *Commonplace*

Protagonists/Accounts and *Preferential Mode of Interpretation*. The ordinariness of the authors and their topics was judged a positive feature of the museum. Interestingly, even though there are no names to prove that the authors of the stories are ordinary people, not a single visitor suggested that someone famous and important might have written some of them.

Visitors stressed that they liked the museum because it shows 'the 'losers' stories' and not love stories from Hollywood or Disney' and that 'It gives a human aspect ... ordinary people got their voice' and 'It's special, because of the stories, they have impact on me, other museums don't have such stories about objects.' The narrative quality of texts was often emphasised as the most evident contrast with other museums: 'It's the stories that makes it special, I have a feeling of entering into some films.' *Intimate Experience* is the category that represents 'the feel' of the museum, which is different: 'It is like sharing secrets with close friends' and 'It's easier to relate to human stories than for example abstract art.' Another noted 'Here, I feel the warmth, and intimacy, personal components; in other museums, everything is factual.'

Substantive Intangibles includes the museums' subject matter, where the focus is not on physical objects but on intangible, immediate, experiential and shared experiences. For example, 'It's not about the thing itself (objects) but about what happened' and 'It's about personal lives of people, stories about something that can happen to everybody.' The last category relates to *Shared Authority* and the participative nature of the museum: 'Unlike conventional museums this one has been created by people with their donations', so that 'Here everybody can be the 'artist'.' All these features were judged positive and even preferable by the visitors interviewed, which suggests that alternative approaches to museum-making and museum communication such as this one deserve the attention of the museum and heritage profession, not only as creative endeavours but also because of their social impact.

Transforming museum communication into affective flow

In the last 10 years, from its initial conceptualisation to its professionally recognised practice,[2] the MBR has gradually developed from a symbolic space of representation of past relationships to a social space where people come to perform the cultural ritual of museum visiting. This conceptual change has resulted from a series of interrelated events, one of which is arguably a growing number of donations and the acquisition of the exhibition space.

The fluid and flexible nature of the museum allows donors to express their emotions through texts and objects in whatever way they want. By doing that they invest their feelings into material forms to externalise them and give them permanence. This is often a social and individual practice of ritual that entails the process of projecting abstract notions onto the external world (Leach 1987). The very act of imbuing an emotional state with a communicative form, which is intended to be seen/read and experienced by other people (made possible by the museum), is a form of performance.

The written, non-corporeal performativity of the donors creates a basis for the communicative efforts and goals of the curators, who also partake in a certain form of performance through what Whitehead (2012) calls museum interpretative frameworks of narration and evaluation. Narration entails the selection of objects from the collection that are then displayed in a specific physical and conceptual way. A narrative can emerge 'from the moments of a topic, where a story is cumulatively constructed through the opening of new dimensions and the gradual layering of strata of interpretation' (Whitehead 2012: 26). This procedure is not uncommon to museums, since the possibilities of multiple interpretations can result in different groupings of objects. At the MBR, however, the curators select donated stories/objects for display, on the basis of their affective impact and by paying attention to what might be called a harmonised emotional rhythm of the display. Their performativity is also non-corporeal but mediated through the technology of display – the grouping of differently emotionally charged objects, and the way they are presented in the exhibition space. In addition to being a cultural performance 'in which certain cultural values and identities are continually rehearsed and thus preserved' (Smith 2006: 68), the process of museum curation is in this case also an emotional performance.

Finally, there is also the emotional performativity of visitors, unrelated to their cultural literacy or competences, which may be drawn on at heritage sites (Bagnall 2003). Here, the emotional content does not form part of a heritage product – it *is* the product. Visitors are in emotional communication with their inner selves, with other people or with donors' stories.

The museum is a place where emotional performance starts with donated objects. Depending on the sort of emotional externalisation of donors, the curators will continue with the practice, which is different with every new act of communication (that is, organisation of the display). Finally, emotional performance by visitors depends both on the stories/objects of donors and on the technology of display. The affective flow is at the same time the performative work done by what can be called participative museum communication, that begins with a donor and ends with a visitor-to-become-donor.

Emotions are what is performed through the museum, not merely at it. They emerge from the relations with material artefacts, social interactions and performed (affective) experiences – which are three mutually connected elements that Michael Haldrup and Jørgen Ole Bærenholdt (2015) find necessary for supporting the paradigm of heritage as performance. Emotions can in this context be defined as universal heritage, which people experience within the affective circle of participative museum communication. The participants in that process form a global affective community in what Urry calls a post-societal era in which 'social life [...] depend upon metaphors of network, flow and travel' (Urry 2003: 23). The MBR is not a social space that is defined by geographical space, but rather a space that helps people position themselves as individuals in relation to other peoples' experiences through emotions.

Conclusion

Considering what the collected 'composite museum objects' represent, the goal for which they are included in the communicative act of the museum, and the ways they affect visitors, we may say that the MBR essentially manages emotions.

The very nature of the museum replaces the usual and widespread museum practices with participative collecting: no authority sets the rules; topics are freely chosen within the interpretative framework loosely defined by the museum's name; the narrative manner of presentation can reach and touch everybody, regardless of their education or cultural background; and the feel of the museum makes everybody welcome.

The stories carry the primary importance for the museum experience. It is the stories, intimate and personal, that produce impact, and the acts of reading and interpretation result in both emotional and intellectual experience. The artefacts, which are displayed with the stories, have their own role in the production of affect in terms of their significance for the creation of a socio-cultural notion of the museum. Without the material component of the objects, stories could be read in a book, under different sets of conditions and less embedded in the social situation of the museum space. The museum space, and the way its communicative role is realised, plays a major role in the affective flow of the group of people involved in the museum's activities.

In comparison with other museums, where emotions are a byproduct, the practice of transforming cultural knowledge into affective displays and, in turn, into emotional engagement with the experience of others is reversed in the MBR. The collecting and communication practices of this museum are completely grounded in and dependent on emotions, without which it would not exist ... be that a benefit or a burden.

Notes

1 People resorted to body language through gestures and facial expressions when they could not express verbally what they felt. Audio–video recording would probably be the best means of data collection for thorough research on the emotional impact of the museum, in addition to speaking with all research participants languages in which they are proficient.
2 In 2011, the museum was awarded the European Museum Forum's Kenneth Hudson Award, www.europeanmuseumforum.info/emya.html [Accessed 12 January 2016].

References

Bonnell, J. and Simon, R. I., 2007. 'Difficult' exhibitions and intimate encounters. *Museum & Society*, 5(2), 65–85.
Bagnall, G., 2003. Performance and performativity at heritage sites. *Museum & Society*, 1(2), 87–103.

Cameron, F., 2010. Introduction. In F. Cameron and L. Kelly, eds. *Hot Topics, Public Culture, Museums*. Newcastle upon Tyne: Cambridge Scholars, 1–16.

Fyfe, G., 2006. Sociology and the social aspects of museums. In S. McDonald, ed. *A Companion to Museum Studies*. Malden: Blackwell, 33–49.

Gregory, K. and Witcomb, A., 2007. Beyond nostalgia: The role of affect in generating historical understanding at heritage sites. In S. J. Knell, S. Macleod and S. Watson, eds. *Museum Revolutions: How Museums Change and Are Changed*. London: Routledge, 263–275.

Haldrup, M. and Bærenholdt, J. O., 2015. Heritage as performance. In E. Waterton and S. Watson, eds. *The Palgrave Handbook of Contemporary Heritage Research*. London: Palgrave Macmillan, 52–68.

Heumann Gurian, E., 2010. Forward. Celebrating those who create change. In F. Cameron and L. Kelly, eds. *Hot Topics, Public Culture, Museums*. Newcastle upon Tyne: Cambridge Scholars, xii–xv.

Hogan, P. C., 2003. *The Mind and Its Stories. Narrative Universals and Human Emotion*. Cambridge: Cambridge University Press.

Jordanova, L., 1989. Objects of knowledge: A historical perspective on museums. In P. Vergo, ed. *New Museology*. London: Reaktion Books, 22–40.

Kirshenblatt-Gimblett, B., 2000. The museum as catalyst. Keynote address at *Museums 2000: Confirmation or Challenge*, organised by ICOM Sweden, the Swedish Museum Association and the Swedish Travelling Exhibition/Riksutställningar in Vadstena, 29 September 2000. Available from www.nyu.edu/classes/bkg/web/vadstena.pdf [Accessed 27 January 2012].

Langellier, K. M., 1999. Personal narrative, performance, performativity: Two or three things I know for sure. *Text and Performance Quarterly*, 19(2), 125–144.

Leach, E., 1987. *Culture and Communication*. New York: Cambridge University Press.

Logan, W. and Reeves, K., eds., 2009. *Places of Pain and Shame: Dealing with Difficult Heritage*. London and New York: Routledge.

Macdonald, S., 2009. *Difficult Heritage: Negotiating the Nazi Past in Nuremberg and Beyond*. London and New York: Routledge.

Schorch, P., 2014. Cultural feelings and the making of meaning. *International Journal of Heritage Studies*, 20(1), 22–35.

Smith L., 2006. *Uses of Heritage*. London and New York: Routledge.

Urry, J., 2000. *Sociology beyond Societies*. London and New York: Routledge.

Wetherell, M., 2012. *Affect and Emotion: A New Social Science Understanding*. London: Sage.

Whitehead, C., 2012. *Interpreting Art in Museums and Galleries*. London and New York: Routledge.

Witcomb, A., 2013. Understanding the role of affect in producing a critical pedagogy for history museums. *Museum Management and Curatorship*, 28(3), 255–271.

Chapter 6

The Battle of Orgreave (1984)

Toby Juliff

Introduction

The coming together of performance, art and heritage is nothing new. However, all too often they are separated out through their own disciplinary concerns, so the opportunity to examine their shared values is less frequent. And whilst performance and heritage studies have explored the affecting potential of coming together to engage with traumatic sites of memory, there is still much more to do to consider what recent participatory art practices can contribute to this subject (Taylor 2008). In particular, whilst performance and heritage studies were exploring the necessity of finding shared values in protecting and safeguarding intangible forms of practice in the first decade of the millennium, contemporary art was similarly engaging in new forms of thinking about participation and documentary forms of history (Bishop 2012; Taylor 2016). The 'participatory turn' in contemporary art seemed to garner little response from critical heritage studies, however. This chapter explores one such project that encouraged the use of participation and performance in exploring a recent historical trauma.

The Battle of Orgreave (1984)

On 18 June 1984, a picket line made up of 5,000–6,000 striking miners set up a barricade outside the Orgreave British Steel coke plant just outside Sheffield, South Yorkshire, in an attempt to achieve a major disruption of the production and transportation of raw materials and to deny access to non-striking mine workers. The picket – organised by the National Union of Mineworkers (NUM) – was met by a large police presence of over 4,000 police officers (the numbers on both sides are still very unreliable) (Bailey 2009; Bailey and Popple 2011).

Throughout the day – at a site that had been peacefully picketed many times before and was now some three months into the national coal mining strike – greater and greater numbers arrived on both sides. Flying pickets from neighbouring strikes added to those supporting the picket at Orgreave.

Mounted police officers drawn from forces around Britain – some fresh from the London riots of Toxteth and Brixton – joined local officers and soldiers wearing police uniforms, who were unfamiliar with public jurisprudence, and had been brought in to support the countermeasures organised by local police unprepared for a full-scale action of this sort. Throughout the day, cavalry charges and long baton containments were met with intimidation on the part of the miners and escalated into what would be a full-scale riot that spilt out into the streets of Orgreave and surrounding suburbs.

Before peace could be restored 93 miners would be arrested. Fifty-one pickets were injured, as were 72 police officers. Of the 93 arrests, none resulted in conviction, and eventually, seven years later, South Yorkshire police paid out over £400,000 in compensation for 39 unlawful arrests (Shaw 2012). There were no arrests or charges brought against the police who had been involved in the events of that day, many of whom were not serving officers, but members of the armed forces placed in uniforms devoid of distinguishing markers (such as insignia denoting rank and personal identifiers).

In 2012, due in part to the considerable coverage of the 25th anniversary of Orgreave three years earlier, renewed campaigns demanding justice for the wrongly accused miners and with regard to the still unprosecuted police began under the banner of the Truth and Justice for Orgreave Campaign. This campaign sought to demand full-scale inquiries into the handling of the day and the criminal proceedings that followed, together with an open review of media coverage of the battle between the pickets and the police.

Orgreave was by no means the only picket that would descend into chaos and violence. The original battle remains symbolic, however, of several skirmishes between the state and the miners that lasted throughout 1984 and 1985. Significant cultural events, publications and charitable concerts, together with heritage events and archives, have kept Orgreave fresh in the public consciousness of the working class in the North of England and more widely (Bailey and Popple 2011). This chapter engages more with the archive of material relating to Orgreave – the Figgis documentary record of the event, Deller's exhibition of his own archive at Tate Britain in 2001, *The Battle of Orgreave Archive (An Injury to One Is an Injury to All)* and Deller's subsequent publication of key articles from the event in *The English Civil War: Part II* (2002) – together with the actual events of 1984. Affect remains a key constituent of anniversary events. In particular, one can observe the emotiveness of the cultural and heritage projects forged in the wake of Orgreave 1984. This chapter argues that the cultural and heritage events constituting the post-millennial remembering of Orgreave continue to resonate within the local community and have only increased in currency throughout recent anniversary campaigns to recognise the injustices of Orgreave 1984. This chapter argues also that Deller's *Orgreave* project continues to resonate both as an artwork and as a work of heritage. This is not in any way to *claim* Deller's project for Critical Heritage Studies, but rather to argue that *The Battle of Orgreave*

The Battle of Orgreave (2001)

In 2001, British artist Jeremy Deller arranged a re-enactment of the battle with a commission from the London-based art agency Artangel. Eight hundred participants drawn from historical re-enactment societies, locals (from the mining and non-mining community) and interested parties restaged the battle using foam bricks and fake batons. Of the 800 re-enactors, 280 were recruited from local mining communities. The 'battle' was recorded by film director Mike Figgis and shown on Channel 4, which partially funded the project. The film included archival footage, extensive footage of the re-enactment and interviews with Deller, Artangel and participants, together with specially commissioned interviews with representatives from the police community present in Orgreave 1984, notable figures in the NUM and a key political supporter of the miners and their cause, the MP for Chesterfield, Tony Benn.

The considerable literature on Deller's iconic event has unsurprisingly been led by contemporary art history. In particular, Deller's *Battle of Orgreave* has been regarded as symptomatic of the rise of participatory art from the late 1990s onwards. Occasionally, however, the broader concerns of the work have been read from a perspective of social history. In the former context, critics have largely read the work as a success, whereas in the latter framework of social history the work has been seen as a troubled mess of living history, contemporary participatory art and ethnography (Correia 2006; Bailey 2009; Bishop 2012).

Despite its having drawn on oral and written histories, academic resources and 18 months of strategic development assistance from numerous historical re-enactment societies (together with participants from the original encounter), Deller's *Battle of Orgreave* has received surprisingly little attention from the critical heritage community. On paper, Deller's project may appear simply enough as a 'living history' re-enactment. In reality, the conditions from which the project emerged – conceptually authored by an individual artist, developed in conjunction with an arts agency – have led to its absence in heritage discourse. This is a premature elision, as we shall see. Throughout the early years of the millennium, numerous heritage projects in proximity to that of Orgreave emerged (Bailey 2009; Bailey and Popple 2011). As Laurajane Smith and Gary Campbell argue, apropos local heritage projects in nearby Castleford, the reason for the exclusion of a number of projects from discourse lies in their opposition to the orthodox models of heritage practices (Smith and Campbell 2011). Heritage projects of this type – emotionally driven traumatic re-enactments of living memory, emerging with bias and privilege (and here I temporarily include Deller's *Orgreave* art project) – exist in opposition to the 'authorised heritage discourse' (AHD)

88 Toby Juliff

(Smith and Campbell 2011). The opposition to the dominant modes of thinking about and practising heritage – with its origins in nineteenth-century Europe – lies in its mobilisations of voices usually excluded from hollowed sites of memorialisation (Smith 2006). In resisting the allure of 'heritage status' and comfortable historical narratives, Deller's project fits within the wider study of heritage as critical ontology. This chapter considers a range of inherent contradictions within the work (Deller's *Orgreave*) and a possible navigation through these inconsistencies by reading the project again through a lens of critical heritage studies and Affect Theory.

The range of responses elicited by Deller's project – emotional and critical in equal measure – is *affecting*, it communicates a set of potentials that may not be present in otherwise 'ethical' forms of participation. This affect is felt both in the participants on the day of the 2001 event and in non-participants reflecting on the strike and the re-enactment. It is this resistance of 'feel good' conciliatory heritage forms that are so often privileged by the AHD that demands a re-reading of Deller's project in the light of recent manoeuvres in affect as it relates to Heritage Studies (Smith and Campbell 2016: 88).

This study argues that Critical Heritage Studies can occupy the discursive gap between the art-historical accounts of the event and the objections to its ethical and authorial frame posited by social history. Deller's project's opposition to AHD and its privileging of 'feel good' histories marks out the project as symptomatic of new critical heritage forms. With its open-ended dialogic, anti-nostalgic elevation of ongoing emotional trauma and emphasis on keeping wounds open rather than sympathetic reconciliation, this project – on paper at least – demands consideration from new perspectives in working-class intangible heritage (Russo and Linkon 2005; Robertson 2008).

Part One: *The Battle of Orgreave* (2001)

> As an artist, I was interested in how far an idea could be taken, especially one that is on the face of it a contradiction in terms, 'a recreation of something that was essentially chaos'.
>
> Deller (2002)

Artangel was founded in 1985 by Roger Took and has been directed since 1991 by James Lingwood and Michael Morris as a prominent commissioner of public art projects (Green 1999). Their most notable work leading up to Deller's commission included the commissioning and production of Rachel Whiteread's *House* (1993). A concrete casting of the interior of an inner-city working-class terrace due to be demolished to make way for a green park and the gentrification of the area, *House* emerged as a temporary project that received considerable critical attention.

The Battle of Orgreave (1984)   89

Signalling a ready commitment to confront and examine the histories of working-class life, Artangel's commissioning of Deller's restaging was – they admitted themselves – incredibly audacious:

> The principal concern of the Orgreave veterans centred on the media (the project was rarely perceived locally as an art event) and whether the re-enactment would merely provide an opportunity to reopen old wounds and the chance to re-iterate historic slurs and injustices. This was a concern we shared ('Lottery-funded riot' being the tabloid headline we dreaded most) so we decided to only send out invitations to attend to the press on the eve of the re-enactment.
>
> (Deller 2002)

Jeremy Deller, still in his early thirties at the point of the commission, had already received considerable attention for a set of projects that explored the practices and histories of working-class British life. *Acid Brass* (1997) explored the imperilled practices of colliery brass bands – as explored in the popular movie *Brassed Off* (1996) – by commissioning new arrangements and performances of traditional brass music fused with the 'acid house' music ubiquitous in underground subcultural music at the time. Performed and arranged by the William Fairy Band – a Stockport-based brass band emerging from the local aviation factory – *Acid Brass* brought about numerous performances, recordings and documents that continue today.

Deller, it must be pointed out, has admittedly no connection to the working-class communities of the former collieries of Yorkshire. Deller was a teenager at the height of the miners' strike of 1984–1985 and the ready trauma of working-class life that was relayed on television made a considerable impression on the young artist (Figgis 2001). Despite his already assured reputation for sensitive and critical projects with working-class communities, a project of this type originated by a privately educated, upper-middle-class London-based artist and organised by a London-based arts agency raised eyebrows in Orgreave and the capital alike.

Deller and Artangel planned for the re-enactment to coincide with the 17th anniversary of the original conflict. Deller and Artangel sought to re-enact Orgreave as close as possible to the site (of which only part remained) and to involve as many of the original participants as possible. Through consultation and the use of several historical re-enactment societies – who were more used to carrying civil-war pikes than modern truncheons – the project sought to replay key moments of the battle. With the histories of Orgreave still being written and several key documents still subject to the Official Secrets Act, Deller's *Orgreave* is only a partial restaging – focusing on just a few key moments of the day, choreographed and played out with fake batons and foam bricks over a few short hours. The project would be supported by displays of archival material – photographs, press clippings, media clips – and brass band music from local colliery bands. On the day, there were talks and presentations from key protagonists from the day, including representatives of the NUM, ambulance men, notable pickets and historians of the conflict. The 'battle' would be observed from behind safety barriers by the wives and children of the striking miners and members of the local community, together with non-participating strikers from the original conflict.

Alongside participants of the original battle, re-enactors would bolster numbers on both sides of the conflict. Using the technologies of re-enactment, period costume, trained horses and fake weapons, the re-enactors took an active role in ensuring the safe replaying of what was a very bloody and violent original. Employing oral histories and archival footage, and in consultation with serving police officers present at the original battle, key scenes were replayed – the opening gambits of stone throwing and baton waving, the horse charge, the first hand-to-hand contacts – following rehearsal the day before.

Participants were recruited from cold-call letters, copies of which circulated among the local communities and workingmen's clubs. Participants would be paid for their contribution, subject to strict codes of conduct and safe behaviour. Participants were paid £80 per day for taking part. Of particular interest to the critics of the project was the very deliberate exclusion of original serving police officers from the re-enactment. The recruitment letter noted the intention of employing former miners to play the police: 'Some of the re-enactors will be acting as miners, some as police. We are hoping that some former miners will play policemen, as they have valuable firsthand experience of police tactics' (Deller 2002).

The event went ahead without causalities and in good humour (even a last-minute intervention by the right-wing tabloid newspaper *The Daily Express* in an adjacent field failed to dampen spirits). The event and its preparation were documented by Deller (present with a video camera in amongst the participants), who also collected archival material pertaining to the event and its preparation. Mike Figgis, already a notable director of Hollywood hits and independent arthouse films, joined the project to record the battle; this film documentation was supplemented by archival material, behind-the-scenes footage of preparations for the re-enactment, interviews with participants, re-enactors, Deller, former police officers and leading Labour politician Tony Benn MP. Deller was keen on distancing Figgis' film document from that of the project, insisting that the event and the artist's own documentation of the event constituted 'the work'.

In 2002, a book was published, edited by Deller and Michael Morris of Artangel, entitled *The English Civil War Part II* and containing in facsimile material drawn from miners' scrapbooks that was used by Deller and Artangel in preparing for the event, interviews with key participants, essays by historians of the event, press clippings following the event, the recruitment letter and an accompanying CD of interviews and songs from participants. The title of the book highlights what for many was to all intents and purposes a replay of the seventeenth-century English Civil War: brothers, fathers and sons, cousins fighting on both sides of *The English Civil War Part II*.

Part Two: Critical receptions

In her early reading of the social and ethical 'turn' in contemporary art, key historian and theoretician of participatory art Claire Bishop noted Deller's (and his contemporaries') commitment to ambiguity over that of that of ethics:

> Deller [... *et al.*] do[es] *not make the 'correct' ethical choice*, they do not embrace the Christian ideal of self-sacrifice; instead, they act on their desire without the incapacitating restrictions of guilt. In so doing, their work joins a tradition of highly authored situations that fuse social reality with carefully calculated artifice.
>
> (Bishop 2006: 183)

More recently, in *Artificial Hells* (2012) – the first dedicated history of participatory art – Bishop expands on these points. Deller's project was the 'epitome' of this new form of practice that explored the generative potential of paradox, contradiction and 'incorrect' ethical choices (Bishop 2012: 30). Bishop noted that, whilst Deller's project may at first glance appear 'therapeutic', with bias clearly being shown to the pickets, the project itself is much more 'ambiguous' (Bishop 2012: 32). The Figgis documentary – in which Deller participated, but which, for him, did not constitute the work – was much less ambiguous, though no less successful in Bishop's view in that its concentration on the historical conditions of the miners' strike took on a much more direct political message than did Deller's multifaceted approach.

For social historian David Gilbert, reviewing *The English Civil War Part II*, there were notable differences between Deller's and Figgis' Orgreave projects. Deller's commitment to the 'event' – in the array of archival materials, music and talks, and in giving up a degree of authority in the 'battle' – is in marked contrast to Figgis' commitment to the 'politics' (Gilbert 2005: 104). As a result, the Figgis film neglected the multiplicity of the event – the parades of union banners, colliery bands – due to its privileging of the political conditions of the original conflict. For Marxist historian Dave Beech, it was precisely Deller's lack of a direct political message – he cites the involvement of the re-enactment societies as compromising its political voice – that marks out Figgis' success and Deller's failure (Beech 2001: 10). Whereas Bishop's reading commends the ambiguity and ethical conundrum of silent voices as an aesthetic and generative potential, many other readers of Deller were unable to locate the positive aspects of elision.

For Alice Correia (2006), an art historian, the absence of key personnel from the event only evidenced bias towards the pickets and Deller's reading of them as martyrs. For Correia, the absence of the police is telling; whereas for Gilbert the absence of 'scabs' (those miners' who refused to join the picket or broke the picket line and returned to work) was crucial: 'Other voices from the strike remain silent – those miners that returned to work in Yorkshire are shadowy figures to be demonized or pitied' (Gilbert 2005: 105).

All these readings have merit. Deller acknowledges that the project *was* political. His refusal to directly name that politics, however, results in a number of problems. This was a practical manoeuvre. A great many of the re-enactment societies were apolitical in their stance and would have refused to participate had this work been labelled a political project rather than an art event. The absence of the original police force from the project was due to a practical concern: the very *real* possibility that they would be identified and vilified, perhaps even physically beaten.

There appears to be a central conflict regarding Deller that all these readings share: *authorship*. As is shown both in the organisation and in the presentation of the event and its archives, the nature of Deller's practice is collaborative. And yet, the archives are presented as the work of a single author. This is somewhat misleading and raises questions about what is meant by 'authorship' in this project. Despite the highly choreographed nature of the event on the day, Figgis' in-field interview of Deller – walking amongst the re-enactors with a camera – revealed the author's standpoint; he would neither intervene in the event nor attempt to direct it. When asked by the interviewer 'How's it going?', Deller responded 'It's going interesting ... This is the first time we've actually got these two groups together, and it's difficult to say what's going to happen. Look at it ... I'm not in charge anymore, really. As you would be in a real situation like this, you'd be a bit excited and a bit worried as well.' (Figgis 2001; quoted in Bishop 2012: 32).

As noted, the early critics of Deller's project are notably much divided – though broadly positive. Although it garnered some initial attention from social history and heritage studies, Deller's project is now curiously absent from more recent histories of working-class projects of the same period. In *Heritage, Labour and the Working Classes* (Smith, Shackel and Campbell 2011) there is no mention of Deller's *Orgreave* project, despite there being several chapters dedicated to intangible heritage and mining communities. Notably, the first chapter – by Michael Bailey and Simon Popple – is focused on the 1984–85 miners' strike and the mobilisation of film archives following the 25th anniversary of the strike. As Bailey was well aware of the Deller project, having reviewed it – somewhat less than favourably in comparison with most – in his earlier edited book *Shafted* (2009), the omission is clearly deliberate. Furthermore – and just as problematic – in Bailey and Popple's argument for 'heritage-based' initiatives engaging with the BBC archive (their project was co-funded by the BBC) they ignore the active role the BBC played in vilifying the Orgreave miners, many of whom still hold the BBC in contempt (Orgreave Truth and Justice Campaign n.d.). Advocating for an

The Battle of Orgreave (1984)   93

expansive view of heritage that resists the AHD, Bailey and Popple seem to misunderstand this point of grievance:

> Heritage-based initiatives such as those outlined above [film projects] offer these communities, *in genuine partnership with cultural organisations*, the opportunity to revise Marx's dictum and to make their own history through heritage on their own terms. The loss of this potent collective memory would be a terrible tragedy for future generations.
>
> (*my emphasis*, Bailey and Popple 2011: 31)

Why then not Deller's *Battle of Orgreave*? The community played an active role in choreographing the 2001 event and the event plays a continued role in defining it more than a decade later. So why then is Deller's *Orgreave* not admissible to this call to arms? Is Deller's project less than *genuine*? This reading of Deller's *Orgreave* is less than generous.

Though Deller and Figgis' projects continue to play an active role both in commemorating Orgreave and in generating political action, they appear to have little significance for Critical Heritage Studies. Given the conditions of the project and its clear similarity to other heritage projects of the period – utilising oral and archival histories, participation, developed in and played out in the community, 'living history' – this is curious. The explanation for this has as many complexities and contradictions as the project itself. As a non-local, well-educated, historically attuned author, Deller's account of the archive must be scrutinised for its adherence to an Authorised Heritage Discourse (Smith 2006). Deller has no immediate connection with the community of Orgreave, and the source of his privilege emerges from his status as artist and historian. This, however, is much more complicated than it at first appears. That the event is 'authored' as an art project marks it out as a different form from that of heritage initiatives and is, we can argue, the key condition for its omission from the literature. This, however, is premature and marks out an erroneous reading of contemporary authorship and its role in the project. It is certainly true that Deller 'authored' the project proposal. It is similarly true that Deller 'authored' the archive of the event. *The re-enactment itself is much more complex*. As noted earlier, Deller was well aware that the participants would determine much of the outcome and that *his authorial control of the events was divested into the performers themselves*. So, if Deller's authorship of the archive – for which he was awarded the prestigious Turner Prize in 2004 – is non-admissible as a 'heritage' project, we could argue that the event itself certainly *is* admissible as it was authored as much by the local participants as it was by Deller, Artangel and the re-enactment societies that took part on the day. Though the resultant art installation of the *Orgreave* archive explored the effect of the original strike and its re-enactment, the staging of Orgreave and its affect was authored by its participants.

Throughout the literature both from art history (Bishop 2006, 2012; Correia 2006) and from social history (Gilbert 2005; Bailey 2009) the same problems arise, albeit demanding different conclusions. For Michael Bailey, the democratic 'coercion' of the former miners was insensitive and ethically unsound (Bailey 2009). And Bailey was not alone in this assessment (Correia 2006). The objections focused on two related conditions of the restaging: (1) the absence of key participants from the original battle (the police); and (2) the deployment of former striking miners to play the part of the police alongside re-enactors. And such objections were – as we shall see – perfectly true.

The press

A continued bone of contention in 1984 was the deliberate bias against the striking miners by the media (a key concern of Truth and Justice for Orgreave). When he was interviewed by Figgis for the accompanying film, Tony Benn MP set out one such instance amongst many. On the evening of the original battle, the BBC news report coverage made a number of edits to the footage so as to make it appear that the horse charge towards the miners was a result of a volley of missiles from the pickets. In reality, as was soon found out, the opposite was true and the footage had in fact been reversed: the pickets threw stones *because they were being charged towards*. Tony Benn demanded a response from several members of the BBC on this, but was told that it was an unintentional error brought about by confusion regarding the original footage (Figgis 2001). There remain deep suspicions that, far from having been unintentional, the reversal of the narrative was a deliberate attempt to elicit sympathy for the police and to cast the pickets as the sole provocateurs. But the active fabrication, distortion and disruptive narrative of the media in 2001 was little better, and Artangel noted the potential for renewed vilification.

At short notice, the politically conservative tabloid *The Daily Express* arranged for its own re-enactment that would be played out in a field adjacent to the Deller–Artangel project. According to the *Express*, 82 were arrested in 1984. The actual figure was 93, and all were acquitted due to unreliable police evidence (the *Express* failed to acknowledge these acquittals). In time, South Yorkshire police paid out significant compensation for over 30 unlawful arrests. This was, again, not mentioned by the newspaper report of Orgreave 2001.

The Express was not content with misreporting the original battle or attempting to deliberately compromise and intervene in the re-enactment. It also sought to deliberately misreport the Deller–Artangel project:

> Yesterday there was more of a carnival atmosphere as the bloody scenes were re-enacted for a TV documentary to be shown next year. Hundreds of spectators gathered at the site near Sheffield. There was musical entertainment, displays, stalls and refreshments.
>
> (*The Daily Express* 18 June 2001)

The Battle of Orgreave (1984)   95

Yes, there was musical entertainment: picket songs, brass bands, music representative of 1984, together with tributes from musicians following the strike. Displays? Yes, of documentary photography, archives of the miners' strike and several historic union banners used by parents to show to their children.

Such media distortions – as alive in 2001 as they were in 1984 – had penetrated the public imagination of the miners' strike to the extent that many of the re-enactors employed to bolster numbers were petrified:

> A lot of the members of historical re-enactment societies were terrified of the miners. During the '80s they had obviously believed what they had read in the press and had the idea that the men that they would be working with on the re-enactment were going to be outright hooligans or revolutionaries. They thought it would turn into one huge real battle.
>
> (Deller 2002)

Reassurances from Deller, Artangel and the fight choreographers placated some (together with the quiet reassurance that this was an art project, not a political one), but distanced others: 'We resolved to abandon the project at the first sign of antagonism' (Deller 2002). In many respects *The Daily Express'* fabrication and false reporting of Orgreave 2001 had the adverse effect of changing the minds of many of the re-enactors who had entered into the project with a less than positive view of the miners but left – after a convivial and safely organised battle – with a greater sense of empathy for the pickets and the continued injustices played out in the national press (Deller 2002).

The literature on Deller's *Orgreave* is extensive and diverse, and the contradictions and its afterlife in the Truth and Justice for Orgreave campaign have failed to put the event and its archive to rest:

> The event was, and is, difficult to describe because it occupied many different cultural categories at once: it was a work of art, a re-enacted battle, an extraordinary celebration, a struggle to represent history and part film set [...]. Overall, it was very difficult to pinpoint the experience in relation to a particular object or 'site' as a work of art, or even to acknowledge where the various components of the 'art' project began or ended. But over time, it became clear that Jeremy Deller had produced an extraordinary artwork, the effects of which are still reverberating.
>
> (Cummings and Lewandowska 2006: 405)

Part Three: Affecting heritage

Contemporaneously with Deller's projects *Acid Brass* and *The Battle of Orgreave* came a renewed interest in 'affect theory' in art and cultural studies. Gregg and Seigworth, leading authors in the field of affect theory, define affect as '[that which] arises in the midst of in-between-ness: in the capacities to act and be acted upon' (Gregg and Seigworth 2010: 1). Furthermore, affect

> is in many ways synonymous with force or forces of encounter. The term 'force', however, can be a bit of a misnomer, since affect need not be especially forceful (although sometimes, as in ... trauma, it is). In fact, it is quite likely that affect more often transpires within and across the subtlest of shuttling intensities: all the minuscule events of the unnoticed.
> (Gregg and Seigworth 2010)

Affect theory in art and its histories arrived almost in sync with Deller's *Acid Brass* and *Battle of Orgreave*. The turn towards studies of objects and events in terms of impact, collision and experience marked out a new field of study and practice in participatory art in the post-millennium era. As historian and artist Simon O'Sullivan remarked at the time,

> Affects are moments of intensity, a reaction in/on the body at the level of matter. We might even say that affects are immanent to matter – they are certainly immanent to experience. [...] As such, affects are not to do with knowledge or meaning; indeed, they occur on a different register – an asignifying register.
> (Sullivan 2001: 135)

Sullivan's working definition of affect is that of a particular embodied intensity that communicates outside of meaning. In the context of Deller's *Orgreave* this employment of affect is somewhat problematic.

Works such as Deller's *Orgreave* not only elicit an effect (an emotional response to a particular event), *they also generate and communicate it* ('affect'). These affects are *not always* traumatic, and can be generated from any range of experiences and encounters. Affect theory determines that emotion is not always causal – 'you are sad, so you cry' – but also communicative and generative – 'your crying makes me sad'. Affective artworks, then, are less concerned with the privileging of 'effect' (crying, joy, indifference, horror) than they are with *the communication of emotion*, what we as an audience might collectively and individually feel and communicate. Sullivan's definition of an *asignifying* register somewhat fails to account for this communicative overspill. Far from evading meaning, Deller's *Orgreave* employs several registers that differ in their production of signification: the register of the participants in 1984; the non-miners participating in 2001; the interviewees; the local community.

Affect exists in multiple registers, which Sullivan's early definition fails to unpick. Sullivan's usage of 'affect', however, is useful in understanding its contemporaneous use in Deller's *Orgreave*. Subsequent critical overhauls of affect by the social sciences in the decade following Sullivan have drawn out a much broader and nuanced set of tools (Wetherell 2012). 'Affect', in

The sense evoked by Sullivan, is a particular concern of art and its practices from the mid-1990s onwards, one that feeds into Deller's mode of practice at this time.

In these terms, the *Battle of Orgreave* (2001) was less concerned with re-enactment and the replaying of historical narratives and more concerned with eliciting a range of affective responses. That affect – on the part of the miners playing police – is considerable: from those miners revealing their discomfort at playing their perceived oppressor; the fear at facing the picket; awareness of the complexity of critical conditions of the day. Of course, this affect is not necessarily concerned with conciliatory gestures. Reconciliation under these conditions would demand the presence of the original participants. The affect is in the broad range of feelings generated on both sides of the battle that would be, this study argues, mediated and muted through a stricter adherence to an ethical framework for participation.

On this, whereas Bishop and Bailey question the ethical conundrum brought about by the pickets playing police, a contemporary reviewer of the work, David Butler, noted its generative potential:

> The participants were either ex-miners, local people or re-enactors. The audience were locals, people who go to re-enactments and the art world. These people were there for different reasons and they looked at the event in different ways. You could see this as a kind of parallel tracking where everyone leaves with what they came for. But, I think it's more complex than that. If, as a re-enactor, you take part in an event that someone says is art *you have to take a look at it in that way even if that's not your language*. So these different worlds impact on each other.
>
> (Butler 2001)

Two particular responses recorded by Figgis from the pickets playing police are particularly noteworthy. The first response was the most common and probably the most expected: 'It goes against t'grain' (Figgis 2001). The very idea of a former picket, vilified and abused (physically and judicially), playing the role of police is – as Bailey points out – insensitive. This response does achieve one thing, however, something that demands a deeper reading: it is symptomatic of the *continued* mistrust of the police and the state that Orgreave 1984 exacerbated.

The second response is even more interesting. The picket – who earlier in the film had spoken very emotionally about his feelings towards the police and their treatment of the miners – took a much more empathetic approach to the role:

> I'd prefer to be a picket again. But I think we were short of a few policemen so I've ended up being one of these. I've no qualms about it, it's going to be quite interesting [to] see what it's going to be like on the other side of the spectrum.
>
> (Figgis 2001)

It is no surprise that there was a shortage of willing participants to play the role of the police. This particular former picket, however, is intelligent in his response, a response that would have been lost under a more 'ethical' framework as demanded by Bailey.

Mac McLoughlin, a former police officer in Orgreave 1984 who acted in a consultancy role, explained through an interview in the Figgis film that, like many of the local police serving that June day, he had a complex relationship with the picket. A former miner himself, from a family of miners, his testimony reveals the wider cost of Orgreave 1984. As he admits, the justices of the peace acted unjustly. In an interview for the documentary, McLoughlin acknowledged that his role in the original battle was flawed and admitted his shame at what happened:

> As police, did we make mistakes? Of course we did. And without doubt, some police officers committed serious criminal offences such as assault.
>
> (Figgis 2001)

It is widely recognised that relationships between the pickets and the local police were, if not cordial, at least respectful. The local police knew about the struggle, and many supported the miners financially. They were the brothers, cousins and sons of the pickets, in what was so aptly named *The English Civil War Part II*. The emotional trauma on both sides of the battle is key to understanding the especially fraught conditions under which the original battle took place. It is not surprising, however, that much attention has been paid to the trauma of the pickets and their families at the expense of the voices of the serving police that day. The aftermath of Orgreave 1984 led to a serious deterioration of local faith in the police and the state. Here, the resistance to the idea of the AHD is both useful and limited. By asking former pickets to play the police, unusual responses can be garnered. Opposition to the AHD demands that we ask the question 'Who is authorised to tell this story?' Rather than offering a critically safe history of Orgreave – as is often demanded of the AHD – the bias here reveals something that, under a more rigorous ethical frame, would not be revealed. The picket playing a policeman is, this study argues, an attempt not to elicit a critical revision – 'The police were maybe not to blame' – *but to reveal through an empathetic and affecting gesture that not just bones were broken on that day*. The bonds between brothers, sons and cousins and the broader trust of the local community were broken on that day *and remain broken*. Though the physical fractures of those injured (on both sides) would in time be healed, the bonds of community and state remain injured.

This is the value of Deller's *Battle of Orgreave* to heritage. The critically intelligent response by the former miner playing the police offer in 2001 is, I think, something that is lost on Bailey. It is not an 'ethical' error on the part of Deller – though in a very real sense it was a decision drawn out of pragmatism – but rather his recognising the potential empathetic responses that such a manoeuvre might elicit.

A little more than a third of the re-enactors had taken part in the original battle. Many more, however, watched along the side and took part in the preparation of the event. Some miners were too infirm to take part in the physical skirmish; others had passed away. Some of the participants were representing their missing family members who could not take part. One interviewee spoke particularly evocatively of the inter-generational trauma and his willingness to expose the open wounds of Orgreave 1984:

> I'm only here doing this for me dad's sake. You know cos he can't be here and I know how he felt about the pits. He were a really strong bloke.
> (Figgis 2001)

It is hard not to be moved by such a gesture. Though he was not present at the original battle, the son playing the role of a picket reminds us of what is at stake and how art and heritage (often in tandem) can explore and revive lost voices.

Conclusion

Interviewed by Figgis for the Channel 4 documentary, Deller revealed that reconciliation and revision were far from his intention for *The Battle of Orgreave*:

> It's going to take more than an art project to heal wounds. But it was definitely about confronting something and not being afraid of looking at it again and discussing it and not being ashamed by what happened to you.
> (Figgis 2001)

Deller was not interested in playing at history with the re-enactment. Recognising the open-ended and dialogic nature of the work, Deller reveals his interest in Orgreave is that of energising recognition and confronting still-to-be-resolved conflicts and traumas. The statement from Deller, it could be argued, has much in common with other similarly antagonistic and agonistic heritage projects. And though the ethical conundrums regarding the participation of some miners acting as the police and Deller's authorship of the work mark it out as an especially difficult work to place, it remains significant in elevating a set of affective conditions that prove useful in examining empathy and emotion in a heritage setting.

That Deller's *Orgreave* is centrally important to participatory modes of art practices is of no importance to the mining community. Deller's *Orgreave*, however, maintains a significance in those communities as they continue to fight for justice and recognition of the wrongs perpetrated more than 30 years

100 Toby Juliff

ago. Deller's *Orgreave* is significant to these communities not in order to advertise and promote their victimhood, but, rather, to remind the world that their voices are still, in many ways, 'striking'.

It is particularly telling that the documentary film of the event directed by Figgis has, more than a decade after the re-enactment and three decades after the original event, gained increasing coverage in mining communities and their support mechanisms. Public showings of the film in former mining communities, together with more 'arthouse' events in London, have been utilised by the Truth and Justice for Orgreave campaign with increasing popular and critical success. Would a more 'ethically' sound and conciliatory re-enactment have proven quite so affecting? I would argue not.

As stated in the introduction, it is not the aim here to claim Deller's *Orgreave* for heritage studies. As Jackson and Kidd (2012) have already noted, the increasing role of performance at heritage sites raises a new set of provocations for critical heritage studies. Deller's *Orgreave* employs a number of different modes of performing heritage. Conceived of as the generative site of an artwork destined for a museum rather than as 'living theatre', *Orgreave* employed both re-enactment (the participants recruited from Orgreave 1984) *and* performance (the participants recruited from re-enactment) in a manner that further questions the role of authorship in the work. Furthermore, *Orgreave* took place beyond museum walls and grounds and used a non-heritage site through which to partially re-enact the event. As Smith (2012: 80) notes regarding the use of a site as a 'prop' for memory, the value of a site need not be dictated by its 'authenticity', but rather depends on its potential for generating new possibilities. In *Orgreave*'s exemplary occupation of the 'grey' areas, its privileging of affect and resistance to the AHD, a more subtle reading of its contradictions and 'wrong ethical choices' might reveal new criteria through which to examine new critical heritage works.

As Smith and Campbell (2016) argue, affect is a practical as well as theoretical concern for heritage studies. Even though it is relatively new as a critical criterion for heritage studies, affect develops an understanding of emotionality across a broad spectrum of responses. Deller's *Orgreave* certainly achieved that.

References

Bailey, M., 2009. Unfinished business: Demythologising the Battle of Orgreave. In G. Williams, ed. *Shafted: The Media, the Miners' Strike and the Aftermath.* London: Campaign for Press and Broadcasting Freedom, 119–128.

Bailey, M. and Popple, S., 2011. The 1984/85 miners' strike: Re-claiming cultural heritage. In L. Smith, P. A. Shackel and G. Campbell, eds. *Heritage, Labour and the Working Classes.* London: Routledge, 19–33.

Beech, D., 2001. The uses of authority: Jeremy Deller interviewed by Dave Beech. *Untitled*, 25, 10–12.

Bishop, C., 2006. The social turn: Collaboration and its discontents. *Artforum*, February.

Bishop, C., 2012. *Artificial Hells: Participatory Art and the Politics of Spectatorship.* London: Verso.

Butler, D., 2001. Battle of Orgreave. *a-n magazine*, September.

Correia, A., 2006. Interpreting Jeremy Deller's *The Battle of Orgreave. Visual Culture in Britain*, 7(2), 93–112.

Cummings, N. and Lewandowska, M., 2006. A shadow of Marx. In A. Jones, ed. *A Companion to Contemporary Art since 1945.* London: Wiley and Sons.

Deller, J., 2002. *The English Civil War Part II: Personal Accounts of the 1984–85 Miners' Strike.* London: Artangel.

Figgis, M., dir., 2001. *The Battle of Orgreave.* Channel 4 Productions.

Gilbert, D., 2005. *The English Civil War Part II: Personal Accounts of the 1984–85 Miners' Strike* by Jeremy Deller. *Oral History*, 33(1), 105–106.

Green, C. 1999. So who is behind Artangel? *The Telegraph*, 7 April.

Gregg, M. and Seigworth, G. J., eds., 2010. *The Affect Theory Reader.* Durham: Duke University Press.

Jackson, A. and Kidd, J. 2012. Introduction. In A. Jackson and J. Kidd, eds. *Performing Heritage: Research, Practice and Innovation in Museum Theatre and Live Interpretation.* Manchester: Manchester University Press.

Orgreave Truth and Justice Campaign. n.d. https://otjc.org.uk/ [Accessed 6 February 2018].

Robertson, I. J. M., 2008. Heritage from below: Class, social protest and resistance. In B. Graham and P. Howard, ed. *The Ashgate Research Companion to Heritage and Identity.* Aldershot: Ashgate.

Russo, J. and Linkon, S. L., eds., 2005. *New Working-Class Studies.* Ithaca: ILR Press.

Shaw, K., 2012. *Mining the Meaning: Cultural Representations of the 1984–5 UK Miners' Strike.* Newcastle upon Tyne: Cambridge Scholars Publishing.

Smith, L., 2006. *Uses of Heritage.* London: Routledge.

Smith, L. 2012. The 'doing' of heritage: Heritage as performance. In A. Jackson and J. Kidd, eds. *Performing Heritage: Research, Practice and Innovation in Museum Theatre and Live Interpretation.* Manchester: Manchester University Press.

Smith, L. and Campbell, G., 2011. Don't mourn organise: Heritage, recognition and memory in Castleford, West Yorkshire. In L. Smith, P. A. Shackel and G. Campbell, eds. *Heritage, Labour and the Working Classes.* London: Routledge.

Smith, L. and Campbell, G., 2016, The elephant in the room: Heritage, affect and emotion. In W. Logan, M. Nic Craith and U. Kockel, eds. *A Companion to Heritage Studies.* Oxford: Wiley Blackwell.

Smith, L., Shackel, P. A. and Campbell, G., eds., 2011. *Heritage, Labour and the Working Classes.* London: Routledge.

Sullivan, S., 2001. The aesthetics of affect: Thinking art beyond representation. *Angelaki*, 6(3), 125–135.

Taylor, D., 2008. Performance and intangible heritage. In T. Davis, ed. *The Cambridge Companion to Performance Studies.* Cambridge: Cambridge University Press.

Taylor, D., 2016. Saving the 'live'? Re-performance and intangible cultural heritage. *Études Anglaises*, 69(2), 149–161.

Wetherell, M., 2012. *Affect and Emotion: A New Social Science Understanding.* London: Sage.

Part II

Belonging and exclusion

Chapter 7

Apologising for past wrongs
Emotion–reason rhetoric in political discourse

Martha Augoustinos, Brianne Hastie and Peta Callaghan

> One of the most insidious developments in Australian political life over the past decade or so has been the attempt to rewrite Australian history in the service of a partisan political cause.
>
> (John Howard, March 1996)

Introduction

National narratives are key resources for shaping constructions of the nation and national identity. The notion of the nation as an 'imagined community' (Anderson 1991) rests on the conception of shared understanding as to the features of national history and how this has shaped the identity of its members. A nation's historical narrative, therefore, provides not only an empirical warrant for the nation's legitimacy but also the building blocks for constructing a shared identity. However, national narratives are far from unproblematic factual accounts accepted by all (White 1978; Condor 2010). Historical narratives that glorify 'nation-building', civilisation and progress, the version to which former Australian Prime Minister John Howard is referring in the opening quotation, are often contested. Such challenges to modernist narratives of progress and civilisation are particularly evident in settler and coloniser/colonised societies like Australia, where the need to confront and reconcile a brutal colonial past with such triumphant accounts challenges political leaders and the wider polity (Curthoys 2006). Similar challenges are seen in other postcolonial nations, including Canada (Winter 2007) and New Zealand (McCreanor 1993; Kirkwood, Liu and Wetherell 2005), and particularly in former colonisers such as Great Britain (Condor and Abell 2006; Condor 2010).

As contested sites, dominant historical narratives that increasingly attract internal and external criticism lead to ideological struggles within the nation state over competing, even contradictory, versions of history (LeCouteur and Augoustinos 2001; LeCouteur, Rapley and Augoustinos 2001; Macintyre and Clarke 2003). This, in turn, can create ontological insecurity for identity,

106 Martha Augoustinos *et al.*

which leads members of majority groups to resist change (Kinnvall and Lindén 2010). In Australia, the rancorous public debate over history during the period of the Howard government (1996–2007) came to be known as the 'History Wars' and pitted two competing accounts of nationhood against each other: the one championed by the political right depicted Australia's history as a triumph over hardship and adversity that is to be celebrated, whereas the other, championed by the left, was a story of British imperialism, Indigenous dispossession and injustice that required reparation and restitution (Manne 2001; Curthoys 2006).

Such division is problematic for national leaders, particularly when not just disenchanted minority groups, such as Indigenous peoples, but also members of majority groups contest history. Hence, it becomes necessary to acknowledge a problematic past, and one primary way of accomplishing this is through providing national apologies to aggrieved groups for historical injustices (Harris, Grainger and Mullany 2006; Nobles 2008).

As Luke (1997: 366) has argued, national apologies can accomplish a 'discursive reframing of history', allowing negative past events to be incorporated into a nation's history. However, this reframing of national history also represents a potential threat to identity; what it means to be a member of a nation that acknowledges such a past. This, therefore, presents a dilemma for national leaders responsible for such reframings: how to maintain a positive, valued national identity in the face of admitted wrongdoing; and how to overcome resistance to redefinitions of national history and identity by those clinging to a hitherto positive but problematic national narrative?

This chapter examines how a discursive reframing of Australia's history was accomplished through a national apology offered to Australia's Indigenous peoples in 2008 by the then Prime Minister Kevin Rudd for the forced removal of Indigenous children during the twentieth century, a practice that was acknowledged as genocide by the Australian Human Rights and Equal Opportunity Commission (HEROC 1997). More specifically, we analyse how this was achieved rhetorically by linking emotion to reason and thus appealing to collective emotions that Australians *should* feel towards the mistreatment of Indigenous people. We also contrast Rudd's reframing of national history and identity with that constructed by the then Leader of the Opposition, Brendan Nelson, in his reply speech, to show how such redefinitions can be contested and resisted, in order to maintain a dominant coloniser version of the Australian national narrative.

Redefining the nation and national identity

Anderson (1991: 3) has argued that 'nation-ness is the most universally legitimate value in the political life of our time'. It is no surprise, therefore, that nationalist discourse has been identified as a powerful means by which to promote and mobilize public support for a variety of political projects (Reicher and Hopkins 2001). Political parties from across the ideological spectrum in western democracies have become adept at presenting their policies and political agendas as consonant with the 'national interest' and as embodying prototypical features of a 'national identity'. Differing narratives of nationhood, however, can be constructed from the same 'facts', 'thereby giv(ing) the facts different significance and meaning' (Polkinghorne 1988: 181). As such, 'narratives are not merely accounts of experience, they are performative, offering frames for human action' (Hiles and Cermak 2008: 149). In this sense, national narratives can be understood as a type of national heritage that is performed by individuals and societies engaged in the negotiation of historical meaning and the legitimisation of cultural and political values (Smith 2006). Remembering and memory-making are critical aspects of this heritage performance; they are bound up with the legitimisation of identity, sense of place and belonging, and are continually reconstituted for the needs of the present (Smith, 2006).

National narratives are not built on facts alone: representations of nationhood gain power and influence when they are able to rouse the emotions and passions of citizens. Significant scholarly attention has been paid to the mobilisation and invocation of emotion in flare ups of 'hot nationalism': emotions such as pride and love of country, which are often accompanied by what Hage (1998) calls 'practices of exclusion' when dominant groups police the boundaries of who does and who does not legitimately belong to the nation. National history and identity as objects are continually reconstructed through their everyday use as discursive resources and practices (De Cillia, Riesigl and Wodak 1999), and over time these can cement themselves into consensual and shared representations as to their defining features. However, significant events can disrupt the everyday-ness, or what Billig (1995) calls the 'banality', of nationalism, leading to respecifications of national identity. These may be sudden, as in the case of the 11 September 2001 attack in New York, or gradual, such as the increasing recognition of the mistreatment of some members of the community such as Indigenous peoples in settler societies. Such recognition grows from the mobilisation of particular versions of social identities by those advocating change (Reicher and Hopkins 2001), usually through presentation of a competing narrative. In the case of many Indigenous populations, their demands for social change and restitution are based on the argument that contemporary experiences of social, economic and political disadvantage are linked to historical experiences of dispossession and subordination (Nobles 2008). An apology, therefore, that officially acknowledges the dispossession and subordination of Indigenous peoples strengthens claims about the source of current disadvantage and the appropriate remedies to address it.

Recognition that the dominant group has caused suffering, however, represents a significant threat to national identity, which is why such recognition is often denied or minimised by members of the dominant group.

Bonnel and Simon's (2007) description of the 'difficult exhibition' in museum research provides a useful framework for understanding how such threats to national identity can generate complex emotional responses. In the museum context, 'difficult exhibitions' are understood as difficult because they present new ways of thinking and reasoning about the past, thereby challenging the viewer's sense of identity in the context of a national history of violence and suffering (Bonnell and Simon 2007). This is achieved through the presentation of historical facts in such a way that feelings of grief, frustration and even guilt may be evoked (Bonnell and Simon 2007). In this way 'difficult exhibitions' are similar to political acts aimed at bringing about reconciliation, such as the apology, because such political acts also challenge us to rethink our nation's past and who we are, thereby evoking emotions such as guilt, sadness, anger or frustration. It is this constructing, assembling and recruiting of emotions through the presentation of historical facts in intricate and subtle ways which achieves the rhetorical goals of the speaker.

Apologies for past injustices do not merely challenge the historical record of a nation, they also challenge and contest the collective emotions of a people that infuse and saturate these stories: that is, they challenge the unrestrained pride and triumph over adversity upon which most nation states are built. As Barkan (2000) has argued in *The Guilt of Nations*, contemporary demands for restitution by aggrieved groups have the potential to unsettle and threaten a nation's identity in ways that can give rise to aversive emotions such as shame and guilt. Indeed, our previous research analysing formal and informal discourse on whether to apologise to Indigenous Australians (well before the actual apology was delivered in 2007) demonstrated that this heated national debate became a site of contestation over what emotions Australians *should* legitimately feel regarding the forced removal of Indigenous children (Augoustinos, LeCouteur and Soyland 2002; LeCouteur *et al.* 2001). Resistance to the actual apology considered here was primarily rationalised by previous Prime Minister Howard's favoured argument that current generations should not be blamed for the mistakes of previous generations and that an apology, by definition, would evoke negative emotions such as guilt and shame, emotions with which current generations should not be burdened. In contrast, those advocating an apology represented this symbolic act as the 'right thing to do': an act of restitution infused with empathy and sorrow for the suffering of Indigenous people.

It is precisely these two contrasting positions that can be seen in the responses of Rudd and Nelson to the national apology to the Stolen Generations in Australia. Both invoke a national identity to substantiate their positions: Rudd (as instigator) to justify his offering of the apology; and Nelson (as resister) to minimise the need for the apology. In order to legitimate their respective positions, they offer competing narratives of Australia's history, drawing on different sets of facts, and the appropriate emotional reactions Australians *should* feel, to construct different versions of

Australia's history. Throughout this chapter we will refer to these strategies as *emotion–reason rhetoric*, because of the way in which reasoned arguments are legitimated by both leaders by appealing to appropriate emotional responses.

Reason and emotion

We draw our theory of emotion from Wetherell (2013), who examined the relationship between affect/emotion[1] and discourse, arguing that the traditional social science view that affect and discourse are disconnected can impede social research. Wetherell draws out the connection between affect and discourse by demonstrating how 'talk, body actions, affect, material contexts and social relations assemble *in situ*' (Wetherell 2013: 351). Wetherell's (2013) proposed notion of *affective practice* implies the need to focus on the integration (or *entanglement*) of expressive forms across multiple modalities, such as discourse, affect and even cognition, which is implicated through memory by the notion that historical influences permeate our everyday practices. In this sense, embodied affective and emotional action is bound inextricably with talk during and even prior to its expression in the moment.

The construction of Australia's history that is our focus here is therefore conceptualised as a situated activity that draws both on discursive and on affective/emotional modalities. While we are not conducting the type of complex and multimodal analysis of discourse and affect/emotion that Wetherell (2013) described, our analysis is primarily a rhetorical one. However, we treat emotion as more than simply constituted and deployed for political purposes. Emotion is understood here as *entangled* with discourse and other psychological modalities *in practice* to produce accounts that have cultural and even moral relevance – they are accounts that resonate with us because we both *feel* and *understand* their relevance. It is this complex merging of emotion with discursive expression that renders such accounts canonical and therefore rhetorically powerful. However, as we will demonstrate, they are also contested in the political context for ideological and political purposes.

Our analysis of the two leaders' respective apologies to the Stolen Generations will demonstrate how this is achieved in a variety of ways. Specifically, we show how emotion and reason are constructed rhetorically (what we refer to from here on as 'emotion–reason rhetoric') as either linked or contrasting (Edwards 1997, 1999), but are always intricately entangled to produce culturally relevant rhetorical accounts. One significant way in which emotions become entangled with reason in discourse is through linking and contrasting 'facts' with 'emotions'. Edwards (1997, 1999) and others (for example, Shields 2005) have identified a number of rhetorical contrasts concerning emotions used recurrently both in everyday language and in formal discourse to ascribe meaning, to evaluate and to manage accountability. These rhetorical contrasts are described as flexible discursive resources for situated occasions of use. One of the contrasts Edwards highlights is emotion versus cognition. The rhetorical contrast between cognition and emotion is not only common within psychology, but also a pervasive common-sense formulation that is widely shared by ordinary members of a society. This contrast is often mobilised to accomplish specific evaluations, in particular, to construct emotions as 'irrational' and 'subjective', in contrast to 'reason' and 'rationality'. In such representations, the emotions are seen as interfering with, and biasing, decision-making and social judgments (Edwards 1999). At the same time, however, reason and emotion can be intricately linked so that rationality itself can be justified and legitimated on the very basis of emotions that are seen to be 'natural' and normative. We will demonstrate below how this rhetorical link and/or contrast between emotion and reason is invoked throughout the two leaders' respective apologies to the Stolen Generations, and specifically address the varied ideological and social-interactional functions this emotion–reason rhetoric serves. Specifically, we focus on the different facts both Rudd and Nelson draw upon, and the subsequent 'appropriate' emotional responses associated with those facts that both men make relevant as they navigate their way through potentially sensitive and dilemmatic matters concerning injustices perpetrated against Indigenous people in Australia's complicated and dilemmatic history.

Analytical approach

In examining the apologies to the Stolen Generations our analysis draws on a critical or synthetic approach to discourse analysis (Wetherell 1998). The synthetic approach that we adopt examines both the interactional and the ideological features of discourse. More specifically, we consider (1) the ways in which discourse and rhetoric actively construct particular versions of social reality (in this case, a nation's history and identity), which, in turn, accomplish particular social and interactional objectives such as explaining, justifying and blaming; and (2) the broader cultural repertoires of understanding and emotion that are drawn upon to argue and debate the contested issue of a national apology for historical injustice, repertoires that draw upon shared patterns of sense-making. These versions of history and national identity are rhetorically designed: they include features that make them robust against disagreement or undermining by others (Billig 1987); and central to their persuasiveness is how this is accomplished by the two leaders by drawing on an emotion–reason rhetoric that justifies and legitimates competing national narratives and political objectives. Drawing on Wetherell (2012), we do not treat emotion or affect as something outside or separate from discourse. Discourse and emotion are treated as inextricably 'woven together' as practices that are oriented towards social action in everyday informal and formal settings to argue and explain. Moreover, as we will demonstrate, such affective–discursive practices function ideologically to justify and legitimate particular versions of the past, the present and the hoped-for future.

Analysis and discussion

The analysis below considers how each leader drew on emotion and facts to define national identity in relation to the apology, redefined or resisted redefining history as a consequence of the apology, and, finally, argued for a particular version of the nation. Rudd's apology can be seen as an attempt to officially instantiate a version of Australia's history that acknowledges the social injustices perpetrated against Indigenous peoples and provides a narrative basis for building a reconciled and inclusive nation for the future. In contrast, Nelson's reply served to reinforce the dominant, colonial narrative that excused and defended past generations for the social injustice experienced by Indigenous peoples.

Rudd's national apology

Extract 1 below presents the beginning of Rudd's speech and the apology he offers to Indigenous Australians.

<u>Extract 1: Rudd (0.00–1.51)</u>

I move that today we honour the Indigenous peoples of this land, the oldest continuing cultures in human history.

We reflect on their past mistreatment. We reflect in particular on the mistreatment of those who were Stolen Generations – this blemished chapter in our nation's history.

The time has now come for the nation to turn a new page in Australia's history by righting the wrongs of the past and so moving forward with confidence to the future.

We apologise for the laws and policies of successive Parliaments and governments that have inflicted profound grief, suffering and loss on these our fellow Australians.

We apologise especially for the removal of Aboriginal and Torres Strait Islander children from their families, their communities and their country.

For the pain, suffering and hurt of these Stolen Generations, their descendants and for their families left behind, we say sorry.

To the mothers and the fathers, the brothers and the sisters, for the breaking up of families and communities, we say sorry.

And for the indignity and degradation thus inflicted on a proud people and a proud culture, we say sorry.

Rudd's apology explicitly acknowledges the suffering experienced by Australia's Indigenous peoples as a consequence of successive government policies: 'profound grief, suffering and loss'; 'pain, suffering and hurt'; 'the indignity and degradation'. These three-part lists of emotion categories are notable for the extremity of emotion they convey. The suffering of Indigenous people is attributed directly to the indisputable fact of institutional practices that forced the removal of Indigenous children from their families and communities. Right at the outset then, Rudd mobilises an emotion–reason rhetoric that positions the apology as necessary given the emotional trauma inflicted on Indigenous people through past government practices. Describing these policies as a 'blemished chapter in our nation's history', Rudd can be seen to be (re)defining the nation's past, incorporating these events into Australia's historical narrative. By doing so he is countering the definition of national history offered by the previous Howard Government, which played up the 'glorious past' and actively rejected historical narratives that emphasised the nation's violent colonial history, derisively referred to then as the 'black-armband view of history' (Augoustinos *et al.* 2002; Macintyre and Clarke 2003).

Rudd is explicit throughout his speech in acknowledging the damaging effects that the removal of children had, not just on the Indigenous children who were removed, but also on their families and communities. Extract 2 below follows the telling of a personal story, that of Nanna Nungal Fejo, who in 1932 at the age of four was removed from her family and community. The personal narrative Rudd recounts is replete with references to emotion and personal suffering, but it also functions as an empiricist warrant to lay the factual foundations of the Stolen Generations.

Extract 2: Rudd (9.29–10.58)

There is something terribly primal about these firsthand accounts. The pain is searing; it screams from the pages. The hurt, the humiliation, the degradation and the sheer brutality of the act of physically separating a mother from her children is a deep assault on our senses and on our most elemental humanity. These stories cry out to be heard; they cry out for an apology. Instead, from the nation's parliament there has been a stony and stubborn and deafening silence for more than a decade; a view that somehow we, the parliament, should suspend our most basic instincts of what is right and what is wrong; a view that, instead, we should look for any pretext to push this great wrong to one side.

Rudd constructs these 'firsthand accounts' as more than just personal stories: they are described as 'primal' stories of human pain, which 'scream from the pages' to be heard. Again a three-part list of emotions, similar to those invoked in Extract 1, 'the hurt, the humiliation, the degradation', is used to explicitly describe the pain inflicted upon Indigenous people. In emphasising the 'basic instincts' involved in responding to these stories, Rudd represents emotional responses to the forced removal of Indigenous children as natural, innate and normal human reactions. Separating children from their

Apologising for past wrongs 113

mothers is described as 'sheer brutality' and a 'deep assault on our senses. And on our most elemental humanity'. Therefore it is our intrinsic humanity upon which our capacity to empathise with the Stolen Generations is based. By invoking this category, and inviting us to engage emotionally with the Stolen Generations, the natural human response to feelings of empathy and sympathy for those affected becomes the basis for apologising, saying 'sorry' to those affected. In contrast, those refusing to apologise are represented as lacking the 'elemental humanity' required to be emotionally responsive to the tragedy of the Stolen Generations. Here emotions, rather than being considered unreasonable and irrational, are constructed as essential to our humanity and the very foundation upon which the apology is offered. This appeal to our common humanity has significant rhetorical power and is deployed repeatedly in the speech to warrant the apology: 'Decency, human decency, universal human decency, demands that the nation now step forward to right an historical wrong. That is what we are doing in this place today'. In deploying this argument Rudd is appealing not only to a nationalist category of identification, but also to a superordinate level of identity as human.

Redefining national history: The truth about the blemished past

Rudd's apology did not only present firsthand accounts of the Stolen Generations, nor did it rely on emotion alone to warrant the national apology. Rudd's speech balances emotion with reason and rationality by mobilising historical facts and figures about the removal of Indigenous children. At stake for a national leader like Rudd is the charge by political opponents that emotion has the potential to distort reason and rationality. As such, Rudd defends these emotions, and indeed the symbolic gesture of apologising, by minimising the rhetorical contrast between emotion and cognition. In arguing that emotion is inextricably linked with reason and facts, apologising is constructed as a *natural* response to the 'truth' of the Stolen Generations and a necessary component to the *act* of reconciliation. These accounts do important identity work in presenting Rudd as both a *compassionate* and a *rational* Prime Minister.

This is accomplished sequentially throughout the speech; each time Rudd mobilises and invokes emotion, it is grounded in 'fact' and 'truth'. This facticity provides the justification for a historically significant motion such as apologising for past injustices. Extract 3 provides an example of how Rudd draws on an empiricist repertoire in which the facts are externalised and validated by the historical record (Potter 1996).

<u>Extract 3: Rudd (11.18–11.38)</u>

But should there still be doubts as to why we must now act, let the parliament reflect for a moment on the following facts: that, between 1910 and

1970, between 10 and 30 per cent of Indigenous children were forcibly taken from their mothers and fathers; that, as a result, up to 50,000 children were forcibly taken from their families

In this extract Rudd allows the 'facts' to speak for themselves. These 'facts' are made manifest in the specific dates and the number of children affected, the latter of which is presented both as a percentage range and in absolute numerical terms, maximising its impact. Such detail arguably constructs Rudd's account as objective and neutral, which functions to legitimise and bolster his descriptions of the emotional experiences of, and responses to, the Stolen Generations. In Extract 4 below, Rudd does further work to minimise the dichotomy between reason and emotion: indeed, emotion here is explicitly equated with the sheer, incontestable 'truth'.

Extract 4: Rudd (15.24–16.13)

In doing so, we are doing more than contending with the facts, the evidence and the often rancorous public debate. In doing so, we are also wrestling with our own soul. This is not, as some would argue, a black-armband view of history; it is just the truth: the cold, confronting, uncomfortable truth – facing it, dealing with it, moving on from it. Until we fully confront that truth, there will always be a shadow hanging over us and our future as a fully united and fully reconciled people. It is time to reconcile. It is time to recognise the injustices of the past. It is time to say sorry. It is time to move forward together.

Again here Rudd orients to the rhetorical contrast between emotion and cognition (Edwards 1997). Specifically, this is reflected in the direct oppositional relationship worked up between the 'facts, the evidence and the often rancorous public debate' on the one hand and 'wrestling with our own soul' on the other. In equating facing the truth with 'wrestling with our own soul', Rudd mobilises a vivid metaphor to strengthen his construction of empathising, and therefore apologising, as a sign of our essential humanity. Edwards (1999) argues that emotion metaphors such as this achieve interactionally important rhetorical work due to their ability to enable a more subtle formulation of feeling than that allowed for by the explicit attribution of emotion. This can also be seen in Rudd's description of the consequence of avoiding the truth as having a 'shadow hanging over us and our future'. This metaphor of a 'shadow hanging over us' neatly sidesteps the explicit mention of negative emotion terms such as 'guilt' and 'shame', emotions which were represented by opponents to the apology as inappropriate and illegitimate (Augoustinos and LeCouteur 2004), while at the same time implying that such negative emotions can be alleviated only by confronting the truth and empathising with the Stolen Generations. Recognising the potential criticism that apologising would in effect legitimate a 'black-armband' version of Australia's history, Rudd fends off such criticism by explicitly denying that 'wrestling with our own soul' over past injustices would function in this way. Instead, engaging with the history of the Stolen Generations on a moral and emotional level is constructed by Rudd again as 'facing the truth': 'just the truth; the cold, confronting, uncomfortable truth'. Here again, despite embracing emotion, Rudd strategically engages in fact construction, working to build an account that is also based on reason and rationality, thereby uniting reason and emotion through a rhetoric that justifies the apology because of the super-ordinate emotions we *should* feel about this injustice, united as human beings.

In legitimating the need to recognise and acknowledge the truth about Australia's past, Rudd is also establishing a base from which to speak about the nation's future: the past must be recognised in order to 'move forward together' to a reconciled future. Previous critical discursive research on 'race' discourse has identified a 'togetherness repertoire', in which members of different social groups are integrated into a superordinate identity, with which they are invited to identify (Wetherell and Potter 1992). Not surprisingly, this identity invariably invokes the 'nation' as a collective and central organising category. In this extract above we see Rudd mobilising the togetherness repertoire of a unified collective national identity that binds all social groups and categories within the nation state, in order to move towards a 'golden future' (Wetherell and Potter 1992). This orientation to the future projects an image of a better, improved and unified nation, a vision of how Australia should be.

Nelson

Defining national identity as past-oriented

In his reply to the apology, Nelson's evoking of Australian identity is accomplished primarily in reference to 'past generations' and their role in 'building the nation'. This rooting of identity in the past is consistent with his political party's conservative ideological platform, as well as its past position on the issue of apologising. Here the story of Australia is one of sacrifice and adversity on the part of white settlers in order to build the nation, with current generations enjoying what they have been bequeathed. Such an account works to protect the security of the dominant group's identity, requiring little change to the dominant historical narrative.

Nelson works to construct an image of those involved in the policies and practices that created the Stolen Generations as noble and decent people with good intentions. This works to mitigate their responsibility for the consequences of their actions, because of their other important contributions. This theme of nation-building and sacrifice, which is recurrently drawn upon throughout the speech, is evident in the following extract.

Extract 5: Nelson (ll. 94–97)

The period within which these events occurred was one that defined and shaped Australia. The governments that oversaw this and those who elected them emerged from federating the nation to a century characterised for Australia as triumph in the face of extraordinary adversities unknown to our generation.

Nelson evokes the importance of the nation-building project that occurred at the turn of the century. Australia is not seen as a nation that is still being built, dynamic and changing, but as something that was created in the past, with current generations enjoying the fruits of past labour. As with many nation-building stories (see, for example, Grant 2008; Tileagă 2008), this one also involves 'triumph in the face of extraordinary adversities'. This extreme-case formulation (Pomerantz 1986) works to characterise these adversities as far greater than those that might be encountered in a similar nation-building project today, and certainly as beyond those that 'our generation' could understand. Casting current Australians as unable to appreciate the adversities of the past here serves to emphasise that they should (1) be grateful to past generations for what they accomplished, rather than apologising for their mistakes (despite good intentions); and (2) recognise the privileged position that Australians currently occupy because of those sacrifices. In this sense, like Rudd, Nelson is drawing on particular facts to elicit emotional reactions of gratitude and national pride to justify his party's position on the apology.

Resisting redefining history: The glorification of 'nation-building'

Even though Nelson is ostensibly apologising, his apology actively resists a redefinition of the past. As noted by Nobles (2008), one of the major aims of apologies for historical injustice is a redefinition of history that allows recognition of the role of past policies and practices in creating current inequality. Notably, Nelson resists this redefinition in two ways: first, by emphasising the familiar narrative of the glorious colonial past (see also former Prime Minister Howard, in Augoustinos *et al.* 2002; LeCouteur *et al.* 2001); and second, by attributing the cause of Indigenous disadvantage to recent (liberal) policies and practices, rather than to past practices such as the forced removal of children.

In Extract 6, Indigenous Australians and 'early settlers' are contrasted: 'early settlers' are constructed as active, determined and responsible for the building of the Australian nation, while Indigenous peoples are 'ancient', proud and passively rather than actively bound to the land.

Apologising for past wrongs   117

Extract 6: Nelson (ll. 11–16)

This chapter in our nation's history is emblematic of much of the relationship between Indigenous and non-Indigenous Australians from the arrival of the First Fleet in 1788.

It is one of two cultures; one ancient, proud and celebrating its deep bond with this land for some 50,000 years. The other, no less proud, arrived here with little more than visionary hope deeply rooted in gritty determination to build an Australian nation; not only for its early settlers and Indigenous peoples, but those who would increasingly come from all parts of the world.

While this 'ancient' culture is described as 'celebrating its deep bond with this land for some 50,000 years', Indigenous peoples are not portrayed as actively using, or developing, the land, in contrast to the 'settlers', who are 'build[ing] an Australian nation'. Nor is Australia described as belonging to Indigenous people ('this land' not 'their land'), despite the Australian High Court's Mabo and Wik rulings that legitimated this fact in law. This passive description of connection to the land further bolsters the construction of Indigenous peoples as without agency, as 'not really doing anything', as though nations had not already been 'built' on the continent, before the colonisers arrived. Hence, Australian history, and the nation, is presented here as beginning with white settlement, reinforcing the dominant narrative of the glorious colonisation project (Reynolds 1996).

In contrast to Indigenous peoples, the British settlers are ascribed an active position in Extract 6. Besides pride, they also possess 'visionary hope deeply rooted in gritty determination'. They also have a goal that they are actively working towards, 'build[ing] the Australian nation'. So a description of the colonisers as active – 'visionary', 'determined', 'build' – is contrasted with a passive, inactive construction of Indigenous peoples – 'ancient', 'deep bond with this land'. It is through such active constructions that emotions such as pride in Australia's colonialist 'nation-building' past exclude Indigenous peoples (and, arguably, also those who were not free 'settlers', such as convicts) from the historical narrative Nelson attempts to construct.

Given that Nelson goes on to talk at length on nation-building, and ends his speech by 'honour[ing] those in the past who have suffered and made sacrifices for us', these constructions of the two groups as active and passive support this political project in two ways. First, this is an account that includes white people (early settlers and, later, those responsible for the removal of children) among those who have suffered, rather than Indigenous people, whose suffering the apology is supposed to be acknowledging. Second, this account excludes Indigenous peoples from nation-building (or at least minimises their role), thus reducing the 'sacrifices' and 'suffering' they have undergone on

118 Martha Augoustinos *et al.*

'our' behalf, and effectively excluding Indigenous Australians from the group to be 'honoured' and apologised to.

Resisting rebuilding the nation: Continuity with the past

In Extract 7, Nelson's praise for past generations of Australians (specifically, those around when the policies of removal were in place) works to negatively contrast 'us' (the current generation) with 'them'. In doing so, Nelson provides a list of positive-other descriptors that work to construct current-day Australians as lacking the laudable traits of previous generations. This 'positive-other' presentation works to excuse the actions of previous generations in removing children: because they did so many other things that benefited all of 'us', to blame them would be to create an 'injustice' as significant as the one the apology is designed to address. The focus on the nation as having been built largely in the past (as in Extracts 6 and 7) furthers the position that there is no justification for rebuilding the nation as there is no redefinition of the past required as part of apologising. Nelson resists the (re) building rhetoric of Rudd's speech, instead arguing that the existing national narrative should not be undermined.

Extract 7: Nelson (ll. 98–111)

In offering this apology, let us not in our language and our actions create one injustice in our attempt to address another.

Let no one forget that they sent their sons to war, shaping our identity and place in the world. One hundred thousand in two wars alone gave their lives in our name and our uniform, lying forever in distant lands; silent witnesses to the future that they have given us. Aboriginal and non-Aboriginal Australians lie alongside one another.

These generations considered their responsibilities to their country and one another more important than their rights.

They didn't buy something until they had saved up for it and values were always more important than value.

Living in considerably more difficult times, they had dreams for our nation but little money.

Theirs was a mesh of values enshrined in God, King and Country and the belief in something greater than yourself. Neglectful indifference to all that they achieved while seeing their actions in the separations only, through the values of our comfortable, modern Australia, will be to diminish ourselves.

The series of positive contrasts here begins with the legacy of past generations, how sending 'their sons to war, shap[ed] our identity and place in the world'. Here a narrative of experience of wars fought overseas, embodied within the 'ANZAC legend', is explicitly evoked as a basis for national identity. The ANZAC (Australian and New Zealand Army Corps) legend is well known in Australia, and is a cornerstone of nation-building mythology (Macintyre and Clarke 2003). It has also been invoked to position positively Australians who have fought in more recent wars, such as the Vietnam/ American War and the war in Iraq, and also victims of terrorism, such as the Bali bombings in 2002 and 2005 (West 2008). Nelson includes Indigenous peoples as part of this ANZAC identity, although at the time they were not considered citizens, and their families were not entitled to any of the benefits non-Indigenous soldiers received. This is a rhetorically useful move, though, as it functions to position Nelson as socially inclusive.

The magnitude of the loss of life during the world wars is emphasised through quantification. This emphasis on the degree of sacrifice is in stark contrast to the lack of numbers when referring to the Stolen Generations. At no point during Nelson's speech is the magnitude of this discussed, and he never mentions the numbers of Indigenous people who died during colonisation and the 'building' of the nation through displacement, disease, incarceration and both state-sanctioned and unsanctioned killings (Reynolds 1996). The loss of life, family and country is silenced, in contrast to Rudd's version of national history, where these issues are made salient and given emotional resonance.

Other aspects of those who 'shap[ed]' Australia's identity, besides willingness to go to war, include caring about 'responsibilities' rather than 'rights'; saving; and concern with 'values' rather than 'value' (money), with these values including respect for 'God, King and Country'. These descriptions can be implicitly heard as indictments of current-day Australians as caring about rights instead of responsibilities, using credit instead of saving, valuing money over 'values' and being selfish rather than believing in 'something greater'. Although such negative-self and positive-other contrasts appear inconsistent with the notion of maintaining a positive self- and national identity, all of these critical constructions are consistent with conservative social values; hence Nelson's invocation of these characteristics allows the working up of a particular, conservative version of the Australian identity, consistent with this narrative. This identity stems from another time, when Australia (like many other nations in the world at the time) was more isolated, and more socially and culturally homogeneous. Indeed, Nelson's nostalgia for the past harks back to a time and place when Australia saw itself first and foremost as a 'white nation' (Curthoys 2006).

The apology itself (an acknowledgment of Indigenous suffering) is constructed by Nelson as leading to the 'neglectful indifference to all they achieved'. Hence, Australians should be ashamed of blaming past generations, rather than feeling guilt or shame for the acts of forced removal of Indigenous children. By casting this blaming as an 'injustice' of the same magnitude as the removals themselves, Nelson further undermines the social and political significance of Indigenous dispossession and suffering. Ultimately, though, by lauding past generations, whether early settlers or those involved in the removal of children during the twentieth century, Nelson's narrative allows the construction of a particular version of national identity and history, thereby implying a particular version of the nation. Nelson's nation offers continuity with the past, specifically, the dominant colonising narrative, whereby the nation was built by white settlers, and the values of the past should prevail, in accord with his conservative party's ideology. His refusal to hold past generations responsible for mistreatment over the last 200-plus years means that there is no need for Nelson to discursively reframe history or rebuild the nation.

Conclusion

In their respective apologies to the Stolen Generations, Rudd and Nelson draw on differing facts and emotions (emotion–reason rhetoric), allowing them to work up competing accounts of national identity, history and the nation's future, and subsequently justify their respective positions on the need for the apology. Specifically, Nelson manages to evade an actual apology through strategies that allow him to maintain a version of Australian history in line with former Prime Minister John Howard – that an apology in the fullest sense is unnecessary, even inappropriate, and not in keeping with the version of the history the Liberal–National Coalition wishes to maintain. In Rudd and Nelson's speeches we see a contrast between a 'future-oriented' version of national identity (Rudd) and a 'continuity with the past' and 'nation-building' version (Nelson) of national identity, and these constructions are achieved through different strategies for defining historical facts and their associated emotional responses. Indeed, these differing constructions have opposing implications for nation (re)building, with Rudd suggesting a new, inclusive Australia that moves towards a 'golden future', while Nelson seeks to preserve and defend the historical continuity between the present and the past narratives of the nation.

The contrast between this future-oriented version of the nation and the version based on continuity with the past, and the types of emotion–reason rhetoric they deploy to achieve these versions, correspond accordingly to the ideological platforms of the two leaders' respective political parties. As leader of the social-democratic Australian Labor Party, Rudd attends to the progressive–reformist political agenda of the party and his Government. In contrast, as leader of the Liberal–National Coalition, Nelson's job is to defend traditional and conservative values. Thus both work to shore up their support within relevant constituencies, as well as to legitimate and justify their specific actions in this particular context, apologising to Indigenous Australians. In both cases, their approach to historical narratives corresponds to particular versions of a national heritage (Smith 2006) that the public rely upon to engage with a social identity that speaks to their emotions. The rhetoric of both leaders is emboldened by the emotional reactions of their audiences, and therein lies the complexity and dilemma that reinforces the debate surrounding what our historical national narrative should be.

The deployment of both these narratives of national history by Australia's political leaders serves to shape the landscape of available political discourse and its associated affect for framing Indigenous and non-Indigenous relations, but also race and identity more broadly. These two competing accounts, adhering to the traditional political divide, leave little room for radical respecifications of Australian identity to be widely available for use by members. Even Rudd's focus on the 'golden future' (Wetherell and Potter 1992) is a device that limits recognition of the sources of continuing Indigenous disadvantage, due to the ongoing legacy of colonisation and sustained institutional and systematic racism in Australia. Despite this, however, the significance of Rudd's apology to the Stolen Generations in rewriting the dominant historical narrative of Australia, traditionally a story of heroic triumph over hardship and adversity, should not be underestimated. The apology represents a significant symbolic moment in Australia's history for acknowledging the sustained dispossession and violence which were perpetrated against Indigenous peoples and upon which Australia as a nation state was built. At the same time, however, and as Nelson's so-called apology speech demonstrates, the ideological struggle over Australia's history and national identity is likely to continue for some time and reflect a complex dialectic of competing emotions and narratives that flag nationhood (Billig 1995). Similarly, other settler (and colonial) nations may find that attempts to discursively reframe history through acts such as national apologies might not be straightforwardly accepted, and, indeed, can be actively resisted as citizens struggle with the embodied and entangled affect they may evoke.

Note

1 We take the perspective that affect and emotion refer here to two slightly different concepts. Affect is described as the embodied experience, while emotions are the descriptions we give them through our cognitive 'sense-making' practices (Watson 2015). This sense-making is largely influenced by the cultural and historical context in which our emotions play out (Watson 2015).

References

Anderson, B., 1991. *Imagined Communities: Reflections on the Origins and Spread of Nationalism.* London: Verso.

Augoustinos, M., LeCouteur, A. and Soyland, J., 2002. Self-sufficient arguments in political rhetoric: Constructing reconciliation and apologizing to the stolen generations. *Discourse & Society*, 13(1), 105–142.

122 Martha Augoustinos *et al.*

Augoustinos, M. and LeCouteur, A., 2004. On whether to apologize to Indigenous Australians: The denial of white guilt. In N. R. Branscombe and B. Doosje, eds. *Collective Guilt: International Perspectives*. Cambridge: Cambridge University Press, 236–261.

Barkan, E., 2000. *The Guilt of Nations: Restitution and Negotiating Historical Injustices*. New York: W. W. Norton and Company.

Billig, M., 1987. *Arguing and Thinking: A Rhetorical Approach to Social Psychology*. New York: Cambridge University Press.

Billig, M., 1995, *Banal Nationalism*. London: Sage.

Bonnell, J. and Simon, R. I., 2007. 'Difficult' exhibitions and intimate encounters. *Museum & Society*, 5(2), 65–85.

Condor, S., 2010. Devolution and national identity: The rules of English (dis)engagement. *Nations and Nationalism*, 16(3), 525–543.

Condor, S. and Abell, J., 2006. Romantic Scotland, tragic England, ambiguous Britain: constructions of 'the Empire' in post-devolution national accounting. *Nations and Nationalism*, 12(3), 453–472.

Curthoys, A., 2006. Disputing national histories: Some recent Australian debates. *Transforming Cultures eJournal*, 1(1).

De Cillia, R., Reisigl, M. and Wodak, R., 1999. The discursive construction of national identities. *Discourse & Society*, 10(2), 149–173.

Edwards, D., 1997. *Discourse and Cognition*. London: Sage.

Edwards, D., 1999. Emotion discourse. *Culture & Psychology*, 5(3), 271–291.

Grant, S., 2008. Reimagined communities: Union veterans and the reconstruction of American nationalism. *Nations and Nationalism*, 14(3), 498–519.

Hage. G., 1998. *White Nation: Fantasies of White Supremacy in a Multicultural Society*. Annandale: Pluto Press.

Harris, S., Grainger, K. and Mullany, L., 2006. The pragmatics of political apologies. *Discourse & Society*, 17(6), 715–737.

Hiles, D. and Cermak, I., 2008. Narrative psychology. In C. W. W. Stainton-Rogers, ed. *The Sage Handbook of Qualitative Research in Psychology*. London: Sage, 147–164.

Kinnvall, C. and Lindén, J., 2010. Dialogical selves between security and insecurity: Migration, multiculturalism, and the challenge of the global. *Theory & Psychology*, 20(5), 595–619.

Kirkwood, S., Liu, J. H. and Weatherall, A., 2005. Challenging the standard story of indigenous rights in Aotearoa/New Zealand. *Journal of Community & Applied Social Psychology*, 15(6), 493–505.

LeCouteur, A. and Augoustinos, M., 2001. Apologising to the stolen generations: Argument, rhetoric, and identity in public reasoning. *Australian Psychologist*, 36(1), 51–61.

LeCouteur, A., Rapley, M. and Augoustinos, M., 2001. 'This very difficult debate about Wik': Stake, voice and the management of category memberships in race politics. *British Journal of Social Psychology*, 40(1), 35–57.

Luke, A., 1997. The material effects of the word: Apologies, 'stolen children' and public discourse. *Discourse: Studies in the Cultural Politics of Education*, 18(3), 343–368.

Macintyre, S. and Clark, A., 2003. *The History Wars*. Carlton: Melbourne University Press.

Manne, R., 2001. In denial: The Stolen Generations and the Right. *The Australian Quarterly Essay*, 1, 113 pp.

McCreanor, T., 1993. Settling grievances to deny sovereignty: Trade goods for the year 2000. *Sites*, 27, 45–73.

Nobles, M., 2008. *The Politics of Official Apologies*. New York: Cambridge University Press.

Polkinghorne, D., 1988. *Narrative Knowing and the Human Sciences*. Albany: SUNY Press.

Pomerantz, A., 1986. Extreme case formulations: A way of legitimizing claims. *Human Studies*, 9(2–3), 219–229.

Potter, J., 1996. *Representing Reality: Discourse, Rhetoric and Social Construction*. London: Sage.

Reicher, S. and Hopkins, N., 2001. *Self and Nation: Categorization, Contestation and Mobilisation*. London: Sage.

Reynolds, H., 1996. *Nowhere People*. Camberwell: Penguin.

Shields, S., 2005. The politics of emotion in everyday life: 'Appropriate' emotion and claims on identity. *Review of General Psychology*, 9(1), 3–15.

Smith, L., 2006. *Uses of Heritage*. London: Routledge.

Tileagă, C., 2008. What is a 'revolution'?: National commemoration, collective memory and managing authenticity in the representation of a political event. *Discourse & Society*, 19(3), 359–382.

Watson, S., 2015. Emotions in the history museum. In A. Witcomb and K. Message, eds. *The International Handbooks of Museum Studies. Volume 1: Museum Theory*, Chichester: Wiley Blackwell, 283–302.

West, B., 2008. Collective memory and crisis: The 2002 Bali bombing, national heroic archetypes and the counter-narrative of cosmopolitan nationalism. *Journal of Sociology*, 44(4), 337–353.

Wetherell, M., 1998. Positioning and interpretative repertoires: Conversation analysis and post-structuralism in dialogue. *Discourse & Society*, 9(3), 387–412.

Wetherell, M., 2012, *Affect and Emotion: A New Social Science Understanding*. London: Sage.

Wetherell, M., 2013. Affect and discourse – What's the problem? From affect as excess to affective/discursive practice. *Subjectivity*, 6(4), 349–368.

Wetherell, M. and Potter, J., 1992, *Mapping the Language of Racism*. London: Sage.

White, H., 1978. *Tropics of Discourse: Essays in Cultural Criticism*. Baltimore: Johns Hopkins University Press.

Winter, E., 2007. Neither 'America' nor 'Québec': Constructing the Canadian multicultural nation. *Nations and Nationalism*, 13(3), 481–503.

Chapter 8

Experiencing mixed emotions in the museum

Empathy, affect, and memory in visitors' responses to histories of migration

Rhiannon Mason, Areti Galani, Katherine Lloyd and Joanne Sayner

Museums and migration

Migration has come to dominate media headlines and political debates in recent years. In these spheres, contemporary migration in Europe is addressed through a variety of conflicting narratives. In some cases, we see expressions of empathy towards those fleeing the horrific conflicts in North Africa and the Middle East. Since the summer of 2015, these expressions have frequently related to emotionally charged news media reports and images that focus on the 'human tragedy' of migrant boats capsized in the Mediterranean, and the ongoing humanitarian crisis in Calais. At the same time, we are also witnessing considerable hostility towards migrants as expressed by certain sections of the media, political figures and right-wing pressure groups. In particular, there has been a noticeable use of what has been called dehumanising language. Take, for example, the language used by the UK's former Prime Minister David Cameron to refer to those attempting to enter Europe as migrant 'swarms' (Elgot and Taylor 2015). Such pre-existing trends have been exacerbated in the more recent context of Brexit and, at the time of writing, US President Donald Trump's rulings on immigration. In view of the above, the opportunity for museums to provide an alternative narrative of migration in the UK has never been more pertinent. This is particularly relevant given that museums are often celebrated as places for public debate and dialogue by those who advocate for their vital role in society. Motivated by a commitment to social justice, a growing number of museums have chosen to address the topic of migration and to provide historical context for these contemporary debates.

This chapter aims to articulate how visitors draw connections between historical and contemporary migration in relation to what they encounter in museum displays. It is based on a small-scale research project conducted over the summer of 2015 with long-term residents whom we invited to visit the permanent display, *Destination Tyneside*, at Discovery Museum in Newcastle, UK. In this chapter, we highlight how these research participants utilised not only resources such as museum objects and interpretive materials, but also childhood memories, debates in the media and narratives about place, in order to make sense of and review their position towards migrants. In so doing, we explore the different ways in which the participants responded to the museum's invitation to empathise, and we investigate how affective responses are part of these experiences.

We argue that looking at the ways in which visitors negotiate empathy in the exhibition space through different kinds of 'memory work' provides a hitherto-underexplored way to understand seemingly complex and contradictory visitor responses to migration displays. We show how, in their responses to stories of migration, some participants drew on particular narratives about post-industrial decline which circulate within the 'mnemonic communities' to which they belong (Zerubavel 1996). Our attention to mnemonic patterning in visitor responses to the museum addresses Margaret Wetherell's call to 'explore the format of patterns in people's affective lives through the practices that cannot be deciphered into separate "psycho" and "social" lines' (Wetherell 2012: 139). We emphasise how a long-term memory discourse of post-industrial decline intersects with time-specific contemporary news media, political debates about migration and autobiographical narratives.

By highlighting the role of different 'memory schemata' and 'narrative templates' in the participants' responses (Wertsch 2012), we identify complex interactions of self and other which show varied, and sometimes competing, empathetic responses to the exhibition. Our point is not to privilege certain responses over others but to highlight an inherent, and productive, instability of hierarchies within these responses. We argue that bringing understandings of the self and other into a new relationality is particularly important in a context where media and political discourses tend to essentialise and reify the distance between those defined as insiders and outsiders; those who are seen to belong in specific places and those who are designated as always 'other'.

Our research emphasises that the museum encounter is experienced by visitors as synchronous relations of past and present, and a constant slippage and relaying between different temporal registers, personal memories, memory communities and personal relationships. Our research aims to explore the situational and relational dimensions of the museum encounter by engaging with a small group of participants on more than one occasion. Our research process included, but was not limited to, a single museum visit. With this approach, our chapter builds upon the arguments around heritage, emotion, empathy and performativity in the work of Smith and Campbell (2016); see also Smith (2006). At the same time, it responds to Bella Dicks' call to investigate intersections between 'cultural framings' and 'narrative appropriations' that pre-exist and go beyond the space of the museum (Dicks 2016: 61 with reference to Macdonald 2002; Wertsch 2012).

126 Rhiannon Mason *et al.*

In the following sections we introduce the conceptualisation of empathy that informed this study, the specific exhibition, *Destination Tyneside*, which formed the basis of the research, and our methodological approach. We subsequently discuss the participants' responses to the exhibition's invitation to empathise, alongside a 'thick' account of the participants' negotiation of meaning around migration, in relation both to their affective response to the exhibition and to their personal and collective memory narratives as they emerged in the course of this study.

Empathy and the museum

Definitions of empathy are contested and contentious, as shown by Amy Coplan and Peter Goldie as they trace the term through decades of philosophical and psychological debate (Coplan and Goldie 2011). Such definitions matter because authors from across disciplines often (but not always) suggest that something is at stake, morally, ethically, or politically. While it is possible to tentatively point to a general consensus that empathy refers to 'affective and cognitive engagement' (Arnold-de Simine 2013: 111), the extent to which these are coterminous is open to debate. This chapter takes Amy Coplan's definition of empathy as its starting point: 'empathy is a complex imaginative process in which an observer simulates another person's situated psychological states [both cognitive and affective] while maintaining clear self–other differentiation' (2011: 5). When successful, empathy results in imaginative perspective-taking or perspective-shifting (Coplan and Goldie 2011: xxxiii–xxxiv). For Coplan, the continued awareness of alterity – the other-orientated rather than the self-orientated perspective – is paramount. In this, she agrees with those critics who warn against problematic over-identification or 'empty empathy' (Kaplan 2011) and advocates instead a productive awareness of the limits of understanding another's position, or 'empathetic unsettlement' (LaCapra 2001: 41).

The role of affect in visitors' meaning-making processes in museum and heritage contexts has long been the subject of debate (Gregory and Witcomb 2007). More recently, an emerging body of literature addresses affect and empathy as interconnected categories by seeking to examine empathy as an affective interpretative strategy (Smith 2011, 2016; Witcomb 2013; Schorch 2014, 2015; Smith and Campbell 2016; Whitehead *et al.* 2015). Exhibitions and display methods that deal with sensitive, contested and difficult histories and heritage(s), including migration, are often seen as the ideal *loci* for curatorial strategies that prioritise empathy. As an interpretive strategy, research suggests, empathy is often intended to be built through enabling the expression of subjectivity, fostering an embodied and visceral experience for the visitors and mobilising visitors' imaginations.

Subjectivity and personalisation as interpretive strategies

Witcomb (2013: 257) argues that the 'affective space is mobilised' when subjectivities come into tension in the exhibition space. In this context, aesthetics and the language of creative practice and art installation that prioritises film, oral histories, talking heads, large-scale photography and art-installation works have become a significant delivery device for affective and empathetic exhibitions. This is because they foreground individual 'expressions' of human experience (Landsberg 2004; Hutchison and Collins 2009: 96; Purkis 2013: 53; Witcomb 2013), although these approaches are not without their critics (Arnold-de Simine 2013). Other authors call for a reflective approach in the use of multimedia in exhibitions that deal with difficult topics (Bonnell and Simon 2007; Brown and Waterhouse-Watson 2014).

In particular, the trope of 'meeting' the other is often deployed to enhance visitors' personal connection with the individuals included in the respective exhibitions. Purkis, for example, discusses this in relation to the exhibition *Destination Donegal*, which she curated:

> [t]he exhibition was designed by the curator to allow visitors to get a sense of meeting the individuals in the exhibition space, with the aim of affecting an emotional response. This, it was posited, might lead to understanding and empathy towards different people's lives and experiences.
>
> (Purkis 2013: 51)

Despite the growing literature and practice in this area, to date only a limited amount of research has analysed actual visitors' responses to museums' attempts to engender empathy (but see Smith 2010, 2011, 2016; Schorch 2014, 2015; Smith and Campbell 2016).

Destination Tyneside

Destination Tyneside opened in 2013 in Discovery Museum, Newcastle, UK, as a permanent gallery that addresses issues of both historic and contemporary migration in the region. The gallery employs many of the interpretative strategies outlined above in an attempt to 'engender an immediate and emotional connection' to the stories of migration being told (Little and Watson 2015: 196). The empathic vision for the exhibition was informed on the one hand by Newcastle City Council's acknowledgement that the gallery had

> the potential to contribute to promoting greater community cohesion and defusing tensions by: [...] encouraging a process of empathy and 'perspective taking', where a group that may previously have been viewed

with fear, distrust and lack of understanding becomes more individuated (Little and Watson 2015: 195).

On the other hand, it also reflected the UNESCO–IOM Migration Museum Initiative's core objective for migration museums to increase empathy by building awareness of why people migrate (Little and Watson 2015: 195).

Five aims were set out in the original brief (Little and Watson 2015: 195).

1. To engage in an informed way with contemporary migration by promoting an historical perspective
2. To encourage people to debate migration and identity
3. To promote tolerance, alter perceptions on immigration and contribute to social cohesion by increasing understanding of the migrant experience
4. To undertake an enabling role to show how the North-East can respond to and benefit from migration
5. To show that Tyneside's history and identity is not fixed or immutable, we have always been an open society

The main interpretive strategy is that of first-person narration and personalisation of the past. Historic and contemporary migration is expressed through the stories of individuals who have migrated to Tyneside. The first part of the gallery is devoted to historic migration in the nineteenth century and follows the stories of six people chosen to represent 'the largest and most significant, immigrant groups at that time' (Little and Watson 2015: 196). They include the stories of Ali Said, one of the first members of the Yemeni community in South Shields; Lena, who moved to Tyneside to escape the persecution of Jews in Poland; Thomas, who came from Ireland in search of work in the chemical works; and Angela, who, with her husband Antonio, started the Mark Toney ice-cream business, which remains a well-known local institution. Upon entering the gallery, visitors are greeted by an audio-visual display featuring these characters, depicted by actors, discussing their motivations for migration and explaining how they ended up in Tyneside. On the wall alongside this display a 'case study' of each of the six characters is provided, situating them within the wider migrant Yemeni, Irish, Italian and Jewish communities, alongside economic migrants from other regions in the UK (figure 8.1).

The volume of people moving into and out of Tyneside is displayed through a wall of graphics with quotes from historians, statistics on population movement and historical documents including adverts for travel to the 'New World' and official migrant documentation. Historic images related to migrations are projected on a large screen. A suitcase interactive encourages visitors to think about what items they would take with them on a journey to start a life in a new country. This is accompanied by a large display case with objects and photographs related to the six characters and their respective communities (figure 8.2).

Experiencing mixed emotions in the museum 129

Figure 8.1 Cinema section of display and interpretive panel featuring the story of Lena Vineberg

Alongside personal everyday objects, the display includes religious objects and objects associated with the characters' professions, including a pair of tailor's scissors and an ice-cream glass, to highlight the economic contribution of migrants through the establishment of businesses in Tyneside. In the centre of the gallery, there is an enclosed 'cinema' space, featuring an audio-visual display with first-person interpretation from each of the six characters, who look at and speak directly to the visitor about their experiences of living and working on Tyneside. These interactions vary in tone, with Ali Said angrily highlighting the injustices the Yemeni community experienced in the form of racial and religious prejudice, before 'remembering his manners' and offering the visitor a cup of tea.

The second half of the gallery depicts contemporary migration, again utilising personal objects and audio-visual stories of individuals from the largest migrant communities in present-day Tyneside. The stories include the experiences of Indian, Bangladeshi, Pakistani and Chinese migrants to Tyneside, alongside those who live in Tyneside as refugees or international students. An adjacent area includes digital interactives such as a surname mapper and a British citizenship test, as well as a community 'showcase' with rotating programming. The gallery concludes with a visitor feedback wall where visitors are invited to write their comments anonymously on luggage labels and affix them to the wall. The overarching interpretive narrative of

Figure 8.2 'Leaving home' suitcase interactive

the exhibition is that migration is 'a process rather than an event' (Little and Watson 2015: 197). According to the curators, visitors are encouraged to consider that 'migration is not an easy activity' (Little and Watson 2015: 201) and through the individual stories review their sense of belonging in the North-East of England and develop greater tolerance towards migrant groups (figure 8.3).

Methodology

Our methodology focused on gaining insights into visitors' 'entrance narratives' (Doering and Pekarik 1996) regarding their sense of place and belonging, and to what extent they consider migration to be relevant to their own lives. The methodological approach prioritised in-depth engagement with a small number of participants, to allow us to obtain a more nuanced understanding of how participants related the themes in *Destination Tyneside* to their own backgrounds (such as experiences of migration, age, ethnicity, length of time or family connections in the North-East, first-, second- or third-generation migration experiences and so forth). Although the overall study involved both long-term residents and recent asylum seekers, in separate groupings, this chapter discusses our insights from our engagement with participants who are long-term residents in Tyneside. This allows us to put the spotlight on personal and collective memory narratives about the North-East of England and how they interface with the exhibition-based experiences of the participants. In addition, a variation in methodology was adopted with the group of participants who were asylum seekers, which can be more aptly explored in future publications.

The study with long-term residents involved a total of 12 participants in two phases: in the first phase nine long-term residents of Tyneside were recruited through an open call to participate in an exploratory workshop about North-East identity in Discovery Museum. In spring 2015, two such workshops took place, with four and five participants, respectively, which were audio- and video-recorded over the course of two hours.[1] The workshops involved a mapping activity, whereby participants were asked to respond to questions about where they felt at home, where they belonged and which other places were significant to them, and to mark these on a map. Throughout the exercise, many participants discussed their connections with places outside the region. This activity highlighted the importance of migration (often within the UK) to the personal histories of long-term residents of Tyneside, demonstrating a high level of mobility even amongst relatively 'settled' contemporary communities. Participants then took part in a broader group discussion about their feelings about living in Tyneside, which encompassed issues such as the changes experienced in the region during their own lives, including changes in employment and population demographics. It is worth noting that most of the long-term residents were retired, an issue that emerged as significant within the narrative responses with regard to changes in employment in the region.[2] The participants were not required to visit the exhibition during this phase of the study, and indeed half of the participants had not visited *Destination Tyneside* at the time of the workshops. We did not discuss the exhibition with the participants at this stage. The purpose of holding these workshops was to attempt to gauge a sense of participants' perspectives on issues of belonging, place and identity before they encountered the exhibition. Similar themes surfaced in the workshops around post-industrial decline, as were subsequently expressed again by participants in the post-visit exhibition.

Following the workshops, participants were invited to take part in the next phase of the study, which involved a visit to the *Destination Tyneside* exhibition with a member of their family or a friend. Four pairs took part in the second phase of the study; each pair was asked to visit *Destination Tyneside* for approximately 15 to 20 minutes wearing glasses with in-built audio-visual capture. The glasses were worn by one participant and recorded everything the wearer saw and said, also capturing the responses of their friend (see also Allen *et al.* 2014).

The key advantage of this approach was that it enabled us to gain insights into the visiting behaviours and types of conversations triggered by the museum visit within the context of an existing relationship. Immediately after the visit, participants took part in a paired interview (lasting between one and a half and three hours) in which they first discussed their initial thoughts about the exhibition before watching and discussing the film of their visit with the researchers. The two-phase approach and the multiple points of engagement with a small number of participants aimed to develop trust among researchers and participants and to capture narratives around place, migration, memory and personhood as they evolved in a set of interactions, including the visit to the exhibition.

The rest of this chapter will provide a rich account of the experiences of three pairs of participants[3] who visited *Destination Tyneside* as part of this study, weaving together biographical elements captured in the first phase of this study with their experiences of their visit recorded through the glasses and their reflections during the follow-up interviews. The participants in these pairs shared commonalities that allowed us to delve deeper into their experiences and identify common threads. They had been born in the region and had lived there all their lives. Furthermore, they had a longstanding link with and personal experience of migration, either through ancestral connections or through their long-term residency in areas with migrant communities in the North-East.[4]

The three pairs comprised a mother and daughter, Linda and Katie, two cousins, John and Elaine, and two friends, Janet and Maureen. Linda (age early fifties) and Katie (21 years old) were both born in the area and currently live in South Shields, a coastal town approximately 20 minutes from Newcastle. Linda describes herself as a 'Geordie' (i.e. someone from Newcastle), whereas her daughter has a much more ambivalent relationship to her North-East roots. Katie says she doesn't feel 'British' and expresses much more of an affinity for her Irish ancestors who migrated to Tyneside three generations ago. She has a strong desire to move to Ireland in the near future.

Cousins John (69 years old) and Elaine (late fifties/early sixties) both live in Hebburn, a town approximately 20 minutes from Newcastle. Elaine was keen to reconnect with her family history since the death of her mother earlier in the year, and has traced Irish and Scottish ancestors who moved to Tyneside in the late nineteenth and early twentieth centuries. John's grandparents were born in Scotland and moved to Hebburn, where his parents were born. He does not have Irish ancestors himself, but is a singer who enjoys Irish music and knows lots of descendants of Irish and Italian migrants living in Hebburn. Both pairs of participants are actively involved in genealogical research, and this was a motivation for visiting the gallery and being involved in the research project.

The friends who made up the third pair of participants, Janet and Maureen, are both retired and in their early to mid-sixties. Janet and Maureen are childhood friends from Gateshead, the town immediately adjacent to Newcastle with a well-established orthodox Jewish population, as well as more recent refugees and asylum seekers from countries such as Syria. Both women are heavily involved in the local church and, through this, with charitable efforts to help and host migrants coming to the area. Maureen knows that her husband's grandfather migrated to the UK from Italy in about 1900. Her own grandparents also moved as internal migrants to Tyneside from Plymouth, although she had not previously considered this as 'migration'. During World War II, her husband's grandfather was temporarily put into an internment camp because of his Italian surname (which Maureen has by marriage) and because he had lost his papers while serving in the British army at the battle of Dunkirk.

Responses to the museum's invitation to empathise

Our research identified a range of emotions present in participants' responses, some of which, following Coplan's definition, could be described as empathetic. Our research showed that the audio-visual and analogue interactive interpretive strategies adopted by the gallery are particularly successful in engaging visitors with the intended themes and with personalised accounts of the past. We identify three main ways in which the six participants above can be seen to respond positively to the gallery's invitation to empathise with migrants, as described in the following three subsections.

1. Perspective-taking

Perspective-taking can be seen in the following exchange by two of the participants, Linda and Katie (mother and daughter, born and brought up in Tyneside), in response to the gallery's prompt 'You are moving to another country with your family. Not all of your things will fit into your suitcase. What do you want to take with you?'

LINDA: I think if I'd take maybe a handkerchief and a mebbes *[maybe]* a small bottle of perfume and a photo. Like a family photo, anything of your parents or your family.

KATIE: Or maybe something for your faith? Like I was seeing like rosary beads, that was a Catholic one, and then there was another one what was it? Was there a Hindu one or something like that as well? So I think something to do with your faith that you would put in there. Well, for me anyway. I think, think that's what got a lot people through when you were travelling to far places. That was something that you could have attached, something you could take from home that they could have. So I think that was something that was really important for them.

Later in the conversation …

RHIANNON (INTERVIEWER): Do you think there's something you'll remember [from the visit]?

KATIE: Probably that suitcase and the compartments. It does make you think, what, you know, we were talking about what we would take with us, but also seeing what they took, from China, or from India or Ireland. You know, what would … the diversity, one person would take that, one person wouldn't. What would a man who was leaving his family behind, what would he take? What would a man with no family behind, what would he take? I think it raises all kinda questions in me head. You know? It does leave you thinking …

As this exchange demonstrates, Katie and Linda both find the suitcase interactive, combined with the textual prompt, a powerful cue to begin imagining what it must have been like for a migrant leaving their home behind. Katie, in particular, describes how she imagined different scenarios and subjectivities; a man with a family, a man without a family, people of different faiths. Other respondents also picked out the suitcase interactive as being particularly memorable and connected with it in similar ways.

2. Humanising 'the migrant'; personalising history

One of the intended consequences of encouraging visitors to imagine what it is like to be a migrant is to humanise the figure of the migrant. This was a key goal for the curators, as discussed above. It is particularly relevant in the context of news media and a broader public discourse which tends to stereotype and abstract the idea of migration through its constant discussion of migrants as either faceless hordes or depersonalised statistics. Our respondents remarked on how it made a change to see the faces and hear the accounts of individuals and to recognise migrants as people with individual stories. In particular, the audio and visual interpretive techniques which used first-person narration and personalisation techniques (film, digital storytelling, large-scale photographic portraits) were identified as powerfully bringing this message home to visitors. Objects relating to named individuals also supported this response. In the post-visit interview, Katie and Linda discuss how the gallery prompted them to think again about views they had encountered in the news media and broader public discourses on economic migration:

KATIE: [...] Because you have so much bad stuff in the newspapers, you want to get to the bottom of it and to the reality of it. It's [*meaning migration*] not anything bad, it's just people looking for work. I mean ...
LINDA: Yeah.
KATIE: And I mean, it really opens your eyes, that these are just genuine people. You know, they've got a family and they want to make a living and that's normal, that's OK, you know [...]
LINDA: When people come from other countries and they're trying to live like that and you've got people going 'there's no room for us' and 'there's no jobs for us'. But you've got them themselves there talking on a screen [gestures in front of her – makes TV shape] and you think 'God it actually happens'. It's like Katie says, you're reading the paper and you think 'nah, that's rubbish' but you see people's faces ... it actually hits home to you.
KATIE: Again, because you've got something that you can relate to as a person, there's something in front of you that makes it real ...

3. Reframing histories

These examples of productive, other-orientated processes of empathetic involvement are accompanied by ways in which some of the interviewees reframed and recontextualised their own lives in relation to migration histories. In the post-visit interview, long-term residents John and Elaine, from Hebburn, reassess their childhood memories of migration within their community:

ELAINE: I think for me it [*meaning the visit to* Destination Tyneside] just prompted, it made me think, ... I've lived in Hebburn all my life ... the Italians came over like Maria Rabbiotti who had the ice-cream parlour and Bracchi's who had the fish and chip shop. When I went to school I sat next to Tony Bracchi. Just things like that that you don't realise, you don't really think about it when you're younger, I don't think. And when you get older you can think about all the people that you spent childhood with ... where their parents came from.

Janet and Maureen also found that the gallery prompted them to reflect again on the region's history in relation to contemporary perceptions of migration:

JANET: And we were just saying as well when we were talking there, people in London seem to think that they invented being the first people to, you know, ... first immigrants and everything, but people in the North-East have just been coming all the time and getting on basically, haven't they?

MAUREEN: I think it was quite interesting because they *[meaning in the display]* had people from Cumbria, as well as the Irish and the Italians and the Polish. I thought that was kind of ... you know, you don't think of immigrants from Cumbria.

As these three examples suggest, the museum's invitation to empathise was successfully accepted by these visitors at these moments and can be clearly identified as such. Yet a focus *only* on these responses fails to capture a series of more complex navigations between embodied experience, empathetic identifications and social relationships that were also happening. The following examples of affective and mnemonic patterning were elicited by the multifaceted methodology which opened up a space within the discussions for its emergence. We would argue that these affective responses may well not have become apparent without this methodology.

To be clear, we are not suggesting that certain responses are somehow more authentic or 'real' than others. Neither are we suggesting that it is possible to ever fully 'capture' an *a priori* account of what the visit means to visitors. What visitors come to think, feel and say about the exhibition experience is situational and realised through the different interactions that we as researchers have with them as well as through their interactions with their companions. This is an inevitability of any research methodology that intervenes in the museum visit in the way ours did and which prompts people to actively reflect upon it. It does, nevertheless, raise the methodological question of whether what the visitors came to articulate was in fact a product of our methodology. However, in our view, the varied responses would not have been articulated as they were without the enabling framework offered by the exhibition. Evidence for this can be found in the way that visitors explicitly reproduced the same three conceptual framings (humanising the migrant, perspective-taking and reframing migration histories) and the general language of the exhibition in their own discussions of what they encountered. The combination of methods that allowed us to take account of the participants' encounter with the exhibition as it happened, without the presence of the researchers, as well as their post-visit reflections through conversation provides a rare opportunity to witness how the visiting experience became a resource for the participants in their effort to make sense both of the exhibition and of contemporary debates around migration.

Emotion and an affective loop

The exchange between the two friends, Janet and Maureen, illuminates both the affective nature of the museum visit and the extent to which the affective aspect of the visit is framed for the pair by the migration crisis of the summer of 2015 and its contemporary media reporting. At the same time, the way that the exchange below plays out within the interview demonstrates how the affecting experience of the visit evolves through a series of interactions, not only during the visit but also post-visit as part of reflection and social interaction. Alternatively, another interpretation is that the following exchange indicates how the participants prefer not to dwell on what might be perceived as upsetting material, leading to a loss of self-control and inappropriate public expression of emotion arising from their empathetic response.

Initially, the interviewer (Katherine) asks about their feelings 4.50 minutes into the post-visit interview:

KATHERINE: And how did you feel after visiting the gallery?
JANET: Nothing in particular.
MAUREEN: Well, I identified with it.
JANET: We're quite museum visitors aren't we?
MAUREEN: Yes. Obviously I quite identified with, I'd never thought about the, about the [my] Grandparents as being immigrants into Tyneside.
JANET: Mmm.
MAUREEN: My grandparents ... because they came from Plymouth, and we discussed that.
JANET: And obviously with having a name like Lorenzo [Maureen's married Italian name] ... cos we looked for the Italians.
JANET: I think always after you've ... visited any exhibition you sort of think differently for a bit after ... for a couple of days and see things differently.

Here Maureen expresses more of an identification with the topic of the gallery, presumably because of her already-confirmed migrant-descendent identity, although she simultaneously states that she had not previously thought of her own grandparents as belonging in the category of immigrants to the area. However, at this point neither mentions what, later in the interview, transpires to be a strongly affecting response. Almost 20 minutes into the post-visit interview, Katherine asks whether their feelings have changed:

KATHERINE: Has the visit changed how you feel about Tyneside in any way?
JANET: No. Well, the reason I've brought Maureen is she spends six months here and six months in New Zealand, so every time she comes back she looks at things differently. *[Referring to a film they are now watching about leaving home which plays outside the cinema space in the gallery and which*

is playing in the film recording of their visit that they are now watching with the researcher]

[The glasses are now recording Maureen looking at a panel]

[She reads aloud in the film] 'Imagine leaving home. Imagine not returning.'

[In the post-visit interview, still commenting on the film of their visit that they are watching] Maureen: Well these people won't nowadays, will they?

[What follows is all in the post-visit interview] Maureen: Didn't I say that that *[referring to the text panel currently in view in the film]* was relevant for today? ... And obviously I compared that to today. I have great difficulty with all these people leaving their homes.

KATHERINE: Is that ... because you're leaving for six months of the year?

MAUREEN: I suppose so, yeah. And I'm thinking then I can come back and all my friends are there to support me.

JANET: It's the upheaval of just going with small children.

MAUREEN: Yes, yes, I couldn't ...

KATHERINE: So were you thinking about the stuff that's been going on over the summer? *[referring back to Maureen's comment above about people leaving their homes]*

MAUREEN: Yes, yes. I've got issues with that, when you see them setting up their camps on those Greek islands in those flimsy tents.

[...]

MAUREEN: And should they stop? *[meaning stay where they are]* ... but with the bombs and things like that ... should they move with their small children? I was quite distressed. You know, when you think of all things that our children have got. OK, you get children that are socially deprived in some ways, but *[goes on to describe how her charitable work with refugees has brought her into contact with people fleeing their own countries]* you're bringing them from witnessing all this aggro and, you know, you're seeing all these police holding them back with kids on their shoulders and babies in their arms! *[sounds tearful]* ... *[sniffs]* ... sorry.

KATHERINE: No, it's really distressing.

[Long silence ... No-one speaks as they all watch the film of Janet and Maureen looking at the museum displays of more recent immigration, including Mela performers and asylum seekers]

MAUREEN: And obviously these people *[meaning recent migrants shown in the media]* came over in the same way *[as those in the display]*. But I don't think they were fleeing from ... well they were, they were fleeing from bad places, weren't they? Would it have been better for them to stop where they were? I dunno.

[Another long pause ... no-one speaks]

JANET: It is a bit artefact-thin.

During this exchange, Maureen becomes visibly and audibly affected as she recalls images she has seen recently in the news and connects them to this larger

Experiencing mixed emotions in the museum   139

history of migration, as represented with the display and through her own experiences of refugees through her charitable work over the years. Mixed in with this, she is also connecting these thoughts to her personal family history, including the memories passed down from her husband and his grandfather, and the reasons she imagines her own family members and other migrants must have had for leaving their homes. She begins to sound tearful and her voice catches with emotion as the images and associations seem to be coming thick and fast, one after the other, and as she recalls the previous emotional experience of being 'distressed'. At the height of the affective episode she apologises to the interviewer for her emotional response and temporary loss of composure. At this point what the transcript does not easily show is that the silences between the comments increase noticeably, to the point that they turn into awkward pauses; both the interviewer and the interviewees seem to be at a loss for words or a way out of this moment.

What happens next is revealing in terms of what it tells us about how museum visitors are situated within a nexus of emotional and personal relationships uniting those visiting together. Maureen's friend, Janet, intervenes to provide a safe route out of this affective moment. She says 'It is a bit artefact-thin.' Her comment is pointing out that the display is lacking the level of objects which might normally be expected in a 'successful' museum display. This is a common criticism of migration displays because museums tend not to be able to access the same level of objects as they might in other subject areas. People fleeing war and hardship are unlikely to be able to bring many objects with them and are often – understandably – unwilling to part with those few precious keepsakes which they do have. However, the primary purpose of Janet's transition into a technical register, and the broader discursive shift she makes towards talking about museum practice, is clearly a deliberate move to put the conversation onto safer, more emotionally neutral ground. It is a kind, understated gesture of friendship from Janet to Maureen in response to her friend's distress and a move which speaks volumes about their longstanding relationship and care for each other.

As a whole, this exchange demonstrates that, when we are attempting to understand museum visiting and emotional, empathetic or affective encounters in these spaces, we need to be attentive to the ways in which such responses will ebb and flow across the time of the visit. We need to be careful about taking self-reporting of the experience at face-value because there may be complex processes of disavowal, embarrassment, self-consciousness and post-hoc rationalisation at play. People's reactions will always be imbricated in a web of experiences, emotions and perceptions which stretches in many different, temporal directions simultaneously. There are processes of rethinking and revisiting long-held memories and histories at work here. Running simultaneously, there are highly contemporary and time-sensitive experiences weighing on the visit, for example, of contemporary media events over the last few weeks and months. And as these are recalled, these triggers send people back

140 Rhiannon Mason *et al.*

to the place – emotionally – where they last engaged with such issues – 'I was distressed'. The affective dimensions of the encounter can therefore be understood as looping forwards and backwards as they play off the triggers in the display. At the same time, these responses are also relayed through the exchanges and relationships of the particular visitor-group combination and – in this case – the personal histories and friendships they bring to the encounter.

Revisiting past–present relations

As we suggested above, the visit prompted Elaine, Janet and Maureen all to reframe their history of Tyneside as a history of migration, but for Maureen the visit and attendant research process also prompted her to emotionally reframe her own family history. What the interview transcripts also show, however, is that accompanying such personalised, autobiographical reframings is a reframing of a different kind, one which draws on wider cultural narratives and memory communities. The curatorial intention had been to focus visitor attention on migration to the local area. The goal was to highlight how this influx of foreign labour was an essential factor in enabling a period of peak industrial productivity on Tyneside from the latter part of the nineteenth century. Our research showed that participants did recognise this narrative of the intertwined nature of past economic growth and the ensuing diversity of the local population. However, for the long-term residents, this discussion of local history also led them to reflect more on the general rise and decline of heavy industries and resulting unemployment.

In the post-visit interview, Katie, for example, expressed a positive sense of pride in the achievements of her individual ancestors and their contribution to the making of modern Tyneside. In comparison, for her mother, Linda, the gallery and subsequent discussion triggered more comments on the contrast with today and the effects of de-industrialisation she had witnessed in her lifetime:

LINDA: … How they travelled from Ireland over here was fascinating and there's a lot of us now going to Ireland looking for work and going to London looking for work. This was, the North-East, a real heart for the jobs like. I tries to explain to you *(to Katie)* didn't I? You says 'Why did they come?' I says 'Cos this is where the jobs were.' And now look it at …

Similarly, in Elaine and John's post-visit discussion, they coupled the post-industrial restructuring of the economy in Tyneside – away from mining, factories and shipbuilding towards culture and leisure – with a discussion of how this had changed the nature of community in their lifetimes and locality:

ELAINE: It must have been, at first there mustn't have been enough shops and places to accommodate all these people you know and houses. All of a sudden the sky opens and well obviously there was more than one shipbuilder wasn't there? There was a few small shipbuilders and as the word spread and they all came around at the same time. It must have been massive. [...] I mean even when I was a kid I can remember you could have set your watch by the buzzers because there was 7:25, and you had 5 minutes to get there and everyone would be running along for 7:30 and then there was 9 o'clock tea break. And then the church bells to be going as well because everybody went to church. Because we were Catholic and you went to church practically every single day. And then 12 o'clock lunchtime ... just the throng of people because hardly anybody had cars. So they'd all walk up the Bank from Hebburn

[...]

ELAINE: I think it's sad to look at how quiet the river is now compared to how busy it was even when I was a child. Because it was so busy ...

JOHN: That is one of the saddest things to, you know, really, the demise of industry, you know what I mean, it's just it's affected the community that much, I think, in a lot of ways.

ELAINE: [...] What attracted people? Well, it must have been the river mustn't it? That attracted all these ...

JOHN: coal-mining

ELAINE: ... people to the area in the first place. And why have they all disappeared? because we don't make anything anymore.

[...]

JOHN: And lads going straight from school to be an apprentice in that sort of environment. And it was just tremendous, really to have that sort of opportunity.

JOHN: ... And now that you have people working in call centres, you know, and zero hour contracts. There's no sort of continuity, it's terrible. But, like I say, it's not exclusive to Tyneside, is it?

ELAINE: I can't imagine they get any work satisfaction out of being in a call centre. [...] Having the different generations coming together and treating each other with respect and looking out for one another, learning a trade. That's lost to us now. And you just think when the river was so busy then, why is it not busy now, why is it not?

JOHN: Well, it's globalisation isn't it, you know what I mean [laughs], the curse.

ELAINE: I mean I certainly wouldn't want to go back to, my youngest son is 12, going down the mines a hundred years ago. I certainly wouldn't want that because it was such a hard life.

JOHN: Ah yeah, there were good sides to it and bad sides to it.

ELAINE: Certainly some things have been lost.

What stands out palpably is the sense of the very visible nature of community and prosperity so that, as Elaine describes it, you could see the community thronging in the streets, all sharing the same routines and schedules. While there is a realism about the dangerous nature of the past industries such as coal-mining, there is a clear sense of a regret over the loss of the cohesive nature of community which certain kinds of blue-collar industries previously generated. The overarching narrative here is one of feeling marginalised by the anonymous forces of 'globalisation', as John says. Elaine elaborates on this theme with a revealing anecdote about where they live, Hebburn:

ELAINE: I can't imagine anyone thinking that 'I want to move to Hebburn, because I want to move to Hebburn'. This guy stopped me and my friend the other day. The guy said 'Is this the through road to Jarrow?' and I says 'No, this is Hebburn'. Because he didn't know, he just thought it was the way to Jarrow. He just thought this was a long road, a through road to Jarrow. Hebburn has just been forgotten about. Whereas 100 years ago, people from Scotland would have known where Hebburn was, because you went there for work.

These exchanges encapsulate people's feelings of being both geographically and economically peripheral, in contradiction to the picture painted in the museum display where Newcastle is very much positioned as a centre point which previously pulled people towards it. This sense of marginalisation clearly evokes sadness and frustration. At the same time, both speakers recognise that Newcastle, as opposed to its suburbs, has undergone significant rebranding and regeneration through culture and leisure. They pick out the River Tyne and the Quayside as focal points where this transition from industry to culture and leisure is manifested through its cluster of art galleries, bars, new bridges, cultural venues and tourist activities.

This discourse about the effects of post-industrialisation on the area is apparent in other respondents' comments too and in the broader conversations which took place in the two workshops that preceded the exhibition visits. Crucially, this discourse is intertwined with people's understanding of contemporary migration and globalisation. In Katie and Linda's post-visit interview comments, for example, they make several references to the idea that there are not enough jobs for local people, 'like us', so they wonder how it will work for migrants coming to look for jobs. In this sense, they appear conflicted between a recognition of how others are understandably looking for work, just like their own relatives did when they migrated to the area, and concern about the lack of jobs in the area today. While the long-term residents to whom we spoke recognised the gallery's depiction of Tyneside as historically heterogeneous, for them this historical diversity was mediated by the shared daily routines and experiences of the mining and shipbuilding

Experiencing mixed emotions in the museum   143

communities. This resulted in the perception of these place- and industry-based communities as also relatively homogeneous, in comparison with the contemporary diversity of ethnically defined communities. These long-term participants regretted this loss of solidarity within present-day communities.

In part, this post-industrial melancholia is arguably a reflection of the more fragmented experience of work patterns and employment opportunities (or lack thereof) in today's globalised societies, rather than a comment about migrants per se. However, it is wrapped up with an underlying sense of how community on Tyneside is different from the more apparently coherent world depicted in the gallery. This is significant given how the gallery was attempting precisely to stress how Tyneside's recent past was itself much more diverse than is usually recognised. The human effects of processes of economic globalisation are, in fact, key to understanding both participants' responses and the stories of migration in the museum gallery, although these linkages are not necessarily foregrounded in this way in the display.

Nostalgias and mnemonic patterning

The fluid combination of sentiments of sadness, regret and pride focalised around the built environment and physical markers we identified in the participants' responses is similarly identified in Bonnett and Alexander's (2012: 399) study of nostalgia and memory amongst ex-residents of Newcastle:

> Repeatedly during our interviews, it was the same specific features of the urban landscapes ... that participants brought up and wanted to talk about at length. These acted as what Meusburger *et al.* call 'mnemonic devices; as the storage vessels of cultural identity and information ... as triggers for sensations, emotions, and sensibilities' (2011, 8), and as 'spatial anchors for historical traditions' (Foote *et al.* 2000, 305).
> (Bonnett and Alexander 2012: 399)

On the basis of our findings at *Destination Tyneside* and earlier research (Mason, Whitehead and Graham 2012), we support Bonnett and Alexander's (2012) observations that nostalgia cannot be clearly separated into 'productive' or 'simple', 'good' or 'bad' types. Instead, participants' responses indicate a complex intertwining of different kinds and scales of collective memory and nostalgic sentiments, some of which are reflective and aware of ambivalence (Boym 2001: xv). In this respect, we argue that the museum display prompted and resonated with wider collective memory discourses beyond those intended by the curatorial team and the interpretive focus of the gallery. As indicated above, the gallery positively celebrates the booming industries that attracted migrants to the region in the past. However, many local visitors expressed emotions of disappointment and sadness about the perceived loss of local and national pride due to the post-industrial decline of the heavy manufacturing industries that has marked this area's recent history. These emotional narratives clearly frame these visitors' responses to the gallery. Moreover, these commonly expressed emotions are articulated through recurring tropes and narrative structures which, we argue, cumulatively function as memory 'schemata' which operate through 'narrative templates' (Wertsch 2012).

For Wertsch, these narrative templates can be identified where a '… storyline is used repeatedly by a mnemonic community to interpret multiple specific events by fitting them into a specific plot line' (Wertsch 2012: 175). Wertsch's point is that, although the details may vary (the exact location in question, the specific time, or the particular community), these 'generalised schematic structures' can accommodate the overarching account (Wertsch 2012: 175). Such accounts are powerful in terms of supporting mnemonic communities and collective memory, as discussed by Zerubavel:

> The collective memory of a mnemonic community is quite different from the sum total of the personal recollections of its various individual members, as it includes only those that are commonly shared by all of them (in the same way that public opinion, for example, is more than a mere aggregate of individuals' personal opinions). It thus involves the integration of various different personal pasts into a single common past that all members of a particular community come to remember collectively.
>
> (Zerubavel 1996: 293–294)

Reiterating Zerubavel's last point about the scope of this mnemonic community, this narrative template of post-industrial decline was only invoked by, and available to, the long-term residents group. The post-visit interviews further emphasised that such schemata are acquired through socialisation. Katie at age 21 has, arguably, little firsthand experience of the direct effects of de-industrialisation, but belongs to the mnemonic community in which that knowledge continues to circulate and through which it is intentionally passed on:

LINDA: I tries to explain to you *(to Katie)* didn't I? You says 'Why did they come.' I says 'Cos this is where the jobs were.' And now look at it.

Conclusion

What emerges clearly from our study is the importance of taking account of other pre-existing, emotionally charged narratives which come to the surface for many long-term local residents when visiting such displays. Visitor analysis needs a methodology that is complex enough to able to begin to identify such different forms of emotional response and affective patterning and to acknowledge that they may evolve through interactions during and after a visit. As Sharon Macdonald has argued, competing processes of 'framing' are always in operation during any museum visit (Macdonald 2002). While the gallery was, as Macdonald has put it in another context, 'concerned with setting the scene so that certain connections [would] be made rather than others' (Macdonald 2002: 250), a different set of broader cultural framings was being referred to by the interviewees to make sense of their visit. As a result the 'visions and work' of the curators 'were set in a context which gave [the exhibition] inflections they had not anticipated' (Macdonald 2002: 255). At one level, we could say this is always the case with museum displays, as Macdonald's (2002) study of the Science Museum amply demonstrates. However, we are specifically concerned with the implications of this argument when thinking about how the museums might be aiming to build and foster empathetic responses around migration stories, as discussed above.

Specific memory schemata related to post-industrial nostalgia result in particular outcomes relevant to empathy and migration. The interviews we conducted, which provided opportunities for reflection by reviewing recordings of the visit with the participants, suggest that the presence of these schemata complicates the way in which empathy is operating; it may result more readily in expressions of empathy for those within one's own memory community rather than outside it. Imaginative identification in this case appears to become refracted through affiliations of class – as epitomised by an understanding of a lost work-community in an alienating globalised world – and, more implicitly, in terms of ethnicity and ideas of 'otherness'. While the synchronic intersections of framing and schemata suggest that it is more appropriate to talk about active communities of *remembering*, the extent to which interpellating such communities through empathetic strategies can be transformative, in the sense envisaged by the gallery, is less certain. Our conclusion is that diverse narratives of migration, and of self and other, compete for prominence as visitors assemble, and then reassemble, their own account of their visit to the museum.

This is where we diverge from the idea as suggested by Wertsch (2012), for example, that memory schemata are inherently politically conservative. At some moments the participants in our study recognised and responded powerfully to the invitation to empathise. Yet, at the next moment, attention and emotion appeared to be heading off in another direction altogether, triggered by specific memory narratives. What is abundantly clear is the extent to which people engage emotionally with museums in multifaceted ways. Sometimes the responses might be complementary, sometimes they might be in conflict. Furthermore, those responses are not explicitly connected to certain interpretive and exhibitionary media. Crucially, they can change throughout the context of the visit – identification and dis-identification, empathy and nostalgia, can happen almost concurrently. One important implication of this finding is that museum and heritage studies, therefore, need better methodologies that can capture the ebb and flow of people's responses across different moments within their visits, and which are able to capture and make sense of the 'felt experience' of the visit. Moreover, we continue to need to understand not only how museum visits relate to people's lives, memories and experiences beyond the museum, but, crucially, also how this connects with wider memory practices and mnemonic communities.

In conclusion, this research has demonstrated the ways in which unanticipated, wider memory schemata interact with the emotional responses expressly invited by the museum display. It thereby raises important questions about the complexity of understanding the museum visit in terms of affective practices and emotional responses. It prompts us to pay more attention to how different kinds of emotions may come into conflict with, frame, or support one another. It also alerts us to the importance of attending to the interplay between individual, personal emotional responses to specific displays and those which are connected to broader discourses of identity and place circulating within certain memory communities.

Acknowledgements

Our thanks to Kylea Little, Curator of *Destination Tyneside*, for her advice and insights and to TWAM for allowing us to carry out this research in their spaces with their visitors. We acknowledge the Newcastle Institute for Social Renewal (NISR) at Newcastle University for its financial support of this research project. We also acknowledge the inspiration for the methodology and this line of enquiry which arose from the EU-funded MeLa project. Thanks to all the colleagues and friends who gave us feedback and encouragement at seminars and conferences. Last, but not least, we gratefully thank all the participants who so generously shared their time, stories and memories with us and without whom this study would not have been possible.

Notes

1 The variation between the total number of participants involved and the numbers attending the initial workshops was due to the fact that some of the initial participants subsequently brought along a friend, who had not been in the first workshop, for the paired exhibition visit and post-visit interview.
2 We acknowledge that the long-term residents' responses are undoubtedly influenced by their age and life-stage; a younger group may well have placed less emphasis on the issue of post-industrial decline. At the same time, it was evident that these participants' were endeavouring to pass on this collective memory to their children, so that younger generations may well still be familiar with this particular memory discourse.
3 Subsequent publications will address the responses of the asylum seekers group and our reflections on the overall methodology.

4 Names of participants have been changed to provide anonymity, as have the names of other people mentioned by participants. All participants were briefed about the purpose of the study and agreed to take part voluntarily. Consent forms cover the use of the data collected in all phases of the study.

References

Allen, A., Bak, J., Whitehead, C. and Gauthier, D., 2014. Seeing yourself in the museum: Experimental actions and methodological potentials for walk-through studies in exhibition contexts. In L. Basso Peressut, C. F. Colombo and G. Postiglione, eds. *Museum Multiplicities: Field Actions and Research by Design*. Milan: Politecnico di Milano, 95–113.

Arnold-de Simine, S., 2013. *Mediating Memory in the Museum: Trauma, Empathy and Nostalgia*. Basingstoke and New York: Palgrave Macmillan.

Bonnell, J. and Simon, R., 2007. 'Difficult' exhibitions and intimate encounters. *Museum & Society*, 5(2), 65–85.

Bonnett, A. and Alexander, C., 2012. Mobile nostalgias: Connecting visions of the urban past, present and future amongst ex-residents. *Transactions of the Institute of British Geographers*, 38(3), 391–402.

Boym, S., 2001. *The Future of Nostalgia*. New York: Basic Books.

Brown, A. and Waterhouse-Watson, D., 2014. The future of the past: Digital media in Holocaust museums. *Holocaust Studies*, 20(3), 1–32.

Coplan, A., 2011. Understanding empathy: Its features and effects. In A. Coplan and P. Goldie, eds. *Empathy: Philosophical and Psychological Perspectives*. Oxford: Oxford University Press, 3–18.

Coplan, A. and Goldie P., eds., 2011. *Empathy: Philosophical and Psychological Perspectives*. Oxford: Oxford University Press.

Dicks, B., 2016. The habitus of heritage: A discussion of Bourdieu's ideas for visitor studies in heritage and museums. *Museum and Society*, 14(1), 52–64.

Doering, Z. D. and Pekarik, A. J., 1996. Questioning the entrance narrative. *Journal of Museum Education*, 12(3), 20–23.

Elgot, J. and Taylor, M., 2015. Calais crisis: Cameron condemned for 'dehumanising' description of migrants. *The Guardian*, 30 July. Available from www.theguardian.com/uk-news/2015/jul/30/david-cameron-migrant-swarm-language-condemned [Accessed 5 April 2016].

Gregory, K. and Witcomb, A., 2007. Beyond nostalgia: The role of affect in generating historical understanding at heritage sites. In S. Watson, S. MacLeod and S. Knell, eds. *Museum Revolutions: How Museums Change and Are Changed*. London: Routledge, 263–275.

Hutchison, M., and Collins, L., 2009. Translations: Experiments in dialogic representation of cultural diversity in three museum sound installations. *Museum & Society*, 7(2), 92–109.

Kaplan, E. A. 2011. Empathy and trauma culture: Imaging catastrophe. In A. Coplan and P. Goldie, eds. *Empathy: Philosophical and Psychological Perspectives*. Oxford: Oxford University Press, 255–276.

LaCapra, D., 2001. *Writing History, Writing Trauma*. Baltimore: Johns Hopkins University Press.

Landsberg, A., 2004. *Prosthetic Memory: The Transformation of American Remembrance in the Age of Mass Culture.* New York: Columbia University Press.

Little, K. and Watson, I., 2015. Destination Tyneside – stories of belonging: The philosophy and experience of developing a new permanent migration gallery at Discovery Museum in Newcastle upon Tyne. In C. Whitehead, S. Eckersley, K. Lloyd and R. Mason, eds. *Museums, Migration and Identity in Europe.* Farnham: Ashgate, 183–205.

Macdonald, S., 2002. *Behind the Scenes at the Science Museum.* Oxford: Berg.

Mason, R., Whitehead C. and Graham, H., 2012. The place of art in the public art gallery: A visual sense of place. In P. Davis, G. Corsane and I. Convery, eds. *Making Sense of Place: Multidisciplinary Perspectives.* Woodbridge: Boydell Press, 133–144.

Purkis, H., 2013. Making contact in an exhibition zone: Displaying contemporary cultural diversity in Donegal, Ireland, through an installation of visual and material portraits. *Museum and Society,* 11(1), 50–67.

Schorch, P., 2014. The cosmohermeneutics of migration encounters at the Immigration Museum Melbourne. *Museum Worlds: Advances in Research,* 2(1), 81–98.

Schorch, P., 2015. Experiencing differences and negotiating prejudices at the Immigration Museum, Melbourne. *International Journal of Heritage Studies,* 21(1), 46–64.

Smith, L., 2006. *Uses of Heritage.* London: Routledge.

Smith, L., 2010. 'Man's inhumanity to man' and other platitudes of avoidance and misrecognition: An analysis of visitor responses to exhibitions marking the 1807 bicentenary. *Museum & Society,* 8(3), 193–214.

Smith, L., 2011. Affect and registers of engagement: Navigating emotional responses to dissonant heritage. In L. Smith, G. Cubitt, R. Wilson and K. Fouseki, eds. *Representing Enslavement and Abolition in Museums: Ambiguous Engagements.* New York: Routledge, 260–303.

Smith, L., 2016. Changing views? Emotional intelligence, registers of engagement and the museum visit. In V. Gosselin and P. Livingstone, eds. *Museums and the Past – Constructing Historical Consciousness.* Toronto and Vancouver: UBC Press, 101–121.

Smith, L. and Campbell, G., 2016. The elephant in the room: Heritage, affect and emotion. In W. Logan, M. Nic Craith and U. Kockel, eds. *A Companion to Heritage Studies.* Oxford: Wiley Blackwell, 443–460.

Wertsch, J., 2012. Deep memory and narrative templates: Conservative forces in collective memory. In A. Assmann and L. Shortt, eds. *Memory and Political Change.* New York: Palgrave Macmillan, 173–185.

Wetherell, M., 2012. *Affect and Emotion: A New Social Science Understanding.* London: Sage.

Whitehead, C., Eckersley, S., Lloyd, K. and Mason, R., eds., 2015. *Museums, Migration and Identity in Europe: Peoples, Places and Identities.* Farnham: Ashgate.

Witcomb, A., 2013. Understanding the role of affect in producing a critical pedagogy for history museums. *Museum Management and Curatorship,* 28(3), 255–271.

Zerubavel, E., 1996. Social memories: Steps towards a sociology of the past. *Qualitative Sociology,* 19(3), 283–299.

Chapter 9

Coming undone
Protocols of emotion in Canadian human rights museology

Jennifer Claire Robinson

Introduction

In the field of heritage studies, particularly with regard to museums, exhibitions, or heritage sites that deal with historically challenging or disturbing subject matter related to human rights violations, the emotional investment of the heritage professionals involved is a relatively under-researched area (Lehrer and Milton 2011; Wilson 2011; Munro 2014). Accounting for the role of emotion has most often come through analyses of visitor engagement; examining how visitors react to certain exhibitions or how they feel when spending time at heritage sites is part of how heritage spaces measure their success (Lehrer and Milton 2011). Studies have also shown that museums, exhibitions and heritage sites have the potential to evoke both positive and negative feelings of nostalgia in visitors as they encounter aspects of history or particular events in these spaces (Gregory and Witcomb 2007). Thus, many studies have begun to unpack how visitors emotionally engage with subject matter that may confront and challenge their understanding of historic events (Gregory and Witcomb 2007; Smith 2011, Smith and Campbell 2015; Melton 2013; Witcomb 2013; Simon 2014), including how emotional reactions help visitors to engage in acts of remembering and meaning-making that come to shape new understandings of shared histories in critical ways (Witcomb 2013; Campbell 2014). New forms of critical thinking about the past are paramount in creating empathy for culturally traumatic histories in visitors. Yet, these emotional reactions are not just happening to visitors. Given the subject matter being discussed, emotional exchanges occurring between those involved in creating a project can often be incredibly deep and personal. However, often traditional models of curatorial work that stress neutrality and objectivity leave little room for the influence of emotional experience. This is part of what Ross Wilson (2011) identifies as 'the curatorial complex', where common practices and expectations can limit the ability of some curators to cope with this strain of museum practice. At times heritage professionals find themselves acting as caregivers, in some cases playing a role like that of a counsellor, but with very little training or institutional support for how best to cope with the intensity of these responsibilities (Wilson 2011; Munro 2013, 2014).[1]

This chapter looks at the affective practices, or emotional responses, that develop between heritage professionals and community partners during curatorial projects dealing with challenging subject matter in a variety of Canadian museums. I take as a point of departure an understanding of *affect* as 'embodied meaning-making' (Wetherell 2012: 4), while *practice* as a descriptive term allows for a kind of fluidity; it implies a sense of ongoing, repetitive actions that accompany the processes of learning and improvisation (Wetherell 2012: 23–24). A practice is also, as Theodor Schatzki defines it, a 'nexus' of 'human activity' that encompasses various actions, relations, meanings, identities, and embodied positions (Schatzki 2012: 59). This nexus is both the physical body and the repeated and habitual actions that come from the body. Given these definitions, this chapter seeks to better understand what kinds of affective practices are produced during the development of projects pertaining to difficult histories in Canadian museums and whether these emotional responses come to produce better museological methods. Drawing on reflections shared by heritage professionals from across Canada, I argue that emotional experiences factor greatly during project development with challenging subject matter. As traumatic life stories are shared between heritage professionals and community partners, affective practices that have the potential to create a space of emotional vulnerability are developed. Though this space may be contentious or at times filled with conflicting opinions, being emotionally vulnerable can also produce stronger bonds of trust and empathy, which can productively shape curatorial work.

I begin by outlining human rights in heritage work as it relates to Canadian museological practice, before presenting a discussion regarding the need to build strong relationships when working with survivors of rights violations in Canada. I take account of any practice-based protocols or guidelines that have been created to safeguard against triggering traumatic experiences for survivors as well as practices put in place to safeguard the good health of all those involved in a project. This research finds that working with survivors of trauma is not just about creating a successful exhibition; in the end the exhibition is but one part of the curatorial process. Rather, this work comes with the belief that healing from trauma can occur through the curatorial process and that this healing is part of the transformative potential of curatorial work.

Exhibiting human rights in Canada

The practice of a human rights museology in Canada, that is, how museums are tackling topics related to cultural discrimination, violence and genocide through the lens of rights and justice (see Carter and Orange 2012; Orange and Carter 2012), sits within the developing national discourse on human rights. Canada has been implicated in several high-profile human rights violations over the last century (Miron 2009; Heathorn and Goutor 2013; Henderson and Wakeham 2013). In the wake of these violations, the federal government has made several 'reconciliatory gestures', including apologies, reparations and commemorative programmes aimed at various cultural communities (Henderson and Wakeham 2013: 7). While researching rights-based issues in Canada could take many forms, my research focused on institutions that have engaged in some capacity with Canada's three official national apologies: The Japanese Canadian Internment during World War II (delivered in 1988); the Chinese Head Tax and Exclusions Laws (delivered in 2006); and Indian Residential Schools (delivered in 2008).[2] Gestures such as apologies make up part of what Henderson and Wakeham (2013: 7) argue is 'the culture of redress' in Canada, which includes a complex network of actors with relationships to different human rights policies and other redress movements. One of the most recent of these redress movements is the Canadian Truth and Reconciliation Commission (TRC) on Indian Residential Schools (IRS). In June 2015, the TRC released its final report to the Canadian federal government, which stated that the IRS system in Canada was an act of cultural genocide (TRC 2015). The *Final Report* includes 94 'calls to action' that factor into various facets of Canadian government and society, including archives and museums, to approach redressing the legacies of these schools in the future (TRC 2015: 319).[3]

Canadian heritage institutions play an important role in this network of redress. Museums provide physical spaces where the public can negotiate what human rights and cultural diversity mean in the context of Canadian nationalism, but they also create and implement the politics of cultural recognition and processes of reconciliation that have been at the forefront of much of the practice of Canadian heritage work over the last 25 years. This is how, as Carter and Orange argue, 'museums not only reflect historical and current human rights but are also participating in the prospective shaping of those rights' (Carter and Orange 2012: 119). A strong example of this is the *Task Force Report on Museums and First Peoples* (Assembly of First Nations and Canadian Museum Association 1992). The Task Force was created in large part due to protest over the exhibition *The Spirit Sings: Artistic Traditions of Canada's First Peoples*, which opened at the Glenbow Museum in January 1988 as a part of the Calgary Olympic celebrations. The exhibition was meant to showcase the unique cultural histories of Indigenous peoples across Canada; however, Shell Oil, one of the major funders for the exhibition, was at the time drilling on the lands of the Lubicon Lake Cree First Nation despite mass protest. A resulting boycott of the exhibition by Indigenous peoples drew national attention to the existing disconnect between Canadian museum practice and contemporary Indigenous issues (see Ames 1992, 2003; Phillips 2011). This protest and the creation of the Task Force demonstrate how the ethics surrounding cultural heritage are deeply entwined in local and national histories; they are, as Smith argues, 'framed by wider struggles for justice and recognition' (Smith 2010: 60). The guidelines set forth in the *Task Force Report* were designed to make museums more inclusive of Indigenous peoples and more accountable to Indigenous cultural needs and rights over cultural representation. To do this, the *Task Force Report* calls on museums to build better relationships with Indigenous peoples. Building better practice cannot occur without building better relationships.

The results shared here are drawn from interviews conducted in 2014–2015 with heritage professionals from eight different institutions across Canada that vary in size and operational structure: three of Canada's national museums, the Canadian Museum of History in Gatineau, the Canadian War Museum in Ottawa and the Canadian Museum for Human Rights in Winnipeg; the Glenbow Museum, which is a municipal museum; two smaller community-driven museums, the Nikkei National Museum and Cultural Centre in Burnaby and the Chinese Canadian Military Museum (CCMM) located in Vancouver's Chinatown; one university museum, the Museum of Anthropology (MOA) at the University of British Columbia in Vancouver; and the Residential and Indian Day School Art Research Program (RIDSAR) from the University of Victoria. Through these interviews I was interested in assessing the processes of 'curating difficult knowledge' (Lehrer and Milton 2011: 3) in Canada; how these processes may differ from but also inform other curatorial work; and the relationships being created to do this strain of curatorial practice. The term *process* has been useful throughout this project, for it implies how 'fundamentally processual in nature' curatorial work with community partners can be (Silverman 2015: 2). Museological work is, at its roots, an experimental process, and, as Silverman stresses, experiments always have the potential to 'succeed and fail' (Silverman 2015: 2). Throughout this research it has been essential to hear my participants discuss the complicated, messy and even failed attempts at project development as often as the positive or successful moments, and to hear how emotion factors into these outcomes.

In some circumstances, exhibitions fail and do not come to fruition or suffer from extreme community backlash and protest in addition to media and academic scrutiny. This was undoubtedly the case with the fallout from *The Spirit Sings* at the Glenbow Museum. MOA suffered from a similar failed exhibition attempt more recently, despite having an institutional reputation of progressive museological practice in Canada (see Ames 2003; Phillips 2011). In 2011, the museum cancelled an exhibition on missing and murdered Indigenous women from Vancouver's Downtown Eastside called *The Forgotten*. Though scholarship has documented how and why this exhibition failed, namely primarily because the exhibition was seen as re-traumatising to women and their families (Pinto 2013), what has not been discussed is what happened after this failure and what has been learned by the institution. Failures can also be catalysts for change where learning opportunities develop out of moments of conflict. Thus, I was interested in speaking with current and former staff at these museums to gain a sense of how institutions in Canada recover from complicated and contentious moments when dealing with matters related to human rights.

Conversely, project success is not just defined as every exhibition that was created without conflict. What struck me in my interviews was to hear how my participants often deemed projects to be successful on the basis of how the process of building an exhibition 'felt' and whether those involved in a project *felt* the experience brought positive change. This was certainly the case from my discussions with those involved with the work of the RIDSAR collective led by visual anthropologist Andrea Walsh and a team of residential school survivors. This project has repatriated a number of paintings done by Indigenous children while they were at residential schools to survivors and their families. Though RIDSAR is not a museum per se, as a research collective this group has taken part in a number of collaborative projects, including exhibitions about residential schools, participated at three national TRC hearings, and taken part as educators in various community and university events. Projects produced by this collective have become important sites for the experiences shared by IRS survivors to be acknowledged and witnessed. I have been very fortunate to have been involved with this work as a researcher since 2012 and have personally witnessed the impact of RIDSAR on the lives of those involved, most importantly in the lives of the survivors whose efforts have guided this work from the beginning, but also the various museum professionals, academics and students, including myself, who have helped with this work. The emotional experiences shared while building these projects have been nothing short of life-changing.

What has remained most clear to me throughout this research when working through complex and emotionally sensitive material related to rights violations in Canada, regardless of the institutional size, structure or exhibition mandate, is that building strong relationships helps to facilitate the creation of respectful working guidelines. Furthermore, time spent being comfortable in the space of being uncomfortable can lead to powerful transformative exhibitions.

The role of relationships

Longstanding relationships in museum work are essential for any successful curatorial partnerships to grow; however, building these relationships takes time. It takes time to foster a level of trust on the part of those sharing stories and it takes time to be a good listener. It also takes time to mend relationships. In the case of the Glenbow Museum, the immediate changes that took place after *The Spirit Sings* were about building new and stronger ties with Indigenous communities in southern Alberta, particularly the Blackfoot Nations. Much of this was done through former curator Gerald Conaty, who throughout his career at Glenbow worked tirelessly with various Indigenous community members from the Blackfoot Confederacy (Carter 2013; Janes

2014, 2006; Schmidt 2014; see also Conaty and Carter 2005; Conaty 2006, 2008). As a result of strategic relationships built from 1990 onwards, the Glenbow Museum has entered into various collections and curatorial projects with Blackfoot members, including the highly successfully permanent exhibition *Niitsitapiisinni: Our Way of Life*, which opened in 2001. As former Glenbow Director Robert Janes reflects,

> [...] to me it is just an offshoot of genuine, authentic human relationships because as our relationships with the Blackfoot progressed we were given more and more of an intimate exposure to Blackfoot [culture] ... all of this peeled back the onion of truth and I think more and more comfort and ability to be honest with each other about what was going on.

This was also the case with the failed *Forgotten* exhibition at MOA, in the aftermath of which it was necessary to mend relationships with members of the Downtown Eastside community and to find ways to work together in order to move forward with potential educational opportunities. This led to a series of group discussions between MOA and members of community organisations about missing and murdered Indigenous women in Canada and how museums and universities can better tackle such a difficult subject in the future.

Another avenue of relationship building finds objects as a central role in processes of remembering and attempting to reconcile with the specific histories of oppression and violence in Canada. Listening, witnessing, talking, touching, all become part of the emotional set of responses humans have with material objects (Edwards 2001, 2005; Langford 2001; Simon 2014). As MOA designer Skooker Broome reflects,

> Being in the presence of an object has an emotional commitment and attachment to the practitioner, especially if touch is involved ... but that is a human condition I think. No matter how much we try to augment the space ... the object just has too much power.

Objects related to human rights violations found in museums across Canada contribute to the 'pedagogy of witnessing' (Simon 2014: 19) of past events of violence and cultural discrimination in Canadian history. In the case of RIDSAR, the children's paintings were for some survivors the only thing they have remaining from their childhood, in addition to being representative of familial relationships within the community. When Walsh reflects on earlier work with Indigenous children's drawings from a previous project (see Walsh 2005), she notes

> I didn't have a sense ... of the importance of names ... how connected people were through names ... how close to the present the drawings

were ... This project and the Aller project [RIDSAR] heighten my awareness ... even though these pieces may have been separated physically from community for decades they remain tightly knit into those social relationships.

The children's paintings have also played a central role in strengthening relationships between those involved in the current RIDSAR work on redressing the IRS system in Canada. With regard to collections that are bound to difficult histories, Walsh notes that

> [...] these collections are people, they are relationships. When you become a curator of these collections you sign on to those social networks and you become part of that for better or for worse. You take the heat for the institution and all its practice, but you also have the pleasure of trying to do things better.

Maintaining good relationships means continuing to work on those relationships when the exhibition comes down. In some cases, this also means helping community members, as is the case at the CCMM, where curators often help elderly veterans with errands and work to keep them socialising with the greater Chinese Canadian community in Vancouver. Going for coffee, making phone calls, and sending emails are all small actions that help to keep aspects of the work in process, but also, more importantly, they are actions that strengthen relationships.

Guidelines and protocols: Creating a methodology of emotion

Many of my participants discussed the responsibility they feel to tell stories appropriately, with their work being cautiously driven by the effort not to re-traumatise those involved with a project. I was interested to hear whether and, if so, how guidelines have been developed to safeguard against re-traumatising. It is curious to note that not one of the institutions I conducted interviews at has begun a process of writing down how to work with challenging subject matter. Whatever institutional protocols or guidelines exist, aside from institutionally specific interpretations of the *Task Force Report*, are really based on 'what to do' versus 'what not to do', which is often learned *in situ*. Commenting on this, Jill Baird, Curator of Education and Public Programmes at MOA, notes that

> That is a real failure ... we don't actually take the time. Instead we have an exhibition review process, someone externally to comment on the exhibition. It doesn't help us really; logistical things are captured ... [but] we don't have a vehicle to have those kinds of conversations.

156   Jennifer Claire Robinson

Almost all those I interviewed noted how little space is allocated to reflect on completed work and to take account of what worked successfully in terms of methods of practice. What was also clear from my interviews and gallery visits is that the protocols that are being captured in a somewhat more official capacity are culturally specific, and these guidelines are fundamentally shaping how some projects are being created. For example, prior to mounting an exhibit of artwork related to RIDSAR at the Legacy Art Gallery in downtown Victoria, the gallery was swept by Coast Salish Elders with cedar branches to cleanse the gallery space to host an exhibition of this nature. All of the RIDSAR work has been intricately guided by protocols put forth by Indigenous advisory members. These protocols include how to enter spaces and speak with elders in communities, as well as how best to look after people involved in the project: those sharing stories, those hearing stories, and those entering the space of the exhibition, including the staff. Robina Thomas (Qwul'sih'yah'maht), UVIC's current Director of Indigenous Academic and Community University Engagement, as well as Associate Professor of Social Work and a RIDSAR collaborator, shares the importance of Indigenous protocols (Thomas (Qwul'sih'yah'maht) 2015):

> [...] we had our own ethical guidelines but then we had cultural guidelines and ethics ... Part of our [Coast Salish] teachings are about witnessing, when you witness significant events it is your responsibility to remember. Those of us in that project have witnessed those stories, we are now responsible for remembering those stories, those places ... it is now our responsibility to remember that and carry it forward.

Well Indigenous knowledges related to better handling of material collections have been entering many museums in Canada steadily since the *Task Force Report*; the examples above are evidence of Indigenous protocols entering gallery spaces to better safeguard emotional experiences. Local Indigenous Elders are being consulted to ensure the *wellbeing of people* together in a space of emotionally challenging subject matter. This is a unique and defining feature of human rights museological work currently being developed in Canada. Protocols of emotion are directly linked to Indigenous knowledges. These protocols emphasise the need to take care of elders, who are numerous among the people who have experiences related to the three official apologies in Canada. Many participants working with Indigenous, Chinese and Japanese Canadians emphasised the importance of meeting people in person, especially elderly people, even if it means driving a distance for the visit to be in their home so that the conversation is as comfortable as it can be. It was also stressed that there is a need to respect when someone does not want to share their experiences, when silence is a protocol. As Curator Paul Lee from the CCMM reflects,

We have one veteran who will not talk about his experiences ... sometimes we go out for lunch ... and he will still not talk about his experiences ... Maybe something he experienced [was] so tragic he just doesn't want to talk about it.

Some of this care entails paying attention to the physical language of those involved in a project in order to read the body for signs of emotional distress. As Linda Kawamoto Reid from the Nikkei notes,

[...] when I started interviewing people, out of nowhere, though it is actually not out of nowhere, [some] people would become emotional and not be able to continue the interview .... I am very, very respectful for their experiences and I don't push it.

MOA Curator Bill McLennan shared a similar experience from his interviews with IRS survivors for a 2013 exhibition titled *Speaking to Memory: Images and Voices from St. Michael's Indian Residential School*:

[...] the worst things people said to me, those people decided they didn't want to put their interviews forward. They really appreciated that they got to speak it, and appreciated the fact that I transcribed it, but they don't want to release it.

In all my interviews, the need was stressed to always remember the hardships that people have gone through; to remember these stories are peoples' lives. As former Curator and Nikkei Director Beth Carter notes,

[...] just because there has been a formal apology doesn't mean there has been healing ... For museum staff, we are talking about these things every day ... We have to always stop and realise that this is real people, and this is real emotion, and real experiences, and painful experiences that people have gone through. We have a very important role in sharing those experiences and provide one way for people to process and move through those experiences.

In hearing these stories, some participants spoke with me, in part, about the need to take care of those sharing the stories but also those hearing the stories. This means recognising not only that these experiences are really challenging for some to share, but also that they are sometimes heart-wrenching to hear. There is a need for heritage professionals to also take care of themselves physically, emotionally and spiritually. As Thomas states,

My rule of thumb: always making decisions based on the relationships I create are lifelong relationships and then it makes you make decisions differently because you are making them with your heart, not always with your head. I think that this heart stuff, this emotional stuff, makes us engage differently. That being said, we always need to be really aware that we take care of this heart stuff. And you know when I teach I say to students all of the time, how are you taking care of yourself today? Go walk under that cedar tree, let it brush you off, let it take your negativity ... I am always really aware that we need to do that.

Some of these protocols or guidelines are essentially very basic but important 'check-ins' to see how people are feeling. Checking-in is part of how to take care of oneself and others during a project.

Comfortable with being uncomfortable

The emotional investment required by heritage professionals working with survivors of violence and cultural discrimination should fundamentally differ from the investment of care given to other curatorial projects. Given that the nature of the content is so emotionally charged, the potential for complication during the working partnership is greater. The possibility of failure could mean drawing further divides between communities of people, or, worse, re-traumatising those involved in a project. This fear of failure was expressed to me on a number of occasions, but what was also emphasised was the potential that comes from entering the space of the unknown or taking on practices that are uncomfortable. As Legacy Art Gallery Director Mary Jo Hughes remembers about first working with RIDSAR,

> [...] I just remember being on a conference call or something and something cracked and I saw a light come through and I was like, it is OK, she [Curator Andrea Walsh] knows what she is doing and it is OK to have the exhibition. Just follow the needs she outlines ... It was so much easier after that ... I just went, it is OK, we will just follow the needs and the exhibition will follow.

Some of this unknown space means having faith to follow the project and to let the work unfold without too much of a set agenda. Letting go of that control is a really challenging task, but it can lead to important transformative experiences. As Thomas stresses,

> [...] we have that word in our own language *'uy shkwaluwuns* 'to be of a good mind and a good heart'. In order for us to be of a good mind and a good heart in this project you have got to let the project do what the project does ... we follow the project, we are not leading the project ... What I am saying is that it is really up to the artists that painted these paintings

to guide us ... My role is to be as much of a support person as I can to the artists as their story unfolds.[4]

In summarising the potential of transformative learning, Regan (2005: 7) notes that 'transformative theory suggests that we do not learn solely or even primarily through reason or rationale, but also through our emotions, physical body, spiritual presence, and imagination'. In Canada, part of this transformation comes through an unsettling process, which involves acknowledging the colonial history in Canada that has left legacies of inequality and injustice (Regan 2010). Part of this transformation comes from emotionally challenging moments, from moments of crying with someone and holding their hand, to dancing and feasting at community events. It comes from moments of being comfortable with the possibility of becoming emotionally undone, that is, emotional vulnerability with those involved in a project. As Walsh states, 'I love that now, I am very comfortable with being uncomfortable ... This is exactly where I want to be ... I like that idea of figuring out how to do things better.'

Final thoughts

Given the intensity of the stories and experiences being shared, taking a step back to evaluate just how heritage work of this nature is being conducted seems an invaluable asset for the practice of future work, but also, more importantly, this critical reflection on the part of heritage professionals is part of acting responsibly and ethically in a working partnership. This reflection should not just be pragmatic, that is, solely accounting for the logistics of how stories are shared in conversation or designed into an exhibition. Rather, this critical reflection should take into account the relational foundation that has made the work possible. Strong relationships are essential in all forms of museological practice; however, they are fundamental when working with survivors of trauma and curating challenging subject matter in a good and respectful way. This chapter has shown how examples of this museum work in Canada are being guided by culturally specific protocols. Procedurally, however, outside of these protocols very little is written down to guide future work. Capturing these guidelines has the potential to help future projects not only in Canada, but also in other settler societies such as New Zealand, Australia and the USA, where processes of decolonialisation are actively taking place through museum spaces. Importantly, the outcome of this research also highlights how the space of uncertainty can be a fruitful place for exhibition work to grow. To work respectfully with emotionally challenging subject matter, it is necessary *'uy shkwaluwuns*, 'to be of a good mind and a good heart'; to be guided by the emotional, physical and spiritual needs of all those involved in a project.

160 Jennifer Claire Robinson

Acknowledgements

This research was funded by the University of Victoria and the Social Sciences and Humanities Research Council of Canada. I am grateful to my supervisor Dr Andrea Walsh for her ongoing guidance and support and to my good friend and colleague John Alexander Pysklywec for his thoughts on this chapter. I thank the editors of this volume for their most helpful feedback and for the opportunity to contribute to this volume.

Notes

1 I have adopted the term 'heritage professionals' to be more inclusive of those I interviewed who are not actually employees of the institutions I visited but who have collaborated in a curatorial capacity. My participants included academics, local historians, community elders and activists, as well as curators, designers, directors and programmers.
2 There have been several apologies in Canada at the federal, provincial and municipal level of government for historical wrongdoings; however, to date these three are the only apologies to have been delivered in the House of Commons.
3 The IRS Settlement Agreement of 8 May 2006 established the Truth and Reconciliation Commission (TRC) of Canada to document the experiences of IRS by survivors and their families, as well as to record and research the histories of the schools through church and state archives (Indian Residential Schools 2006; Regan 2010; TRC 2015). The public face of this commission has largely been survivor statements at TRC regional and national events and hearings.
4 The term *'uy shkwaluwuns* is from the Hul'qumi'num dialect of the Coast Salish language. The term can mean both 'being of a good mind and heart' and 'being of a good mind and spirit' (Robina Thomas (Qwul'sih'yah'maht), personal communication, 15 August 2016).

References

Ames, M., 1992. *Cannibal Tours and Glass Boxes the Anthropology of Museums*. Vancouver: UBC Press.
Ames, M., 2003. How to decorate a house: The renegotiation of cultural representations at the University of British Columbia Museum of Anthropology. In L. Peers and A. Brown, eds. *Museums and Source Communities: A Routledge Reader*. London: Routledge, 171–180.
Assembly of First Nations and Canadian Museum Association, 1992. *Turning the Page: Forging New Partnerships between Museums and First Peoples*. Ottawa: Assembly of First Nations and Canadian Museums Association.
Campbell, S., 2014. *Our Faithfulness to the Past: The Ethics and Politics of Memory*. Oxford: Oxford University Press.
Carter, J., 2013. Human rights museums and pedagogies of practice: The Museo de la Memoria y los Derechos Humanos. *Museum Management and Curatorship*, 28(3), 324–341.

Carter, J. and Orange, J., 2012. Contentious terrain: Defining a human rights museology. *Museum Management and Curatorship*, 27(2), 111–127.

Conaty, G., 2006. Glenbow Museum and first nations: Fifteen years of negotiating change. *Museum Management and Curatorship*, 21(3), 254–256.

Conaty, G., 2008. The effects of repatriation on the relationship between the Glenbow Museum and the Blackfoot people. *Museum Management and Curatorship*, 23(3), 245–259.

Conaty, G. and Carter, B., 2005. Our story in our words: Diversity and equality in the Glenbow Museum. In G. Conaty and R. Janes, eds. *Looking Reality in the Eye: Museums and Social Responsibility*. Calgary: University of Calgary Press, 43–58.

Edwards, E., 2001. *Raw Histories: Photographs, Anthropology and Museums*. Oxford: Berg.

Edwards, E., 2005. Photographs and the sound of history. *Visual Anthropology Review*, 21(1–2): 27–46.

Gregory, K. and Witcomb, A., 2007. Beyond nostalgia: The role of affect in generating historical understanding at heritage sites. In S. Knell, S. MacLeod and S. Watson, eds. *Museum Revolutions: Museums and Change*. London: Routledge, 263–275.

Heathorn, S. and Goutor, D., eds. 2013. *Taking Liberties: A History of Human Rights in Canada*. Don Mills: Oxford University Press.

Henderson, J. and Wakeham, P., eds., 2013. *Reconciling Canada: Critical Perspectives on the Culture of Redress*. Toronto: University of Toronto Press.

Indian Residential Schools, 2006. *Indian Residential Schools Settlement*. Available from www.residentialschoolsettlement.ca/settlement.html [Accessed 1 March 2016].

Janes, R. R., 2014. Interview with J. Robinson on 5 December 2014, Canmore [Recording in possession of author].

Janes, R. R., 2015. *Museums without Borders: Selected Writings of Robert R. Janes*. London: Routledge.

Langford, M., 2001. *Suspended Conversations: The Afterlife of Memory in Photographic Albums*. Montreal: McGill-Queen's University Press.

Lehrer, E. and Milton, C., 2011. Introduction: Witnesses to witnessing. In E. Lehrer, C. Milton, and M. Patterson, eds. *Curating Difficult Knowledge Violent Pasts in Public Places*. New York: Palgrave Macmillan, 1–19.

Melton, A., 2013. Comfort and connectivity: The museum as a healer. *Museums & Social Issues*, 8(1–2), 6–21.

Miron, J., 2009. *A History of Human Rights in Canada: Essential Issues*. Toronto: Canadian Scholars' Press.

Munro, E., 2013. 'People just need to feel important, like someone is listening': Recognizing museums, community engagement programmes as spaces of care. *Geoforum*, 48, 54–62.

Munro, E., 2014. Doing emotion work in museums: Reconceptualising the role of community engagement practitioners. *Museum & Society*, 12(1), 44–60.

Orange, J. and Carter, J., 2012. It's time to pause and reflect: Museums and human rights. *Curator: The Museum Journal*, 55(3), 259–266.

Phillips, R., 2011. *Museum Pieces: Towards the Indigenization of Canadian Museums*. Montreal: McGill-Queen's University Press.

Pinto, M., 2013. Pamela Masik and the forgotten exhibition: Controversy and cancellation at the museum of anthropology. *Museum Anthropology*, 36(1), 4–17.

Regan, P., 2005. A transformative framework for decolonizing Canada: A non-Indigenous approach, Paper presented at the IGOV Doctoral Symposium, 20 January 2005.

Regan, P., 2010. *Unsettling the Settler Within: Indian Residential Schools, Truth Telling, and Reconciliation in Canada.* Vancouver: UBC Press.

Schatzki, T., 1996. *Social Practices: A Wittgensteinian Approach to Human Activity and the Social.* Cambridge: University of Cambridge Press.

Schmidt, J., 2014. Interview with J. Robinson on 3 December 2014, Calgary [Recording in possession of author].

Silverman, R., ed., 2015. *Museum as Process: Translating Local and Global Knowledges.* New York: Routledge.

Simon, R., 2014. *A Pedagogy of Witnessing: Curatorial Practice and the Pursuit of Social Justice.* Albany: SUNY Press.

Smith, L., 2010. Ethics or social justice? Heritage and the politics of recognition. *Australian Aboriginal Studies*, (2), 60–68.

Smith, L., 2011. Affect and registers of engagement: Navigating emotional responses to dissonant heritage. In L. Smith, G. Cubitt, R. Wilson and K. Fouseki, eds., *Representing Enslavement and Abolition in Museums: Ambiguous Engagements.* London: Routledge, 260–303.

Smith, L. and Campbell, G., 2016. The elephant in the room: Heritage, affect and emotion. In W. Logan, M. Nic Craith and U. Kockel, eds. *A Companion to Heritage Studies.* Oxford: Wiley Blackwell, 443–460

The Truth and Reconciliation Commission of Canada, 2015. *Honouring the Truth: Reconciling for the Future. Summary of the Final Report of the Truth and Reconciliation Commission of Canada.* Toronto: Lorimer.

Thomas, R. (Qwul'sih'yah'maht), 2015. Interview with J. Robinson on 12 March 2015, Victoria [Recording in possession of author].

Walsh, A., ed., 2005. *Nk'Mip Chronicles: Art from the Inkameep Day School.* Oliver: Osoyoos Indian Band.

Wetherell, M., 2012. *Affect and Emotion: A New Social Science Understanding.* London: Sage.

Wilson, R., 2011. The curatorial complex: Marking the bicentenary of the abolition of the slave trade. In L. Smith, G. Cubitt, R. Wilson and K. Fouseki, eds. *Representing Enslavement and Abolition in Museums: Ambiguous Engagements.* London: Routledge, 131–146.

Witcomb, A., 2013. Understanding the role of affect in producing a critical pedagogy for history museums. *Museum Management and Curatorship*, 28(3), 255–271.

Chapter 10

Touring the post-conflict city
Negotiating affects during Belfast's black cab mural tours

Katie Markham

> If the role of political tourism is developed, what will the additional experience be? Will the tourist experience mock kneecappings – maybe even the recorded screams of the supposed victims? What about the dummy bomb runs? What about the political beatings – hurley sticks provided? Even more ghoulish, what about the activities of the IRA's infamous nutting squad? With a bit of blindfolding and torture, the tourist could relive the experience of the terror victim.
>
> Robin Newton MLA, *Hansard* 2008

Introduction

Railing against a recent surge of interest in Northern Ireland's conflict, which in 2007 accounted for 9% of Belfast's visitors (*Belfast Tourism Monitor* 2007), Robin Newton's inflammatory response to a 2008 Assembly debate that focused on the growth of political tourism in the city was neither unexpected nor out of keeping with other Unionist sentiments on the subject. Responding to Sinn Fein's request for formal investment in the sector, the perspective of Newton and other DUP MLAs was that so-called 'political', 'terror' (*Hansard* 2008) or 'troubles' tourism (*Cultural Tourism Strategy* 2006) 'confuse[d] the political process [...] present[ing] a biased and prejudiced approach to the events of the past' (Newton, *Hansard* 2008). The debate, catalysed by a favourable review of West Belfast's murals in the *Independent* (Calder 2007), quickly degenerated into a sectarian squabble over which party had the most to gain from this form of tourism, with the result that the amendment for further investment in the sector was ultimately tabled (*Hansard* 2008). And yet, in spite of its treatment within parliament, the popularity of Troubles tourism, which, as this essay will discuss, is largely concentrated around tours of Belfast's murals, has yet to decline, with more people visiting areas associated with the conflict in 2014 than the capital's own state-approved Ulster Museum (*Belfast Tourism Monitor* 2014).

Newton's underlying suggestion, that adding tourism to the already-contested arena of conflict heritage risks perpetuating political violence, is an opinion shared by many other academics working on Troubles tourism in Northern Ireland. Unequivocal in her rejection of mural tours in particular, Sara McDowell (2008: 408) summarises the entire industry as a 'spatial practice' that 'reinforces territorial politics' and 'transforms the conflict into a war by other means'. Particularly critical of the monopoly which ex-prisoners and paramilitaries seem to have on the trade, McDowell articulates Newton's fear that 'agents within local communities such as community or ex-prisoner groups see the landscape as a political tool through which they can vie for external support or sympathy', concluding that through this mechanism 'Republican and Loyalist symbolic landscapes can be sold as Republican places or Loyalist places' (McDowell 2008: 406–407).

McDowell's concerns about the way in which tourist 'sympathies' intersect with divergent political agendas during these tours are echoed by other academics and a range of community groups, who see the choice of routes and narratives on offer as an extension and re-assertion of Belfast's sectarian landscape. Madeleine Leonard (2011: 123), who analyses concepts of 'authenticity' in relation to the tours, remains cautious about exhorting its positives, noting that 'tourism can also strengthen political and ethno-sectarian identities', whilst Wendy Ann Wiedenhoft-Murphy (2010: 555) declares that 'the expansion of tourism in Northern Ireland fundamentally [....] enables the reproduction of symbolic violence, particularly through the process of territoriality'.

Notable across these accounts is the authors' shared preoccupation with the characteristic proximity of the tour guides to the conflict itself. Part of the perceived problem with mural tourism in West Belfast is, as McDowell highlights, that apart from the City Bus tours, which have been in operation since 1995 (Thompson 1999), and the occasional package coach trip, tourist encounters with Belfast's murals are generally mediated through localised perspectives, either whilst taking part in the walking tours organised by Republican and Loyalist ex-prisoner groups, or whilst on one of the avuncular 'black cab' taxi tours of the area. In the case of the latter two options, tour guides are not only likely to have grown up in the local ethno-national community, and possibly participated in paramilitary activity, but they are also, as Jonathan Skinner (2015: 3) notes, disarmingly charismatic, which runs contrary to most visitors' expectations of how ex-militants should behave. It is this charisma which McDowell and others appear to have in mind when accusing tour guides of 'compet[ing] for the attentions and sympathies of the tourist', in order to 're-presen[t] and transmit[t] a selective past to an external audience' (McDowell 2008: 414–415). And yet, in spite of the obvious impact that guides' interpersonal relationships with tourists have on their first-time experiences of West Belfast, very few of those who criticise the tours actually engage with this element. As Sharon Pickering (2001: 485) notes, in the quagmire of socio-political debate around the Troubles, room is rarely made for discussion of the 'softer', more speculative aspects of the conflict, such as the emotional, the affective or the interpersonal, as work on emotions and 'emotionality' is 'systematically excluded in most academic work in Northern Ireland'.

By addressing the affective gap in conceptualisations of post-conflict heritage in Northern Ireland, this essay aims to situate Wetherell's (2012) concept of 'affective practice' alongside Sara Ahmed's (2004) work on 'affective economies' in order to discuss the intersection of affect and emotion that shapes mural tour guides and their communities in West Belfast. Placing these discussions in the context of work done elsewhere on emotionality in contested, or difficult, heritage (Ballantyne and Uzzell 1993; Landsberg 2004; Bonnell and Simon 2007; Simon 2011; Smith 2011; Arnold-de Simine 2013; Dowler 2013), this chapter argues that the uniquely spatial nature of emotion during these tours requires an alternative model of affect, distinct from practice or economy, that I term 'affective synecdoche'. Insofar as affective synecdoche is a working concept, specific to observations about the black cab mural industry in Belfast, this essay should be considered a position piece, designed to provoke further questions about how as researchers we develop and apply particular theoretical frameworks to work on conflict heritage.

Methodology

The findings for this research are the result of a series of trips made to Belfast between September 2014 and February 2016, during which time I participated in 12 cab tours of West Belfast's murals, both as an individual and as part of a group, and conducted 10 semi-structured interviews with black cab tour guides. These participants were drawn from seven private tour companies, all of which advertised their services in the Visit Belfast Welcome Centre and had received consistently high reviews from local hotels and review sites such as *TripAdvisor*. Of these companies, only one is explicitly rooted in a contemporary Nationalist perspective, and beyond this the majority of companies employ a mixture of Republican/Nationalist, Loyalist/Unionist, Protestant/Catholic drivers. Amongst the most successful black cab companies there tends to be a culture of sharing their best drivers (jauntily referred to as 'tour whores') during the peak seasons and as a result, many of the guides I interviewed worked across several of my chosen companies. As suggested by the 2008 Assembly debate, although undertaken by representatives on both sides, the urge to espouse community narratives to a wider public is strongest amongst Nationalists in Northern Ireland (Jarman 2005 [1997]; Graham 1998; Graham and Whelan 2007), with the result that those from a Republican/Nationalist/Catholic background tend to outnumber those from Loyalist/Unionist/Protestant ones. In terms of my own participants, of the 10 interviewed, three identified as being from a broadly Unionist background (with varying degrees of paramilitary involvement), four counted themselves as Republicans, two were from mixed backgrounds (a mixture of Catholic, Protestant and British army), and one was not native to Ireland at all, but since moving to Belfast had aligned himself with Nationalist interests.

The decision to focus solely on those tours being run by black cab companies was a strategic one, given my early interests in tracing emotionality and affect within the industry. On a pragmatic level, it soon became evident that, although previous research on mural tourism has tended to focus on the more controversial Republican (Coiste) or Loyalist (EPIC) ex-prisoner walking tours (McDowell 2008; Leonard 2011; Dowler 2013; Skinner 2015), the sheer number of black cab tour companies in operation, combined with their ability to be more flexible in terms of pick-up points and times, meant that the majority of tourists actively seeking engagement with the Troubles (as opposed to seeing the murals as part of a generic city bus tour) were more likely to come to West Belfast by taxi than on foot. Although precise figures for those taking part in cab tours of West Belfast are hard to come by (a result of Belfast council's tacit boycott of the 'Troubles tourism' industry), one of the major companies has recently started maintaining logs of its activities. With records from this company indicating that 2,000 tours were processed during one peak season month in 2015 (which, if extrapolated across the year, accounts for 27% of the council's overall figure for those going to Troubles-related areas), there is reason to believe that the black cab mural industry has considerably outgrown council and tourist board estimates.

On an epistemic level, mural tours that are undertaken in a black cab are significantly different from the walking tours so heavily criticised by McDowell and others, in that, unlike their antecedents, which tend to stay based in either the Nationalist or the Unionist side of West Belfast, black cab tours explicitly bridge the ethno-cultural divide, starting in one community before crossing the peace wall and going into the heart of the 'other' community for the conclusion of the tour. For the purposes of thinking about the affective shifts and negotiations that can occur during a tour, I have identified this act of crossing as the methodological key for assessing how clashes of memory, culture and emotion are translated into the briefly held affective moment, a moment which can be partially unpacked through the notion of affective practice.

Affective practice and the 'ordinary flows' of sectarianism

'Affective practice', writes Margaret Wetherell, is a concept long overdue within academia. Critiquing affect's over-theorisation within the academy, Wetherell (2012: 4) observes that the relationship between affect and qualitative fieldwork is complex, as 'the turn to affect in social research currently struggles to deliver a way of working that is consistently productive and generative'. Particularly critical of post-structuralist philosophers such as Massumi and Deleuze, whose work, she argues, has created a radical disconnect between affect,

Touring the post-conflict city 167

emotion and the intricacies of social reality, Wetherell (2012: 77) advocates for a return to affect that is located in discourse, embodiment and 'the flow of ordinary life'. Offering burgeoning social researchers what she modestly calls a 'portmanteau' (Wetherell 2012: 96) approach, affective practice is thus outlined by Wetherell as a tracing of 'embodied meaning making' and recognition of the social dynamics of 'activity, flow, assemblage and relationality' (Wetherell 2012: 4). Using this approach as a method for exploring the 'emotional as it appears in social life', Wetherell (2012: 4) suggests that affective practice seeks 'shifting, flexible and often over-determined figurations rather than simple lines of causation, character types and neat emotion categories'.

This pragmatic approach to affect and emotionality has deep resonances for academic understandings of the 'ordinary flows' that are present within West Belfast, and which often intrude onto mural tours. Too often, as Debbie Lisle (2006: 29) has noted, academic writing on Belfast's murals has been overly driven by a 'two-communities thesis', which fundamentally denies the 'complex and competing networks that function throughout the urban landscape of Belfast', effectively precluding engagement with the myriad other 'social cleavages' such as race, gender and class which have always acted in tandem upon the city's sectarian landscape. Just as academic work on the socio-cultural experiences of living in these urban spaces has tended to fall into this bicultural paradigm, so too has work on conflict commemoration, with understandable concerns about ethno-national bias at certain museums, memorials or murals often occluding the effects that a quietly changing demographic in the area has on the readings and experiences of these places and events (Crooke 2007; Flynn 2011; McGrattan 2014; Braniff, McDowell and Murphy 2015). Using affective practice to trace the varying emotional and discursive confluences which are built into mural tours therefore becomes a way of disrupting these 'simple lines of causation' (Wetherell 2012: 4), whilst offering a more nuanced, theoretically charged way of exploring the phenomena of Troubles tourism. However, it is also necessary to recognise that, in spite of the changing nature of sectarianism in Belfast, many communities, particularly those defined as 'interface', are still held hostage to a familiar repertoire of emotions (such as hate, fear, suspicion) that supports the bilateral thesis, and which themselves require their own affective unpacking.[1] In order to address mural tourism as a simultaneously bilateral and multiplicitous phenomenon, I argue it is useful to consider Sara Ahmed's (2004) conceptualisation of the boundary-making work done by affect, which she explores through her nominalisation of affect-as-economy.

Surprisingly, Wetherell (2012: 159) is somewhat suspicious of Ahmed's work on affective economies, suggesting that it contains a 'quite narrow [...] almost completely disembodied account' that 'completely miss[es] the situated domain of daily life'. Part of Wetherell's dissatisfaction with Ahmed's foray into the affective mechanics of culture, economics and politics is, as she indicates, that the latter's 'seamless' movement 'across a number of affective–discursive domains' makes the concept vulnerable to 'transposition errors', particularly when these ideas are translated into the practicalities of social research (Wetherell 2012: 159). Nevertheless, in spite of Wetherell's (2012: 159) suggestion that 'affective economies' are better suited for textual analysis than quotidian, situated affects, it is my contention that this particular framework has powerful resonances for contemporary discussions about the intersections between tourist cultures and everyday emotionality in West Belfast. Therefore, within my own work on affective synecdoche, I use Ahmed's concept of an economy to access the kind of situated, social paradigms that Wetherell agitates for in her discussion of affective practice, in order to provide a more nuanced account of the social and emotional relations that shape stakeholder experiences of these tours.

The emotional economies of West Belfast

Emotions, writes Sara Ahmed (2004: 121), are not individually experienced or discrete phenomena, but should be understood as products of a bio-economic model of affect, which distinguishes itself through the over-accumulation and displacement of emotion onto certain individuals and societal groupings. Like Wetherell, Ahmed's interest in affect lies in its intersection with the material and the social; however, unlike Wetherell, these variables are not the starting point for understanding emotion, but are themselves products of affect's circulation in the socio-political economy. Like all efficient economies, Ahmed declares the displacement of affect to be hegemonic, as it is 'stuck' (through discourse, media and politics) to certain bodies and communities in ways that create visible indices of difference (Ahmed 2004: 118). Within Ahmed's schemata, emotions therefore 'work as a form of capital' that, heightened by these affective circulations, begins to 'shape the surfaces of bodies and worlds' (Ahmed 2004: 119–121.).

Like Wetherell, Ahmed is concerned with the power dynamics governing affect. However, whereas Wetherell's reading of affect is deeply invested in the social conditions of power's production, Ahmed is particularly attentive to the ways in which culture and representation predetermine such conditions and relations in the first place. Within the context of interface spaces in Northern Ireland, which are differentiated by discourses of 'culture' that have traditionally been mediated through violent social encounter, it is my argument that a theory that incorporates both Wetherell's and Ahmed's approaches to affect is necessary in order to fully appreciate the socio-political impacts of tourism on West Belfast.

Research conducted by Peter Shirlow and Brendan Murtagh (2006) exploring the lived realities of interface communities across Belfast indicates that, in line with Ahmed's declaration that the material is symptomatic of the emotional, the separations between Catholic and Protestant communities in Belfast are determined less by physical walls than by a series of psycho-social geographies that determine people's patterns of living in these areas. Using in-depth surveys to trace the daily habits and interactions of those living in divided communities across Belfast, Shirlow and Murtagh paint a picture of a 'post'-conflict city in which ethno-sectarian antagonisms are on the rise, and fear continues to be a dominant factor in the structuring of people's social lives. Revealing that 58.9% of their respondents were afraid of crossing the peace walls that separate Catholic and Protestant domiciliaries, and an additional 78% actively avoided using public services which might take them into the other's community, Shirlow and Murtagh (2006: 85–86) ultimately conclude that, in the light of decreased paramilitary activities since the Good Friday Agreement, it is not physical violence that precludes Nationalist and Unionists from co-habiting, but the circulation of fearful 'emotional landscapes' (Shirlow and Murtagh 2006: 84).

Viewing these emotional landscapes as the product of affective economies (an anticipation, rather than direct experience of violence), whilst useful, does not by itself account for why some figures, such as tourists and non-residents in Belfast, are able to traverse these physical and psychic barriers, without apparent fear. Indeed, so popular has West Belfast become as a tourist destination that these days it is not uncommon to see rogue flocks of tourists casually crossing the gateways between the communities, as many choose to take themselves on self-directed tours of the Shankill and Falls Roads. Ahmed again has an explanation for this phenomenon. Detailing the concept of 'stickiness', Ahmed (2004: 118) notes that, within the affective economy, circulation of affect is not always evenly distributed, with some bodies becoming more value-laden than others. For Ahmed, those (usually queer, racialised or gendered) bodies already vulnerable to the accumulation of negative affects become 'sticky' as they enter into a cycle of aggregation whereby they cannot shift these negative valuations, ultimately resulting in ostracisation from wider society (Ahmed 2004: 119).

Within West Belfast and other, similar interface areas, the role of stickiness in upholding segregation is fairly evident. Now the stuff of on-tour 'craic', as drivers exchange jokes with tourists about how to distinguish Catholics and Protestants ('Catholics have big ears, Protestants have a big nose. I'm both, so I've got a big willy!' [Tour Guide 5]), at the height of the Troubles, such physiognomic details (alongside clothing choice and linguistic inflections) held serious mythological sway over the reading of an individual's political or religious affiliation (Barritt and Carter 1962; Burton 1978; Milroy 1981; Harris 1972). So ingrained are these physical misnomers in contemporary cultural narratives of difference in Belfast that all the tour guides I interviewed spoke of the initial fear of being (mis)recognised ('crossing the political divide at the start I was nervous. Very nervous' [Tour Guide 3]) when they first started doing these tours, as though their allegiances were indeed written on the body. In contrast tourists, made conspicuous by the tell-tale cameras around their neck, or wide-eyed stares at the murals in front of them, are usually excluded

170   Katie Markham

from these particular physiognomic readings, and consequently tend to be sheltered from some of their more pernicious effects. This is not to say, however, that tourists on black cab mural tours in West Belfast are completely immune from sectarianism's emotional and affective turns. In fact, as this chapter will now explore, the affective economies of West Belfast tend to take centre-stage during the average mural tour in ways which, when explored through the concept of synecdoche, offer a radically different understanding of the area's emotional topography.

Problematising the economy: Affective synecdoche and black cab tours

Affective synecdoche, in its broadest form, is the process through which the affects attendant, or 'stuck', on certain bodies begin to speak *to* other bodies and self-reflexively *of* the sticking process. Inspired by Ahmed's relativist approach to affect, but underpinned by Wetherell's pragmatic focus, affective synecdoche also borrows from Michel de Certeau's (2011) definition of synecdoche as a cartographic element, which he describes in *The Practice of Everyday Life*:

> Synecdoche expands a spatial element in order to make it play the role of a 'more' [...] Synecdoche makes more dense: it amplifies the detail and miniaturizes the whole.
>
> (de Certeau 2011: 101)

Re-centering the individual, the banal and the quotidian in his analysis of urban geographies, de Certeau deploys synecdoche to describe the anarchic potential of individual experiences of the city. As a 'walking rhetoric' (de Certeau 2011: 100), synecdoche is characterised by de Certeau as the replacement of 'totalities with fragments', and a contusion of space and place into 'enlarged singularities and separate islands' (de Certeau 2011: 101). Understanding synecdoche as a splintering device, which separates and camouflages the connections between parts, is perhaps useful when trying to articulate the fractured geographies that have been created through sectarianism in Northern Ireland (Boal 19691967; Shirlow 2003; Shirlow 2006). However, as noted by social psychologist Cameron Duff (2010: 881), de Certeau's extended metaphors for place building, which focus on the 'doing' or 'making' of place, are less useful when one is trying to consider the experiential, affective dimensions of living in that place, and as a concept de Certeau's synecdoche almost certainly reinforces the bicultural paradigms that Lisle and this paper are trying to avoid. However, by thinking about synecdoche as a spatial experience that is mobilised by affect, I argue that we can simultaneously resist these binaries whilst beginning to unpick the raw complexity of feelings that shape the contours of West Belfast. Approaching emotionality in mural tourism through the framing of affect as synecdoche, rather than practice or economy, is also a more approximate representation of the role that space plays in catalysing emotion during these tours, and throughout interface communities in Belfast.

Indeed, in spite of persistent myths around the reading of Catholic and Protestant bodies (Feldman 1991; Finlay 2001; Kelleher 2003: 72), the most 'sticky' of sectarianism's qualities is not physiognomic, but spatial. As Shirlow and Murtagh's (2006) study already indicates, it is not so much fear of other bodies that prevents sectarian communities from effectively integrating as fear of the space that those bodies inhabit. Brian Graham (1998: 130) notes that around interface communities the dogma that 'landscapes embody discourses of inclusion and exclusion' in Belfast has proven hard to shift. These evaluations of the spatial politics that govern individual movements across interface areas stand in stark contrast to the metropolis of Belfast's city centre, where Catholics, Protestants, Unionists and Nationalists are not only present, but affably mixed (Boal 1982; Neill 2006; Nagle 2009; Hocking 2015). As Sara McDowell and Catherine Switzer's (2009: 350) review of memorialisation in the city centre indicates, commemoration of Northern Ireland's conflict is conspicuously absent in the heart of the city, which they suggest is part of an effort to maintain its appearance as a conflict-free, neutral space. The coexistence of an antonymic space just on the periphery of this new metropolis is therefore a significant source of curiosity for those visitors whose early encounters with Northern Ireland were conveyed by media coverage of bullets, bombs and riots. As such, for the general tourist population, mural tours in West Belfast are a legitimate, convenient and 'safe' way of exploring those areas made famous by this history (Jarman 2005: 182).

The typical route taken by a black cab tour is the product of a continual negotiation between West Belfast's ever-changing landscape, the political energies of the guides and the whims of the clients in the car. However, as a general rule tours start either in the Loyalist Lower Shankill Estate or in the Republican Divis Tower blocks, where a backstory to the Troubles is woven that, depending on the narrative's orientation, either stretches back to Ireland's colonisation in the sixteenth century or begins with the 1690 Battle of the Boyne. After using murals as 'stepping stones' (Tour Guide 2) for explaining the socio-cultural history of the community being introduced, drivers then take visitors to the site of Belfast's longest peace wall on Cupar Way, where they are offered the opportunity to inscribe their signatures in the concrete, alongside the likes of Justin Bieber and Bill Clinton. After admiring this particular megalith, tourists then cross over to the 'other' community, where their itinerary may include stops at Bombay Street Memorial Garden, the Crumlin Road Courthouse or the 'International Wall' on Divis Road. Contrary to Wiedenhoft-Murphy's (2011: 547) suggestion that standard practice across the tours discourages visitors from leaving their cabs at these stops, only one of the 12 tours I took part in conformed to this agenda, and that was at my own request, on a rainy day. In fact, the act of leaving the vehicle and walking around the sites and communities being addressed is an essential feature of many black cab tours, and many of my participants were scornful of those less official companies and city bus tours, which they believed prevented visitors from doing this. Allowing tourists to leave the taxi at will and walk around the mural sites is an important feature of the tour for many drivers, who see the interactions which visitors have with the local landscape as being what makes their tours different and more 'real' (Tour Guide 1) for their participants. Part of that 'realness', I argue, and a factor which is also the source of Robin Newton's anxiety about the industry, is that, by inviting paying customers to immerse themselves in the geography of the area, they become indirect and sometimes disruptive participants in the emotional landscapes they are paying to see, thereby unsettling the traditional imaginings of West Belfast as a biculturally affected place which have long served sectarian politics.

One of the ways in which tourists become disruptive on these tours is through their informal occupation as ethnographers of the interactions between guides and members of the local communities (Widenhoft-Murphy 2010: 548; Leonard 2011: 120; Skinner 2015: 11). As Neil Jarman (2005: 182) has already suggested, the tradition of entering interface areas in order to view the murals is usually pursued by those who, drawn in by the 'seductive effect' of media coverage of the conflict, tend to represent a more knowledgeable demographic than the average consumer. The council's acknowledgement that 32% of Belfast's visitors are motivated by post-ceasefire 'curiosity' supports this thesis (*Belfast Tourism Monitor* 2007), suggesting that whether in a cab, on foot or mediated through the glass plate of a bus window, many mural tourists are attuned to the religious and cultural divides in Belfast. Thus, it is a reasonable assumption that those on black cab tours will be particularly alert to signs of hostility between their guide and the local community, who, despite being dogged by accusations of perpetuating 'terror' tourism (*Hansard* 2008), remain explicit about their desire to impart a 'positive' (Tour Guide 7) 'post-conflict' narrative to their tourists. What distinguishes interactions on black cab tours from the other forms of Troubles tourism is that, unlike the walks organised by Coiste or EPIC, where guides transfer the tour to someone from the 'other side' when they reach the peace wall (Skinner 2015: 5), the same guide delivers the entire black cab experience, guaranteeing that at some point they will enter territory which may be unfamiliar, and possibly hostile to their presence. In terms of wading through the affects that circulate in West Belfast, this means that guides on black cab tours must internalise the emotional shifts that occur as they cross the invisible boundaries between communities, all the while engaging in congenialities with locals under the watchful eye of the tourist. This ability not just to engage with those from the 'opposing' community, but also to maintain an affable exterior in the face of inquisitorial tourists is explored in an anecdote from an interview with Tour Guide 1, who identified as a Republican, and who had been running his own tour company since 2010:

Actually, there's a guy over on the Shankill road and he's stopped me a few times. And he's a typical Belfast character – wee small man, always walks a dog – and for some reason he has, since the first time he saw me, assumed I was a Protestant from a Protestant neighbourhood not far from his. And he says to me 'Alright John?' [...] and I just say 'Are you alright?' And he asked me this guy's name – he says 'What about Billy Bloggs – is he still living up beside you there?' And rather than go through the whole conversation and tell him he's got the wrong person I say 'Oh he's doing fine, I'll tell him you were asking', and he says 'Just tell him Joe's asking' and I'll say 'Okay Joe, I'll tell him.' And every time I've been on the Shankill Road, this guy has come up with the dog and stopped and he'll start talking to the guests too and telling them stories.

So we were standing at this mural one day [...] And this old hand as we say comes up with the dog and he stands there as we are standing by the Billy McCullough mural, and Joe started talking to me and the guests and he started telling me about him and some of the funny stories of the things he did [...] I thought it was brilliant that a local had told me that. And it learned me to listen to other people [...] But that wee guy Joe I'll have to thank him for that because he has given me another narrative in a sense to tell a local person.

What sticks out in this interview is not so much the reported details of the guide's conversation with this local, which after all rests on the kind of 'after-the-event' 'heroic' narrative that Wetherell suggests limits understandings of 'situated affect' (Wetherell 2012: 96), but the series of affective moments that are built into this exchange, which are ripe with 'over-determined figurations' (Wetherell 2012: 4) discernible only through spatial understandings of affect. Indeed, whilst readable across both Ahmed's and Wetherell's analogies, the insertion of the witnessing tourist into this moment makes the incorporated affects resistant to traditional discursive and economic interpretations, and it is this moment, and others like it across mural tours, which I suggest should be read through the framework of affective synecdoche.

Present in my participant's encounter with 'Joe' is precisely the kind of spatialised deconstructive work that affective synecdoche aims to capture. Occupying a space where 'ordinary flows' (Wetherell 2012: 77) clashed with his self-stylisation as a Republican, in the presence of a tour group the guide was forced to negate affective stickiness and assume the role of someone who was familiar with, and comfortable within, the Shankill. Contrary to Lisle's (2006: 45) assertions that 'each company is affiliated with a specific community', the majority of taxi tour companies hire a variety of guides from across the communities in Belfast, in order to be able to market themselves as genuinely non-biased to the hotels advertising them. In the same spirit of neutrality, most guides also withhold details of their own political allegiance from clients until the conclusion of the tour, whereby the opportunity to guess 'which side' of the divide they grew up on becomes a means of assessing the impact of their own bias on the tour's narrative. As a result, moments like the one described above make the tourist central to the creation of synecdochal affects as, in order to uphold their commitment to neutrality, guides must present themselves as representatives of both communities, becoming inadvertently responsible for circulating emotional and affective economies on both sides.

As the above interview extract demonstrates, in order to maintain the affective circulations across Belfast's interfaces, the driver not only downplayed his personal discomfit, but was obliged to engage in an active performance of belonging whilst in the Shankill. Affective synecdoche thus works on simultaneous levels in this moment. On the one hand affective stickiness, which circulates through the reading of bodily signs, but is dependent on being presented with a readable body in the first place (Ahmed 2004: 120), is devalued the instant the driver publicly negates his Republicanism in front of the tour group. Synecdochal fragmentation and occlusion then takes place, as the guide engages in a hyperbolic performance of localism, which is both shaped by, and conceals, his own discomfit. The presence of an audience in this moment solidifies these ontological entanglements, as the repetition of this performance over a series of tours eventually translates into a real engagement with the affective terms and economies of 'Joe' and the wider Shankill community through which, by his own admission, the guide 'learned [...] to listen to other people'. On the other hand, the fact that this encounter also yielded narrative material for other tours further justifies the framing of this moment through affective synecdoche as tourists, clearly involved in the remaking of West Belfast's affective economy, become participants in, as well as witnesses to, these new emotional narratives.

Indeed, so familiar have tourists become within West Belfast's landscape that in recent years a number of incidents involving mural tourists have made headlines, suggesting that, far from being platonic observers of post-Troubles culture, visitors are gradually being 'stuck' with the kinds of affects and emotions usually reserved for interface locals. In a wry confirmation of Robin Newton's fears that the development of political tourism would lead to 'ghoulish' re-enactments of Troubles-style violence, in August 2016, a private-hire bus containing Chinese tourists was pelted with stones as it travelled down the Falls Road (BBC 2016). Although this story was picked up by national media, other previously under-reported incidents involving the violent targeting of tourists in West Belfast have featured in local news over the past decade, again suggesting that emotional experiences of conflict heritage in Northern Ireland are far less bicultural than had previously been believed (McDonald 2007; BBC 2008; Hughes 2014). It should also come as no surprise that, given sectarianism's propensity to direct aggressive acts towards obvious 'others', there is a tendency amongst anti-tourist stakeholders to re-imagine these unwanted figures as East Asian, signified in descriptions of 'Japanese tourists [...] clicking through your front window' (interview, Lower Community Worker). Whilst buoyed by a general culture of racism in Belfast's most deprived areas (STEP 2010; McVeigh 2015), what such racialised anti-tourist agendas also reveal is a desire to incorporate tourist bodies into pre-established affective narratives of recognition and belonging. The fact that black cab mural tours unwittingly expose these incorporations through their spatial work does not just signify the uniqueness of this particular form of Troubles tourism, but also hints at the radical potential that further engagements with tourist emotions and affect might bring to research on conflict heritage in Northern Ireland.

Conclusion

Uncovering this more nuanced understanding of tourist participation in conflict heritage is the real advantage of exploring black cab tours through the concept of affective synecdoche. During a period when sectarian politics frequently blocks attempts to represent and work through the Troubles in museums (Crooke 2001), and commitments to creating cross-community audiences for heritage centres are ultimately rebuffed (Young 2015), black cab mural tours in Belfast are one of the few avenues through which memories and narratives about the conflict can be circulated and exchanged on both sides of the interfaces. Using these tours to integrate space into our discussions of emotion helps develop this critical barometer of affect in a way that acknowledges the diversity of socio-cultural experiences in West Belfast. Whereas much work on emotion in conflict-heritage prefers to diminish the intensity of these factors in favour of speculating on macro-analytic concepts such as empathy and reconciliation (Landsberg 2004; Arnold-de Simine 2013; Dowler 2013), affective synecdoche targets the micro-moment, bringing transitory relationships and hardened identities into critical dialogue with each other. Viewing such moments through the more ambiguous lens of affective synecdoche also supports the paradigm shifts argued for by Debbie Lisle (2006), opening up discussions about 'post'-conflict emotion in Belfast and providing scope for their exploration within the context of contemporary global relations.

Note

1 An 'interface' is a term specific to segregation in Northern Ireland, defined as 'the common boundary between a predominantly unionist area and a predominantly nationalist area' (Belfast Interface Project 1998: 4). Feldman (1991: 28) also describes it as 'the topographic–ideological boundary sector that physically and symbolically demarcates ethnic communities in Belfast from each other. The "interface" is a spatial construct preeminently linked to the performance of violence.'

References

Ahmed, S., 2004. Affective economies. *Social Text*, 22(2), 117–139.

Arnold-de Simine, S., 2013. *Mediating Memory in the Museum: Trauma, Empathy, Nostalgia*. Basingstoke: Palgrave Macmillan.

Ballantyne, R. and Uzzell, D., 1993. Viewpoint: Environmental mediation and hot interpretation: A case study of District Six, Cape Town. *The Journal of Environmental Education*, 24(3), 4–7.

Barritt, D. and Carter, C., 1962. *The Northern Ireland Problem*. London: Oxford University Press.

BBC, 2008. Tourist 'may now avoid Belfast'. *BBC News*, 11 February. Available from http://news.bbc.co.uk/1/hi/northern_ireland/7236558.stm [Accessed 25 August 2016].

BBC, 2016. Chinese tourist family left shaken after Belfast bus attack. *BBC News*, 4 August 2016. Available from www.bbc.co.uk/news/uk-northern-ireland-36964908 [Accessed 25 August 2016].

Belfast Interface Project, 1998. *Interface Communities and the Peace Process*. Belfast: Belfast Interface Project.

Belfast Tourism Monitor, 2007. Belfast: Belfast City Council.

Belfast Tourism Monitor, 2014. Belfast: Belfast City Council.

Boal, F. W., 1969. Territoriality on the Shankill–Falls divide, Belfast. *Irish Geography*, 6, 30–50.

Boal, F. W., 1982. Segregation and mixing: Space and residence in Belfast. In F. W. Boal and J. H. H. Douglas, eds. *Integration and Division: Geographical Perspectives on the Northern Irish Problem*. London: Academic Press, 249–280.

Bonnell, J. and Simon, R. L., 2007. 'Difficult' exhibitions and intimate encounters. *Museum & Society*, 5(2), 65–85.

Braniff, M., McDowell, S. and Murphy, J., 2015. Spacing commemorative-related violence in Northern Ireland: Assessing the implications for a society in transition. *Space & Polity*, 19(3), 231–243.

Burton, F., 1978. *The Politics of Legitimacy: Struggles in a Belfast Community*. London: Routledge and Kegan Paul.

Calder, S., 2007. Simon Calder's best of Britain. *Independent*, 2 August 2007. Available from www.independent.co.uk/news/uk/this-britain/simon-calders-best-of-britain-460125.html [Accessed 10 February 2016].

Crooke, E., 2001. Confronting a troubled history: Which past in Northern Ireland's museums. *International Journal of Heritage Studies*, 7(2), 119–136.

Crooke, E., 2007. Museums, communities and the politics of heritage in Northern Ireland. In S. Watson, ed. *Museums and Their Communities*. Oxon: Routledge, 300–312.

Cultural Tourism Strategy, 2006. Belfast: Belfast City Council.

de Certeau, M., 2011. *The Practice of Everyday Life*. Trans. S. Rendall. London: University of California Press.

Dowler, L., 2013. Waging hospitality: Feminist geopolitics and tourism in West Belfast Northern Ireland. *Geopolitics*, 18(4), 779–799.

Duff, C., 2010. On the role of affect and practice in the production of place. *Environment and Planning D: Society and Space*, 28, 881–895.

Feldman, A., 1991. *Formations of Violence: The Narrative of the Body and Political Terror in Northern Ireland*. Chicago: University of Chicago Press.

Finlay, A., 2001. Reflexivity, the dilemmas of identification and an ethnographic encounter in Northern Ireland. In M. Smyth and G. Robinson, eds. *Researching Violently Divided Societies: Ethical and Methodological Issues.* London: Pluto Press, 55–77.

Flynn, M. K., 2011. Decision making and contested heritage in Northern Ireland: The former Maze Prison/Long Kesh. *Irish Political Studies*, 26(3), 383–401.

Graham, B., 1998. Contested images of place amongst Protestants in Northern Ireland. *Political Geography*, 17(2), 129–144.

Graham, B. and Whelan, Y., 2007. The legacies of the dead: Commemorating the Troubles in Northern Ireland. *Environment and Planning D: Society and Space*, 25, 476–495.

Hansard, 2008. NIA Debate, 19 February. Available from http://archive.niassembly. gov.uk/record/reports2007/080219.htm [Accessed 9 February 2018].

Harris, R., 1972. *Prejudice and Tolerance in Ulster: A Study of Neighbours and 'Strangers' in a Border Community.* Manchester: Manchester University Press.

Hocking, B., 2015. *The Great Reimagining: Public Art, Urban Space, and the Symbolic Landscapes of a 'New' Northern Ireland.* Oxford: Berghahn.

Hughes, B., 2014. Tourist violently robbed at new mural. *Irish News*, 6 May. Available from www.irishnews.com/news/2014/05/06/news/tourist-violently-robbed-at-new-mural-90864/ [Accessed 25 August 2016].

Jarman, N., 2005 [1997]. Painting landscapes: The place of murals in the symbolic construction of urban space. In M. E. Geisler, ed. *National Symbols, Fractured Identities: Contesting the National Narrative.* London: University Press of New England, 172–193.

Kelleher, W., 2003. *The Troubles in Ballybogoin: Memory and Identity in Northern Ireland.* Ann Arbor: University of Michigan Press.

Landsberg, A., 2004. *Prosthetic Memory: The Transformation of American Remembrance in the Age of Mass Culture.* Chichester: Columbia University Press.

Leonard, M., 2011. A tale of two cities: 'Authentic' tourism in Belfast. *Irish Journal of Sociology*, 19(2), 111–126.

Lisle, D., 2006. Local symbols, global networks: Re-reading the murals of Belfast. *Alternatives*, 27–52.

McDonald, A., 2007. Canadian visitor hit on head with baseball bat. *Belfast Telegraph*, 31 December. Available from www.belfasttelegraph.co.uk/news/canadian-visitor-hit-on-head-with-baseball-bat-28071527.html [Accessed 25 August 2016].

McDowell, S., 2008. Selling conflict heritage through tourism in peacetime Northern Ireland: Transforming conflict or exacerbating difference? *International Journal of Heritage Studies*, 14(5), 405–421.

McDowell, S. and Switzer, C., 2009. Redrawing cognitive maps of conflict: Lost spaces and forgetting in the centre of Belfast. *Memory Studies*, 2, 337–353.

McGrattan, C., 2014. Policing politics: Framing the past in post-conflict divided societies. *Democratization*, 21(3), 389–410.

McVeigh, R., 2015. Living the peace process in reverse: Racist violence and British nationalism in Northern Ireland. *Race & Class*, 56(4), 3–25.

Milroy, J., 1981. *Regional Accents of English: Belfast.* Belfast: Blackstaff Press.

Nagle J., 2009. The right to Belfast City Centre: From ethnocracy to liberal multiculturalism? *Political Geography*, 28, 132–141.

Neill, W., 2006. Return to Titanic and lost in the maze: The search for representation of 'post-conflict' Belfast. *Space and Polity*, 10(2), 109–120.

Pickering, S., 2001. Undermining the sanitised account: Violence and emotionality in the field in Northern Ireland. *British Journal of Criminology*, 41, 485–501.

Shirlow, P., 2003. Ethnosectarianism and the reproduction of fear in Belfast. *Capital & Class*, 80, 77–93.

Shirlow, P., 2006. Belfast: The 'post-conflict' city. *Space and Polity*, 10(2), 99–107.

Shirlow, P. and Murtagh, B., 2006. *Belfast: Segregation, Violence and the City*. London: Pluto Press.

Simon, R. L., 2011. A shock to thought: Curatorial judgment and the public exhibition of 'difficult knowledge'. *Memory Studies*, 4(4), 432–449.

Skinner, J., 2015. Walking the Falls: Dark tourism and the significance of movement on the political tour of West Belfast. *Tourist Studies*, 1–17.

Smith, L., 2011. Affect and registers of engagement: Navigating emotional responses to dissonant heritage. In L. Smith, G. Cubitt, R. Wilson and K. Fouseki, eds. *Representing Enslavement and Abolition in Museums: Ambiguous Engagements*. New York: Routledge, 260–304.

STEP, 2010. *Research to Identify Additional Difficulties Faced by Minority Ethnic Groups and Migrant Workers Because of the Conflict in N. Ireland*. Belfast: STEP.

Thompson, S., 1999. The commodification of culture and decolonization in Northern Ireland. *Irish Studies Review*, 7(1), 53–63.

Wetherell, M., 2012. *Affect and Emotion: A New Social Science Understanding*. London: Sage.

Wiedenhoft-Murphy, W. A., 2010. Touring the Troubles in West Belfast: Building peace or reproducing conflict? *Peace & Change*, 35(4), 537–559.

Young, D., 2015. Orange Order 'baffled' as billboard removed after complaints. *Belfast Telegraph*, 19 June. Available from www.belfasttelegraph.co.uk/news/northern-ireland/orange-order-baffled-as-billboard-removed-after-complaints-31313629.html [Accessed 14 February 2016].

Chapter 11

Performing affection, constructing heritage?

Civil and political mobilisations around the Ottoman legacy in Bulgaria

Ivo Strahilov and Slavka Karakusheva

Introduction

'We do not want anything foreign; we shall not give away anything that is ours!' This slogan led some of the protests in 2013–2015 against the claims of the Grand Mufti's Office (the formal representation of the Islamic community in Bulgaria) for property which was in the possession of state or municipal authorities in the country. The same slogan welcomed us on a huge poster at the entrance of the town of Karlovo in February 2016. The issue that had mobilised the anger of the community there concerned the mosque in the town centre. This mosque was built in 1485 and declared a 'cultural monument with local significance' in 1964 (Tsoleva-Ivanova 2006: 115), but was closed and left to decay, used neither as a tourist site nor as a place of worship. When we visited the town, we saw various vulgar messages drawn on its walls and dome; the building had even been used as an unauthorised public toilet. At the end of 2012, however, the Grand Mufti's Office initiated legal proceedings to restore ownership of property that had been nationalised, expropriated or confiscated by the state. Thus, the mosque in Karlovo, along with Muslim places of worship in other Bulgarian towns, became a symbolic and emotionally charged battlefield that initiated a lively public debate on who should take possession of the religious buildings. The local, predominantly Orthodox Christian, communities refused to 'return' the mosques to the Muslim Denomination, organised numerous protests and petitions, and made statements in the media, declaring the buildings 'ours' (that is, Bulgarian) and defending them as national cultural heritage.

Although Muslims are estimated to constitute around 10–14% of the population of Bulgaria (Census 2011: 4; Hackett 2016),[1] the demands of their official religious representative body were perceived as 'foreign' and very quickly unleashed a public outcry. In our chapter, we explore the massive civil and political mobilisations that gained momentum in many towns throughout the country as a reaction to the claims of the Grand Mufti's Office. We are particularly interested in the emotional charge of the actions, and the role affect and emotions played in the mobilisations. Further, the research tries to understand the paradoxical use of the cultural heritage argument: the local communities in general reject and dis-identify themselves from the Ottoman past and ruins, and yet insist on the fact that mosques are part of the cultural heritage of the country. Taking into account first that heritage mobilises individual and collective emotions (Fabre 2013); and second, that affect and emotion, recognised or not, are 'essential constitutive elements of heritage making' (Smith and Campbell 2016: 444), we therefore analyse the switch from aggressive refusal to paternalistic affection, asking whether emotions could influence, reframe or renegotiate the notion and the boundaries of the national heritage discourses in Bulgaria. The research considers heritage as 'a resource in the interplay of the politics of representation and recognition' (Smith and Campbell 2016: 450), which is especially valid in the (re-)production of national identity (Smith 2006: 30, 48–53) and 'a key locus for realising the nation' (De Cesari and Herzfeld 2015: 175). Following on from this, our chapter highlights the intensity and the impact of feelings and affects, alongside what might more commonly be called 'rationality', on the selection, creation and narration of cultural heritage. In this context, we agree with Michael Herzfeld (2013: 380–381) that it might be more relevant to talk about emotions not (only) as psychological drivers of ethnic or national mobilisation, but as simulacra, in Baudrillard's sense. Although they do not match lived experience, emotions serve to subject individuals to the imperatives of identity policy by depriving them of alternative versions.

The text is based on ethnographic fieldwork conducted in the period September 2014 to February 2016 at the main foci of public sensitivity – the towns of Karlovo, Samokov, Dupnitsa, Gotse Delchev and Stara Zagora. The analysis is supported by a review of media reports, both local and national, legislative acts, court decisions, political utterances and official statements of the religious denominations.

The Ottoman past in the Bulgarian present

The lands of contemporary Bulgaria were part of the Ottoman Empire for almost five centuries (from the end of the fourteenth century to the late nineteenth century). Nevertheless, the tangible and intangible remains from this period, which reference the historical presence of the Empire, are perceived with reluctance as part of the national cultural heritage. Simultaneously, and uncomfortably, it is also a necessary past, as it is part of the construction of the modern national identity discourse, through the framing rhetoric of the 'liberation' from the Ottomans (in 1878), and plays a crucial role in building emotional belonging to the Bulgarian nation. As such, the Ottoman period is currently seen and characterised mainly in negative tropes of cruelties and forced Islamicisation (Todorova 2004), characterised as 'dark ages' (Lory 2015: 366), and publicly narrated as a 'yoke'. Paradoxically, however, it remains little known – apart from the Bulgarian revolutionary decades of the late nineteenth century, the period is accorded just a few pages of the school history textbooks. It is often understood as a monolithic historical construction, lacking any public recognition of internal periodisation, contradictions or developments.

Can we therefore talk about an Ottoman heritage in the Balkans (and in Bulgaria particularly) at all if we agree that heritage suggests 'heritagising', in other words, recognising and valuing something as part of the history of a nation? On the one hand, Maria Todorova (1995: 55, see also 2009a:162) argues that 'it is preposterous to look for an Ottoman legacy in the Balkans. The Balkans are the Ottoman legacy.' On the other hand, the memories of the Ottoman Empire on the peninsula are far from positive (Lory 2015: 355); the Christian populations see it 'in a negative light, without any positive features and it is pushed to the periphery' (Aretov 2008: 71). Many of the architectural sites, such as mosques, schools and public baths, have been destroyed during the establishment of the modern Bulgarian state, been rebuilt and adapted as museums, churches and other public buildings, or abandoned to natural decay (Lory 1985; Valtchivova 2005; Koyuncu 2006; Aretov 2008). In this sense, one might speak of 'deottomanisation' (Lory 1985; Hartmuth 2006), implying a purposeful ideological 'clearance' of the urban space; as erasure, demolition, conversion or appropriation of the main signs of Ottoman presence (Kiossev 2008: 58) in the architectural profile of the cities.

In this controversial and complex historical and social background, what is important for our research is the sensitivity of the majority of the Bulgarians towards the Ottoman past and how this emotionality infuses the different layers of the heritage discourse. If we understand that a crucial role of heritage is its use in policies for constructing national memory that include a process of selecting and narrating historical facts, and demonstrate political and social willingness for creating, maintaining and negotiating cultural meanings, the 'Ottoman' seems to be excluded from the hegemonic Bulgarian 'authorised heritage discourse' (Smith 2006). Hence it is 'contested' (Smith 2006: 35–42; Silverman 2011), 'dissonant' (Tunbridge and Ashworth 1996) or 'rejected' (Aretov 2008), yet ironically it is a necessary heritage that serves as 'a medium which makes the history [of the Ottoman past of Bulgaria] tangible in everyday life' (Rihtman-Auguštin 2004: 193) and prevents its falling into oblivion.

Angry nation

When we began our fieldwork in September 2014 the possible 'restitution' of the Muslim religious sites – a remainder from and reminder of the Ottoman times – had already received huge public attention and become a polarised, politicised and mediatised scandal. Many different actors were involved in the debates, and their voices in local and national media shared a concern about an Islamic provocation threatening the territorial integrity of the state. Local Christian communities were presented as 'victims of their own tolerance', which was being used by the Muslims for the realisation of the frightening project of neo-Ottomanism, understood literally as an attempt by neighbouring Turkey to reclaim the lands of its former empire.

The protests exploded in the spring of 2013 in towns where the local mosques were subject to the ownership claims initiated by the Grand Mufti. Indicative for our research was the fact that the legal representative of the Muslim Denomination submitted claims for 83 properties by the end of 2012, some of which were mosques. Of all the different types of property, which also included forests, agricultural lands and so on, the claims on the mosques were those that provoked strong public reaction and were most prominently covered in the media.

At first, the protests were spontaneous, dispersed and at a local level, relying on the personal initiative of frustrated citizens who started online petitions and created Facebook groups. At that time, the reactions seemed to be similar to the 'Not in my backyard' protests which often unify the inhabitants of an area against some undesirable external intervention (Fabre 2013: 77). Shortly thereafter, these formerly separate actions proceeded as coordinated campaigns, engaging both civil stakeholders and municipal authorities. The prominent participation of the latter was also motivated by the fact that they officially owned the properties in question. One can assume that the 'loss' of the buildings would be not only a symbolic but also an economic dispossession. Several months later the protests became more intense, better focused and well attended. Mayors, town councillors, local governors and members of the national parliament were leading the public anger, and trying to find political solutions of the issue. Posters with messages such as 'We protect our history, we protect Bulgaria' and 'We shall not give up a single stone of Bulgarian land!' were raised in the town squares and widely circulated in the media. These examples support Fabre's hypothesis that connection with heritage transcends the attachment to a particular place (Fabre 2013: 78). The notion of heritage thus goes beyond the characteristics of the cultural object, i.e. the mosque, and encompasses the collective subject that identifies itself through this object. Then the revolt becomes total, expressing the complexity of everyday existence and defending the right to be oneself in harmony with one's understanding of the past. By using the case of a monument 'in danger', Bulgarians articulate their resistance to the instability of their lives, especially in smaller provincial towns: 'If we lose the court proceedings, this will mean that the state has been lost' (interview with a citizen of Dupnitsa, September 2014).

An illustration of such absolute thinking was evident in February 2014, when, after the only court decision transferring the possession of a mosque (the one in Karlovo) to the Muslim Denomination, people from all over Bulgaria went to express their outrage in front of the regional court in Plovdiv. Football fans, public figures and local leaders of nationalist parties were amongst the demonstrators. Unable and unwilling to hold their temper, the crowds marched to the city's mosque and Regional Mufti's Office, threw stones at it and set the cafeteria on the ground floor on fire. A catalyst for these widely expressed emotional outbursts was Karlovo's status as a famous historical town, a topos of the uprisings at the end of the nineteenth century that led to the liberation of Bulgaria from the Ottoman Empire and the birthplace of the national hero and freedom fighter Vasil Levski (see Todorova 2009b). It is thus a symbolic *lieu de mémoire* (Nora 1986), recollecting a memory of the valiant past of the nation. The 'returning' to the Muslims of the mosque there, which meant in the nationalist discourse the simultaneous deprivation of a topological space of the collective memory, was read as a provocation and suspected of being an attempt to 'rewrite history'. Furthermore, Karlovo was given a dominant position in media coverage, becoming again an epicentre of some kind of national revolution, just as it had been in the past. With its petition signed by more than 8,000 local citizens (more than a third of its population), the town was held up as an exemplar amongst the other rebellious communities.

The claims submitted by the Grand Mufti's Office coincided with suggestions of amendments of the Denominations Act which were discussed in the National Assembly. The legislative project suggested that buildings built for religious purposes could only be the property of the registered denominations. Although Christian churches would also be subject to these changes, local communities surmised that the project was a political favour to the Muslim Denomination, which exacerbated their anger. Consequently, public figures, local authorities and the media composed and started narrating a syncretic story in which facts, rumours, emotions and juridical interpretations intertwined and resonated in a strong expression of moral panic.

The anger was expressed, explained and, more importantly, felt as a defence of the nation, as shown for example during the demonstration in the town of Dupnitsa. The residents of the town made a human chain around the former mosque, to symbolically protect it from the danger of being converted back into an active place of worship. Bulgarian flags were hung on the building, while patriotic songs were played in the square in front of it. The symbolism of these performative acts was obvious – the building, which until some time ago had been perceived as part of the complex historical and often rejected picture of the Ottoman past, was then narrated, defended and legitimised as 'Bulgarian'. Depending on the local circumstances, various references to the cultural property surfaced, and were used to justify the protective behaviour seen in many towns – from sharing personal memories and evoking local history, through emphasising aesthetic, historical and architectural qualities, to proclaiming the Ottoman Muslim temple a city emblem or a monument that belongs to everybody. Needless to say, the emotional complexity of this response is quite extreme, and is a rather ironic example of Herzfeld's (2013) analysis of nostalgia and nationalism.

Going further, it is intriguing to explore the limits of this apparent identification with mosques, their acceptance as public presences in the urban space and their vernacularisation as buildings. It is known that local histories and folklore in the Balkans talk about Christians who participated in the building process (Aretov 2008: 75; Hartmuth 2008: 702–703), or the Bulgarian origin of some local Muslim ruler, or the existence of a Christian temple on the site of the mosque. It is possible that this approach of 'nostrification' (Hartmuth 2008: 702; Marinov 2010) would valorise the externalised Ottoman legacy. During the ongoing affair, however, the widely shared legends were exploited in order to serve specific ideological and political goals. Local stories helped thus to appropriate the remains and evidence of the inconvenient past – a crucial task for sustaining the dominant position of the national majority, but also a means of forging an emotional commitment to the previously disregarded buildings.

When the revindication claims made the mosques visible in the urban space as their 'loss' became conceivable, the municipal authorities were obliged to undertake more determined actions, so that now the museumification of the sites has entered a more definitive stage. Previously, as the most harmless solution, some of the formerly religious buildings were maintained by the local museums and often kept locked. Recently, a new tendency for dealing with mosques is being established by means of archaeological investigations (Ruggles 2011). The pioneering example of such archaeological 'neutralisation' in Bulgaria was the temple in Stara Zagora. After the excavations, which found remains from different historical periods related to different religious legacies, the mosque there was restored and marketed as a museum of religions, exhibiting the ruins of an ancient Thracian sanctuary,[2] and Christian and Muslim temples. This strategy was consequently appropriated by the Municipality of Karlovo, which organised archaeological works in and around the local mosque in an attempt to discover an older Orthodox church on the site, the possibility of which was suggested by urban legends. Once equipped with such proof, the mayor would have easily contested the revindication and legitimised the museumification. Whose property should the land be if temples of two or more religions occupy it? This also shifts the potentially hostile emotional tone of the tensions over the building onto the more familiar terrain of the museum or heritage site, where a more 'considered' and less febrile affective practice is the norm. It is of course no accident that museums are often seen as dealing with a 'dead' past, so this strategy cleverly sidesteps the emotional 'affront' to nationhood by making it a problem of the past, best presented in a context of 'learning'.

The emotional intensity of the crowds was further captured in policy strategies applied by the political authorities. These strategies incorporate and use the potential of the public excitement and disquiet to create a complex socio-political amalgam, where different actors and their presumed interests or hidden aims can barely be distinguished, where people's moods and

Performing affection 185

necessities are presented as a monolithic totality and where political actions or their absence are legitimised as a natural expression of all that fictitious integrity. That is why municipalities, which had initially underestimated the public gravity of the revindications, gained time and allies during the court hearings precisely by raising the alarm about the imagined forthcoming Islamicisation or the deprivation of the national land and cultural heritage. At the same time, the emotional invocation passed over the unattractive legal arguments, and the mobilisations – civil and political – were not late in coming. Emotions, practically, have been recruited to strengthen and justify political action. Although they look authentic and spontaneous, one should not forget, however, that they are inherently social, and are very likely to be consciously manipulated (see Thrift 2004: 58, 64–68) to serve rational interests. Emotions acquire culturally specific forms and meanings (Frevert 2011), and civil and political initiatives could be motivated by an 'affective rationality' (Clavairolle 2011: 180–183). This explains why the feelings on display were those which the 'true' Bulgarian should maintain about the Ottoman past – something that became clear through the respondents' mistrust towards attempts to address the religious rights of Muslims or the aesthetic characteristics of the mosques.

Whose legacy? What heritage?

While labelled with the same word[3] by all actors, narrated as heritage or legacy and presented as valuable, religious buildings concentrate various meanings. Apart from being cultural property, they are important because of their religious significance – a position expressed by both Muslim and Orthodox denominations (the latter had also claimed possession of some churches). In terms of religion, Islam in particular, the building is a legacy rather than a heritage – it is something that should belong in perpetuity to the pious ideals to which it had been dedicated. Understood as an inheritance requiring eternal care, the temporal perspective in a theological sense is much longer – it is believed that 'sooner or later, whatever is a temple, will be a temple. With or without the law.'[4] What is determinative in this case, however, is not the preservation of the authenticity of the monument, but the persistence of the designation according to the will of the donor, i.e. an allotted place of worship should perform this function. 'We have to protect the mosque, to fulfil the will of its founder, otherwise we will be traitors in the eyes of Allah', explained the imam of Karlovo (interview with Kemal Rashid, February 2016).

The local authorities, on the other hand, frame and introduce the mosques only as cultural sites, denying them recognition as religious buildings and disregarding the theological arguments of the Muslim Denomination. In their understanding, cultural monuments cannot belong only to a single denomination because that would undermine the heritage status of the sites. Conversely, the latter will be guaranteed if the authorities maintain their ownership. Thus, their statements draw a strict line between religious buildings and cultural properties.

The gap between these two positions, and their unshakable assertion, which extends the 'battle' to every single religious building, also excite public opinion. In fact, the Cultural Heritage Act in Bulgaria does not see a contradiction in a cultural property being owned by the registered denominations and, what is more, expressly includes the latter in the preservation system. But these discrepant notions lead to a cleavage in safeguarding priorities. The excerpt from a heated debate at the National Assembly cited below illustrates the collision between the religious and the 'monumental' point of view:

HH: Who owns the building [of the ancient mosque in Gotse Delchev]?

BP: The building is a cultural property.

HH: Right! How can the Grand Mufti's Office [...] conduct repairs on the building itself?

BP: It's very simple: it should apply to the Ministry of Culture requesting a subvention; then a commission will come, an architect will come and say 'Yes, here you can do this, this and this.' In that way, you will save it.

HH: Great! And afterwards, it can be used for its purpose?

BP: Conceivably, yes.

HH: Even for prayers? This is permitted, as I understand?

BP: Is that your final goal, or to save that which is inside?

HH: What else would a religious institution fight for when trying to restore the temple?

BP: I will explain to you. For the tombs of its sacred people, which are inside.

HH: No, for praying!

BP: Why are you not listening to me? For the tombs of its sacred people, for the sacred tuğras inside, for the cultural heritage which is preserved within this mosque. Why not take care of those things? Is this the only goal – to go there only to pray?

HH: Because it is a religious institution. It will restore the temple and will use it for its purpose, as had been prescribed by the donors.[5]

The court proceedings of the Muslim Denomination are motivated by, and grounded in, this eschatological perspective for the preservation of the religious meaning and usage of the building. 'We have the moral obligation for Muslim people at least to try to recover the ownership of the mosques', admitted the Deputy Grand Mufti, while expressing his suspicions that the court could ever make such an unpopular decision (interview with Murat Pingov, January 2016). At the same time, this narrative supplies the Grand Mufti's Office with another legitimisation, alongside the legal right.

Although the degree was lower, and its voice was often silenced or neglected, the counterpart in the protests also introduced arguments that might influence the feelings of the public, and eventually create a more 'appropriate' image of the revindications and the confession. Official statements attempted to integrate Islam in the discourse of the nation, to address the cultural and human rights of its followers, and, therefore, to overcome their marginality. It was recalled that Muslims were not foreigners and, if restituted, the mosques would stay in Bulgaria because the Denomination was a Bulgarian institution (interview with Hayri Emin, Department of Public Relations and Protocol, Grand Mufti's Office, September 2014). Their cultural heritage argument, on the other hand, was not common. A responsibility for the preservation of the Ottoman monuments exists amongst Muslim communities, but it is not articulated in a distinct way. It is rather evoked in order to rebuke the state, or particular municipalities, for the poor condition of the mosques used as museums in their possession.

When an ancient building is vandalised or destroyed, emotions are often aroused (Fabre 2013:29), but in our case it also confers legitimacy on the religious institution, and permits it to act and criticise the care of the building. This criticism made local authorities realise their own interests and be enterprising, which further changed the strategy of the Grand Mufti's Office. When the Municipality of Karlovo funded the archaeological excavations at the mosque, a counter-protest was organised. It was coordinated by the head office in the capital, and supported mostly by Muslims from other cities, who gathered to pray in front of the former mosque in Karlovo. They thus expressed their disagreement, and rejected the ongoing museumification of the religious buildings. The museumification was qualified as 'islamophobic, discriminative and antidemocratic actions', which were not supposed to occur in a 'European Bulgaria' (Muslim Denomination 2015), that is understood as guarantying religious plurality and human rights. In the context of such contestation and raised tension, in 2015 another demonstration was organised in the city of Razgrad. The base of the local mosque, a cultural property and object of long-lasting excavations, was concreted in an attempt to prevent its museumification.

Analysing the confrontations between the different perceptions, it turns out that the dispute over cultural heritage embodies several conflicting meanings and interdependent narratives which, by interacting publicly, exchange emotional energy, feed each other and become polarised. It also seems that the place reserved for the cultural properties themselves within this framework makes these monuments susceptible to manipulation, speculation and instrumentalisations. On the other hand, it is highly questionable whether there is any genuine care for the historic or other values.

Valorisation?

As we pointed out at the beginning of this chapter, one of our research questions was whether we could trace a process of reframing of the national heritage discourse, especially in relation to the place of the Ottoman legacy within the 'grand narrative' of the nation. This would mean that there is a tendency for positive re-evaluations of cultural sites remaining from this undesirable past. In this context, we can consider the words of the Bulgarian Minister of Culture in his speech during the inauguration of the mosque of Stara Zagora, newly restored as a museum: 'What we have here is more valuable than Jerusalem. Whereas in Jerusalem only two religions are presented, here everything goes back to Ancient Thrace' (Georgiev 2011). However, what he indicated as valuable was the fact that historical artefacts were exhibited, whereas current religious coexistence was not mentioned, implying that the real presence of the religions is less important than their representation.

Another example of museumification occurred when the Municipality of Karlovo submitted documents to change the heritage status of the mosque – from a cultural monument with local significance to a national one – which would allow them to apply for funding for its restoration. We were told that, even if the grant applications were unsuccessful, 'the mayor promised that the Municipality would assure finance every year' for archaeological work and conservation of the formerly religious building (interview with Petya Naydenova, Department of Humanitarian and Social Activities, Municipality of Karlovo, February 2016). This care for the cultural and historic values of the monument and the attempts to ensure funding for its preservation constitute a new phase in the municipal policies. Until recently the mosque has been neglected, and the attempts of the local museum to restore the building have met with reluctance, ostensibly due to the town's budget (interview with Petya Tsoleva-Ivanova, specialist on Ottoman history, Museum of History, Karlovo, February 2016).

Perhaps threatening a culturally significant place with destruction might eventually reveal the degree of its importance to the local communities. It was not the fear of destruction of the mosque, though, that provoked the massive protests, but the fear of losing control over the basic markers of national identity. When asked what was going to happen if the Grand Mufti's Office gained possession of the mosques, the residents of Karlovo and Samokov answered in a similar way: 'They will burn it down … One night people will go out and burn the mosque down', 'It's better if we put potatoes inside rather than having the imam sing' (interviews with citizens of Samokov, September 2014); and 'If it falls into ruin, I will not miss it. It is just a popular place for meetings in the town centre, we say "Let's meet at the mosque." But I don't care whether there's a hole in its place' (interview with Svetlozar Yankov, town councillor, Karlovo, February 2016).

These answers suggest that the 'Ottoman' continues to be excluded from the national heritage discourse and is rejected by the local communities. Apparently, on an everyday basis ancient religious buildings operate as a shortcut to a dark and unwanted past, shortening its distance from the present (Heinich 2013: 203, 206). Moreover, being a religious legacy, they are the most visible signs of the victory of Islam over Christianity, of 'foreign' over 'ours'; and as such are constantly and continuously used for deliberate 'actualisation of history' (Giordano 2005). As a site with strong relevance to identity, the local mosque becomes then a 'monument-trace' (Debray 1999: 31–34) that functions in the register of memory. In a retroactive and vivid manner, it testifies that the 'horrors' of the 'yoke' were real, by re-affirming the national mythology about forced Islamicisation and the cruelties of the Ottomans, who are presented as those who have destroyed 'our' Christian temples in order to build 'theirs'. In this sense, the returning of the property to the Muslim Denomination is perceived as interference in the history of the nation. Because this act was promoted as such, for the general public, it constituted an attack against the national identity (cf. Herzfeld 2013: 383).

The official interpretation of the past is in the hands of the intellectual and political elites. Although the Ottoman period in general is perceived as culturally insignificant, the experts clearly admit the value of the mosques in scientific and historical terms. In a comparable manner, laymen, local and national authorities domesticate and instrumentalise the discourse used by heritage professionals, underlining the cultural importance of the sites. This apparent valorisation and heritagisation of the mosques is actually the only appropriate narrative that could block the revindications sought by the Grand Mufti's Office. By declaring publicly that the religious buildings are heritage, and arguing for their ownership, municipalities imply that they will put effort into the sites' preservation and accessibility for all citizens. This logical argument could hardly be challenged, and a counter-argument (by the Muslim Denomination) would be difficult to mount, and would be unlikely to be heard or accepted.

Conclusion

There is no doubt that the engagement of the Bulgarians with the Ottoman heritage in general is shallow. The shock of the possible loss, or more accurately the threat of 'giving' the mosques over to 'foreign' hands, however, unleashed a wave of negative emotions which mobilised local communities, authorities, politicians, experts and media in a collective battle against the revindications. The initial concern metamorphosed into a rebellious discontent, the emotions into motions, the monuments into *moviments* (Dufrêne 1999). Our analysis has shown that the Ottoman cultural heritage was rather a 'hostage' in a broader discussion involving and influenced by different projections of religion, memory, history and heritage. Multiple instrumentalisations and uses have shaped it, elaborating a specific concept, which is summarised in the words of an elderly Bulgarian man living next to the remains of the ancient mosque in the town of Gotse Delchev:

> The mosque can be restored but there must be a plaque on it saying that at the beginning it had been a church which was later transformed into a Muslim temple. People have to see that everything was turned upside

down during the Ottoman rule. We cannot demolish it. Signs must be preserved, history should not be erased (September 2014).

By insisting on the safeguarding of the mosques as national heritage, Bulgarians – despite the plasticity of their imagined 'us' – actually give a contextual response (cf. Smith and Campbell 2016: 445) and try to sustain their own way of reading the past. The latter can be illustrated with another example from our fieldwork – people, even representatives of local elites, see the traces of the Ottoman legacy as memories of a traumatic period of the national history, rather than as an architectural monument: 'The bullet holes and the skulls, that people here are still exhuming, are the Ottoman legacy' (interview with Stefan Filchev, Museum of Ivan Vazov, Sopot, February 2016). This historicity is, therefore, valuable. For the majority, a particular Ottoman building is important insofar as the memory is preserved: the mosque should remain a place which will reinforce what people 'already know, believe and feel about the past and its relationship with the present' (Smith and Campbell 2016: 445).

As a starting point, we hypothesised that the paternalistic claims could unconsciously construct more positive images of the rejected Ottoman legacy and eventually valorise it. In fact, the observed performative practices deconstruct the Ottomanness of the mosques, forgetting their religious meaning and putting their foreignness in a passive position, while re-imaging a symbol of a traumatic event and a collective suffering, which at the end reaffirms the dominant discourse. Despite supposedly being based on the monumental value of the mosque, the ongoing strategy of performative emotional heritagisation silences its forbidding original purpose, decontextualises it, (re-)appropriates it and makes out of it a new monument implying commemorative practices. Beyond the loudly proclaimed cultural sites, the Ottoman legacy does not transform into Heritage, but remains rejected and subverted into a specific counter-monument, an evidence of a history that 'must never be repeated'. The subversion thus allows contestation of the existence of the monument itself and the values attributed to it (cf. Stevens, Franck and Fazakerley 2012), protecting it from its reassessment or 'historical' neutralisation (Fabre 2000), reacting against 'the end of memory-history' (Nora 1986).

On the other hand, these feelings should not be undervalued as, aside from their social origin and political catalysts, they are based on traumatic historical events, which have been safeguarded and developed as painful stories within the collective memory. In this sense, the public anger is understandable. According to Fabre (2010), such disassociation with a legacy is expected when it refers to a hated past which nobody wants to experience again. The building, or the mosque in our case, should first lose its initial function (of a place of worship) to allow the appearance of the past (in a place of memory). The abandonment of the place and the vandalism, together with the declassification of the monument, could be seen by the national subjectivity, in this regard, as an historic judgment (Fabre 2010).

Yet the complex mixture of the low-prestige and dangerous Ottoman has become visible and recognisable, if not recognised, as heritage, precisely because it has been narrated as such: 'emotions are the proof of the heritage', states Nathalie Heinich (2013: 195). What is more, this articulation has been made not only by experts and policy makers, but also by non-specialists, who have mobilised the concept of heritage while supporting the monolithic and exclusive interpretation of the past and the status quo of the social geography. The picture seems, however, much more complicated, and includes mutual distrust and tension between different communities and authorities, embodied with historical stereotypes, economic instability, social insecurity and political disappointment. This general anxiety provokes the feeling of a loss of control and a weakening of the power of the nation, where the battle for the past is possibly an emotional reaction to, and compensation for, the uncertainty of the present. Thus, heritage, as an important field for constructing, reproducing, realising and feeling the nation, appears to be an arena for social engagement. It becomes a vehicle through which local people assert their resilience (cf. Creed 2011: 205), but also a resource for various political instrumentalisatons.

Notes

1 The Muslims are the second-largest religious community in Bulgaria. The vast majority of Bulgarians self-identify as Eastern Orthodox Christians, which according to the Constitution of Bulgaria is the 'traditional religion'. Islam was officially declared as their religion by 10% of the population in 2011, but 21.8% of all citizens refused to answer the question about their religious self-identification (Census 2011: 4). The Pew-Templeton Global Religious Futures Project estimates a 13.7% Muslim population in Bulgaria (Hackett 2016). The official institution which represents the Islamic community in Bulgaria is the Grand Mufti's Office of the Muslim Denomination.
2 Ancient Thrace is a historical region in southeastern Europe that was inhabited by Indo-European populations during the late second millennium and first millennium BCE. Currently, Bulgaria presents itself as a proud heir of the Thracian civilisation, trying in this way to root its culture in a prestigious ancient heritage.
3 In Bulgarian the word for 'heritage' and 'legacy' is the same ('nasledstvo'), meaning also 'inheritance', 'patrimony', etc. (see Aretov 2008; Kiossev 2008).
4 A representative of the Holy Synod's intervention during the debates in the Parliamentary Commission on Culture and Media discussing amendments of the Denominations Act, July 2013.
5 Part of the debate in the Parliamentary Commission on Culture and Media between Hyusein Hafazov (HH), Member of the National Assembly and former Secretary General of the Grand Mufti's Office, and Associate Professor Boni Petrunova (BP), at that time Deputy Director of the National Archaeological Institute and Museum, discussing amendments of the Denominations Act, December 2013.

References

Aretov., N., 2008. The rejected legacy. In R. Detrez and B. Segaert, eds. *Europe and the Historical Legacies in the Balkans*. Brussels: PIE Peter Lang, 69–79.

Census, 2011. *Population Census in the Republic of Bulgaria (Final Data)*. Sofia: National Statistical Institute. Available from www.nsi.bg/census2011/PDOCS2/Census2011final_en.pdf [Accessed 31 January 2017].

Clavairolle, F., 2011. La Borie sauvée des eaux. Ethnologie d'une émotion patrimoniale. *Les Carnets du LAHIC 7*. Paris: LAHIC/DPRPS – Direction générale des patrimoines. Available from www.iiac.cnrs.fr/lahic/sites/lahic/IMG/pdf/carnet_7.pdf [Accessed 4 February 2016].

Creed, G. W., 2011. *Masquerade and Postsocialism: Ritual and Cultural Dispossession in Bulgaria*. Bloomington: Indiana University Press.

De Cesari, C. and Herzfeld, M., 2015. Urban heritage and social movements. In L. Meskell, ed. *Global Heritage: A Reader*. Chichester: John Wiley and Sons, 171–195.

Debray, R., 1999. Trace, forme ou message? *Les Cahiers de médiologie*, 7, 27–44.

Dufrêne, B., 1999. Monument ou moviment? *Les Cahiers de médiologie*, 7, 183–191.

Fabre, D., 2000. Ancienneté, altérité, autochtonie. In D. Fabre, ed. *Domestiquer l'histoire. Ethnologie des monuments historiques*. Paris: Ministère de la Culture/Maison des sciences de l'homme, 195–208. Available from http://books.openedition.org/editionsmsh/2893 [Accessed 15 February 2016].

Fabre, D., 2010. Introduction. Habiter les monuments. In D. Fabre and A. Iuso, eds. *Les monuments sont habités*. Paris: Ministère de la Culture/Maison des sciences de l'homme. Available from http://books.openedition.org/editionsmsh/3483 [Accessed 15 February 2016].

Fabre, D., 2013. Le patrimoine porté par l'émotion. In D. Fabre, ed. *Émotions patrimoniales*. Paris: Éditions de la Maison des sciences de l'homme, 13–98.

Frevert, U., 2011. *Emotions in History – Lost and Found*. Budapest: Central European University Press. Available from http://books.openedition.org/ceup/1496 [Accessed 20 August 2016].

Georgiev, R., 2011. Borisov otkri Eski dzhamiya i obeshta na starozagortsi plazh [Borisov inaugurated Eski Mosque and promised a beach to the citizens of Stara Zagora]. *Stara Zagora Info*, 16 September. Available from http://stara-zagora.info/borisov-otkri-eski-dzhamiya-i-obeshta-na-starozagortsi-plazh [Accessed 30 January 2017].

Giordano, C., 2005. The past in the present. Actualized history in the social construction of reality. In D. Kalb and H. Tak. *Critical Junctions. Anthropology and History beyond the Cultural Turn*. New York and Oxford: Berghahn, 53–71.

Hackett, C., 2016. *5 Facts about the Muslim Population in Europe*. Pew Research Centre. www.pewresearch.org/fact-tank/2016/07/19/5-facts-about-the-muslim-population-in-europe [Accessed 30 January 2017; no longer available].

Hartmuth, M., 2006. Negotiating tradition and ambition: Comparative perspective on the 'DeOttomanization' of the Balkan cityscapes. *Ethnologia Balkanica*, 10, 15–33.

Hartmuth, M., 2008. De/constructing a 'Legacy in stone: Of interpretative and historiographical problems concerning the Ottoman cultural heritage in the Balkans', *Middle Eastern Studies*, 44(5), 695–713.

Heinich, N., 2013. Esquisse d'une typologie des émotions patrimoniales. In D. Fabre, ed. *Émotions patrimoniales*. Paris: Maison des sciences de l'homme, 195–210.

Herzfeld, M., 2013. À la recherche du temps écrasé: Patrimoine et suppression des liens sociaux d'émotion (Grèce, Italie, Thaïlande). In D. Fabre, ed. *Émotions patrimoniales*. Paris: Maison des sciences de l'homme, 377–392.

Kiossev, A., 2008. Legacy or legacies. Competitions and conflicts. In R. Detrez and B. Segaert, eds. *Europe and the Historical Legacies in the Balkans*. Brussels: PIE Peter Lang, 49–67.

Koyuncu, A., 2006. Bulgaristan'da Osmanlı Maddi Kültür Mirasının Tasfiyesi (1878–1908). *Osmanlı Tarihi Araştırma ve Uygulama Merkezi Dergisi OTAM*, S. 20. Güz 2006, 197–243. Available from http://dergiler.ankara.edu.tr/dergiler/19/1335/15460. pdf [Accessed 22 February 2016].

Lory. B., 1985. *Le sort de l'héritage Ottoman en Bulgarie. L'exemple des villes bulgares, 1878–1900*. Istanbul: Isis.

Lory. B., 2015. The Ottoman legacy in the Balkans. In R. Daskalov and A. Vezenkov, eds. *Entangled Histories on the Balkans, Volume 3: Shared Pasts, Disputed Legacies*. Leiden: Brill, 355–405.

Marinov, T., 2010. Chiya e tazi kashta? Izmislyaneto na balgarskata vazrozhdenska arhitektura [Whose is this house? The invention of the Bulgarian Revival architecture]. In St. Dechev, ed. V tarsene na balgarskoto: Mrezhi na natsionalna intimnost (XIX–XXI vek) [*In Search of the Essentially Bulgarian: Networks of National Intimacy (19th–21st Centuries)*]. Sofia: Institut za izsledvane na izkustvata [Institute of Art Studies], 325–404.

Muslim Denomination [Myusyulmansko izpovedanie], 2015. Glavno myuftiistvo podkrepya mirniya protest na myusyulmanite ot Karlovo [Grand Mufti's Office supports the peaceful demonstration of the Muslims from Karlovo]. Available from www.grandmufti.bg/bg/home/news-room/novini/1319-glavno-myuftiistvo-podkrepya-mirniya-protest-na-myusyulmanite-ot-karlovo.html [Accessed 30 January 2017].

Nora, P., 1986. Entre mémoire et histoire. La problématique des lieux. In P. Nora, ed. *Les lieux de mémoire, tome 1, La République*. Paris: Gallimard, xvii–xlii.

Rihtman-Auguštin, D., 2004. The monument in the main city square. Constructing and erasing memory in contemporary Croatia. In M. Todorova, ed. *Balkan Identities: Nation and Memory*. New York: New York University Press, 180–196.

Ruggles, F., 2011. The stratigraphy of forgetting: The Great Mosque of Cordoba and its contested legacy. In H. Silverman, ed. *Contested Cultural Heritage: Religion, Nationalism, Erasure, and Exclusion in a Global World*. New York: Springer, 51–67.

Silverman, H., 2011. Contested cultural heritage: A selective historiography. In H. Silverman, ed. *Contested Cultural Heritage. Religion, Nationalism, Erasure, and Exclusion in a Global World*. Urbana: Springer, 1–49.

Smith, L., 2006. *Uses of Heritage*. London: Routledge.

Smith, L. and Campbell, G., 2016. The elephant in the room: Heritage, affect and emotion. In W. Logan, M. Nic Craith and U. Kockel, eds. *A Companion to Heritage Studies*. Oxford: Wiley Blackwell, 443–460.

Stevens, Q., Franck, K. A. and Fazakerley, R., 2012. Counter-monuments: The anti-monumental and the dialogic. *Journal of Architecture*, 17(6), 951–972.

Thrift, N., 2004. Intensities of feeling: Towards a spatial politics of affect. *Geografiska Annaler*, 86B, 57–78.

Todorova, M., 1995. The Ottoman legacy in the Balkans. In G. G. Özdoğan and K. Saybaşılı, eds. *Balkans. A Mirror of the New International Order*. Istanbul: Eren, 55–74.

Todorova, M., 2004. Conversion to Islam as a trope in Bulgarian historiography, fiction and film. In M. Todorova, ed. *Balkan Identities: Nation and Memory*. New York: New York University Press, 129–157.

Todorova, M., 2009a. *Imaging the Balkans* (updated edition). New York: Oxford University Press.

Todorova, M., 2009b. *Bones of Contention. The Living Archive of Vasil Levski and the Making of Bulgaria's National Hero*. Budapest: Central European University Press.

Tsoleva-Ivanova, P., 2006. Arhitektura i istoriya na Kurshun dzhamiya spored osmanski i drugi iztochnitsi [Architecture and history of Kurshun Mosque according to Ottoman and other sources]. In R. Kovachev, P. Todorova and P. Tsoleva-Ivanova, eds. Obshtestveni i religiozni sgradi XV–XIX vek [*Public and Religious Buildings of the 15th–19th Centuries*]. Karlovo: Istoricheski muzei [Museum of History], 115–124.

Tunbridge, J. E. and Ashworth, G. J., 1996. *Dissonant Heritage: The Management of the Past as a Resource in Conflict*. London: Wiley.

Valtchinova, G., 2005. Le passé, la nation, la religion: La politique du patrimoine en Bulgarie socialiste. *Études balkaniques*, 12, 194–209. Available from http://etudesbalkaniques.revues.org/118 [Accessed 22 February 2016].

Part III

Learning, teaching and engaging

Chapter 12

Understanding the emotional regimes of reconciliation in engagements with 'difficult' heritage

Michalinos Zembylas

Introduction

In recent years, there has been an increasing number of museum and public exhibitions that deal with 'difficult' heritage, namely, the dark histories of genocide, wars, colonialism and racism (Simon 2006a, 2006b, 2011a, 2011b, 2014; Bonnell and Simon 2007; Witcomb 2010, 2013, 2015). As Witcomb (2013: 256) points out, the work of understanding what might be achieved through engagements with 'difficult' exhibitions 'is slow and patchy', yet it is beginning to recognise that affect and emotion are essential elements of heritage and museum visitors' experiences (Smith and Campbell 2016). The recent call for the development of 'critical heritage studies' shows the urgent need for a critical engagement with what can be accomplished by making painful histories public (Witcomb and Buckley 2013). My own work so far has included attempts to engage with the challenges of 'difficult knowledge' and 'difficult history' in the context of teaching and learning about/from traumatic events (Zembylas 2014, 2015, 2017). This chapter is a further contribution to this work by focusing on a topic that has not received much attention in heritage and museum studies: the 'emotional regimes' that may be invoked, moulded or used in engagements with 'difficult' heritage, especially when these engagements become part of reconciliation processes in the aftermath of historical brutality.

'Emotional regime' is a concept borrowed from the perspective of the history of emotions and refers to the norms that are imposed by political regimes, prescribing specific 'feeling rules' (Hochschild 1983), ideals, rituals and vocabularies (Reddy 2001; Plamber 2010). Heritage and museum visitors have emotional agency and make choices about how and where they express themselves emotionally; in other words, people manage their emotions, and that management will be influenced by their personal, social, cultural and political contexts (Smith and Campbell 2016). Feeling rules and emotional regimes are unavoidable, then; but what are the implications for heritage and museum visitors' experiences when the envisioned goal of museum curators is to elicit emotions of empathy in the name of reconciliation? What sort of emotional regimes might be moulded and with what consequences in relation to visitors' perceptions of 'victims' and 'perpetrators'? In using the concept of an 'emotional regime' in this chapter, I am interested in pursuing how the engagement with difficult heritage in the context of reconciliation processes may invoke certain emotional regimes in heritage and museum visitors' experiences. My effort is situated within wider attempts in history education (Trofanenko 2010) to make exhibitions forms of critical history practice (Witcomb 2013); therefore, I want to show how emotional engagement with difficult heritage might often have unintended consequences, even when the intentions are 'good', such as invoking reconciliation.

The chapter is divided into the following parts. In the first part, it reviews briefly how 'difficult knowledge' is emotionally relevant in heritage and museum visitors' experiences, and looks at my approach on emotion and affect in engagement with difficult heritage. Then, the chapter draws on work from history education, especially in the area of textbook revisions, to outline the different options that might be available in the context of reconciliation efforts. Then, the last part of the chapter discusses the implications of considering these options in the context of heritage and museum visitors' experiences and the emotional regimes that might be elicited. It is argued that the affective dimensions of engagement with difficult heritage, especially in reconciliation efforts, require critical analysis to understand the complex and often ambivalent nature of emotional regimes that might be invoked through such efforts.

'Difficult knowledge' in heritage and museum visitors' experiences

I want to begin by outlining some of the insights emerging from the literature on 'difficult' knowledge and how these ideas might be relevant to heritage and museum visitors' experiences. Britzman (1998) used the term 'difficult knowledge' in the context of discussing Holocaust education to highlight the learner's painful encounter with trauma and victimisation from the past. In particular, Britzman's notion of difficult knowledge refers *both* to representations of social and historical traumas in a curriculum *and* to the learner's encounters with them in pedagogy (see also Pitt and Britzman 2003). Knowledge becomes difficult, as Simon (2011a: 433) explains further in the context of curatorial judgment and public exhibitions, when it 'appears disturbingly foreign or inconceivable to the self, bringing oneself up against the limits of what one is willing and capable of understanding'. Difficult knowledge, then, is difficult not only because of the traumatic content of knowledge, but also because one's encounter with this content is emotionally and conceptually unsettling.

An important element of difficult knowledge, therefore, has to do with the fact that museum and heritage sites can be places that elicit emotional encounters with traumatic histories; someone (for example, a learner; a museum visitor) experiences negative affect and related dissonance and struggles to understand loss: a loss of agency (one's feeling of helplessness); a loss of meaning (one's inability to accommodate affective dissonance); and the 'loss of the idea of the social bond' (Britzman 2000a: 33). As Britzman explains, 'What makes trauma traumatic is the incapacity to respond adequately, accompanied by feelings of profound helplessness and loss, and a sense that no other person or group will intervene. What makes trauma traumatic is the loss of self and other' (Britzman 2000b: 202). In facing affective dissonance and loss in museums, classrooms and public exhibitions, we are confronted with the impossibility of undoing the harm and suffering that has taken place. Therefore, a related element of difficult knowledge has to do with the *pedagogical* treatment of our affective dissonance and loss. Britzman (2000a) is particularly concerned with the question of how to make trauma 'pedagogical', namely, how to organise the learning experience in such a way that it creates new openings from which individuals can reclaim trauma from the past in productive (e.g. reconciliatory) ways.

A number of scholars in recent years, especially in social studies education and heritage and museum studies, have further theorised the concept of difficult knowledge in relation to difficult heritage and the wider pedagogical implications for learning spaces (for example, schools and museums). Simon (2006a, 2006b, 2011a, 2011b, 2014), in particular, suggests that a pedagogy that accommodates difficult knowledge would have to entail uncertainty and disruption in how affective dissonance and loss are understood: 'In such a pedagogy,' he writes, 'affect is understood as mobilizing thought about the substance and limitations of any given historical narrative and its significance, without attempting to guarantee in advance what this thought might be' (Simon 2011b: 200). This conception of pedagogy requires the development of a new vocabulary for describing the affective legacies of difficult heritage (Simon 2011a, 2014). It is through the exploration to develop this new vocabulary, maintains Simon, that we might attain a deeper understanding of what is gained and what is lost in pedagogies addressing difficult heritage.

Overall, it is clear that museums and heritage sites are places where people engage with some sort of emotion management through which certain insights about the past may be reinforced or questioned (Smith and Campbell 2016). A growing body of research in heritage and museum studies, suggest Smith and Campbell, 'has documented how emotions can be used to destabilize received narratives and understandings of history, so that greater engagement with hidden or marginalized histories and contemporary group sympathy may occur' (Smith and Campbell 2016: 450). Recognising the role of emotions and affects in heritage and museum visitors' experiences requires some clarifications about how emotions and affects are understood and how they are 'managed'.

My theoretical approach on emotions

My approach in this chapter is informed by literature that emphasises the historical, political and cultural dimensions of emotion and affect. A crucial distinction that is often made in this literature is that between 'affect' and 'emotion' (see also Zembylas 2008). For post-Deleuzian scholars, in particular (for example, Massumi 1996), emotion signals cultural constructs and conscious processes, where affect marks precognitive sensory experience, relations to surroundings, and generally the body's capacity to act, to engage, to resist and to connect. Hence emotion represents a form of assimilation, a closure and containment of affect within symbolic means, whereas affect is considered along the lines of a bodily intensity resistant to domestication, always evading a final structuration (Hook 2011). A possible error that comes to light, however, as Hook explains, is the assumption that affect bypasses or exists prior to the symbolic and 'that it hence warrants distinctive analytical attention potentially set aside from [the] symbolic' (Hook 2011: 111). Similarly, emotion might be perceived as socially determined, the effect of social conventions – an interpretation that fails to account for the emotion's disruptive and transformative potential. In general, I agree with those scholars (e.g. Cvetkovich 2012) who use affect in a generic sense, rather than in the more specific Deleuzian sense. Affect, then, can be seen as a category that encompasses affect, emotion and feeling, and 'includes impulses, desires, and feelings that get historically constructed in a range of ways' (Cvetkovich 2012: 4). Affects are always embedded in acts and practices; they are not psychological or mental processes, but they constitute an integral part of the practical activities with which bodies relate to other subjects and objects (Wetherell 2012). Also, emotions can be defined in terms of both a social and a psychic dimension (Braunmühl 2012).

Along these lines, Ahmed's (2004) work on how emotions bind subjects together into collectivities is valuable in theorising what the sociality of emotions and affects means in terms of historical changes and power configurations. This work shows us that what is felt 'is neither internally produced nor simply imposed on us from external ideological structures' (Rice 2008: 205), but rather this scholarship theorises that affects and emotions cannot be thought outside the complexities, reconfigurations and re-articulations of power, history and politics (Athanasiou, Hantzaroula and Yannakopoulos 2008). This scholarship highlights how psychic elements of relationality as responses to suffering, violence and trauma are entangled with historical, cultural, social and political norms and conventions. Affects and emotions shape and are shaped by 'the political contours of our social imaginaries' (Rice 2008: 206). This means that, instead of arguing that a person either buys into racist or nationalist beliefs wholesale or has them imposed wholesale, as Rice says characteristically, we are enabled to theorise affects and emotions – and thus difficult heritage – as intersections of language, desire, power, bodies, social structures, subjectivity, materiality and trauma.

Particularly useful for my examination of the role of emotions in engagement with difficult heritage is Reddy's (2001) concept of an 'emotional regime'. Reddy defines an 'emotional regime' as the set of normative emotions and the official rituals, practices and expressions that underpin any political regime or community – at the micro- or macro-level. 'Feeling rules' (Hochschild 1983) are inevitable in any emotional expressions within a community as these rules are expressions of power relations. Needless to say, these rules might change over time, or it is possible that different feeling rules might clash within a certain socio-political setting (Stearns and Stearns 1985; Rosenwein 2002). The boundaries of emotional regimes are not permanent but rather movable; these regimes are defined by the emotion norms and practices of emotional expression. For example, museum and heritage sites within particular cultural and political settings set rules of 'appropriate' emotion management; these norms certainly interact with personal and subjective habits of emotional expression. These conceptualisations highlight the interplay between the social and the psychic in emotional engagement with heritage and museum sites.

One recent example that shows the power and implications of emotional regimes in relation to difficult heritage is the emerging movement of reconciliation processes taking place in many parts of the world. There is a fundamental dilemma underlying these processes: how can one respond emotionally and politically to the difficult heritage of past atrocities (for example, the dark histories of genocide, wars, colonialism and racism) while promoting reconciliation processes? What if these reconciliation processes constitute departure points for emotional regimes that provide a shallow rather than rigorous historical understanding – all in the name of 'good' intentions for promoting reconciliation?

In her analysis of humanitarian and human rights movements on human suffering, Flam (2013) concluded that the moral feeling rule produced for dealing with the past/distant suffering is to place the burden on the victim from whom more is demanded in terms of courage, endurance and emotion management than from the perpetrators. The victims, then, are caught in a double bind: on the one hand, they are told they should testify for the sake of reconciliation, even if it is painful for them and they might face consequences; even if they would rather forget, they are told they should remember, tell and heal. On the other hand, the victims are told that they should leave their trauma behind and that they must not degrade or deny the dignity of the wrongdoer. The burden of reconciliation, then, is placed on the victims, who, although they have the right to rage, are told that they can only achieve empowerment when they forgive the perpetrators (Flam 2013). This joint therapeutic–reconciliation perspective establishes an emotional regime which imposes certain emotions on the victims and discourages other emotions in the name of reconciliation.

The above example highlights two ideas that are valuable in heritage and museum practices. Firstly, it is important to pay careful attention to the development of 'pedagogies of feeling' (Witcomb 2015) in museum and heritage sites, namely, curators need to engage with the idea that emotional experiences play a significant role in what visitors take home from their visits to museums and heritage sites. But this is not enough. The critical engagement with the pedagogical aspects of heritage and museum practices needs to seek a deeper understanding of the emotional regimes that might be evoked through these practices. A greater understanding of the intended and unintended consequences of potential emotional regimes elicited in museums and heritage sites is important for the project of revisionist agendas and political activism.

Contributions from critical history education

Generally speaking, history and museum education can play an important part in the process of reconciliation by addressing the legacies of conflict and trauma and by helping to overcome prejudice, resentment and hatred. Recent studies examining the potential of history education to make a contribution to reconciliation processes highlight that critical history education, especially the critical approach towards history textbooks and the narratives they present, is related to important components of reconciliation (Cole 2007a; Paulson 2011; Korostelina and Lässig 2013). Similar efforts in museum education focus on visitor's learning, meaning-making, experience and response to address in productively pedagogical manners different instances of difficult heritage (Witcomb 2013, 2015; Smith and Campbell 2016).

In relation to history education specifically, McCully (2010) refers to four contributions in the development of skills and dispositions that promote reconciliation and peace-building in the aftermath of conflict and trauma: critical thinking, multiperspectivity, caring and democratic values. The third contribution, caring, is particularly relevant to this chapter because it refers to fostering empathetic understanding and deals with the importance of addressing the emotional dimensions of reconciliation processes. Empathetic understanding, that is, the ability to identify (to at least some degree) with the experiences and situation of another person, is considered important in perspective-taking and caring with and about other people. For example, school history curricula, teaching and textbooks may function as a form of recognition of victims' suffering, thus 'giving voice' to the victims and allowing them to regain their sense of dignity. In a similar manner, difficult exhibits may offer openings to acknowledge the suffering of the Other (for example, an 'enemy') in public and museum exhibitions rather than a mono-perspectival recognition of the suffering of one's 'own' community.

At the same time, there are important challenges emerging when considering the contribution of history education in reconciliation processes.

Cole (2007b), for example, refers to the chicken-and-egg problem: history education can potentially promote reconciliation, yet a certain stage of reconciliation needs to be reached before textbooks and curricula are revised, and the public can accept these revisions, while teachers need to become able to challenge discredited narratives and take this risk in the classroom. Another problem, continues Cole (2007b), is the perennial tension in history education between the need to support patriotism and the need to provide young generations with a critical history – a tension that has become known in various countries (from the United States to Japan and Russia) as 'history wars' (Wertsch 2002). This problem raises many challenges regarding the clash between different needs and visions in a post-conflict society; balancing the need to avoid reigniting conflict with the need to foster social cohesion without creating a falsely (and, I would also add, sentimentalised) positive narrative is extremely difficult (Cole 2007b). Finally, another problem concerns how the aspirations from history education and the institutional realities of promoting reconciliation are not materialised. That is, the hopes raised by the larger movement of reconciliation may turn into bitter frustration and disappointment (Flam 2013), impacting expectations and realities at the micro-level.

I will take now as point of departure a measure that is often proposed and enacted in post-conflict societies to promote reconciliation processes – namely, the revision of history textbooks – and explore the different options that are available. My goal is to show not only how these options are relevant to heritage and museum practices, but also how they elicit different emotional regimes of reconciliation that need to be carefully considered by heritage and museum curators. In relation to history education, then, there are three options that can be undertaken in reconciliation processes, according to Pingel (2008, 2009). The first option is 'separation', that is, to choose one group, either the victors or the defeated, and defend its cause (Ahonen 2013). According to this option, conflicting sides promote different 'truths' and, therefore, it is very likely that the narratives of conflict will be perpetuated. This option seems to have been followed by educators in Bosnia-Herzegovina after the war of 1992–1995. The Dayton Agreement of 1995 confirmed the separate education systems of the three main ethnonational groups (Bosniaks, Bosnian Serbs and Bosnian Croats) and perpetuated cultural separatism; each side emphasised its own history and victimhood, while neglecting or disparaging those of the 'others' (Pingel 2008). This option, as will be discussed later, promotes obligations and feeling rules formulated for the victims of each side, while one's own perpetration is, for the most part, ignored.

The second option is 'harmonisation', in which there is an effort to impose a unifying 'truth' on the difficult past. The 'harmonisation' option aims at strengthening social cohesion and avoiding contested issues that might threaten the one and only 'truth' that is promoted. In the process, though, of constructing this one and only 'truth', it is possible that young generations in school are educated in the spirit of the rules of the existing political order. Ahonen (2013) writes about the case of Finland, in which the victors' values were initially imposed, followed decades later by a truly reconciliatory ethos that aimed to harmonise history narratives between conflicting sides. A similar effort in the case of Rwanda failed because the harmonisation effort glossed over the period of massacres, finding consolidation in a more distant, 'harmonious' past (Pingel 2008). The danger with this option is that it might promote a therapeutic, sentimental history of a harmonious past, while ignoring the 'difficult history' and the 'difficult emotions' experienced by the victims.

Finally, the third option is 'multiperspectivity', whereby 'truth' is seen as a communicative process; in this option, the goal of history education is to facilitate dialogue between the antagonistic memory communities (Ahonen 2013). This way was pursued in the case of South Africa after the end of apartheid in 1994 and in the German–French reconciliation efforts after World War II. This option, as will be discussed next, often promoted a politics of empathy and caring, while emphasising 'psychological' rather than 'historical' truth (Minow 1998). As McCully (2010) explains, when stories are told from multiple perspectives, they can have a cathartic effect and can generate caring, while 'unlocking the emotional barriers that resist the scrutiny of the recent past, thus facilitating recognition, redress, and repair. Yet, at this point, it may be difficult to verify such testimony through the more distanced vista of historical investigation' (McCully 2010: 219).

The questions that might be raised at this point are the following. What are the implications of these three different options – separation, harmonisation and multiperspectivity – in terms of the emotional regimes that might be invoked? And how can this analysis help curators reconsider the wider emotional regimes that might be elicited in reconciliation efforts to deal with difficult heritage? I would argue that these three options are available beyond textbook revisions to include critical engagement with difficult heritage in reconciliation processes more generally. Thus, the narrative possibilities of curatorial forms that promote reconciliation might include these three different options. A major challenge underpinning these different options is the need to respond to the legitimate request of victims that their suffering should be acknowledged, while at the same time ensuring that this acknowledgement does not perpetuate hatred and resentment (Cole 2007b). The acknowledgment of *all* victims' sufferings in engagement with difficult heritage potently raises the issue of fostering empathetic understanding (McCully 2010; Zembylas 2015). Through empathetic identification with victims' sufferings, as it is suggested, one can open oneself to differing ways of knowing and feeling and thus overcome feelings of resentment, animosity and hatred for 'others' that are commonly associated with difficult heritage. But how do questions about empathetic understanding with 'others' (who may be 'enemies') intersect with demands not to forget victims' suffering, and how do these questions map onto history and museum education efforts so that resentment is not perpetuated? What feeling rules might be invoked in efforts to promote the separation, harmonisation or multiperspectivity options? Finally, what are the perils of empathy and resentment when they become feeling rules? These are complex questions to address in a single piece of writing, therefore in the remainder of this chapter I focus on a discussion of the feeling rules formulated for perpetrators and victims in each of the three aforementioned options. My purpose is to explore some of the potential consequences when these options are pursued by curators in heritage and museum education practices; it remains to examine empirically, of course, whether and how these options are manifested in specific settings.

The emotional regimes elicited in reconciliation efforts to deal with difficult heritage

One of the mechanisms used to create 'us-and-them' categorisations is the constant fabrication of collective identity through the production of spaces of resentment for the Other (McCarthy and Dimitriadis 2000). A voluminous literature in sociology, psychology and philosophy deals with the emotional experience of resentment and its implications (see Barbalet 1998; Pedwell 2014 for reviews of some of this work). In common usage, 'resentment' refers to a feeling of displeasure as a result of being offended (Meltzer and Musolf 2002). Resentment is a reaction induced by feeling discredited in the eyes of others (Barbalet 1998). As argued by Barbalet (1998), personal experience and a direct relationship between perpetrator and victim are not necessary; direct relationships and personal experience, though, are likely to intensify the feeling of resentment and blend it with a desire for revenge. Those who are resented are conceived as hostile, as receiving undeserved advantage (Barbalet 1998), possibly 'gained at the expense of what is desirable or acceptable from the perspective of established rights' (Solomon 1990: 137). For Brown (1995), there is a paralysing tendency inflecting the logic of wound attachment; a preoccupation with past suffering risks forcing people and communities to get stuck in a present with no hope and a future that puts the past before everything.

The above ideas urge us to consider how emotions (for example, resentment) organise the social, emotional and pedagogical spaces in heritage and museum sites, creating powerful emotional boundaries between 'victims' and 'perpetrators'. Perpetrators, for example, are resented by victims through a discourse on emotions that assumes *they* (perpetrators) cause pain and injury to *us* (victims), especially if pain and injury are not recognised by the perpetrators. But victims may also be resented by perpetrators because victims may insist that their victimhood is remembered in order to score moral and political points (Ahmed 2004; Zembylas 2015). Thus, for example, the option of harmonisation and certainly the option of separation discussed earlier may perpetuate the politics of resentment, albeit from different angles. If harmonisation entails a harmonised discourse of 'truth' that avoids the recognition of victimhood and demands from the victims that they manage their emotions in the name of a common (reconciliatory) narrative, it is possible that victims' feelings of resentment might be kept alive (see, for example, Bekerman and Zembylas 2012; Noor *et al.* 2012). The perpetrators within a post-conflict society will be resented and conceived as hostile, because the victims will feel that in the name of reconciliation perpetrators get away with their crime – something that would be unacceptable to the victims from the perspective of human rights (Cole 2007b).

The politics of resentment as an emotional regime is more forceful, though, in the case of the separation option, in which a strong distinction between victims and perpetrators is drawn, according to which different 'psychological truths' (Minow 1998) are promoted by these collective groups. On the one hand, the victims are embittered and trapped in their resentment, as they find no recognition from perpetrators (Flam 2013). Sometimes the victims may be portrayed as heroic for their nation's history, yet, with the lack of recognition of their victimhood, it is unlikely that victims' feelings of resentment will be eased. On the other hand, the perpetrators do not offer any apology or ask for forgiveness, as the separation option does not allow for such a possibility. Arguably, then, both in the harmonisation option and in the separation option, more feeling rules are placed on the victims than on the perpetrators, confirming Flam's (2013) argument that victims in reconciliation situations are told more often than not that they should remember and tell with no assurance for recognition, while doing all the work to heal and forget.

A number of social theorists and scholars argue that, to intercept the politics of resentment, we need to learn how to empathise with the Other (Boler 1999; Nussbaum 2001; Pedwell 2014). While empathy is defined differently across various disciplines, it is generally understood as the imaginative experiencing of the feeling and perspectives of another person. That is, empathy is a *process* that unfolds over time and is informed by the work of the emotions to learn more about the Other's emotional states and perspectives. This process requires dialogue, imagination and affective attunement; thus, one's emotional engagement with another person through communication helps one to imagine how and why the Other acts or feels the way she or he does (Halpern 2001).

However, theorists from various disciplines, including heritage and museum studies (see, for example, Lowenthal 2009), warn us about the dangers of projecting one's own feelings and experiences onto others (Hollan and Throop 2008; Throop 2010). Claiming to 'know' the Other's experience across cultures and historical circumstances may involve forms of projection and appropriation that lead to 'empty' or 'sentimental' empathy (Zembylas 2013), that is, superficial forms of empathy that reify existing social and political structures. The term 'cheap sentimentality' was used by Hannah Arendt (1994: 251) to refer to what she saw as misplaced expressions of guilt among German youth after World War II. 'Empty sentimentality' is a similar term which refers to a superficial feeling of empathy and solidarity with those who suffer (see, for example, Kaplan 2005). Moreover, empathy is not boundless but rather always has a limit point, through which distinctions between subjects (for example, 'victims' and 'perpetrators') may be inevitably reinforced (Hemmings 2011). Finally, gaining empathetic insight into the life of one's collective 'enemy' may not always be considered a positively valued practice by members of one's community (Halpern and Weinstein 2004). In other words, we cannot assume that empathy is automatically and necessarily productive, as it intersects with the broader relational, interactional and discursive contexts and the opportunities and sites available for the Other. Arguably, then, there are complex personal, interpersonal, historical and political influences that are always at play in the process of constructing empathetic imagination in museum and heritage sites.

The 'multiperspectivity' option and, to a lesser extent, the 'harmonisation' one are the options which are more likely to engage heritage and museum visitors with mutual (rather than one-sided) empathetic understanding. Promoting reconciliation and empathy at the expense of truth and justice can tilt the balance towards less empathy for the victims and more for the perpetrators (Flam 2013). For example, if the harmonisation option entailed the construction of one and only 'truth', which is a 'felt truth' (Pedwell 2014), it would seem that the equation of the imaginative experience of the 'victim' and the 'perpetrator' – in the name of balance or compromise or avoidance of contested issues – 'puts the suffering of the victim on an equal footing with that of the bystander and the perpetrator' (Flam 2013: 375).

A similar peril exists for the multiperspectivity option, if curators and museum educators fail to consider the asymmetries in the suffering of victims or the interchange of roles between victims and perpetrators in some contexts. That is, if multiperspectivity simply puts the different perspectives side by side without engaging in a critical analysis to understand the emotional complexities in which 'victims' and 'perpetrators' are immersed, then it is unlikely that multiperspectivity will rise above a superficial 'sentimental history'. Sentimental history, according to Salber Phillips, is the history which wants to know not so much 'what happened' as 'what did it feel like to be there?' (Salber Phillips 2008: 52).

All three options outlined above highlight the need to take into consideration that neither the empathy for the victims nor the resentment for the perpetrators should be 'impulsive' (Flam 2013: 377). Instead, there ought to be a critical examination of the intended and unintended consequences of each option in terms of the possible emotional regimes that might be evoked or moulded through history or museum education within each setting.

Therefore, even if our intentions are 'good' – that is, promoting empathy for reconciliation – empathy and emotional sharing are not uncontested 'goods', whatever the context, outside any emotion regimes or normative framework. These efforts are always embedded in particular emotional regimes as they gain meaning within these regimes; however, the boundaries of these regimes are not permanent but fluid and changeable. The boundaries of these regimes are formulated by the norms, ideals, rituals and vocabularies developed through different options; if we want to change the boundaries, we need to develop new vocabularies and practices for dealing with the affective legacies of difficult heritage (Simon 2011a, 2014).

Concluding remarks

This chapter has explored the possible set of feeling rules specifying how different options in reconciliation processes might elicit different emotional regimes in dealing with difficult heritage. Drawing on work conducted in history education, I focused in particular on the rules proposed by the options of separation, harmonisation and multiperspectivity in relation to victims and perpetrators. Crucially, downplaying the suffering of the victims in the name of reconciliation or fostering empathy on the basis of which victims are promised some form of recognition while perpetrators receive compassion is likely to *re*produce existing 'structures of feeling' (Williams 1977) that place the burden on victims.

The task of curators and museum educators is – or at least ought to be – to create spaces where grievances can be freely expressed, and corresponding emotions can be productively worked through (cf. Hutchison and Bleiker 2008). The aim of heritage and museum practices would then be, according to Hutchison and Bleiker, 'to draw out and work through the collective, politicized forms of emotion that may unknowingly constitute animosity and divisive relations' (Hutchison and Bleiker 2008: 396). Facilitating such a critical analysis in the context of visitors' experiences in heritage and museum sites is certainly not easy, yet it will lead to a more thorough understanding of how emotions such as resentment and empathy operate as regimes and how they help to shape configurations of dealing with difficult heritage. A great obstacle to such critical reflection and analysis is constituted by those options that prevent heritage and museum visitors from recognising and delving into the emotional complexities of victimhood and perpetration. These observations highlight the need to continue working to enrich the different options available in dealing with difficult heritage in reconciliation processes, without getting stuck in certain regimes – a challenge that constantly raises new questions not only about the extent to which visitors can empathise with 'others' (in the light of distinctions between 'victims' and 'perpetrators') or work through their resentment, but also about what it means to take into account the contexts in which this happens, which are defined by trauma, political norms and 'structures of feeling'.

References

Ahmed, S., 2004. *The Cultural Politics of Emotion*. Edinburgh: Edinburgh University Press.

Ahonen, S., 2013. Post-conflict history education in Finland, South Africa and Bosnia-Herzegovina. *Nordidactica – Journal of Humanities and Social Science Education*, 1, 90–103.

Arendt, H., 1994. *Eichmann in Jerusalem: A Report on the Banality of Evil*. New York: Penguin.

Athanasiou, A., Hantzaroula, P. and Yannakopoulos, K., 2008. Towards a new epistemology: The 'affective turn'. *Historein*, 8, 5–16.

Barbalet, J., 1998. *Emotion, Social Theory and Social Structure*. Cambridge: Cambridge University Press.

Bekerman, Z. and Zembylas, M., 2012. *Teaching Contested Narratives: Identity, Memory and Reconciliation in Peace Education and Beyond*. Cambridge: Cambridge University Press.

Boler, M. 1999. *Feeling Power: Emotions and Education*. New York: Routledge.

Bonnell, J. and Simon, R., 2007. Difficult exhibitions and intimate encounters. *Museum and Society*, 5(2), 65–85.

Braunmühl, C., 2012. Theorizing emotions with Judith Butler: Within and beyond the courtroom. *Rethinking History*, 16(2), 221–240.

Britzman, D. P., 1998. *Lost Subjects, Contested Objects: Toward a Psychoanalytic Inquiry of Learning*. Albany: SUNY Press.

Britzman, D. P., 2000a. If the story cannot end: Deferred action, ambivalence, and difficult knowledge. In R. I. Simon, S. Rosenberg and C. Eppert, eds. *Between Hope and Despair: The Pedagogical Encounter of Historical Remembrance*. Lanham: Rowman and Littlefield, 27–57.

Britzman, D. P., 2000b. Teacher education in the confusion of our times. *Journal of Teacher Education*, 51(3), 200–205.

Brown, W., 1995. *States of Injury: Power and Freedom in Later Modernity*. Princeton: Princeton University Press.

Cole, E., ed. 2007a. *Teaching the Violent Past: History Education and Reconciliation*. Lanham: Rowman and Littlefield.

Cole, E., 2007b. Introduction: Reconciliation and history education. In E. Cole, ed. *Teaching the Violent Past: History Education and Reconciliation*. Lanham: Rowman and Littlefield, 1–28.

Cvetkovich, A., 2012. *Depression: A Public Feeling*. Durham: Duke University Press.

Flam, H., 2013. The transnational movement for Truth, Justice and Reconciliation as an emotional (rule) regime? *Journal of Political Power*, 6(3), 363–383.

Halpern, J., 2001. *From Detached Concern to Empathy: Humanizing Medical Practice*. New York: Oxford University Press.

Halpern, J. and Weinstein, H. M., 2004. Rehumanizing the other: Empathy and reconciliation. *Human Rights Quarterly*, 26, 561–583.

Hemmings, C., 2011. *Why Stories Matter: The Political Grammar of Feminist Theory*. London: Duke University Press.

Hochschild, A. R., 1983. *The Managed Heart: Commercialization of Human Feeling*. Berkeley: University of California Press.

Hollan, D. and Throop, J. C., 2008. Whatever happened to empathy? Introduction. *Ethos*, 36(4), 385–401.

Hook, D., 2011. Psychoanalytic contributions to the political analysis of affect and identification. *Ethnicities*, 11(1), 107–115.

Hutchison, E. and Bleiker, R., 2008. Emotional reconciliation: Reconstituting identity and community after trauma. *European Journal of Social Theory*, 11(3), 385–403.

Kaplan, A., 2005. *Trauma Culture: The Politics of Terror and Loss in Media and Literature*. New Brunswick: Rutgers University Press.

Korostelina, K. and Lässig, S., eds. 2013. *History Education and Post-conflict Reconciliation: Reconsidering Joint Textbook Projects*. New York: Routledge.

Lowenthal, D., 2009. Patrons, populists, apologists: Crises in museum stewardship. In L. Gibson and J. Pendlebury, eds. *Valuing Historic Environments*. Farnham: Ashgate, 19–31.

Massumi, B., 1996. The autonomy of affect. In P. Patton, ed. *Deleuze: A Critical Reader*. Oxford: Blackwell, 217–239.

McCully, A., 2010. The contribution of history to peace building. In G. Salomon and E. Cairns, eds. *Handbook on Peace Education*. New York: Psychology Press, 213–222.

McCarthy, C. and Dimitriades, G. 2000. Governmentality and the sociology of education: Media, educational policy and the politics of resentment. *British Journal of Sociology of Education*, 21(2), 169–185.

Meltzer, B. and Musolf, G. R. 2002. Resentment and ressentiment. *Sociological Inquiry*, 72, 240–255.

Minow, M., 1998. *Between Vengeance and Forgiveness: Facing History after Genocide and Mass Violence*. Boston: Beacon Press.

Noor, M., Shnabel, N., Halabi, S. and Nadler, A., 2012. When suffering begets suffering: The psychology of competitive victimhood between adversarial groups in violent conflict. *Personality and Social Psychology Review*, 16(4), 351–374.

Nussbaum, M., 2001. *Upheavals of Thought: The Intelligence of Emotions*. Cambridge: Cambridge University Press.

Paulson, J., ed. 2011. *Education and Reconciliation: Exploring Conflict and Post-conflict Situations*. New York: Continuum.

Pedwell, C., 2014. *Affective Relations: The Transnational Politics of Empathy*. New York: Palgrave Macmillan.

Pingel, F., 2008. Can truth be negotiated? History textbook revision as a means to reconciliation. *The ANNALS of the American Academy of Political and Social Science*, 617(1), 181–198.

Pingel, F., 2009. *UNESCO Guidebook on Textbook Research and Textbook Revision*. Paris: UNESCO.

Pitt, A. and Britzman, D. P., 2003. Speculations on qualities of difficult knowledge in teaching and learning: An experiment in psychoanalytic research. *International Journal of Qualitative Studies in Education*, 16(6), 755–776.

Plamber, J., 2010. The history of emotions: An interview with William Reddy, Barbara Rosenwein, and Peter Stearns. *History and Theory*, 49(2), 237–365.

Reddy, W. M., 2001. *The Navigation of Feeling: A Framework for the History of Emotions*. Cambridge: Cambridge University Press.

Rice, J., 2008. The new 'new': Making a case for critical affect studies. *Quarterly Journal of Speech*, 94(2), 200–212.

Rosenwein, B., 2002. Worrying about emotions in history. *American Historical Review*, 2, 821–845.

Salber Phillips, M., 2008. On the advantage and disadvantage of sentimental history for life. *History Workshop Journal*, 65, 49–64.

Simon, R. I., 2006a. The terrible gift: Museums and the possibility of hope without consolation. *Museum Management and Curatorship*, 21(3), 187–204.

Simon, R. I., 2006b. Museums, civic life, and the educational force of remembrance. *Journal of Museum Education*, 31(2), 113–122.

Simon, R. I., 2011a. A shock to thought: Curatorial judgment and the public exhibition of 'difficult knowledge'. *Memory Studies*, 4(4), 432–449.

Simon, R. I., 2011b. Afterword: The turn to pedagogy: A needed conversation on the practice of curating difficult knowledge. In E. Lehrer, C. E. Milton and M. E. Patterson, eds. *Curating Difficult Knowledge: Violent Pasts in Public Places*. New York: Palgrave Macmillan, 193–209.

Simon, R. I., 2014. *A Pedagogy of Witnessing: Curatorial Practice and the Pursuit of Social Justice*. Albany: SUNY Press.

Smith, L. and Campbell, G., 2016. The elephant in the room: Heritage, affect and emotion. In W. Logan, M. Nic Craith and U. Kockel, eds. *A Companion to Heritage Studies*. Oxford: Wiley Blackwell, 443–460.

Solomon, R., 1990. *A Passion for Justice*. Reading: Addison-Wesley.

Stearns, P. N. and Stearns, C. Z., 1985. Emotionology: Clarifying the history of emotions and emotional standards. *The American Historical Review*, 90, 813–836.

Throop, J., 2010. Latitudes of loss: On the vicissitudes of empathy. *American Ethnologist*, 37(4), 771–782.

Trofanenko, B., 2010. The educational promise of public history museum exhibits. *Theory and Research in Social Education*, 38(2), 270–288.

Wertsch, J., 2002. *Voices of Collective Remembering*. Cambridge and New York: Cambridge University Press.

Wetherell, M., 2012. *Affect and Emotion: A New Social Science Understanding*. London: Sage.

Williams, R., 1977. *Marxism and Literature*. Oxford: Oxford University Press.

Witcomb, A., 2010. The politics and poetics of contemporary exhibition making: Towards an ethical engagement with the past. In F. Cameron and L. Kelly, eds. *Hot Topics, Public Culture, Museums*. Newcastle upon Tyne: Cambridge Scholars Publishing, 245–264.

Witcomb, A., 2013. Understanding the role of affect in producing a critical pedagogy for history museums. *Museum Management and Curatorship*, 28(3), 255–271.

Witcomb, A., 2015. Toward a pedagogy of feeling: Understanding how museums create a space for cross-cultural encounters. In K. Message and A. Witcomb, eds. *The International Handbooks of Museum Studies. Volume 1: Museum Theory*. Chichester: Wiley Blackwell, 321–344.

Witcomb, A. and Buckley, K., 2013. Engaging with the future of 'critical heritage studies': Looking back in order to look forward. *International Journal of Heritage Studies*, 19(6), 562–578.

Zembylas, M., 2008. *The Politics of Trauma in Education*. New York: Palgrave Macmillan.

Zembylas, M., 2013. The 'crisis of pity' and the radicalization of solidarity: Towards critical pedagogies of compassion. *Educational Studies: A Journal of the American Educational Studies Association*, 49, 504–521.

Zembylas, M., 2014. Theorizing 'difficult knowledge' in the aftermath of the 'affective turn': Implications for curriculum and pedagogy in handling traumatic representations. *Curriculum Inquiry*, 44(3), 390–412.

Zembylas, M., 2015. *Emotion and Traumatic Conflict: Re-claiming Healing in Education.* Oxford: Oxford University Press.

Zembylas, M., 2017. Teacher resistance to engage with 'alternative' perspectives of difficult histories: The limits and prospects of affective disruption. *Discourse: Studies in the Cultural Politics of Education*, 38(5), 659–675.

Chapter 13

Affective practices of learning at the museum
Children's critical encounters with the past

Dianne Mulcahy and Andrea Witcomb

Introduction

STUDENT 1: *It unsettled me that I could make those judgements and see them as different people. Like the difference between the people – people have bad days, people have good days. Like it happens. They change, but it unsettled me that I could make the two different stereotypes about the same people.*

STUDENT 2: *I like it too because … when they were really cold and unwelcoming, it seemed like people were discriminating against them and stereotyping them, and I was like a third person watching their reaction, while not hurting them, if you know what I mean. So I felt sympathy for them, but then I kind of felt like they were being mean to me by having that cold, unwelcoming kind of reaction, and they were kind of really judgemental, and I felt like I could have been like discriminated against as well, but it was really nice when they were welcoming. And as Rose said, it was really interesting how the same people, but based on their actions, you can stereotype them differently.*

These comments, made by two Year 10 students during an interview about their experiences of the *Identity: Yours, Mine, Ours* exhibition at the Immigration Museum in Melbourne, usefully open up the intellectual terrain that we wish to explore in this chapter. Made in response to the Welcome Wall – a video installation by Lynette Wallworth which consists of groups of people from a wide variety of ethnic and cultural backgrounds making both welcoming and pushing-away gestures – these comments point to the ways in which embodied forms of learning occurring in response to affective and emotive situations can open up a critical disposition in which relations between self and others become the ground of critical inquiry. Our aim here is twofold – to demonstrate the value of museum exhibitions for providing embodied learning opportunities aimed at developing critical capacities and, at the same time, to demonstrate the central role of affect in this learning practice.

In doing so, we want also to contribute to nascent discussions on the role of affect in the fields of museum studies and education. These discussions are part of a much larger interest in emotions and affect in the humanities and social sciences over recent decades (Brooks 2014; Lemmings and Brooks 2014), with affect, in particular, emerging as a key site for social and cultural research (Wetherell 2015). Accompanying this turn to affect is a renewed interest in registers of the material and the bodily (Blackman 2012), which has led to an understanding that affect is generated in interactions between bodies, a point that the comments from the students support, given their close attention to how the bodies of other people, when positioned in relation to their own, made them feel. Scholars are recognising also that there is no fundamental difference between reason, emotion and affect as 'each elicits responses from the body' (Isin 2014). Emotion, reason and affect are mutually implicated; each term shapes and informs the others and leads to forms of thinking, a point also supported by the students' comments, as they move from articulating how they felt to what this feeling made them think about – in this case, how easy it was to stereotype others.

Despite this, it is widely acknowledged that a cognitivist bias continues to play out in education (Zembylas 2007; Saito 2010; Mulcahy 2015) taking attention away from the ability of affect to promote the desire and capacity to learn (Mulcahy 2016), including the capacity to foster critical forms of thinking that can assist museum visitors to negotiate significant social and historical issues (Witcomb 2013). Importantly, this affective capacity also activates learners' ethical and political imaginations and induces attentiveness to otherness (Mulcahy 2016). Affect can prompt a practice of engaging ethically with the Other which, for Andreotti (2007: 74), involves establishing a responsibility *to* the Other (as answerability or accountability). Within cultural heritage and museum studies there is a growing interest in how emotions and affect are mobilised in contemporary processes of drawing on the past to undertake social, cultural and political work in the present (Trofanenko 2014; Witcomb 2013, 2015). This interest is relatively recent. As Smith (2015) claims, museums and heritage sites are, above all, places where people go to 'feel', yet curators at these institutions have traditionally paid little attention to emotion and affect. Knowledge, which is taken to be a form of cognitive engagement, has commonly been considered the result of attending any museum exhibition. Dominant discourses about museum visitation assume that museum visitors will take away information learned. As a consequence, and as Smith and Campbell (2016) state, affect and emotion is 'the elephant in the room'. The intricate interconnections between the cognitive and the affective go unrecognised. Guided by the idea of affective practice (Wetherell 2012, 2013), we explore how the close relationship between the cognitive, the affective and learning at the museum can produce critical changes in knowledge and understanding. We consider not only what the embodied museum visit may *mean* for (children's) learning, about which, as Smith (2015: 461) states, there has been little examination to date, but also what it *does* – what it stages, performs and enacts. We assume from the outset that learning involves affective relations and ask the following question: *how do affective practices of learning at the museum work?*

The structure of the chapter is as follows. Initially, we provide a practice-oriented account of the concepts of affect and learning. Here, we draw from a tradition of work on affect that, while challenging the foundational model of autonomous subjectivity which underlies the psychological sciences, retains the importance of the psyche or psychological (Blackman 2012; Walkerdine and Jimenez 2012; Wetherell 2012, 2013). We give an account of learning as learning to be affected, attending to how affect, and, in concert, learning, extend beyond the subjective and subjectivities, while being given meaning by the subject (Dragojlovica 2015). Leading with an affective *practice* approach (Reckwitz 2002, 2012; Wetherell 2012, 2013), and drawing selectively on the work of Deleuze and Guattari (1987, 1994), we proceed to study affectivity at the museum practically. We do so by deploying data from video-based case studies of 40 school students' experiences of learning when visiting Museum Victoria, Australia's largest public museum organisation, focusing on how their affective learning practices within the exhibition space enabled them to achieve specific kinds of social understandings. Finally, the insights that these analyses offer for better understanding encounters with the past are discussed, with particular attention given to the character of learning as an affective practice. We argue that this practice can potentially provide an unsettling of existing understandings and attachments and open a space through which issues of social justice can be addressed.

On affect and learning as learning to be affected: A practice-oriented perspective

Affect is framed in multiple ways depending on the intellectual traditions that are brought to bear. A distinction can be drawn between traditions in which affect is construed as mediated by human consciousness, intentionality and interpretation and traditions in which it unfolds free of the human subject, as an impersonal force or flow. For Wetherell (2013: 228), the latter tradition promotes a 'subjectless' approach to affect, the most provocative expression of which can be found in the work of Nigel Thrift (2008a). Affect, writes Thrift (2008b: 116), 'is not … reducible to the affections or perceptions of an individual subject'. It is 'a passionate, shared, and embodied intensity that erupts beyond the register of consciousness' (Gibson-Graham 2006: 203). Or, as Rice (2008: 201) has it, 'affect describes an energetics that does not necessarily emerge at the level of signification'. In this chapter, we draw selectively on both designations of affect, showing most particularly through the empirical material how they can play out in relation to each other and in relation to the situation or circumstances at hand. In company with Dragojlovica (2015), we consider how affect operates through and across the binary oppositions of cognitive and affective, intentional and non-intentional, and how it is given meaning by the subject, echoing arguments made by Blackman (2012: 22) that affect is always subject to mediation. We hold to the idea that affective relations can be interpreted and serve self-making – such as the making of the museum learner, among other subjectivities. Accordingly, we lead with the concept of affective practice (Wetherell 2012, 2013). Drawing on the social practice approach articulated by the social philosopher Theodore Schatzki (2002; Schatzki, Knorr Cetina, and von Savigny 2001), the affective practice approach emphasises the embedded and embodied character of affects. As Reckwitz (2012: 251) has it,

> affects are always embedded in practices which are, in turn, embedded in tacit schemes of interpretation. Affects are thus not psychological or mental processes, but they constitute an integral part of the practical activities within which human bodies relate to other objects and subjects.

Affect can thus be understood 'as a form of embodied cognition or thinking, a processual engagement with the world' (Conradson and McKay 2007: 170). This kind of engagement implies a shift in focus from affect as an inner psychological state of *human* being to affect as embodied practice. Wetherell (2012: 159) sees 'affective practice as a moment of recruitment and often synchronous assembling of multimodal resources, including, most crucially, body states'. An affective practice approach

> takes as its focus and units of analysis patterns and cycles of activity that at a particular historical moment have become 'emotionalised' ... An affective practice typically pulls together or orders in relation to each other patterns of body/brain activity, patterns of meaning-making, feelings, perceptions, cognition and memories, interactional potentialities and routines, forms of accountability, appraisals and evaluations, subject positions and histories of relationships. In this sense, an affective practice can be usefully seen in Anderson's terms as a kind of flowing assemblage, an articulation or a dynamic figuration (Wetherell 2013: 235–236).

Here, reference is made to the work of the cultural geographer Ben Anderson, who holds to the Deleuzian idea of *assemblage*. As discussed by Deleuze and Guattari (1987), the idea of assemblage directs attention to the many, diverse and contesting actors, agencies and practices through which human subjects and material objects take form. And, as they (Deleuze and Guattari 1987: 22–23) write,

> an assemblage, in its multiplicity, necessarily acts on semiotic flows, material flows, and social flows simultaneously ... There is no longer a

tripartite division between a field of reality (the world) and a field of representation (the book) and a field of subjectivity (the author). Rather, an assemblage establishes connections between certain multiplicities drawn from each of these orders.

Affect is rendered radically differently in social practice and Deleuzian philosophic accounts, most particularly with regard to the place they accord the human subject within analyses. 'A social practice perspective on the social basically focuses on human activity' (Reckwitz 2012: 248). While important differences between these approaches exist, specific emphases are shared, for example the focus on relationality: affective practice 'is an organic complex in which all the parts relationally constitute each other' (Wetherell 2012: 19). A certain commensurability also exists between the terms affective practice and assemblage. An affective practice is 'a kind of flowing assemblage' (Wetherell 2013: 236). As Wetherell (2012: 4) states, 'practice is also capacious enough to extend to some of the new thinking available about activity, flow, assemblage and relationality and to follow translations of aspects of Deleuzian and other philosophical projects into social research'. Thus, 'a practice is an assemblage for now which draws on past assemblages and influences the shape of future activity' (Wetherell 2015: 148).

The terms assemblage and affective practice are also illuminating when considering learning. Contrary to currently well-established cognitivist, constructivist and representational conceptions[1] of learning in education, we argue that learning is a matter of both body and mind – or, as Semetsky puts it, of 'learning with bodymind' (Semetsky 2013). An affective, intensive and material process, learning establishes 'the bond of a profound complicity between nature and mind' (Deleuze and Guattari 1994: 165). In an oft-cited claim, Deleuze (2004: 139, original emphasis) stated that

> Something in the world forces us to think. This something is an object not of recognition but of a fundamental *encounter*. What is encountered may be Socrates, a temple or a demon. It may be grasped in a range of affective tones: wonder, love, hatred, suffering. In whichever tone, its primary characteristic is that it can only be sensed.

Here, 'affect' is the catalyst for thinking and a form of encounter. Learning is the change effected as a result of encounters: a coming together (assemblage) of affects, objects and material practices such as a shock to thought (Massumi 2002). Conventional distinctions between subject and object are dismantled: a subject is not separable from its relations with the world. Instead of considering a learner as a subject, the focus falls on *affects* as forms of *encounter* through which lines of force or power pass: animate affects (Niccolini 2016). Switching the interpretive frame, learning as an affective *practice* is 'a figuration where body possibilities and routines become recruited or entangled together with meaning-making and with other social and material figurations' (Wetherell 2012: 19). Bodies and meaning-making are 'the main things that an affective practice folds or composes together' (Wetherell 2012: 20). Affect is disclosed predominantly in embodied action and meaning-making, but also in 'atmospheres, fleeting fragments and traces, gut feelings and embodied reactions and in felt intensities and sensations' (Blackman 2015: 25). In the final analysis, it is affective phenomena and how they are performed in practices that we are most concerned to investigate. Our interest lies in ways of thinking about affect that might be especially generative for achieving an empirical understanding of how museum-based learning occurs.

Data and methods

Our analysis draws on three bodies of data collected over the course of a small-scale, one-year study (2013–2014) sponsored by the University of Melbourne in collaboration with Museum Victoria. The methodological approach adopted was informed by the emerging interest in education research in materialist perspectives that provide purchase on sociomaterial practice and affect as a distributed and dynamic phenomenon (Fenwick, Edwards and Sawchuk 2011; Hickey-Moody 2013; Mazzei 2013).[2] Initially, video-based case studies of 'naturally' occurring interactions in selected exhibition spaces at each of Museum Victoria's three venues, Melbourne Museum, the Immigration Museum and Scienceworks (see http://museumvictoria.com.au/) were conducted by the first author and her co-researchers. Subsequently, interviews were undertaken with lead curators on these exhibitions (three altogether), museum educators and participating teachers (six altogether) and participating students (six altogether). Finally, documentary data were collected from the visiting schools towards gaining a sense of the preparations made for the museum visit and the educational intent of it. More specifically, extensive use was made of video, including (i) whole-group camerawork by two technicians of student groups (40 students altogether) within exhibition spaces and (ii) individual body camerawork via GoPro action cameras which recorded students' embodied movement through these spaces and 'captured' what they saw and said individually over the course of the filming. Paired interviews were conducted with two children (selected by the visiting teacher) immediately after the filming. These interviews were both video-stimulated and video-recorded. Using as catalyst the video record from the GoPro cameras, the children were invited to make a reconstructive account of these encounters with regard to their learning. Their commentary was directed by questions such as 'Can you tell me about what you *best liked doing* during the activity filmed?' and 'As you made your way through the exhibition, what jumped out at you as something you might like to look at again or take part in? *What left the strongest impression* on you? Can you say why?' Altogether, 40 students took part in the filming, ranging in

Affective practices of learning   219

age from eight to 16, with the filming at each museum taking approximately one hour. Students and visiting teachers were drawn from a Catholic primary school, an independent (non-government) girls' secondary school and a government secondary college. The exhibitions in which the school visitors were filmed at each of the museums above were, respectively, *The Melbourne Story*, *Identity: Yours, Mine, Ours* and *Think Ahead*. These exhibitions invite embodied engagements, making them ideal for the study of affective practices of learning. Given limitations of space, we will discuss only the data collected from Melbourne Museum and the Immigration Museum.

Affective practices of learning at the museum: Contemporary engagements with the past

Case 1. Little Lon: 'Like [they] shared their stuff because they were really poor'

A historic recreation of two workers' cottages (figure 13.1) in an inner-city area of Melbourne with a reputation for being a slum, riddled with poverty, prostitution and drug addiction, the Little Lon exhibit at Melbourne Museum[3] offers an immersive sensory experience. Recreating two types of lived experience of the working poor, one cottage shows extreme poverty (figure 13.2) while the other is the home of a family who have some material comforts (see figure 13.3). The cottages are 'peopled' through audio stories that provide a sense of the lives of their occupants and of the broader social history of the area and are dressed with props and collection objects (home furnishings, cooking and washing utensils, a sanitary pan toilet). Little Lon affords the opportunity to show how embodied capacities to learn are 'increased or decreased by sounds, lights, smells, the atmospheres of places and people' (Hickey-Moody 2013: 80). It also serves to show that affect is a public and communal event (Wetherell 2014: 147).

Upon entering the two cottages, children were observed handling domestic items and trying out items (stools, sofas, beds) for size and comfort towards, getting, we think, a 'fix' on the experience of living as a family in past times and in what was taken at the time to be an unwholesome slum. The children were engaged with their bodies, showing immediate responsiveness to the material world they were encountering. Affect as the act of affecting and being affected was in evidence through connections made between children's bodies, for example, directions given gesturally by some children to others to attend to certain items, and between children's bodies and the cottages' objects. These connections are crucial for inducing certain bodily arousals (Reckwitz 2012: 250) such as anxiety, joy, wonder, surprise and distaste, each of which was captured on camera over the course of the exploration of the cottages. Thus, looks of alarm appeared initially on the faces of some chidren upon entering the dark and seemingly squalid space of the poorer cottage, as

Figure 13.1 Recreated cottages with laneway in the distance, Little Lon display in *The Melbourne Story*, Melbourne Museum. Photographer: Ben Healley
Source: Museums Victoria.

Figure 13.2 Interior of poorer cottage, Little Lon display in *The Melbourne Story*, Melbourne Museum. Photographer: Ben Healley
Source: Museums Victoria.

did grimacing and turning up of noses when the clothes hung in the bedroom of this cottage were touched. As Pyyry (2016: 9) has it, reflection and learning arise via relations between sensing and the sensed. Expressing distaste for the crowded conditions in the poorer cottage and specifically for the sanitary pan toilet, the conversation of one group of students progressed thus:

> I couldn't live in this place ... so small and, we all have bigger houses and it makes us feel better like, what if we lived here, bit worried ...
> Look, it's the toilet.
> That's the toilet! Oooh.
> Look at the toilet. Imagine ...
> Just imagine.
> Maybe I don't want to look in there (sanitary pan).
> Yeah!
> I'm already expecting that this house is poorer than the other house ... just makes you feel so bad for them.
> Like the two beds in there are just like squished into each other, there's like barely any space.

This small-group conversation demonstrates the idea of affective–discursive meaning-making. The children are coming to a view of whether

Figure 13.3 Interior of more aspirational cottage, Little Lon display in *The Melbourne Story*, Melbourne Museum. Photographer: Ben Healley
Source: Museums Victoria.

they could live in such cramped conditions, and this view is formed affectively: their meaning-making is produced as embodied *action* as they move from one cottage to another, interacting on route with objects such as washing hung on the washing line, the outside toilet which one of the children enters and the sanitary pan upon which she sits, eliciting a comment from the accompanying museum educator of 'Oooh, you're brave.' The affective force of objects is shared and amplified through language. As Dawney (2011: 601, original emphasis) claims, 'language can operate *as* affect: it has the power to impact materially on the body, to course through and between bodies', as is evident in these data through the repetition of phrases such as 'Look, it's the toilet' and 'Just imagine.' Affect is performative: it directs the children's attention to the material conditions of inner-city life in times of 'so small' houses and provokes thinking about and judgement of these conditions: 'Just imagine.' The two cottages impel thought regarding the size of housing, present and past, and the social issues attaching to housing such as its affordability, as discussed further below. This thought is *felt thought* – 'I couldn't live in this place'; 'just makes you feel so bad for them'.

From observation, the depth of affective engagement with, and by extension, learning from, the challenges presented by Little Lon was different for different children. A unitary, singular and shared response to these challenges cannot be assumed, given the children's different histories of relationship with the museum,[4] among many other matters (socio-economic status, ethnicity, gender, children's knowledge and interests). In the case of one of the children interviewed, the felt thought expressed was particularly critically inflected:

> Little Lonsdale Street wasn't really rich, and they didn't have, you know, that good houses. So they lived and they … yeah they lived in such small houses, but they still … they still lived in it and they didn't care if it was big or not, they just wanted a house.

Joseph observed a little later in the interview that Little Lon reflected

> things that represented fairness, like some of the objects and (living in) Little Lonsdale Street was like (they) shared their stuff because they were really poor … if you looked at the backyard(s), they were both connected … In the rich house, part of the window was like curtained, which is like it wasn't connected.

Here, Joseph appears aware of the exclusionary and privatising impulses of rich houses; the curtained window in the rich house and the desire it embeds produces a capacity to engage the ethical and social justice dimensions of this situation – 'things that represent(ed) fairness'. Since the children hailed from a Catholic primary school where the current curriculum focus is 'Australia – A fair place for all?', the ground for an affective practice of learning at the museum had been pre-prepared. In this instance, the encounter with the cottages can be claimed to have prompted a critical and ethical engagement with the past and possibly its legacies in the present (Witcomb 2013). Joseph's report on his learning at interview implies a socio-political and ethical education induced in part through his embodied and affective response to the cottages. He was filmed putting up curtains that had fallen down in one of the cottages, towards, we take it, making a more 'homely' family life for a family, not members of a city slum. Here, affect is disclosed in embodied action, in discourse (the discursive shift from city slum to family home) and in material practice, the affective ties of putting up curtains. We were 'witness' to a body through which affects give rise to learning – 'they didn't care if it was big or not, they just wanted a house' – with the potential for affects to be directed in productive ways for social justice.

Case 2. Tram Scenario: *Breaking out in 'swear' words*

Opened in 2011, the exhibition *Identity: Yours, Mine, Ours*, within which the filming at the Immigration Museum was undertaken, attempts to address issues around diversity, difference, prejudice and racism. In the words of the museum educator at interview, 'the whole exhibition works on pulling at *you* and *your* awareness, and your self-awareness'. This 'pulling work' is very evident in the affect engendered by one of the exhibition's exhibits, the *Tram Scenario*, a video that invites viewers to 'see a racist incident that takes place on a tram'.[5] The scenario plays out in a tram-like structure in which museum visitors can sit and aims to have school visitors address the following questions: How do we feel when difference moves in next door? Or sits next to us on the train or in the classroom? One of the Year 10 student visitors from the independent girls' secondary school described the *Tram Scenario* at interview in these terms:

> Well ... this guy ['Rob'], he walks on a tram, and this [other guy, 'Ibrahim'] ... I think he's Aboriginal, or I think that's what I took from it, but he makes like ... I think he makes a spare seat for the guy to sit down next to him, but then the man doesn't sit next to him. And so ... and then he [Rob] starts ... he starts drinking, and then the Aboriginal guy gets on the phone and he starts talking in his native language to someone, and he [Rob] goes – 'oh excuse me, you're too loud, can you lower the volume?' And he still wasn't sitting next to him, and then he ... and then he just crushed his can and walked out of the tram.

In addressing the question 'how does the *Tram Scenario* work and for whom?', we hold a copy of the transcript of the scenario, which is available on the Museum Victoria website (see note 5 below), against a copy of the conversation held by a small group of Year 10 girls while watching the *Tram Scenario* video. Many of the girls' remarks are made as a direct address, the addressee, in all cases, being the figure of Rob.

224 Dianne Mulcahy and Andrea Witcomb

Transcript: Tram Scenario	Transcript: Viewing the video of Tram Scenario
[Tram sounds and hum of conversations] [Tram door opening and closing beeps] [Can cracking open] [Phone rings] [Ibrahim speaks in Tigrinya language] [Drinking sounds] Rob: Hey, mate ... Hey, hey! Can you keep it down a bit? You're a bit loud. [Can crushing] [Tram door opening and closing beeps]	[Background chat amongst girls] [Rob enters tram] Aaah. Excuse you! *Get out!* Oh, my god ... he's so weird. He's slurping really loudly. Oh my god, just sit down! Oh! Jeeez. *You're* a bit loud! Your slurping's louder than he's talking! Oooh. He looks drunk ... oh, my god!

Affect is central. Again, language operates *as* affect. It courses through and between bodies as is evident in these data through the repetition of phrases such as 'Oh my god', 'Jeeez' and 'Aaah'. It brings both righteous indignation and empathy into effect. Underwritten perhaps by gender, age and class markers, the righteous indignation directed by the girls at Rob has particular valence as implied in the utterances 'Excuse you!' and 'Get out!' Affect *is* a form of encounter that circulates between and within bodies (human and otherwise), yet it is not free-floating. It is anchored in words and in already available subject positions of perpetrator, victim and bystander of racial abuse that are inscribed in the *Tram Scenario*. As Wetherell (2012: 125) puts it, 'Practice draws attention both to a transpersonal "ready-made" we confront and slip into, as well as to active and creative figuring.' Recruited to, and caught up in, the practice of calling out racism, albeit as virtual bystanders to a racist incident, these girls engage affectively/discursively, towards bringing a new configuration of social relations into effect. Their outrage at the unfair treatment of Ibrahim can be considered to produce an opening up to difference, evident in the affective response of Nelly, one of the students interviewed, to the *Tram Scenario*:

> I felt terrible. Like I really felt the side of the victim watching that, and so I felt really bad, and I felt maybe like guilty for doing the same thing, like maybe I do that. So it made me think about my actions in relation to like what was happening.

What is important here is that Nelly did not stop her reflection at the point at which she expressed her feelings but went on to articulate how those feelings caused her to think about her own practices. As Ahmed (2014: 201, original emphasis) cautions, 'emotional struggles against injustice are not about finding good or bad feelings, and then expressing them' but rather 'about how we are moved by feelings into a different relation to the norms that we wish to contest, or the wounds we wish to heal'. This can happen, she argues, when we are moved by an affective response to a 'sticky' object or situation – something is left behind which makes us be or do otherwise. As Simon (2006) argued in relation to the 'terrible gift' embodied in the testaments offered by Holocaust survivors in museum settings, the challenge on the part of those using affect as a pedagogical tool for altering social relations is to make us feel sufficiently differently that we want to act in the present for a different future. Being moved to action is a form of work 'which opens up different kinds of attachments to others, in part through the recognition of this work *as* work' (Ahmed 2014: 201, original emphasis), much as the student above recounts as she continues:

> Oh I interpreted it [Rob *not* taking the seat next to Ibrahim] as ... well at first I thought of all the people on my bus, 'cause I catch the bus every day, and how they just ... I don't know why, they just don't sit down in spare seats. I think it's because they don't want to sit next to ... I don't think it's the person, but I think it's just like they don't want to ... they want to sit by themselves or with their friends, not someone they don't know ... [W]hen I first started catching the bus, I was like those people, and I didn't want to sit next to other people because they were strangers and I didn't know them, not because they were a different race or something. But then I just started to learn that ... I don't know ... it doesn't really matter, yeah, it's a seat, it's a person, like there's nothing wrong with sitting next to whoever. So it kind of made me think back to that, and how people on my bus still do that.

These data well illustrate Reckwitz's (2012: 251) claim that 'affects are always embedded in practices which are, in turn, embedded in tacit schemes of interpretation' and, we add, embedded in body politics. In learning to sit next to whoever, Nelly opens herself up to 'creative affective connections with the Other' (Zembylas 2006: 313). Affect circulates in the embodied action of sitting next to other people on the bus and in the meanings to be made with regard to this action, which are not easy to articulate: 'I don't know why ... I think it's because ... I don't think it's ... I think it's just like ...'. It is also disclosed in objects and 'atmospheres' such as the confined space that a tram or a bus can produce. Sitting 'next to whoever' on the bus is a process and product of learning and, at the same time, an *affective intervention*, an 'explicit mobilisation of affect to produce new understandings of social interactions' (Zembylas 2006: 312). Albeit mundane, it is a political and ethically inflected act.

Conclusions: Affective practice and animate affects

Working across multiple modalities (the psychic *and* the social, the affective *and* the discursive), the concept of affective practice is rightly argued to enable a 'useful and pragmatic empirical approach' to analysing affective, embodied engagements (Wetherell 2012: 20). Affect is embodied, situated and operates (socio)psychologically: 'I couldn't live in this place ... so small ... what if we lived here, bit worried.' Contrary to the Deleuzian emphasis on flow, both change and continuity can be accounted for, as evidenced in Nelly's narrative of when she first started catching the bus. As Wetherell (2012: 125) indicates, the affective practice approach allows us to grasp 'the ongoingness of a particular subject, their repetitions and continuities, and the ways in which their present practice intertwines with their past practice'. This is illustrated in reflections such as Nelly's 'But then I just started to learn that ... I don't know ... it doesn't really matter, yeah, it's a seat, it's a person, like there's nothing wrong with sitting next to whoever.' We are sensitised to the idea that learning affectively at the museum and beyond it involves both body routines and a good deal of interpretive work. Affects are 'closely intertwined with social norms and shared meanings and, as such, they are (also) something that we learn and do as part of our socialization into our respective community' (Johansen 2015: 49). They are also materially inflected.

Affect provides richly generative, but often overlooked, pedagogic and political sites such as the spare seat offered by Ibrahim to the bullying Rob in the *Tram Scenario* and taken in time by Nelly on her bus towards 'sitting next to whoever'. As Wetherell (2012: 159) has it, it is the 'participation of the emoting body that makes an assemblage an example of affect rather than an example of some other kind of social practice'. The empirical material attests to the centrality of this body, yet the possibility that bodies other than (human) emoting ones also constitute affective assemblages could, with profit, be kept in view. It is the animating capacities of affect, carried not only in human bodies, but also in material objects (spare seats, 'slum' dwellings, curtained windows) and material practice ('sitting next to whoever', can crushing, putting up curtains), the prosaic netherworlds of affective practice, that help us comprehend what the embodied museum visit means for learning, and also what it does; what it brings into effect. Returning to the empirical material, learning opens up only if museum visitors are sufficiently *attracted* to want to invest their labour long enough to gain insight into the issues at hand. As one of the students at interview commented,

> I liked the tram because it's a real-life situation and like I could actually see that happening, so it was really realistic, so you could like relate to it ... I thought it was entertaining, so that's why I liked it, and I liked it because it made me think because otherwise if it's just too straightforward, then, as I said, it doesn't interest me. So then I won't want to keep reading it or watching it.

The point this Year 10 student is making is worth pausing on. It is all too common an assumption that museums only reinforce that which is already known; that they rarely, if ever, offer opportunities to think again, in ways that challenge received understandings. The assumption is always that the function of museums is to celebrate collective identities in ways that reinforce established power relations by operating within established comfort zones. In many situations this is undoubtedly true. It is also true that both affect and emotion are tools that are used to achieve these ends. This student, however, alerts us to the fact that representing established ways of looking at things is boring and will not catch their attention. They want a challenge, they want to be interested by being attracted to something that they have not yet felt their way around, even if that is through something that is, at first sight, recognisable, like the tram setting. What these students found exciting and what provoked them to new thoughts was that these exhibitions caused them to think anew about themselves and their relations to others – whether in the past or in the present. The exhibitions did so by providing the students with an opportunity to engage in affective learning practices that invited new relations, new assemblages between themselves and the social realities they encountered. Affective practices of learning at the museum, then, can provide an opening for unsettling existing understandings and attachments through which issues of social justice can be addressed.

Notes

1 While cognitivist, constructivist and representationalist accounts take a variety of directions and follow a number of influences, they share the understanding that a traditional knowing subject lies at the heart of learning and that this subject is separable from its relations with the world.
2 Interest in materialist, and relatedly, affective methodology, is burgeoning in education research. A number of publications now provide accounts of it. See, in particular, Hickey-Moody and Page (2016), Snaza *et al.* (2016) and Zembylas and Schutz (2016).
3 Melbourne Museum is a natural and cultural history museum located in Melbourne, the capital city of the Australian state of Victoria. Little Lon forms part of a single exhibition on the history of Melbourne, *The Melbourne Story*, and comprises a display that includes two cottages which are physically identical to those that would have populated the lanes of an inner-city area adjoining Lonsdale Street, in the mid-to-late nineteenth century.
4 Of the two children interviewed for the case study at Melbourne Museum, one had visited the museum with her family once and the other 'a couple of times, and a couple of times with my family'.
5 See http://museumvictoria.com.au/immigrationmuseum/discoverycentre/identity/videos/tram-scenario-videos/tram-scenario/.

References

Ahmed, S., 2014. *The Cultural Politics of Emotion* (2nd edn). Edinburgh: Edinburgh University Press.
Andreotti, V., 2007. An ethical engagement with the other: Spivak's ideas on education. *Critical Literacy: Theories and Practices*, 1(1), 69–79.
Blackman, L., 2012. *Immaterial Bodies: Affect, Embodiment, Mediation.* London: Sage.
Blackman, L., 2015. Researching affect and embodied hauntologies: Exploring an analytics of experimentation. In B. T. Knudsen and C. Stage, eds. *Affective Methodologies: Developing Cultural Research Strategies for the Study of Affect.* Basingstoke: Palgrave Macmillan, 25–44.
Brooks, A., 2014. 'The affective turn' in the social sciences and the gendered nature of emotions: Theorizing emotions in the social sciences from 1800 to the present. In D. Lemmings and A. Brooks, eds. *Emotions and Social Change: Historical and Sociological Perspectives.* New York: Routledge, 43–62.

Conradson, D. and McKay, D., 2007. Translocal subjectivities: Mobility, connection, emotion. *Mobilities*, 2(4), 167–174.

Dawney, L., 2011. The motor of being: A response to Steve Pile's 'Emotions and affect in recent human geography'. *Transactions of the Institute of British Geographers*, 36(4), 599–602.

Deleuze, G., 2004. *Difference and Repetition*. London: Bloomsbury.

Deleuze, G. and Guattari, F., 1987. *A Thousand Plateaus: Capitalism and Schizophrenia*. Trans. B. Massumi. Minneapolis and London: University of Minnesota Press.

Deleuze, G. and Guattari, F., 1994. *What Is Philosophy?* London: Verso.

Dragojlovica, A., 2015. Affective geographies: Intergenerational hauntings, bodily affectivity and multiracial subjectivities. *Subjectivity*, 8(4), 315–334.

Fenwick, T., Edwards, R. and Sawchuk, P., 2011. *Emerging Approaches to Educational Research: Tracing the Sociomaterial*. London and New York: Routledge.

Gibson-Graham, J. K., 2006. *A Postcapitalist Politics*. Minneapolis: University of Minnesota Press.

Hickey-Moody, A., 2013. Affect as method: Feelings, aesthetics and affective pedagogy. In R. Coleman and J. Ringrose, eds. *Deleuze and Research Methodologies*. Edinburgh: Edinburgh University Press, 79–95.

Hickey-Moody, A. and Page, T., eds., 2016. *Arts, Pedagogy and Cultural Resistance: New Materialisms*. Lanham: Rowman & Littlefield International.

Isin, E., 2014. Acts, affects, calls. *openDemocracy*. Available from www.opendemocracy.net/can-europe-make-it/engin-isin/acts-affects-calls [Accessed 2 February 2008].

Johansen, B. S., 2015. Locating hatred: On the materiality of emotions. *Emotion, Space and Society*, 16, 48–55.

Lemmings, D. and Brooks, A., 2014. The emotional turn in the humanities and social sciences. In D. Lemmings and A. Brooks, eds. *Emotions and Social Change: Historical and Sociological Perspectives*. New York: Routledge, 3–18.

Massumi, B., ed., 2002. *A Shock to Thought: Expression after Deleuze and Guattari*. London and New York: Routledge.

Mazzei, L. A., 2013. Materialist mappings of knowing in being: Researchers constituted in the production of knowledge. *Gender and Education*, 25(6), 776–785.

Mulcahy, D., 2015. Body matters: The critical contribution of affect in school classrooms and beyond. In B. Green and N. Hopwood, eds. *The Body in Professional Practice, Learning and Education: Body/Practice*. Dordrecht: Springer, 105–120.

Mulcahy, D., 2016. 'Sticky' learning: Assembling bodies, objects and affects at the museum and beyond. In J. Coffey, S. Budgeon and H. Cahill, eds. *Learning Bodies: The Body in Youth and Childhood Studies*. Singapore: Springer, 207–222.

Niccolini, A., 2016. Animate affects: Censorship, reckless pedagogies, and beautiful feelings. *Gender and Education*, 28(2), 230–249.

Pyyry, N., 2016. Learning with the city via enchantment: Photo-walks as creative encounters. *Discourse: Studies in the Cultural Politics of Education*, 37(1), 102–115.

Reckwitz, A., 2002. Toward a theory of social practices: A development in culturalist theorizing. *European Journal of Social Theory*, 5(2), 243–263.

Reckwitz, A., 2012. Affective spaces: A praxeological outlook. *Rethinking History*, 16(2), 241–258.

Rice, J., 2008. The new 'new': Making a case for critical affect studies. *Quarterly Journal of Speech*, 94(2), 200–212.

Saito, H., 2010. Actor-network theory of cosmopolitan education. *Journal of Curriculum Studies*, 42(3), 333–351.

Schatzki, T. R., 2002. *The Site of the Social: A Philosophical Account of the Constitution of Social Life and Change*. University Park: Pennsylvania State University Press.

Schatzki, T. R., Knorr Cetina, K. and von Savigny, E., eds., 2001. *The Practice Turn in Contemporary Theory*. New York: Routledge.

Semetsky, I., 2013. Learning with bodymind: Constructing the cartographies of the unthought. In D. Masny, ed. *Cartographies of Becoming in Education: A Deleuze–Guattari Perspective*. Rotterdam: Sense, 77–92.

Simon, R. I., 2006. The terrible gift: Museums and the possibility of hope without consolation. *Museum Management and Curatorship*, 21(3), 187–204.

Smith, L., 2015. Theorizing museum and heritage visiting. In A. Witcomb and K. Message, eds. *The International Handbooks of Museum Studies. Volume 1: Museum Theory*. Chichester: Wiley Blackwell, 459–484.

Smith, L. and Campbell, G., 2016. The elephant in the room: Heritage, affect and emotion. In W. Logan, M. Nic Craith and U. Kockel, eds. *A Companion to Heritage Studies*. Oxford: Wiley Blackwell.

Snaza, N., Sonu, D., Truman, S. E. and Zaliwska, Z., eds., 2016. *Pedagogical Matters: New Materialisms and Curriculum Studies*. New York: Peter Lang.

Thrift, N., 2008a. I just don't know what got into me: Where is the subject? *Subjectivity*, 22(1), 82–89.

Thrift, N., 2008b. *Non-representational Theory: Space, Politics, Affect*. London and New York: Routledge.

Trofanenko, B., 2014. Affective emotions: The pedagogical challenges of knowing war. *The Review of Education, Pedagogy, and Cultural Studies*, 36(1), 22–39.

Walkerdine, V. and Jimenez, L., 2012. *Gender, Work and Community after De-industrialisation: A Psychosocial Approach to Affect*. Basingstoke: Palgrave Macmillan.

Wetherell, M. 2012. *Affect and Emotion: A New Social Science Understanding*. Los Angeles: Sage.

Wetherell, M., 2013. Feeling rules, atmospheres and affective practice: Some reflections on the analysis of emotional episodes. In P. Aggleton and C. Maxwell, eds. *Privilege, Agency and Affect: Understanding the Production and Effects of Action*. New York: Palgrave Macmillan, 221–239.

Wetherell, M., 2014. Affect and banal nationalism: A practical dialogic approach to emotion. In C. Antaki and S. Condor, eds. *Rhetoric, Ideology and Social Psychology: Essays in Honour of Michael Billig*. Hoboken: Taylor and Francis, 137–150.

Wetherell, M., 2015. Trends in the turn to affect: A social psychological critique. *Body and Society*, 21(2), 139–166.

Witcomb, A., 2013. Understanding the role of affect in producing a critical pedagogy for history museums. *Museum Management and Curatorship*, 28(3), 255–271.

Witcomb, A., 2015. Cultural pedagogies in the museum: Walking, listening and feeling. In M. Watkins, G. Noble and C. Driscoll, eds. *Cultural Pedagogies and Human Contact*. London: Routledge, 158–170.

Zembylas, M., 2006. Witnessing in the classroom: The ethics and politics of affect. *Educational Theory*, 56(3), 305–324.

Zembylas, M., 2007. *Five Pedagogies, a Thousand Possibilities: Struggling for Hope and Transformation in Education*. Rotterdam and Taipei: Sense.

Zembylas, M. and Schutz, P. A., eds., 2016. *Methodological Advances in Research on Emotion and Education*. Basel: Springer.

Chapter 14

White guilt and shame

Students' emotional reactions to digital stories of race in a South African classroom

Daniela Gachago, Vivienne Bozalek and Dick Ng'ambi

> One is undone, in the face of the other, by the touch, by the scent, by the feel, by the prospect of the touch, by the memory of the feel. We are touched by stories we tell.
>
> (Butler 2004: 19)

Introduction

Since 1994, South African higher education (HE) has undergone major transformations, driven by the twin imperatives of racial transformation and pressures for efficiency (Department of Education 1997, 2001). However, research into the progress of transformation, such as the 2008 Ministerial Committee into Transformation and Social Cohesion in Higher Education (Soudien *et al.* 2008), draws a dire picture of the state of South African HE, confirming the pervasiveness of race and racism in educators' and students' lives. The ongoing protests at South African universities, which started in 2015 at the University of Cape Town around the removal of the Rhodes statue – experienced as a symbol of the colonial oppression, the continued legacy of apartheid and the lack of transformation – are a powerful reminder of the discontent and alienation black students and staff feel (Hodes 2015).

Authors such as Jansen (2009) and Zembylas (2013) define South Africa as a post-conflict society. Post-conflict societies have to respond simultaneously to the consequences of current conflicts and to the factors which gave rise to conflicts in the past (Pattman 2010). These authors argue that what keeps students from engaging across difference is 'indirect knowledge' (Jansen 2009: 52), the 'powerful ideas and constructs about the past, present, and future' (Jansen 2009: 260) passed on from generation to generation. This 'knowledge in the blood' is 'habitual, a knowledge that has long been routinized in how the second generation see the world and themselves, and how they understand others' (Jansen 2009: 171). This knowledge unconsciously impacts on our choice and negotiations of social engagements. It is 'troubled', as it is steeped in discourses of power and privilege and draws out the 'worst racial stereotypes, prejudices and aggressions among students'

(Jansen 2004: 121). This indirect knowledge is also deeply defensive and can evoke strong emotions both in white and in black students, such as guilt, defensiveness and anger, further complicating or preventing an engagement across difference.

This chapter is drawn from the first author's PhD study (Gachago 2015), which reflects on a digital storytelling project set in a pre-service teacher education programme at a large University of Technology in South Africa and this project's potential to contribute to a post- conflict pedagogy. Drawing on a growth in interest in emotions as a central concern in the context of critical citizenship and social justice education, this chapter explores how, in student responses to *difficult knowledges*, such as the legacies of apartheid, the entanglement of knowing, feeling and doing was brought to the surface.

We focus on the process of storytelling and on the audience response to the stories in and beyond the digital storytelling workshop. In particular, we are interested, to use Shuman's words, in how 'these stories and the storyteller change when people empathize with each other's experiences' (2005: 4). Stories shared in this space reflect on what Frankish (2009: 89) calls the 'systemic traumas of [South African] contemporary life': students tell stories of gender-based violence, domestic abuse, drugs, gangsterism, poverty and discrimination. What happens to students when these often painful stories are being told? What happens to their engagement across difference? Do these stories help to shift power dynamics in the classroom? What kind of empathy do these stories elicit: empathy that keeps the distance between the storyteller and story listener, or the sort of empathy that troubles any distance between the self and the 'Other',[1] what Boler (1999) would call witnessing or Curtin (2014) compassion? These are the questions guiding this chapter. We thus focus on the performative nature of stories, rather than using the stories as a 'portal into the mind of storyteller' (Frank 2010: 13), which has been the usual focus of narrative inquiry (Kohler Riessman 2008).

While this chapter is set in the context of teacher education, the literature on the role of museums in transformative learning by their audience shares common concerns. Both education and museums aim at changing a learner's or a visitor's view or understanding. In both cases, however, there is a growing understanding that an educational intervention – be it a lecture or a museum visit – can elicit a variety of responses in the learner/visitor. Rather than automatically leading to new understanding, it may more often than not reinforce dominant narratives and discourses (Smith 2015).

Framed by a belief that feelings, implicit prejudices and bodily responses constitute our racialised, gendered, classed subjectivities, we argue that the unlearning, the transformative process, also requires work through feelings and bodily reactions, to move towards an active empathy or witnessing which implies taking on responsibility and holding oneself complicit, co-responsible for the other's plight.

The role of emotions in post-conflict classrooms

Underpinned by a critical pedagogy perspective but also by post-structural thought, a pedagogy of discomfort proposes that, for both educators and students to develop a deeper understanding for their own and their shared past and present, it is necessary to move outside their comfort zones (Boler and Zembylas 2003). Boler and Zembylas (2003: 112) explain that experiencing discomforting emotions can help one to challenge dominant beliefs, social habits and normative practices that sustain social inequities, and might ultimately lead to individual and social transformation. Their work draws from Boler's seminal book on emotions and education (Boler 1999: xii), where she highlights the link of emotions and social justice education: 'the 'risky' business of addressing emotions within our classrooms is a productive and necessary direction for the exploration of social justice and education'. Her aim is to develop a theory of emotions and education that begins from an examination of power relations: 'how structures and experiences of race, class, and gender, for example, are shaped by the social control of emotion, and how political movements have resisted injustice by drawing on the power of emotions' (Boler 1999: 5).

Throughout her book, she draws attention to how gendered emotional rules have been used to keep women in subordinate roles. She points to the deliberate absence of attention to emotions in the educational literature to demonstrate how they have become an unchallenged site of social control. She argues that 'culturally patterned, inscribed habits of inattention' (Boler 1999: 17) are accountable for this silence. However, once this silence is challenged and 'outlaw' emotions are expressed, they can empower an oppressed group to resist their subordinate status (Boler 1999: 12). She notes that Foucault and post-structural thought can help us view emotions not as internal, individualised states, but as shaped by dominant discourses and ideologies, allowing us the possibility to resist these through emotional knowledge and critical inquiry. Challenging these emotional rules and reclaiming emotions 'as part of our cognitive and ethical inquiry' could 'provide the students hope for changing the quality of their lives and taking action towards freedom and social justice' (Boler 1999: xi).

For transformation that could lead to improved relationships among diverse and differently positioned groups of students, it is crucial that the educator directly confront underlying problems that render relationships among students from different backgrounds difficult – such as issues around historical origins of power and privilege. This can lead to deep unsettlement in learners, a sense of personal loss and highly charged emotions, such as anger, grief, disappointment and, most importantly, resistance. However, Boler and Zembylas (2003) argue that it is exactly these discomforting emotions and the process of critically reflecting on their origins that is so powerful. They insist that only through this process of reflection can dominant beliefs, social habits and normative practices that sustain social inequities be challenged and possibilities for individual and social transformation be created.

While this process can be deeply unsettling, a critical engagement with the emotions experienced can also lead to critical thinking and inquiry (2003: 128), as well as 'self-discovery, hope, passion and a sense of community' (2003: 129). These are hopeful assumptions, since, once we acknowledge that we are a product of hegemony, we are better placed to accept the ambiguity and messiness of power relations and for spaces for transformation to open up.

Boler and Zembylas (2003) and other authors warn that a pedagogy of discomfort might not necessarily be successful. More often than not, it might not be transformatory in the way educators intend it to be. Educators who have attempted it (such as Macdonald 2013) remain cautious, arguing that introducing a pedagogy of discomfort to disrupt some of the discourses, assumptions and beliefs governing our classrooms and engagements with the 'Other' is a difficult and messy task. South African authors Leibowitz *et al.* (2010: 126) suggest that 'learning to talk about difference is a *process*, during which students may require sufficient support and a level of *explicit enquiry* to break through the polite "rhetoric" of the "rainbow nation"'.[2]

White guilt, shame and other reactions to stories of race

While Boler (1999) engages particularly with gendered emotions, the focus in this chapter is on the emotions following stories of race and in particular the emotions of guilt and shame which are often encountered in classrooms struggling with understanding the legacies of systemic historical trauma such as apartheid. The argument throughout this chapter is that emotions such as pity, guilt and shame are learned and that, to unlearn these emotions, one needs to critically reflect on these emotions – learn through these emotions. Here we draw from scholars following the affective turn, who are concerned with the entanglement of seeing, being and knowing, the entanglement of ontology and epistemology (Young 1997; Ahmed 2004; Hemmings 2012). As Hemmings explains,

> *in order to know differently we have to feel differently.* Feeling that something is amiss in how one is recognised, feeling an ill fit with social descriptions, feeling *undervalued*, feeling that same sense in considering others; all these feelings can produce a politicised impetus to change that foregrounds the relationship between ontology and epistemology precisely because of the experience of their dissonance (Hemmings 2012: 150, our emphasis).

Shotwell's work is helpful in understanding the entanglement of feeling and knowing: she argues that, if feelings, implicit prejudices and bodily responses

234   Daniela Gachago et al.

constitute our racialised, gendered, classed subjectivities, then the unlearning and transformation also has to work through feelings and bodily reactions. She classifies affective knowing as what she calls 'non-presentational knowledge' (Shotwell 2011: xix), i.e. the type of knowledge that is not immediately accessible to us. Her example of an emotional outbreak around white guilt in a lecture, leaving the class and the professor under an 'affective shock' is useful in understanding the role of affect to block or unblock understanding:

> These feelings don't themselves constitute understanding. Seen in the context of a matrix of implicit understanding shot through with propositional knowledge, though, we can see how affect might be important to the epistemic situation. If the purpose of the class was as it was titled 'Theorizing Whiteness', it matters if having a feeling, like guilt about whiteness, attaches to panic about discussing the topic evoking this feeling. Depending on one's political perspective, the feelings, including the ways they might show up through embodied understanding and including the previously unspeakable knowledge they might disclose, can enable or block the process of coming to a conceptual understanding.

An analysis of guilt and shame in particular highlights the way that these emotions can be seen to be relational and performative (Ahmed 2004). Shotwell (2011: 75) argues that, while guilt and shame are interlinked, guilt is backward-looking, making us defensive and paralysed, without an opportunity to connect. She describes shame, on the contrary as 'an active, transitive practice' (Shotwell 2011: 79), a practice that is relational and one that connects people: 'Shame turns on an inter- and intra-subjective hinge, which is to say that I see myself in relation to others' (Shotwell 2011: 79). Once participants in difficult dialogues manage to move from guilt to shame, which we understand as actively taking responsibility for systemic injustices, they may, in a further step, take action. This echoes Young's more recent work (Young 2011: xv) on social justice, where she calls for a detachment of guilt and responsibility. In similar fashion to Shotwell, she describes guilt as backward-looking and individualised:

> The function of guilt is to locate fault, to single out for either moral or legal blame. It is usually not appropriate to ascribe guilt to a group as such, unless we have some reason to conceive of the group as a collective agent (as in the case of guilt ascribed to corporations, for example).

In the context of Germans' engagement with their past, instead of feeling guilty for crimes previous generations have committed, she calls for them to take up responsibility (Young 2011: xv):

> Responsibility, by contrast, is a forward-looking concept. To ascribe responsibility to a person is to say that they have a job to do. We can hold

White guilt and shame 235

either individuals or groups responsible, and responsibility for social ills is typically shared among many agents. People can be responsible without being guilty.

This is of crucial importance in our particular context, where students often get stuck within white guilt, but where some manage to transform this guilt into shame, which in turn allows them to open up and recognise their responsibility and complicity in past injustices.

Context and methodology

This study is set within the Faculty of Education and Social Sciences at a large university of technology in South Africa. The digital storytelling project was introduced in order to allow students to reflect on their diverse backgrounds and to develop a heightened understanding of their own and their peers' social positioning vis-à-vis personal, institutional and systemic structures. A digital story as defined in this study is a personal narrative that documents a wide range of culturally and historically embedded lived experiences combining voice, sound and images into a short video, developed by non-professionals with non-professional tools within the context of a digital storytelling workshop (Lambert 2010; Reed and Hill 2012). For more information on the project and the pedagogical intervention, including the structure of the workshop, see Gachago (2015) and Gachago *et al.* (2013; 2014).

The demographic composition of the class was diverse in terms of gender, age, race, ethnicity, religion and language. The three students introduced in this chapter were part of a five-day digital storytelling workshop in August 2013, in which they were guided in the development of their digital stories. The brief for the digital story encouraged students to tell a counterstory (Solorzano and Yosso 2002) about one critical incident they encountered in their teaching practice and which related to an issue of social justice in education. For this study, we have adapted the term 'counterstorytelling' slightly to encourage the sharing of stories both of privileged and of less privileged students to challenge hegemonic discourses within a pedagogy of discomfort framework, where it is assumed that *no one* can escape hegemony.

On the basis of the belief that, rather than there being a unified, solid subjectivity, subjectivities are fluid and performed according to the context into which they are embedded, we have chosen a methodological approach to narrative inquiry that recognises that the role of the audience is crucial in the construction and performance of a narrative: performance analysis (Kohler Riessman 2008). As Salmon explains (Salmon and Kohler Riessman 2008: 80),

All narratives are, in a fundamental sense, co-constructed. The audience, whether physically present or not, exerts a crucial influence on what can and cannot be said, how things should be expressed, what can be taken for granted, what needs explaining, and so on. We now recognize that the personal account, in research interviews, which has traditionally been seen as the expression of a single subjectivity, is in fact always a co-construction.

Performance analysis is useful in this study as it explores how identities are situated and constructed within specific contexts for a specific audience. As Kohler Riessman (2008: 105) explains, performance analysis 'interrogates how talk among speakers is interactively (dialogically) produced and performed as narrative'. In this project, the notion of the audience is complex and multi-layered. The audience does not only consist of the researcher. It includes fellow students in the digital storytelling workshop; parents, family members and former teachers invited to the public screening of the stories; an audience as imagined by a storyteller when he/she develops the digital story; and finally the anonymous audience – what Berlant (2008) calls 'an intimate public' – that may access the digital story once it has been published or presented in workshops, conference presentations or research publications. Storytelling thus becomes a relational practice, in which a story is co-created between the storyteller and a physical, virtual and imagined audience (Kohler Riessman [2008: 113] calls it the 'ghostly' audience).

This chapter focuses on one story in particular, created by Noni,[3] one of the black students in the class, and how two of her white peers reacted to her story, their audience response collected in narrative interviews, to exemplify the kind of affective engagements that were enacted in this project.

Noni's story – you might get uncomfortable ... but will you please listen to me?[4]

We have been together for a week now. A week full of uncomfortable, awkward moments where I had to share personal stuff about my life with you and be and feel with you although we have never talked before. In these moments I realised how little I knew about you, although I have been with you for four years. I became conscious of how for four years we have been avoiding interacting with each other on a personal level; we only spoke to each other when we needed to, like for group work.

This 'uncomfortable safe space' made me aware of how we are trying so hard to run away from our truth, running away from the fact that our past still has effects on our present, our today, how we do not want to admit that there is still an advantage to being you in this country and there is a disadvantage in being me in this country ... like how the best schools in the country are your schools, like how being you gets you first preference for a job over people like me. It got me thinking about how we are turning a deaf ear on the fact that you and I in this country still do not have the same opportunities. Do not get me wrong I am not focusing on who is more privileged and who is less privileged or whose fault it is. I am not accusing you ...

This got me thinking about how we can laugh and joke together, but are not making real friendships ... you may say 'oh I have friends that look like you' ... but really ... how often have you invited me into your home to come and dine with you?

We are running away from admitting that we have unfinished business with each other; we have stuff to admit to each other, stuff we need to talk about to each other.

When are we going to create spaces where we can talk about the truth, where I can be honest and admit that I feel inferior to you and you can admit that you sometimes feel superior to me ...? When are we going to admit that South Africa has a standard that everyone has to meet, and that standard is your standard? Look at how I needed to learn to speak English so I can speak with you, whilst you cannot even speak a few sentences of my language.

We need to start creating these uncomfortable spaces wherever we go; in social groups, at work, in schools, at home with our children. I mean everyone has to be part of this, in this South Africa of today ... So that we can talk about these kinds of things, and find a way forward and a way to forgive each other. A space where we can be as honest and brutal as we can about how all of this makes you and me feel, without the fear of hurting mine and your feelings. We are both wounded! Will you come to this place with me?

White students' reactions to Noni's story

Noni's story is a reflection on the digital storytelling workshop process and her engagements with her white peers. Noni's story is written in poetic form. It has a certain rhythm and poetic elements, such as repetition of words and phrases, i.e. her addressing an imaginary 'you' or repeatedly using the phrase 'This got me thinking.' In her movie, there is a series of images from life in the township that she has taken herself: scenes of children and women, literally on her doorstep, depicting the inhuman, brutal conditions that people experience in these areas, but also the innocence of children playing in the street and the care these children display for each other. She first showed these pictures during the workshop while trying to find a focus for her story, to emphasise a life maybe not often enough seen in her classroom and to counter what she perceived as an inability or unwillingness of her peers to recognise ongoing systemic inequalities in today's South Africa.

Noni's story is an uncomfortable one, and prompted differing responses from her peers. In this chapter we will focus on two of these peers' reactions, two white women, differently positioned in class and age, whose affective reactions are useful in understanding the role of emotions in difficult conversations.

238 Daniela Gachago et al.

Lauren is a young female white student. She comes from a privileged middle-class and rather conservative family background. In the interview below, Lauren reflected on the guilt she experienced and the anger at what she perceived as her peers' reaction to Noni's story: both the belittling of and the pity expressed in relation to Noni's story and experience.

DANIELA: *OK emm so what were the most uncomfortable moments for you in that process?*

LAUREN: *Emm, when Noni showed those photos of where she comes from. I felt not guilty but in a sense guilty, because I mean, I can't help that am [I am] white. But I don't know, the way that they have lived, it's not their fault either but that's just how they live ... so it was this kind of confusion of 'How has this happened? How do some people have to live like that and I lived so comfortably?' And it made me made guilty in a sense, even though I am not in control of the fact that I was born as I am, you know? And I just felt angrier as well because it was like, I could see that the other black people in the room were going 'That's where we live too, you know, it's not a big deal!' And the white people were going 'Ooooh shame!' Like that it's horrible you know? And it made me feel so uncomfortable in that moment. (Interview with Lauren)*

Lauren's reaction to the everyday trauma of living in South Africa mirrors students' reactions to what Britzman calls 'difficult knowledge': the encounter with traumatic experiences and the coming to terms 'with various kinds of trauma, both individual and collective' (Britzman 2000: 202). This encounter with past and present trauma leaves students with feelings of helplessness, loss, 'a sense that no other person or group will intervene' (Britzman 2000: 202). The interview, continued below, shows the powerful emotions that circulated between Noni and Lauren, and Lauren's overwhelming feeling of helplessness in the light of black students' stories.

DANIELA: *Why were you angry?*

LAUREN: *Because I just don't think that it's going away. I don't know how it is gonna go away. Like it's happening around us all the time. I mean the townships are growing – growing and growing – and nothing is happening. So it's just like this, it's an anger, I can't do anything about it and that people have to live like that.*

DANIELA: *So you don't feel that you have a personal responsibility to change this?*

LAUREN: *Yes, I think in a sense there's a personal responsibility to make people aware ... because some people aren't aware of it still. Even though it's out there, like right in front of their eyes. They are just so closed in their own bubble and everyone is so busy with their own little life. I think it's good to, you know, to tell people that they need to start reacting. Otherwise nothing is gonna change and I mean, I do my bit, like I will go out and help the poor*

> *people and go and take food to shelters and things like that. [...] And it's like, I think like, if I took it on and said: I need to do something about this, it will actually stress me out more because I wouldn't even know where to start, you know? It's such a big problem and people have been trying to change for years. So that immediately puts you in a position where you are like: what can I do, you know? (Interview with Lauren)*

Lauren's account shows the entanglement of thinking, feeling and doing – what Watkins (2015) calls a 'moment of pedagogic affect'. We see a student struggling with difficult knowledge; and the confusion, helplessness and despondency experienced by young white people born into a life of privilege. Lauren's use of the third person plural both for the 'Other' who is distant from her ('This is how they live …') and for the 'other' who is close, but whom she doesn't want to be associated with ('They are just so closed in their own bubble …'), allows her to distance herself from all of these 'Others'. Although she sees the need to take action, to take responsibility for changing what are deeply unfair systems, she struggles to see *how*.

As a mature white – self-defined as working class – student who had lived through apartheid, Beatrice, the second student we focus on in this chapter, was also deeply affected by and voiced her respect for Noni's story. In her interview, she mentioned that she had to remove herself by leaving the room to go to the bathroom and have a 'good cry'. The story made her recognise what white privilege means – made it 'real'. Unlike Lauren, who distanced herself from 'racist others', Beatrice positioned herself as one of those whites who consciously or unconsciously mistreat blacks, saying 'What do we do as whites to make people feel like they're nothing?':

BEATRICE: *When we had that discussions in the circle with Noni, when she started talking about how she had to learn the English language in order to communicate with white people, she had to learn to be white in order to … to relate to white people and to mix with them and to be seen as one of them. Oh my goodness gracious me, I was so uncomfortable I wanted to cry myself out.*
DANIELA: *Why?*
BEATRICE: *Because I am comfortable being white and I am comfortable speaking English. I am comfortable with my whiteness and I only realised when Noni was talking about it how white people unconsciously make black people feel. I had to leave the room to go to the bathroom, have a good cry in the bathroom and then splash my face with cold water and then come back to class. And that's why my nose was blocked when I did my recording because that was the day I did my recording. But at the same time I was thinking about Noni's discomfort. I was thinking about my father who was a poor white who was not welcome in wealthy people's homes. Even in his own extended family, as a boy he was given a chocolate wrapper and was thinking there was a piece of chocolate in it. He found nothing, only little strips of melted*

240 Daniela Gachago et al.

> *chocolates which he still licked in the street and afterwards he realised what he had done. He was: It's like, I don't know how to explain it, it's like such total rejection ... and that's what went through my mind for the whole of that day. I was out of it for the whole of that day. I was just thinking about the things we do to reject other people. Some people do it explicitly and some people don't ... What do we do as whites to make people feel like they're nothing?*
>
> DANIELA: *And you've never thought about this before?*
>
> BEATRICE: *No! I've never thought of the black/white issues, never! (Interview with Beatrice)*

To allow herself to understand Noni's experience, Beatrice needed to normalise Noni's story by constructing a connection to her own life, in this case represented by her father's sense of isolation as a 'poor white'. She ultimately connected to Noni's story through what she perceived as *shared* emotional experiences: she connected to what she knew. In this moment, Noni stopped being the 'Other' for her. Noni, in becoming the same, became 'human', someone who has 'feelings' and that one can 'be intimate with on ... very close terms':

> BEATRICE: *I would actually almost want to give Noni the credit, she made me realise that we are all the same, we are all the same, we all feel the same. And again, in my mind, I was thinking: But you can make the difference! You can be the one to take the first step! Because this workshop showed us, that article actually showed me, where my weakness is. And it's noted, I am not hesitant. It's not that I don't trust black people. It's just that I have never thought of them as being intimate, somebody to be intimate with on very close terms. That's, that's about it. I can't say, I can't say, that I don't want black people in my life. But the workshop made me more aware that they have feelings. And then maybe there's something that stops them from approaching me. But maybe they can see something in me that stops them from approaching me and making the first contact. It should come from me – you know? I can make it happen. (Interview with Beatrice)*

Why was it easier for Beatrice to connect to Noni's story than for Lauren? Lugones' (1987) concept of 'world-travelling' is useful in unpacking questions concerning the complexity of privilege and responsibility. Lugones writes from an experience of an outsider, a black Latino woman among a White/Anglo organisation of life in the USA. She argues that for engaging emotionally with the other, learning to love the 'other', *it is necessary to travel into her world.*

What is of particular interest for this chapter is her suggestion that such travelling might be more difficult for those who are most at ease and comfortable in their lives. Lugones here offers an explanation for the relative ease with which Beatrice can open herself up and travel to somebody else's world. She links ease and comfort to (1) being a fluent speaker in a 'world', knowing all the words and moves, and being confident; (2) being normatively happy, agreeing with all norms; (3) being humanly bonded and being with those one loves; and (4) having a shared daily history. This ease and comfort is attributed to those who are positioned within normative standards. Looking at Beatrice, one could argue that her being a mature, working-class student and thus positioned slightly on the margins of the normative space of this classroom might make it easier for her to accept responsibility, to open herself up for the other stories and the other world, a prerequisite for travelling into somebody else's world.

Conclusions

The power of digital storytelling lies in connecting the personal to broader structural, social and political inequalities, as Poletti argues (2011). We introduced Noni's story above, told out of a deep-seated wish for change: to be seen differently by her peers on a personal level, and to promote social and cultural change on a political level. Noni's story about race relationships in South Africa divided her class, making it uncomfortable for both black and white students to engage with.

In the interview extracts shown above, students reflect on their engagement with 'difficult knowledges' (Britzman 1998, 2000): the social and historical trauma of apartheid and how its legacies play out in today's South Africa. During these difficult conversations, they experience a range of explosive emotions: anger, sadness, defensiveness, resentment, relief, sorrow, guilt and shame. The reactions shown above exemplify the difference between guilt and shame as backward- and forward-looking emotions (Shotwell 2011). Both students struggled with Noni's story, both reacted with strong emotions. However, there was a difference in their responses: while Lauren positioned herself outside the problem, Beatrice saw herself as part of the problem. In their answers we saw both the opportunities and the limitations for empathy and storytelling, and they exemplified how emotions are both relational and performative. These emotions *do* something to both the storyteller and her audience.

The excerpts above also showed that, when telling personal stories, it is difficult to move beyond the personal. When sharing their often painful stories, students get seemingly stuck in emotional moments of engaging with their own and the other's story, and might lose sight of the larger socio-economic and cultural context, the power relationships that impact on their relationships across difference. This is dangerous, as Boler (1999: 162) warns: 'Passive empathy absolves the reader through the denial of power relations. The confessional relationship relies on a suffering that is not referred beyond the individual to the social.'

242   Daniela Gachago *et al.*

Shuman warns that personal stories can elicit empathy, but that this empathy is steeped in power relationships between storyteller and story listener, maintaining for the story listener a safe distance that is often characterised by pity. On the contrary, witnessing troubles this distance, changes the power dynamics between storyteller and story listener. Active empathy or witnessing assumes taking on responsibility and holding oneself co-responsible for the other's plight (Boler 1999). It also assumes acknowledging and recognising the 'Other' from a position of 'asymmetrical reciprocity' (Young 1997), based on different experiences and from being differently positioned in life, but also valuing these differences, seeing them as affirmative, rather than being 'less than'.

How could this critical reflection on emotions be taken further? What would need to happen for Lauren to reflect on her own role in this unjust system beyond the feeling of guilt towards a feeling of shame, and to establish an affective engagement or investment – a strong enough interest for the 'Other' (Probyn 2005) – outside firmly established roles and power differentials (such as bringing food and shelter to the poor)? What would make it easier for her to travel into somebody else's world?

The conversations with students that happened in and outside the workshop space, the reflection on these 'moments of pedagogic affect' (Watkins 2015), were a crucial start for us to reflect on the emotions experienced by the students and unpack the socio-historic roots of such emotions. Through this unpacking an understanding of how their social positioning affects their emotions may emerge and allow students a grasp of how the legacy of apartheid still plays itself out in today's classrooms. Introducing critical literature around subjects such as empathy and witnessing could further deepen students' understanding of how their own emotional responses are historically and socially situated. If we see compassion, as Curtin (2014) argues, as a cultivated practice, then reflecting on one's emotions is a lifetime process, that can start in the classroom but needs to eventually move beyond the classroom into students' social and professional lives.

What does this mean for museum practice? While in recent years more emphasis has been put on drawing on visitors' emotions to elicit empathy, such as designing multimodal, multisensory experiences to allow visitors to identify and establish a closer emotional engagement with the exhibits (Watson 2015), not enough work is done to critically engage with the registers of this engagement (Smith 2016). As Smith argues, emotional engagement does not equate to transformative learning. What would active empathy or witnessing look like in a museum visit? How could one use emotional responses during a museum visit to critically reflect on one's emotions and use this as a moment of pedagogic affect? How can one facilitate dialogue and self-reflection? These are questions that need further research.

We end this chapter with a quotation from Butler (2004), which started our thinking about why and how we are affected by other people's stories: 'one

White guilt and shame 243

is undone, in the face of the other, by the touch, by the scent, by the feel, by the prospect of the touch, by the memory of the feel. We are touched by stories we tell.' While we believe in her statement, the analysis of students' responses to Noni's story has revealed the complexities of an affective engagement with other people's stories. A reflection on the emotions experienced allowed us insights into how these students' emotions and affects are 'individually experienced but historically situated' (Zembylas 2014: 397), as well as insight into the ways their relationships were 'compromised' (Shuman 2005). This reflection served as a powerful reminder of the entanglement of feeling, thinking and doing.

Notes

1 We use 'Other' with a capital letter and quote marks to foreground the socially and discursively constructed nature of the other – a 'distant other' who in this case not only doesn't look like me but in comparison with whom I am always in some ways differently positioned in relation to power and privilege. This 'Other' is always positioned as either more or less privileged than I, and our relationship is always based on an unequal power distribution.
2 The concept of the 'Rainbow Nation' was introduced by Nelson Mandela, who envisioned a non-racial South Africa where people of all colours could live peacefully and respectfully with each other. This vision has been deconstructed in the recent student protests, highlighting the ongoing institutional and systemic racism and lack of transformation and redress previously disadvantaged population groups are experiencing.
3 Because of the narrative focus of this study, and the use of digital stories as part of the data collection methods, granting complete confidentiality to students proved difficult. In this case Noni and Lauren gave permission for their real names to be used, as their digital stories were analysed multimodally and their images formed an integral part of the data. All other participants' names are pseudonyms. Their written permission to do so was obtained before the start of the study and this was discussed at various stages of the project. This involved negotiating the terms of publishing their images, such as not showing or blurring images of friends and family in the write-up of the study.
4 See Noni's story on https://vimeo.com/130008975.

References

Ahmed, S., 2004. *The Cultural Politics of Emotion*. Edinburgh: Edinburgh University Press.
Berlant, L., 2008. *The Female Complaint: The Unfinished Business of Sentimentality in American Culture*. Durham and London: Duke University Press.
Boler, M., 1999. *Feeling Power: Emotions and Education*. New York: Routledge.
Boler, M. and Zembylas, M., 2003. Discomforting truths: The emotional terrain of understanding difference. In P. Trifonas, ed. *Pedagogies of Difference: Rethinking Education for Social Change*. New York: RoutledgeFalmer, 110–136.

244 Daniela Gachago *et al.*

Britzman, D. P., 1998. *Lost Subjects, Contested Objects: Toward a Psychoanalytical Inquiry of Learning*. Albany: SUNY Press.

Britzman, D. P., 2000. Teacher education in the confusion of our times. *Journal of Teacher Education*, 51(3), 200–205.

Butler, J., 2004. *Undoing Gender*. New York and London: Routledge.

Curtin, D., 2014. Compassion and being human. In C. J. Adams and L. Gruen, eds. *Ecofeminism: Feminist Intersections with Other Animals and the Earth*. London: Bloomsbury, 39–58.

Department of Education, 1997. *Education White Paper 3: A Programme for the Transformation of Higher Education*. Pretoria: Department of Education.

Department of Education, 2001. *Education White Paper 6: Special Needs Education, Building an Inclusive Education and Training System*. Pretoria: Department of Education.

Frank, A. W., 2010. *Letting Stories Breathe: A Socio-narratology*. Chicago and London: University of Chicago Press.

Frankish, T., 2009. *Women's Narratives of Intergenerational Trauma and Post-Apartheid Identity: The Said and Unsaid*. Master's Thesis. University of KwaZulu-Natal.

Gachago, D., 2015. *Sentimentality and Digital Storytelling: Towards a Post-conflict Pedagogy in Pre-service Teacher Education in South Africa*. PhD Thesis. University of Cape Town.

Gachago, D., Cronje, F., Ivala, E., Condy, J. and Chigona, A., 2014. Using digital counterstories as multimodal pedagogy among South African pre-service student educators to produce stories of resistance. *Electronic Journal of e-Learning*, 12(1), 29–42.

Gachago, D., Ivala, E., Condy, J. and Chigona, A., 2013. Journeys across difference: Pre-service teacher education students' perceptions of a pedagogy of discomfort in a digital storytelling project in South Africa. *Critical Studies in Teaching and Learning*, 1(1), 22–52.

Hemmings, C., 2012. Affective solidarity: Feminist reflexivity and political transformation. *Feminist Theory*, 13(2), 147–161.

Hodes, R., 2015. 'The Rhodes statue must fall': UCT's radical rebirth. *Daily Maverick*, 13 March.

Jansen, J., 2004. Race and education after ten years. *Perspectives in Education*, 22(4), 117–128.

Jansen, J., 2009. *Knowledge in the Blood: Confronting Race and Apartheid Past*. Stanford: Stanford University Press.

Kohler Riessman, C., 2008. *Narrative Methods for the Human Sciences*. London: Sage.

Lambert, J., 2010. *Digital Storytelling Cookbook*. Berkeley: Center for Digital Storytelling.

Leibowitz, B., Bozalek, V. G., Carolissen, R., Nicholls, L., Rohleder, P. and Swartz, L., 2010. Bringing the social into pedagogy: Unsafe learning in an uncertain world. *Teaching in Higher Education*, 15(2), 123–133.

Lugones, M., 1987. Playfulness, world-travelling, and loving perception. *Hypatia*, 2(2), 3–19.

Macdonald, H. M., 2013. Teaching in Higher Education inviting discomfort: Foregrounding emotional labour in teaching anthropology in post-apartheid South Africa. *Teaching in Higher Education*, 18(6), 670–682.

Pattman, R., 2010. Investigating 'race' and social cohesion at the University of Kwa-Zulu Natal. *South African Journal of Higher Education*, 24(6), 953–971.

Poletti, A., 2011. Coaxing an intimate public: Life narrative in digital storytelling. *Continuum*, 25(1), 73–83.

Probyn, E., 2005. *Blush: Faces of Shame*. Minneapolis and London: University of Minnesota Press.

Reed, A. and Hill, A., 2012. 'Don't keep it to yourself!': Digital storytelling with South African Youth. *International Journal for Media, Technology and Lifelong learning*, 8(2), 268–279.

Salmon, P. and Kohler Riessman, C., 2008. Looking back at narrative research: An exchange. In M. Andrews, C. Squire and M. Tamboukou, eds. *Doing Narrative Research*. London: Sage, 78–85.

Shotwell, A., 2011. *Knowing Otherwise*. University Park: Pennsylvania State University.

Shuman, A., 2005. *Other People's Stories: Entitlement Claims and the Critique of Empathy*. Urbana: University of Illinois Press.

Smith, L. 2015. Theorizing museum and heritage visiting. *The International Handbooks of Museum Studies*, 3(22), 459–484.

Smith, L. 2016. Changing views? Emotional intelligence, registers of engagement and the museum visit. In V. Gosselin and P. Livingstone, eds. *Museums as Sites of Historical Consciousness: Perspectives on Museum Theory and Practice in Canada*. Vancouver: UBC Press.

Solorzano, D. G. and Yosso, T. J., 2002. Critical race methodology: Counter story-telling as an analytical framework for education research. *Qualitative Inquiry*, 8(1), 23–44.

Soudien, C., Michaels, W., Mthembi-Mahanyele, S., Nkomo, M., Nyanda, G., Nyoka, N., Seepe, S., Shisana, O. and Villa-Vicencio, C., 2008. *Report of the Ministerial Committee on Transformation and Social Cohesion and the Elimination of Discrimination in Public Higher Education Institutions*. Pretoria: Department of Education.

Watkins, M., 2015. Gauging the affective: Becoming attuned to its impact in education. In M. Zembylas and P. Schutz, eds. *Methodological Advances in Research on Emotion in Education*. New York: Springer, 71–81.

Watson, S., 2015. Emotions in the history museum. In A. Witcomb and K. Message, eds. *The International Handbooks of Museum Studies. Volume 1: Museum Theory*. Chichester: Wiley Blackwell, 283–301.

Young, I. M., 1997. Asymmetrical reciprocity: On moral respect, wonder, and enlarged thought. *Constellations*, 3(3), 340–363.

Young, I. M., 2011. *Responsibility for Justice*. New York: Oxford University Press.

Zembylas, M., 2013. Critical pedagogy and emotion: Working through 'troubled knowledge' in posttraumatic contexts. *Critical Studies in Education*, 54(2), 176–189.

Zembylas, M., 2014. Theorizing 'difficult knowledge' in the aftermath of the 'affective turn': Implications for curriculum and pedagogy in handling traumatic representations. *Curriculum Inquiry*, 44(3), 390–412.

Chapter 15

Settler–Indigenous relationships and the emotional regime of empathy in Australian history school textbooks in times of reconciliation

Angélique Stastny

Introduction

In 1991, the report from the Royal Commission into Aboriginal Deaths in Custody connected ongoing injustices faced by Aboriginal and Torres Strait Island people to history education in schools and recommended that

> curricula of schools at all levels should reflect the fact that Australia has an Aboriginal history and Aboriginal viewpoints on social, cultural and historical matters. It is essential that Aboriginal viewpoints, interests, perceptions and expectations are reflected in curricula, teaching and administration of schools (Australia 1991a: 308).

That same year, Australia officially pursued a policy of reconciliation as a way to engage with the country's contentious historical legacy and foster relationships between Indigenous and non-Indigenous people. Since then, as Angela Pratt (Pratt and Australia 2005:1) puts it, 'reconciliation has become the dominant way of talking about relations between Indigenous and non-Indigenous people in Australia'. Education about Australia's history, Indigenous people and cultures became one of the pillars for reconciliation, and schools were to be one of the key sites where this education was to be fostered. At a time when Australia, like several other societies, has been trying, under the aegis of reconciliation, to grapple with its colonial past and present, and the tensions inherent in its diversity, empathy has found many champions and supporters, and has been widely called on to foster understanding and altruism (see Batson 2010). Luke Briscoe (2015) argues that, although the word was not necessarily used, empathy has been put 'at the heart of all of our great steps towards reconciliation'.

Empathy remains a broad, blurry and often misunderstood concept. Social neuroscientists Tania Singer and Claus Lamm (2009:82) observe that 'there are almost as many definitions of *empathy* as there are researchers in the field'. Empathy is understood here as the practice of adopting (or the attempt to adopt) the point of view and emotional disposition of another individual or group. Empathy for people from other time periods and/or from other cultures has been considered an important means to achieve reconciliation. Empathy has come to be seen as an attribute of pro-social attitudes, if not almost synonymous with morality (Hoffman 2000, Slote 2007, Rifkin 2009, 2010). In Museum and Heritage studies, empathy has been defined as a strategic conceptual framework which uses memory and imagination to understand oneself and the other; a strategy that Keightley and Pickering (2012) call 'mnemonic imagination'. Likewise, memory scholar Alison Landsberg (2004) stresses the importance of historical narratives in inducing empathy to engage with another and bridge differences. According to a similar logic, a lack of empathy has often been used to explain racism, and empathy presented as its remedy (Gair 2013; Westaway 2014). Consistently with these views, in schools – a state apparatus and a key cite of education for reconciliation – the capacity to empathise has been considered to be an important skill in historical inquiry and reconciliatory practices (Portal 1983; Zembylas 2007b; this volume). Educationalist Michalinos Zembylas (2007b: 220) argues that, by developing empathy 'for the Other's humanity', a 'process of transforming polarized trauma narratives of the past is initiated'. He adds that, 'in this sense, empathy is an expression of being in relationship with the Other'. According to Zembylas, empathy and reconciliation allow dismantling of 'the system of entrenched myths and antagonistic trauma narratives that perpetuate divisions between communal groups' (Zembylas 2007b: 220; see also this volume). In the Australian context, Pedersen et al. (2004) found that negative attitudes towards Indigenous Australians were due to a lack of empathy, and that fostering empathy could reduce prejudice. Likewise, Susan Gair (2013) suggests that empathy is needed from non-Indigenous practitioners working with Indigenous people. Yet, critiques of empathy argue that empathy is biased by abiding to social norms and favouring one's kin and affiliations (Decety and Cowell 2014). Others, such as Pedwell (2013), also suggest that empathy as it is used in neoliberal discourses towards marginalised people and groups does not fundamentally challenge power relations. Informed by this literature and with the particular interrogations and observations of Pedwell (2013) and Zembylas (2007b) in mind, this chapter investigates the particular manifestations of empathy in Australian secondary school history textbooks. It asks whether, in the specific space of these textbooks, empathy fosters 'relationship with the Other' and functions to dismantle 'entrenched myths', transform 'polarised narratives' (Zembylas 2007b: 220), and challenge power relations. It explores the ways in which empathy has been articulated in these specific educational media, and considers the repercussions that this emotional regime has had on the ways in which people may engage within settler–Indigenous relationships. The concept of an 'emotional regime' has been defined by historian and anthropologist William Reddy (2001: 129) as

248 Angélique Stastny

'the set of normative emotions and the official rituals, practices, and emotives that express and inculcate them'. He argues that 'any enduring political regime must establish as an essential element a normative order for emotions, an "emotional regime"' (Reddy 2001: 124). Historian Barbara Rosenwein (2010: 22) adds that 'the notion of an emotional regime closely tracks that of an emotional community – as long as that community dominates the norms and texts of a large part of society'. This chapter builds on Barbara Rosenwein's reflection on the function of texts produced by a dominant community in establishing an emotional regime, by looking at the forms that this emotional regime of empathy takes in the institutional context of the school. The dominant community – also referred to as 'settler' in this chapter – is defined here as an agglomerate of highly diverse people who have come to Australia from the early days of colonisation to the present, and who inhabit the Europe-inherited settler colonial polity.

For the purpose of this analysis, six secondary school history textbooks published between 1991 and the present have been selected. Selection was made on the grounds that textbooks were produced in Australia and for use in Australian public schools, and that their content covers Australian history from 1788 (the start of the settler colonisation of Australia) to the date of their publication. Two textbooks from the series *History Alive* have been selected for the year 2012, considering that, under the Australian Curriculum, the colonial history of Australia has been divided between Year 9 (until 1918) and Year 10 (from the inter-war period to the present) and that the whole colonial history of Australia is no longer covered within a single textbook.[1] The textbooks on which this analysis is based are

Anderson, M. and Ashton, P., 1993. *Focus on Australian History*. South Melbourne: Macmillan Education Australia.
Shafer, M., 1996. *Visions of Australia. Exploring Our History*. Melbourne: Oxford University Press.
Swinton, J., Georgevits, S. and Proud, A., 2000. *World History and Citizenship*. South Yarra: Macmillan Education Australia.
Anderson, M. and Low, A., 2007. *History 2*. Milton: John Wiley and Sons.
Darlington, R., Smithies, G. and Wood, A., 2012. *History Alive 9 for the Australian Curriculum*. Milton: Jacaranda plus.
Darlington, R., Jackson, L. and Hawkins, T., 2012. *History Alive 10 for the Australian Curriculum*. Milton: John Wiley and Sons Australia.

This chapter addresses the following three key questions. How do textbooks engage empathy in settler–Indigenous relationships? What forms does this call for empathy take in these history textbooks? And what repercussions does it have for the power relations between settlers and Indigenous people? In doing so, this chapter analyses the emotive description of settler and Indigenous people in textbooks and the prescriptive emotional regime of empathy that guide the reader into specific modes of relationships between settlers and Indigenous people. To conduct this analysis, four analytical criteria have been developed: (a) discourses of colonial differences, (b) emotive representations of Indigenous people, (c) emotive invisibility of settlers, and (d) empathy as an emotive project and projection. After a brief outline of the interplay between empathy and reconciliation in educational policies, this chapter explores history textbooks' emotional emphases, in particular the notions of loss, lack and invisibility. It will then consider how these emotional emphases serve to articulate an empathetic emotional regime. Particular attention will be given to the function of empathy as an emotive practice that serves to negotiate the purported emotional, cultural and political distance and colonial difference between settlers and Indigenous people. Finally, this chapter closes on a reflection on the limits of empathy in building relationships between settler and Indigenous people in the particular context of these textbooks. It suggests that the ways in which empathy is mobilised in these texts may, on the contrary, impede these relationships and reinforce existing colonial power relations. It will therefore consider the possibilities that lie beyond empathy.

Political and emotional regimes: Empathy in reconciliatory educational policies

Following the *Report of the Royal Commission into Aboriginal Deaths in Custody* (Australia 1991a), which showed the link between the injustices that Indigenous people continue to face in today's Australian society and the history of dispossession, the federal government pushed for a policy of reconciliation. This shift towards reconciliation was translated into a marked historiographical and emotional shift. The Council for Aboriginal Reconciliation Act of 1991 set out 'to promote, by leadership, education and discussion, a deeper understanding by all Australians of the history, cultures, past dispossession and continuing disadvantage of Aborigines and Torres Strait Islanders and of the need to redress that disadvantage' (Australia 1991b). At the national level, political leaders such as Prime Ministers Paul Keating and Kevin Rudd led the way for recognition by non-Indigenous people of the country's colonial history and the continuing injustices faced by Australia's Indigenous people.[2] These official forms of recognition were paralleled by local efforts to educate the Australian population at large, and schools became one of these key local educational sites. The shift towards reconciliation had a visible impact on the official historical narrative disseminated in schools (Seddon 2001; Clark 2006; Parkers 2007). Australian historiography was going through great transformations since the 1970s as the dominant white settler narrative of Australian history was being challenged. These transformations faced strong opposition by conservative historians and politicians (Blainey 1993; Windschuttle 1994, 2002; Howard 2006), who condemned revisionist historians for articulating a mournful, 'black-armband' view of

250 Angélique Stastny

history (Blainey 1993) – a historiographical debate commonly known as the 'history wars'. Despite the critique, these historical and historiographical changes made their way into the school system, where they took root and influenced the development of history curricula from the 1990s onwards. The works of historians such as Henry Reynolds (1972, 1982, 1989), Robert Manne (2003), Bain Attwood (2005) and Ann McGrath (1995) refuted the idea of a largely peaceful European settlement of Australia and re-examined the history of colonial contacts. They shifted, more markedly, the focus to frontier conflict, Aboriginal resistance and the long history of oppressive policies directed against Indigenous people. Lorenzo Veracini (2003: 224) identifies a marked change in the historiography during the 1990s and 2000s, and observes that 'the debate has shifted dramatically, dealing specifically with the genocidal nature of white Australia's policy towards Aboriginal peoples'. The shift towards reconciliation therefore did not happen in a vacuum, but was buttressed by the slow and deep gestation of a new 'interpretative paradigm' (Veracini 2003: 225) within the historiography. These political and historiographical shifts often involved contentious and emotionally charged meaning-making processes of the colonial past and present. Emotions have therefore been 'an intensely political issue' (Anderson and Smith 2001: 7) and have infused this reconciliatory process of historical and cultural recognition and understanding.[3] Empathy became the dominant emotional regime and interpretative paradigm to engage within settler–Indigenous relationships.

As a result, school history curricula have played a key role in inculcating empathy. Changes to history curricula in Australia and the recent introduction of the national Australian Curriculum have entailed the teaching of empathy. Empathy has been utilised as a way of knowing and stepping across the colonial divide between settlers and Indigenous people and engaging with a diversity of experiences and perspectives. For instance, the Melbourne Declaration on Educational Goals for Young Australians issued by the council of Federal, State and Territory Ministers of Education stated that 'confident and creative individuals develop personal values and attributes such as honesty, resilience, *empathy* and respect for others' (Ministerial Council on Education, Employment, Training and Youth Affairs 2008: 9, emphasis added). Ahead of the implementation of the Australian Curriculum, one of the eight core components of historical understanding outlined in the National History Curriculum Framing paper was 'historical empathy and moral judgement: the capacity to enter into the world of the past with an informed imagination and ethical responsibility' (National Curriculum Board 2008: 5). The guidelines for the Australian Curriculum, which has gradually been implemented in Australian schools since 2011, state that 'the content provides opportunities to develop historical understanding through key concepts, including evidence, continuity and change, cause and effect, perspectives, *empathy*, significance and contestability' (Australian Curriculum, Assessment and reporting Body n.d., emphasis added). The political and historiographical shifts towards reconciliation have therefore been mediated by this specific emotional regime: empathy.

History textbooks' emotional emphases

This marked shift in the historiography was reflected in school history textbooks. Alexandra Sauvage (2010) notices a marked evolution in the content of textbooks between 1991 and 2001, and observes that, by the turn of the twenty-first century, textbooks had included sections on land rights, Indigenous social movements and institutional racism. A similar observation has been made for the six textbooks analysed here (figures 15.1 and 15.2). Discrimination and injustices towards Indigenous people and their struggles for rights are among the most common characteristics defining Indigenous people in the history of Australia since colonisation across the six textbooks. Indeed, Indigenous people are predominantly represented in terms of loss, as discriminated against, fighting for their rights, receiving gain and compensation and experiencing pain and suffering.

Textbooks mention, for instance, the discrimination that Indigenous people faced in the legal system, which did not allow them to testify about massacres in law courts; the discrimination that Indigenous soldiers faced during and after World War II; the segregation of public spaces; the lack of civil rights; and ongoing racism. *History Alive 10* (Darlington, Jackson and Hawkins 2012: 146) for instance acknowledges that

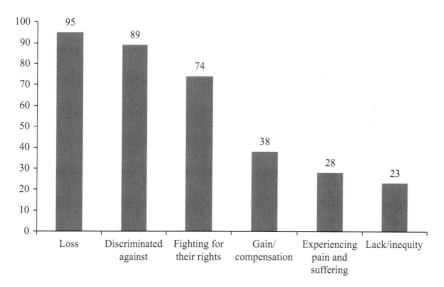

Figure 15.1 Occurrences of the most common themes used to describe Indigenous people across the textbooks

252 Angélique Stastny

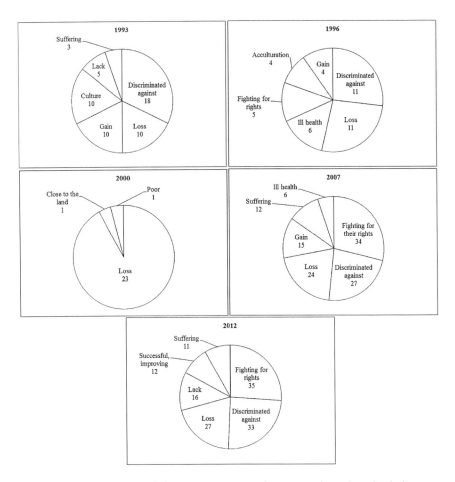

Figure 15.2 Occurrences of the most common themes used to describe Indigenous people in each textbook

Australia's Indigenous people lost much of what they had considered to be theirs with the arrival of European settlers in 1788 and beyond. Over the next 150 or so years, Indigenous people became used to injustice, even racist hostility, from those who had taken their land and denied them their civil and human rights.

This emphasis on discrimination and injustices translates into an emotive representation of Indigenous people around the notions of loss and lack. These notions of loss and lack are embedded within a modern temporal trajectory, articulated around three evolutionary stages: before (the pre-colonial, traditions), in between (a supposedly transitional phase between traditions and modernity, characterised by the experience of loss and by discriminatory practices and the struggle to overcome them) and after (a phase during which equity and rights have been gained). The notion of loss may include the loss of land and resources, the loss of pre-colonial diplomatic and trade practices, and the loss of cultures, people, spirituality and dignity. In the 1996 textbook *Visions of Australia*, for instance, loss is represented as inherent to contemporary articulations and understanding of what it means to be Indigenous:

> By the 1940s and 1950s, Aboriginal Australians had collectively suffered enormously at the hands of white people. Many had lost vital connections with their culture, land and spirituality. They had been treated as inferior and had been forced to live in poverty. The Aboriginal community generally began to acquire a new identity which recognised a common identity of European invasion and dispossession, which formed a basis for a new national Aboriginal identity (Shafer 1996: 33).

Textbooks mention the 'myth of terra nullius' (Shafer 1996: 2) that led to the dispossession of Indigenous people and unanimously relate Indigenous people's loss of control over their land. This emotive emphasis on loss is the result of (1) traumatic past experiences of colonisation and dispossession, (2) contemporary rejections of Indigenous claims to land that perpetuate dispossession and impart an added sense of loss, and (3) the persistence of the colonial notion of cultural authenticity. To a large extent, the emotive emphasis on loss rests largely on a settler colonial projection of cultural essentialism and authenticity onto Indigenous people (as is the case with the native title tribunal, which demands evidence of authenticity and continuing connection to the land from Indigenous applicants) *and* on the unchallengeable legal superiority of the settler polity within existing land claim procedures. Instances of the latter can be seen in the bauxite mining plan in Kakadu and the Yirrkala bark petition (Anderson and Ashton 1993; Shafer 1996: 37; Anderson and Low 2007: 210; Darlington *et al.* 2012: 134) and in the Wik case (Darlington *et al.* 2012: 138). A section in *History 2* (Anderson and Low 2007: 210) reads as follows:

> On 26 January 1972, the Liberal Party Prime Minister, William McMahon, announced that 'land rights would threaten the tenure of every Australian'. He said that his government would grant neither land rights nor compensation to Australia's indigenous people. They could lease land, but only for what his government considered *worthwhile* economic or social purposes. McMahon also said that his government would allow mining on Aboriginal reserves (emphasis added).

Another prominent characteristic conveyed about Indigenous people across the six textbooks is that of lack. Lack is characterised in textbooks

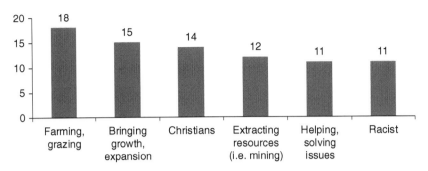

Figure 15.3 Occurrences of the most common themes used to describe settlers across the textbooks

by a pre-colonial Indigenous world that has frayed away, and an equality and equity between settlers and Indigenous people not yet attained in contemporary Australia. Across the textbooks Indigenous people are largely depicted against settler standards as lacking civil rights, experiencing social and economic inequities, and fighting for justice. Taken together, loss and lack assign Indigenous people to a fundamentally fixed, in-between position.

On the other hand, and in comparison, settlers are largely defined with self-constituted characteristics and only to a lesser extent in relation to Indigenous people. Settlers are predominantly characterised as farming the land, bringing growth, being Christians, and extracting resources, but also as either 'helpers' or racist towards Indigenous people (figures 15.3 and 15.4).

While Indigenous people are defined as having 'culture', an essence that can be 'lost', settlers are more likely to be represented as modernity and progress personified. The former remain fixed but the latter are dynamic. When looking at the number of occurrences, settlers are less often the object of characterisation or categorisation than Indigenous people are. The most common characteristic defining settlers (farming and grazing) occurs 19 times in total across the six textbooks – a meagre number in comparison with the 95 occurrences for the most common theme (loss) defining Indigenous people. The emotive representation of settlers is therefore considerably limited. Settlers are largely positioned in relation to Indigenous people as unproblematic and unproblematised emotive agents: they are working the land, bringing growth and progress. The 2007 and 2012 textbooks, however, started to problematise settlers' emotive agency and mentioned issues of racism, for instance. Yet, such occurrences in textbooks focus on attitudes and policies before the 1970s (i.e. the Stolen Generation, the racism faced by 1965 Freedom Riders in Australian country towns), and feed off the myth that racism was, once, more widespread or acceptable and that it is now marginal or inexistent (Anderson and Low 2007: 206–207, 220; Darlington *et al.* 2012: 127, 146). Across these

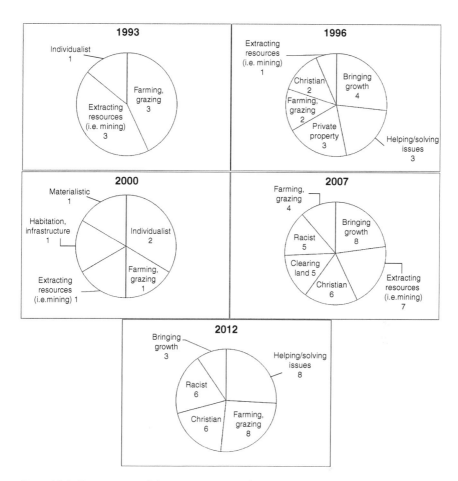

Figure 15.4 Occurrences of the most common themes used to describe settlers in each textbook

textbooks, settlers are therefore characterised by their contemporary emotive invisibility.

Therefore, while textbooks have articulated notions of conflicts, Indigenous resistance and injustices under the new interpretative framework, those articulations consist more of an emotive projection and less of an emotive self-reflection. On the basis of my analysis of textbooks, I suggest that empathy – an emotive projection onto Indigenous people – allows both responding to, and supporting, this new interpretative paradigm. Empathy allows engaging with, and embracing, contentious history while not engaging the responsibility of the reader. In that sense, the emotive representation of Indigenous people around notions of loss and lack, together with the emotive invisibility of settlers, provide fertile ground for this empathetic emotional regime to take place.

Engaging with the past in the present through empathy: A plural meaning-making process or a settler's fantasy space?

Following the introduction of empathy in educational guidelines and curricula, the emotional practice of empathy has been consistently promoted in history textbooks. Literature scholar Suzanne Keen (2006: 208) suggests that empathy 'can be provoked by witnessing another's emotional state, by hearing about another's condition, or even by reading'. Evidence of empathetic practices could therefore be found in the diversity of perspectives and experiences in textbooks that would allow the reader to consider a variety of historical interpretations and to adopt the perspective of a particular individual or group. With the historiographical and political shifts under way since the 1980s, as mentioned at the start of this chapter, textbooks made a break from the unilateral (the settler's) view of history that had characterised decades of history writing in Australia. Textbooks in the 1990s included a greater diversity of perspectives in the sources used to articulate and illustrate the historical narrative. Although the six textbooks analysed here are authored by settler authors exclusively, the sources in these educational texts started including some Indigenous perspectives (figure 15.5).

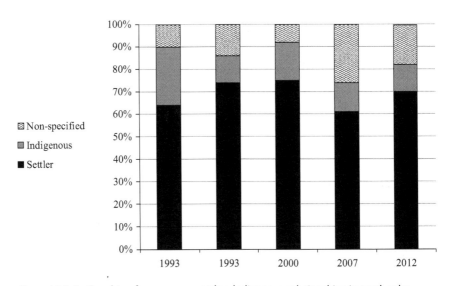

Figure 15.5 Authorship of sources on settler–Indigenous relationships in textbooks

According to Anderson and Ashton (1993: 186),

> it is only in recent years that historians have attempted to include the Aborigines, the first inhabitants of our country, in accounts of Australian history. To do this successfully, historians need to look at Australia's history from an Aboriginal perspective or, better still, to have Aboriginal people tell history from their point of view.

The authors further explain that 'seeing something from someone else's point of view is called empathy' (Anderson and Ashton 1993: 187). Their textbook *Focus on Australian History* contains the highest proportion of Indigenous sources across the sample (26 per cent), and could therefore be interpreted as a strategy to expose readers to other perspectives and encourage empathetic practices. Yet, despite these changes, there remains a great disparity between sources of Indigenous authorship and sources of settler authorship. The proportion of sources from Indigenous people never exceeds 26 per cent of the total number of sources relating to settler–Indigenous relationships. *History Alive 9* (Darlington, Smithies and Wood 2012) that covers the colonial history of Australia until World War I has only one source presenting an Indigenous perspective. In this selection of textbooks, the history of the relationships between settlers and Indigenous people therefore remains predominantly told by settlers. While this limited diversity of primary sources may reflect an effort to foster empathy, drawing conclusions from such data would have the limitation of being overly speculative. For this reason, this chapter focuses on dominant discursive constructions employed by authors to foster empathy through textbooks and their effects on existing colonial power relations. It specifically focuses on explicit appeals to empathic dispositions. These explicit appeals are usually found in the activities section of textbooks. Some of these activities are specifically dedicated or disposed to empathetic exercises. *Focus on Australian History* (Anderson and Ashton 1993) includes sections on 'empathetic understanding', *World History and Citizenship* (Swinton, Georgevits and Proud 2000) has a section on 'Interpretation, Analysis and Empathy', *History 2* (Anderson and Low 2007) has sections titled 'Communicate' and *History Alive 9* (Darlington *et al.* 2012) has 'perspectives and interpretations', all of which involve empathetic exercises. A specific strategy of these empathetic exercises is to foster empathetic modes of relating between settlers and Indigenous people through character identification (Keen 2006: 216) or embodiment. Readers are encouraged to embody historical figures – both settlers and Indigenous people, although predominantly Indigenous (figure 15.6).

Embodiment involves a relatively informed empathetic practice where the reader has built sufficient knowledge of the person or group to empathise with (i.e. name, character, experience, social/political positions).

258 Angélique Stastny

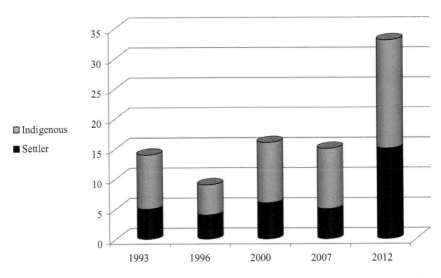

Figure 15.6 Occurrences of empathetic practices of embodiment in textbooks according to their targeted 'embodied' individual

These practices of embodiment take the form of role play and simulation. Activities to encourage empathetic understanding are most effectively based on real historical figures, supported by historical accounts, and require the reader to examine the various existing perspectives within a particular context. For instance, in *History Alive 10* (Darlington *et al.* 2012: 154), a practice of embodiment suggests that the reader should do as follows:

> Imagine yourself on the Freedom Ride either as an Indigenous or a non-Indigenous man or woman, and be sure to detail:

- the reason for the Freedom Ride
- the towns you visited (one blog entry for each town). *Note:* One of the towns must be either Walgett or Moree.
- the reactions of people when you visited those towns (search for newspaper reports on the internet)
- what you want people who read your blog to do to help you
- what you hope to achieve.

> It is important that you display an understanding of the event and the reasons for the Freedom Ride and place it in the context of the campaign for change and the 1967 referendum. You should also research and mention the part played by Charles Perkins in the Freedom Ride.

Such exercises of embodiment encourage historical enquiry and attention to historical accuracy. However, although practices of embodiment call upon the reader's historical knowledge and analytical skills, assessing the empathic accuracy resulting from such practices is difficult. Inaccuracy, fallacy and appropriation are even more likely, considering that many affective practices of embodiment found in the textbooks do not rely on precise and acute identification but rather on the reader's subjective assumptions of broadly defined subjects and historical context. For instance, a question in *World History and Citizenship* (Swinton *et al.* 2000: 284) asks the reader 'how do you think the aboriginal [*sic*] people might have felt when Cook and others rowed ashore?' In a more recent textbook, the authors ask

> What do you think the men in Source 5 [a group of Indigenous people in chains arrested for stealing beef] would have thought of the kinds of ideas expressed in Source 6 [a letter in the Sydney Gazette saying that Indigenous people should be treated just like any other British subject]?.
>
> (Darlington *et al.* 2012: 135)

In other instances, practices of embodiment consist of a speculative (and at times nonsensical) exercise of rewriting history or a task more like creative writing, calling on the reader's partialities rather than encouraging a more complex understanding of the historical context:

> Why do you think Indigenous activists such as William Ferguson, William Cooper and Jack Patten decided to use the theme of 'mourning' for 26 January 1938? How else could they have presented their protest to create a different effect? Do you think this would have been more or less effective than the protest they made?.
>
> (Darlington *et al.* 2012: 121)

> Imagine you are a nine-year-old Indigenous girl or boy and have just been taken into the custody of the state. Which do you think would be hardest to leave behind: your family, your language or your culture? Explain your choice.
>
> (Darlington *et al.* 2012: 123)

These empathetic practices may result in the reader taking their interpretation at face value and failing to question whether their interpretation of someone else's feelings and experiences could be fallacious. Suzanne Keen (2006: 222) calls this 'a particularly invasive form of selfishness. (I impose my feelings on you and call them your feelings. Your feelings, whatever they were, undergo erasure.)' Empathy, imagining ourselves in someone else's shoes, is a process of self-projection into someone else's position while being conscious that this is not one's own position. Empathy does not bring about any shift in existing power relations, as the reader is 'positioned in a relative position of power by virtue of the safe distance provided by the mediating text' (Boler 1999: 166). Empathy therefore exists within a persistent structure of domination and privilege that largely articulates settler responses to Indigenous loss and suffering. At the core of empathy, therefore, lies a process of *ontological detachment*. This ontological detachment is twofold. First, through their performance of embodiment the reader obliterates their position and becomes detached from themselves. Empathic understanding of someone else's difference or suffering does not bring into the equation the question of self and responsibility. Second, while the intention might be to foster greater understanding between settlers and Indigenous people, empathy may have the adverse effect and may instead sever one's connection to the people one tries to empathise with, as empathy is an imaginary – rather than actual – mode of relating. Empathy turns into a fantasy space and the actual conversation does not take place. One particular instance of empathetic practices in a textbook illustrates how a (missed) opportunity for understanding between settlers and Indigenous people gets trapped into the settler's fantasy space. In *History Alive 10*, a practice of empathy based on a speech by the first Indigenous police officer, Colin Dillon, mentioning the racism he faced at his swearing-in ceremony instructs the reader to 'write three questions you would most like to ask Colin Dillon about his time on the police force or his experience since. Then answer them yourself, doing your best to imagine what his responses would be.' (Darlington *et al.* 2012: 119). While empathetic practices are sometimes used in textbooks as a way to explore gaps in historical evidence and as an exercise of historical inquiry, Colin Dillon's personal accounts of his time in the police force and of his experience thereafter were accessible at the time that that textbook was published (Anon. 1989; Aiken 2000; Filder 2009). Such a practice of empathy therefore translates into the further erasure of Indigenous experiences and perspectives.

Final reflections: Beyond empathy?

This chapter has explored, briefly, the emotional emphases and the emotional regime of empathy underpinning the emotive representations of settlers and Indigenous people at a time when reconciliation has been the dominant political framework for settler–Indigenous relationships. After looking at practices of embodiment in Australian school history textbooks as strategies for greater historical understanding and reconciliation, this chapter suggests that the forms that empathy takes in these particular school texts may entrench differences and impede the coeval inward processes of self-introspection and outward processes of self-positioning necessary to encourage conversation, build connection and heal. Instead, the ways in which empathy has been articulated in history textbooks result in an ontological detachment that obliterates self-responsibility, severs connections, and further silences Indigenous voices within a historical narrative that continues to be told from a predominantly settler perspective. Patrick Dodson, Chairperson of the Council for Aboriginal Reconciliation from 1991 to 1998, asked during his Wentworth Lecture in 2000

> What are the protocols to provide the relief to the causes of the mourning and trauma flowing from the intertwined history? There is no easy cultural match up. This is not about a fresh event, it is about a continuing state of being for the Government and the society [...] We have offered on occasions the deepest secrets of our societies to those in highest authority who claimed to be seeking empathy and understanding only to have that encounter and the gift to be diminished, as of no account.
>
> (Dodson 2000: 17)

Engaging with this 'intertwined history', the contentious past in the present, would seem to necessitate 'a continuing state of being', rather than a relentless self-projecting. Megan Boler's words seem particular pertinent here: 'at stake is not the ability to empathize with the very distant other but to recognize oneself as implicated in the social forces that create the climate of obstacles the other must confront' (Boler 1999: 189). The ways in which empathy has been mobilised in these history textbooks, however, are embedded in colonial articulations of difference, supported by settler's emotive invisibility. Thus, these textbooks fail to problematise the mechanisms that created those differences and obstacles. Therefore, in the particular context of these textbooks, empathetic practices that would encourage self-introspection and positioning, and would ultimately lead to taking responsibility and transforming existing colonial power relations, seem to be wanting.

Notes

1 For consistency and greater accuracy, the two 2012 textbooks are grouped together as one datum in the quantitative analysis and figures that support my argument in this chapter.
2 In 1992, Prime Minister Paul Keating publicly recognised, in his Redfern speech, the injustices done to Indigenous people as well as non-Indigenous people's ignorance and prejudice that maintained these injustices. In 2008, Prime Minister Kevin Rudd formulated an apology to the Stolen Generation, for the forced removal of Aboriginal children from their families and their placement into institutional care where they faced discrimination, abuse and assaults on their dignity.
3 There is no scholarly consensus on what is meant by emotions. Michalinos Zembylas (2007a: 58–59), who has written extensively on emotions and education in post-conflict regions, observes that 'in dealing with emotions, many fields [...] are involved in ongoing debates about the extent to which emotions involve the mind or the body, meaning or feeling, or whether these dichotomous poles can be transcended.' For the purpose of this chapter, I use and understand the term emotions as individual interpretations of experience informed by one's understanding of one's specific location within 'modes of relationships' (Myers 1979: 347).

References

Aiken, K., 2000. Highest-ranking Indigenous police officer retires. *ABC PM*, 22 June. Available from www.abc.net.au/pm/stories/s142894.htm [Accessed 24 March 2016].

Anon., 1989. *Police State*, Australian Screen. Available from http://aso.gov.au/titles/tv/police-state/clip1/ [Accessed 24 March 2016].

Attwood, B., 2005. *Telling the Truth about Aboriginal History*. Crows Nest: Allen & Unwin.

Australian Curriculum, Assessment and Reporting Authority, n.d. 7–10 History. *Australian Curriculum*. Available from www.australiancurriculum.edu.au/humanities-and-social-sciences/history/curriculum/f-10?layout=1 [Accessed: 21 March 2016].

Anderson, K. and Smith, S., 2001. Editorial: Emotional geographies. *Transactions of the Institute of British Geographers*, 26(1), 7–10.

Anderson, M. and Ashton, P., 1993. *Focus on Australian History*. South Melbourne: Macmillan Education Australia.

Anderson, M. and Low, A., 2007. *History 2*. Milton: John Wiley and Sons.

Australia, 1991a. *Royal Commission into Aboriginal Deaths in Custody and Johnston, National Report, 4*. Canberra: Australian Government Publishing Service.

Australia, 1991b. *Council for Aboriginal Reconciliation Act of 1991*. Canberra: The Commonwealth of Australia.

Batson, C. D., 2010. *Altruism in Humans*. New York: Oxford University Press.

Blainey, G., 1993. Drawing up a balance sheet of our history. *Quadrant*, 37, 10–15.

Boler, M. 1999. *Feeling Power: Emotions and Education*. New York: Routledge.

Briscoe, L., 2015. Sorry Day is about empathy and reconciliation. *NITV*, 29 June. Available from www.sbs.com.au/nitv/article/2015/05/26/comment-sorry-day-about-empathy-and-reconciliation [Accessed 26 March 2016].

Clark, A., 2006. *Teaching the Nation: Politics and Pedagogy in Australian History*. Carlton: Melbourne University Press.

Darlington, R., Jackson, L. and Hawkins, T., 2012. *History Alive 10 for the Australian Curriculum*. Milton: John Wiley and Sons Australia.

Darlington, R., Smithies, G. and Wood, A., 2012. *History Alive 9 for the Australian Curriculum*. Milton: Jacaranda plus.

Decety, J. and Cowell, J. M., 2014. Friends or foes: Is empathy necessary for moral behavior? *Perspectives on Psychological Science: A Journal of the Association for Psychological Science*, 9(4), 525–537.

Dodson, P., 2000. *Beyond The Mourning Gate: Dealing with Unfinished Business. The Wentworth Lecture*. Canberra: Australian Institute of Aboriginal and Torres Strait Islander Studies.

Filder, R., 2009. Col Dillon reflects on his experience as Australia's first Indigenous police officer. *ABC Conversations*. Available from www.abc.net.au/local/stories/2009/03/17/2518524.html [Accessed 24 March 2016].

Gair, S., 2013. Inducing empathy: Pondering students' (in)ability to empathize with an Aboriginal man's lament and what might be done about it. *Journal of Social Work Education*, 49(1), 136–149.

Hoffman, M., 2000. *Empathy and Moral Development*. Cambridge: Cambridge University Press.

Howard, J., 2006. Address to the Quadrant Magazine 50th Anniversary Dinner. Four Seasons Hotel, Sydney, Australia, 4 October. Speech Transcript. Available from www.pm.gov.au/media/speech/2006/speech2165.cfm [Accessed 23 July 2007].

Keen, S., 2006. A theory of narrative empathy. *Narrative*, 14(3), 207–236.

Keightley, E. and Pickering, M., 2012. *The Mnemonic Imagination: Remembrance: Re membering as Creative Practice*. Basingstoke: Palgrave Macmillan.

Landsberg, A., 2004. *Prosthetic Memory: The Transformation of American Remembrance in the Age of Mass Culture*. New York: Columbia University Press.

Manne, R., 2003. *Whitewash: On Keith Windschuttle's Fabrication of Aboriginal History*. Melbourne: Black Inc.

McGrath, A., 1995. *Contested Ground: Australian Aborigines under the British crown*. St Leonards: Allen & Unwin.

Ministerial Council on Education, Employment, Training and Youth Affairs, 2008. *Melbourne Declaration on Educational Goals for Young Australians*. Available from www.curriculum.edu.au/verve/_resources/National_Declaration_on_the_Educational_Goals_for_Young_Australians.pdf [Accessed 26 March 2016].

Myers, F. R., 1979. Emotions and the self: A theory of personhood and political order among Pintupi Aborigines. *Ethos*, 343–370.

National Curriculum Board, 2008. *National History Curriculum: Framing Paper*. National Curriculum Board.

Parkes, R. J., 2007. Reading history curriculum as postcolonial text: Towards a curricular response to the history wars in Australia and beyond. *Curriculum Inquiry*, 37(4), 383–400.

Pedersen, A., Beven, J., Walker, I. and Griffiths, B., 2004. Attitudes toward Indigenous Australians: The role of empathy and guilt. *Journal of Community and Applied Psychology*, 14, 233–249.

Pedwell, C., 2013. Affect at the margins: Alternative empathies in *A Small Place*. *Emotion, Space and Society*, 8, 18–26.

Portal, C., 1983. Empathy as an aim for curriculum: Lessons from history. *Journal of Curriculum Studies*, 15(3), 303–310.

Pratt, A. and Australia, 2005. *Practising Reconciliation?: The Politics of Reconciliation in the Australian Parliament, 1991–2000*. Canberra: Department of Parliamentary Services.

Reddy, W. M., 2001, *The Navigation of Feeling: A Framework for the History of Emotions*. Cambridge: Cambridge University Press.

Reynolds, H., 1972. *Aborigines and Settlers: The Australian Experience 1788–1939*. Melbourne: Cassell Australia.

Reynolds, H., 1982. *The Other Side of the Frontier. Aboriginal Resistance to the European Invasion of Australia*. Melbourne: Penguin.

Reynolds, H., 1989. *Dispossession: Black Australians and White Invaders*. Sydney: Allen and Unwin.

Rifkin, J., 2009. *The Empathic Civilization: The Race to Global Consciousness in a World in Crisis*. New York: Tarcher/Penguin.

Rifkin, J., 2010. 'The empathic civilization': Rethinking human nature in the biosphere era. *The Huffington Post*, 3 August. Available from www.huffingtonpost.com/jeremy-rifkin/the-empathic-civilization_b_416589.html [Accessed 31 August 2016].

Rosenwein, B. H., 2010. Problems and methods in the history of emotions. *Passions in Context, International Journal for the History and Theory of Emotions*, 1, 1–32.

Sauvage, A., 2010. Teaching the frontier: Shifting narratives and cultural boundaries in 1990s school textbooks. In R. West-Pavlov and J. Wawrzinek, eds. *Frontier Skirmishes: Literary and Cultural Debates in Australia after 1992*. Heidelberg: Winter, 277–294.

Shafer, M., 1996. *Visions of Australia. Exploring Our History*. Melbourne: Oxford University Press.

Seddon, T., 2001. National curriculum in Australia? A matter of politics, powerful knowledge and the regulation of learning. *Pedagogy, Culture & Society*, 9(3), 307–331.

Singer, T. and Lamm, C., 2009. The social neuroscience of empathy. *Annals of the New York Academy of Sciences*, 1156, 81–96.

Slote, M., 2007. *The Ethics of Care and Empathy*. Oxford: Oxford University Press.

Swinton, G., Georgevits, S. and Proud, A., 2000. *World History and Citizenship*. South Yarra: Macmillan Education Australia.

Veracini, L., 2003. Of a 'contested ground' and an 'indelible stain': A difficult reconciliation between Australia and its Aboriginal history during the 1990s and 2000s. *Aboriginal History*, 27, 224–239.

Westaway, M., 2014. Why our kids should learn Aboriginal history. *The Conversation*, 13 March. Available from https://Theconversation.Com/Why-Our-Kids-Should-Learn-Aboriginal-History-24196 [Accessed 26 March 2016].

Windschuttle, K., 1994. *The Killing of History: How a Discipline Is Being Murdered by Literary Critics and Social Theorists*. Sydney: Macleay.

Windschuttle, K., 2002. *The Fabrication of Aboriginal History*. Paddington: Macleay.

Zembylas, M., 2007a. Theory and methodology in researching emotions in education. *International Journal of Research and Method in Education*, 30(1), 57–72.

Zembylas, M., 2007b. The politics of trauma: Empathy, reconciliation and peace education. *Journal of Peace Education*, 4(2), 207–224.

Chapter 16

'Head and heart' responses to Treaty education in Aotearoa New Zealand

Feeling the timeline of colonisation

Ingrid Huygens

The Indigenous and coloniser understandings of history intersect in ways that are crucial to learning about the present in Aotearoa New Zealand, as the following statements reveal:

> [T]here have been two remembered histories of New Zealand since 1840: that of the colonizers, and that of the colonized. Their visions and goals were different, creating memories which have been patterned by varying hopes and experiences (Binney 2002: 3).

> An increased knowledge of the 'big picture' has created an empathy. [I learned] How we have dominated the other – for Māori this was never an intended outcome of signing the Treaty (Pākehā participant in Treaty workshop, Tangata Tiriti – Treaty People programme 2016).

Here a Pākehā[1] (white settler) New Zealander describes their emotional response to learning about both remembered histories. Yet, museums and heritage sites in Aotearoa, as in many other settler–coloniser societies, have tended to present the two remembered histories independently of each other, largely avoiding critical or emotional responses to the relationship between them. References to adverse impacts of Pākehā settlement are confined within Māori accounts, as historical events that are sad but inevitable, and thereby allow the 'standard story' of a benign and successful colonisation to prevail (Nairn and McCreanor 1991). However, calls for Pākehā to consider and respond appropriately to Māori (Indigenous) remembered history are increasingly being made by Pākehā as well as Māori: former Prime Minister Bolger (2016) recently encouraged the teaching of 'an honest history of the settlement period in New Zealand' in schools; historian Tom O'Connor (2016) argued that the 'Land Wars were a civil war', and the dead on all sides deserved open acknowledgment and memorialising.

Until recently, responses of empathy and emotion have been considered somehow 'dangerous' in achieving a balanced understanding of the past in the present (Smith and Campbell 2016: 6). However, there is a growing emphasis

266 Ingrid Huygens

on risk-taking with 'forgotten histories', and recommendations to pay more attention to the emotional content of displays (Pekarik 2002). Recent research suggests that visitors to heritage sites or museums are engaged in 'embodied, emotional performances' of negotiating the meaning of the past for the present (Smith 2006: 10), and indeed value ' "feeling" more often than "learning"' (Pekarik 2002, as cited in Watson 2015: 292).

When Pākehā New Zealanders are exposed to a Māori understanding of the Treaty of Waitangi (1840) and subsequent European settlement, they often experience the learning as revealing and emotional. 'Treaty education' workshops are sites of heritage interpretation that present the relevance of Māori history to non-Māori, and invite emotional responses to such learning. Typically, the historical background and texts of the Treaty are used to illustrate the different visions and goals held by Māori and Pākehā at the time, and a timeline of colonisation is used to illustrate their differing experiences since the Treaty signing. Clarity about Māori aspirations may be found in the parent document for the treaty, He Wakaputanga o te Rangatiratanga o Nu Tireni (1835), where Māori leaders stated their intentions for peace and prosperity for themselves and their country under the guidance of tikanga (principles, law). Māori leaders went on to sign a treaty in their own language (Te Tiriti o Waitangi 1840[2]) retaining their overall lawmaking authority, while allowing the incoming settlers to govern themselves in a relationship of delegated authority (Healy, Huygens and Murphy 2012). Māori have consistently explained Te Tiriti as setting up a committed relationship, or covenant, between Indigenous and settler populations to take care of each other (Healy et al. 2012), and to this day insist that Pākehā 'honour the Treaty'.

Pākehā settler society, in contrast, understood the Treaty of Waitangi as a cession of sovereignty, placing Māori under British, and eventually settler, control. From 1860 onwards, settlers used their numbers to dominate government, acquire land and pass assimilative legislation imposing their aspiration of a 'better Britain' with themselves the primary beneficiaries. Today this vision finds expression in institutional and cultural racism (Came 2012), harrowing statistics for ill-health, poverty and cultural loss for Māori (Ministry of Social Development 2010), and a preponderance of negative news stories about Māori in public media (Moewaka Barnes et al. 2012; McCreanor et al. 2014). Reese (2013: 1) has described the current situation as an 'uneasy relationship' between Māori and Pākehā.

In this chapter I 'talk the walk' experienced by Pākehā and other Tauiwi who participate in Treaty education as both learners and educators. The chapter begins with theory positing emotional practices as essentially relational – integral to constructing relationships and evaluating them, including evaluations of morality and justice in society. There follows a brief review of the role of emotional practices in both maintaining and dissolving colonialism. Next, I present data from Treaty educators and learners in workshops about the emotional experience of Treaty education. The discussion foregrounds the Treaty educators' conclusions about the necessity for both 'head and heart' responses to historical representations, and draws out issues of guilt, responsibility and belonging for coloniser groups. The chapter concludes by considering implications for museum, heritage and commemorative settings. I speak as a long-time Pākehā Treaty educator who has experienced the emotional processes I write about, and also studied those processes in and with other Treaty educators and participants (Huygens 2007).

Emotions as affective practices within relationships

While comparatively neglected in politics, history, cultural studies and geography, emotion has remained a topic of interest for the psychological, sociological and biological sciences. Recently, Wetherell (2012) has argued that emotions and affective practices are woven into all discursive practice. When emotions are viewed as crucial partners in the affective–discursive practices that construct social formations, they become constitutive features of relationships over time. Engaging with emotions becomes crucial for understanding the history and significance of a relationship for two reasons: emotional practices (1) construct and preserve relationships and (2) guide moral evaluations.

Emotional practices construct and preserve relationships

Researching sequences of emotional interchanges in a domestic relationship, Gergen (1994) found that, when anger elicited further anger or defensiveness in another, hostility escalated. When anger or challenge elicited enquiry or empathy from another, then further explanation was possible, and remorse was enabled, thereby allowing the relationship to be preserved. Interestingly, Gergen found that, if one party responded with guilt, this created an end-point in the interactional sequence. Similarly, Weber and Carter (2003) considered emotions to be relational phenomena learned and interpreted in terms of social relationships: 'to derive meaning from an emotional act in the present, individuals must draw on past experiences and anticipated futures'. They considered trust and betrayal of trust as structures within which emotions are experienced – the affective or emotional component of a trusting relationship is a feeling of optimism in the goodwill of the other, whereas betrayal of trust creates a feeling of pessimism about the relationship and the other. They concluded that there must be a 'shared moral code' in the social milieu to enable the construction of trust, so that we strive to 'live up to the placement of trust by the other, that has its focus in the preservation of the relationship' (Weber and Carter 2003: 9).

Emotional practices guide moral evaluations

Emotions also provide prompts for evaluations of justice and morality, since 'all emotion involves imagination' (Morton 2013: 3), where imagination allows us to grasp and comprehend possibilities and potential consequences. For instance, Smith and Campbell (2016) have argued that, although empathy has been criticised as a 'stand-in' for action on social justice, empathy coupled with moral imagination creates emotional engagement and sincerity, and becomes a necessary condition for justice and ethics. Campbell also argues that significance is important in emotional engagement, and that a feeling for both accuracy and integrity allows people to gauge what they consider 'emotional truth' (Smith and Campbell 2016: 453). When a person experiences a sense of 'emotional truth', it helps them re-evaluate what was previously understood about past and present relationships in their context.

The engagement between British colonisers and Māori leaders can equally be understood in a Māori philosophical framework. Ngāpuhi scholars explained to the Waitangi Tribunal in 2010 how Māori approached the treaty negotiations on the basis of the centrality of relationships in tikanga:

> Fundamental to understanding is to know that Māori culture is a culture of relationships. Our culture is based on relationships with everything and everyone in Te Ao Mārama [the world of light].
>
> (Porter, as cited in Healy *et al*. 2012: 31)

All relationships, actual and potential, are governed by tikanga (law, correct way of doing things), which concerns ethics and balance in relationships (Jackson, in Healy *et al*. 2012). Māori leaders expected these ethics of balanced relationships, which are clearly asserted in He Wakaputanga and assumed in Te Tiriti o Waitangi, to continue to provide the overarching moral framework for inter-group relationships in Aotearoa (Healy *et al*. 2012). That the Treaty commitments were broken through colonising actions becomes a deep, and ongoing, betrayal of trust that requires an emotional and restorative response.

In summary, emotional responses are crucial to the interpretation of heritage presentations. Emotional responses allow viewers to re-evaluate their understanding of a relationship. Experiencing new 'emotional truths' allows participants to re-evaluate the ethics in a historical relationship and their own subjective and dialogic positions.

Emotions for colonising and decolonising

Emotional practices have been theorised as an essential element in colonial social orders.

Early theorists of colonisation saw colonial dominance as held in place through psychological and emotional legitimation by the colonists, alongside economic and military means (Memmi 1965; Fanon 1967; Césaire 1972). In their view, the colonial relationship requires specific psychological and emotional practices of the colonists to justify its usurpations and to allow the

'Head and heart' responses   269

colonisers to 'relax, live benevolently' (Memmi 1965: 76) as 'custodians of the values of civilisation and history'. Affective practices of complacency and indifference become colonial privileges defended by the colonist. Similarly, Irish psychologist Moane (1999) argues that colonial orders construct a limited repertoire of emotions for both the colonised and the coloniser to obscure emotional responses to oppression. These patterns of affect become cultural habits, or 'emotional regimes' at particular periods in a culture's history (Reddy 2001; Nandy 1983). The emotional climate after Pākehā settlers had asserted control in Aotearoa New Zealand has been described by one experienced Treaty educator as 'brutal indifference' to the fate of Māori (M. Nairn, personal communication, 2007), and by another Pākehā academic as a 'sedimented comfort with colonising dominance' (Bell 2007: 7).

Researchers have found that Pākehā emotional practices of complacency and indifference have been staunchly defended over the past 40 years. When a Māori and Pacific group of activists challenged the annual lampooning of the haka by Auckland University engineering students in 1979, the ensuing submissions from non-Māori to the Human Rights Commission excused Pākehā for being 'insensitive' on the grounds of ignorance, while Māori were heavily criticised for being unjustifiably 'over-sensitive' about their culture (Nairn and McCreanor 1990). Such a defended ignorance continues to be reproduced by contemporary mass media in Aotearoa. Abel (1997) found that New Zealand media typically produce Māori challenges as unreasonable, threatening and frustrating, generally in an overtly ahistorical and decontextualised way. Analyses of colonisation as disrupting Māori culture, health, education, legislation and social fabric are 'virtually absent' (Moewaka Barnes et al. 2004: 36), and discourses by Pākehā about sovereignty and the Treaty supportive of Māori interests are 'often silent' (Tuffin, Praat and Frewin 2004: 107). Thereby coverage of Treaty content and systematic breaches by the government over the past 170 years is avoided, and Māori views of history and Māori aspirations are under-reported (Moewaka Barnes et al. 2012; McCreanor et al. 2014). Such discursive practices help to reinforce affective practices of indifference, defensiveness and hostility to Māori claims and histories. McConville et al. (2014: 144) conclude that such familiar presentations limit the emotional possibilities for citizens and 'restrict the emotional capital required for citizens to engage in biculturalism'. In these ways, particular affective–discursive practices of ignorance (lack of historical memory), indifference (lack of emotional response) or defensiveness (resistance to an empathic emotional response) are maintained by Pākehā in their relationships with Māori.

Decolonisation theorists consider that emotional responses can and should be recruited to assist decolonisation, because of the complementarity in the colonial relationship. Recommended practices for the coloniser include 'recovery of historical memory' (Martin-Baro 1994: 30) and a 'full and clear narrative of abuse' (Herman, as cited in Moane 1999: 113), alongside

270 Ingrid Huygens

interpersonal work such as the lifting of emotional suppression, communication and support (Moane 1999). Wevers (2002: 8) recommends that Pākehā need to hear 'what they do not already understand', where being Pākehā is not an expression of fear and entitlement but an 'acceptance of a foundational relationship which describes ... the grounds on which we are here and what we should do about it'. Pākehā theologian Reese (2013) considers that the Treaty, when understood as a covenantal relationship, offers an ontological and ethical structure that gives Pākehā opportunity for reconciliation and belonging.

Māori scholars have theorised reconciliation processes based on tikanga of ethics and balance in relationships, and some give priority to emotional work. For instance, Māori psychologist Cooper (2012) recommends empathy and remorse as highly appropriate emotions when hearing about the Treaty and the subsequent trauma of colonisation. Indeed, she recommends hearing about it over and over again, in different ways, in more depth, and through more specific stories relevant to particular areas or families. She considers this approach of emotional engagement with understanding as promoting the restoration of wellbeing for Māori, and as a form of 'restorative practice' for the Māori–Pākehā relationship. Pākehā theorists Humphries and Martin (2005) argue in a similar way that a relationship-centred view of the world, as in the Māori worldview, changes the ethics of conduct in relationships. If a shared moral code is built on such a relationship-centred ethic, the emotional sequences and affective practices of the indifferent or defensive coloniser become unacceptable.

Emotions in Treaty education

Usually considered a form of political or civic education, Treaty education has aims that are similar to those of museums and heritage sites – to present history in ways that allow interpretations of the past that are relevant to the present. Through discussions among Māori, Pacific and Pākehā activists, Treaty education was designed for groups of Pākehā learners to discover historical information together and share emotional responses with their peers in culturally appropriate ways (Huygens 2011). The aims of Project Waitangi: Pākehā debate the Treaty (1986) specified that educational workshops would help Pākehā to understand their commitments under the Treaty by 'getting to know the texts and historical context, and examining fears, misconceptions and confusions' and by 'becoming aware of Pākehā culture and feeling confident within it; by expressing feelings of threat or confusion about racism, going beyond guilt in coming to terms with racism; and by deciding to act, make goals, challenge racist structures and practices' (Huygens 2007: 126). As Treaty workshops have developed in the past 30 years, a typical coverage of historical issues now includes (following Barron and Giddings 2002 [1989]; Treaty Education for Migrants 2006)

- Māori authority and agency from the time of first contact to the 1835 Declaration
- Understanding the Māori text (Te Tiriti) and the English version, in their political and cultural contexts
- The timeline of settler legislation dispossessing Māori of authority, land and culture
- Action steps towards implementing Treaty-based relationships

The methods of presentation are similar to those used in heritage interpretation – stories, texts, images, timelines, role-plays and other audiovisual techniques for imaginative empathy building. A common technique used in Treaty workshops is to construct a timeline of legislation that breaches the Treaty,[3] together with a timeline of relevant Māori actions. Participants see a growing picture leading from 1840 to the present day of land-alienation, suppression of cultural forms and assimilatory legislation. Alongside, they see the initiatives and resistance by Māori in their efforts to enact the intended Treaty relationship with the settlers, to protect their culture and people, and to assert their view of a mutually beneficial future.[4] The chapter's opening quotes are typical responses to such a timeline activity.

Treaty education is undertaken by public services, organisations and communities to help them respond to Māori expectations and challenges. Treaty education today has expanded to include participants from other non-Māori groups, and is typically a component of tertiary, professional and organisational training (Huygens 2016).

To examine emotional experiences in Treaty education, two sources of data were used.

1. Theorising by experienced Treaty educators about how Pākehā change – I facilitated meetings with 10 regional groups of Treaty educators and also a shared national meeting to find consensual views developed over several decades. Our theorising was recorded and published as part of my doctoral research (Huygens, 2007), and samples are presented here.
2. Feedback from participants after Treaty workshops – workshop participants are typically asked for written feedback after a workshop, with one study using face-to-face interviews. A sample of feedback gathered between 1989 and 2016 is included here. The participants were personnel from social and health services, regional and city councils, museums, schools and tertiary education providers. Most participants were Pākehā, some were new immigrants from non-European countries and a few were Māori.

When participant feedback is examined over three decades, almost all participants acknowledge significant learning and emotional responses to

Treaty workshops. While a few participants gave neutral or negative feedback ('I learned about history', or 'Colonisation is normal, everyone does it' and 'This workshop seemed biased', cited in Huygens 2004: 28), the majority acknowledged that they 'learned a lot!' and in other ways communicated enthusiasm about what they perceived as significant and valuable learning. A proportion explicitly reported their emotional responses. A selection of the participant feedback and educators' theorising most relevant to the brief encounters in heritage and museum settings is shown below, grouped under theme headings.

Fear and hostility upon entering the learning process

A typical affective–discursive position for many Pākehā entering a learning situation about the Treaty was summarised by one group of educators: 'Angry about Māoris, resistant, fearful about not having a place, feeling inadequate about not knowing much about colonial history, based on misinformation' (Network Waitangi Otautahi, in Huygens 2004: 11–12). Fearing that their values and beliefs would probably be challenged, some participants commented that they felt 'threatened and on guard' (Barron and Giddings 2002 [1989]: 15–22). Educators affirmed this, explaining that Pākehā people are terrified about what they will lose: 'on a conscious level they may express the fear that they will lose property, while at a subconscious level the fear is probably more about losing their known worldviews' (Waitangi Associates, in Huygens 2004: 17) or losing their valued identity of being a 'good person'.

Shock and emotion at discovering a hidden history

Learners clearly interpreted their emotional responses in the context of new historical information about New Zealand society: the historical information often 'puts a hazy feeling into words' (Network Waitangi Whangarei, in Huygens 2004: 8) and 'the historical events gave credence to the emotional response I feel now, about the injustices of the system that has kept the Māori race at a low ebb' (Barron and Giddings 2002 [1989]: 18). Indeed, participants reported that the historical information was 'spine-tingling in that it was so revealing' (Barron and Giddings 2002 [1989]: 29), and for some it became a call to action: 'What I vaguely felt to be unjust I now knew to be real. Although shocked, I felt a sense of relief at knowing the truth and a real challenge to do more in future' (Consedine and Consedine 2005: 192).

Excitement and inspiration about new worldviews

Responses to new information were not necessarily negative, with some Pākehā 'getting excited by new information' (Network Waitangi Whangarei, in Huygens 2004: 8).

'Head and heart' responses   273

Learners shared new, often inspiring insights about a new perspective: 'The historical perspective that allowed me to truly look at it from a Māori worldview' and 'The Māori perception is that the treaty of Waitangi is about the future – I had never considered this before' (Tangata Tiriti – Treaty People programme 2016).

Empathy and anger about injustice

As in the opening quotes, learners often offered explicit statements of their new awareness and feelings in response to learning about injustices of colonisation. While appreciating their own group's intentions, they described new critical understandings: 'How European law and way of living crippled the Māori unfairly'. Others explicitly described their feelings of empathy: 'More knowledge of the issues and empathy with how Māori have felt and feel' and 'Better understanding of those who have strong opinions in anger'. Their critical understanding and empathy extended to contemporary tensions: 'Better understanding of why grievances/issues still live today' and 'Appreciation of "feelings" being expressed in NZ context/society' (Tangata Tiriti – Treaty People programme 2016).

Sadness, shame and humility about Pākehā treatment of Māori

Some participants reported a deeper intensity of feelings, such as 'It is a profound realisation of injustice' (Huygens 2004: 54) and felt sad or humbled at the Māori experience of colonisation: 'A humbling experience' and 'Very sobering, helping to feel issues that arose from treaty breaches' (Tangata Tiriti – Treaty People programme 2016). Others felt ashamed at the realisation that they had been unaware of the Māori experience – one participant was appalled at her 'ignorance, in fact ashamed of it really' (Barron and Giddings 2002 [1989]: 18).

Reflecting on trust, betrayal and restoration in relationships

Some learners gained new understandings about betrayal and mistrust in the Māori–Pākehā relationship. One reflected 'That there are valid reasons for "mistrust" (towards Pākehā from some Māori)' and another resolved 'To more deeply respect the betrayal feeling of Māori that the treaty has not been honoured'. Another shared their insight 'That the perception people in society have today is wrong. The treaty was not adhered to and if it was we would have a peaceful place' (Tangata Tiriti – Treaty People programme 2016).

Overall, the workshop participants' feedback and educators' theorising show that, in tandem with new critical understandings about history, Pākehā reported excitement at new, revealing information, humility and regret upon realising that Māori experiences have been ignored and their trust betrayed, and also resolutions to approach the relationship with Māori afresh. Differing reports came from Tauiwi other than Pākehā and from Māori participants, but again emotional practices were significant. A participant from the Philippines gave feedback typical of those from countries that have experienced colonisation:

> I have learned amazing information from the training today. I felt like a sponge absorbing information, but at the same time emotion was overflowing. I feel that I can relate to what the Māori people have been through because of the Philippine history of colonisation.
>
> (Tangata Tiriti – Treaty People programme 2016)

Observing such intense emotional responses from Pākehā and other Tauiwi, a Māori participant said that she appreciated 'Knowing that others could feel the way Māori feel', while another simply expressed her 'Relief. Now you know!' (Tangata Tiriti – Treaty People programme 2016).

'It is simultaneously head and heart'

These findings showed that emotions were a significant feature of interpreting the history of an intercultural relationship. While a few participants maintained hostile or dismissive affective practices, most experienced Treaty education as both informative and emotionally moving. Indeed, reflecting on their work over 30 years, educators theorised that 'It is simultaneously head and heart' (Huygens 2004: 35). They described the process of Treaty education as a balancing act of 'feelings and knowledge' (Network Waitangi Whangarei, in Huygens 2004: 9) for facilitators and participants alike. As one educator explained, 'It's that intertwining of feelings, thoughts and knowledge that has been our workbench – in ourselves and with others' (R. Nairn, personal communication, April 2016). They theorised that 'Feelings are early in the sequence of change and need to include positive feelings such as inspiration, hope, sharing and consciousness of our own culture and other cultures' (Huygens 2004: 35), and that this led to 'an awakening' in the head or the heart, or both, depending on the individual (Network Waitangi Whangarei, in Huygens 2004: 7).

'Emotional truth' and significance

Educators agreed that 'The timeline is the single most important tool' in Treaty education, because it provided participants with the greatest intensity of Pekarik's (2002) 'learning and feeling'. Revealing both the historical promise of the Treaty agreements and the injustices of colonisation enabled Pākehā to appreciate the betrayal of trust experienced by Māori, and to make their own evaluations of new 'emotional truths'.

Responsibility or guilt?

The educators theorised that 'integration of learning about the Treaty and colonisation happens partly "in response" to Māori and partly through Pākehā feeling and taking "responsibility"' (Waitangi Associates, in Huygens 2004: 19). They acknowledged that a sense of responsibility could lead to feelings of guilt, and warned that a Pākehā person could become stuck in cycles of denial, guilt and blame, and not proceed to further learning. They identified guilt in particular as a 'stopper' in interactional sequences, as had Gergen (1994) in his experimental work. Ahmed (2004) agrees that guilt works as a 'block' to hearing the claims of the other, in that it returns attention to the (white) self, and therefore functions as a form of self-centredness. However, the educators used specific strategies to deal with immobilising guilt, for example 'Each feeling has an obverse side which may be tapped into, e.g. a sense of guilt can switch to a sense of responsibility' (Network Waitangi Otautahi in Huygens 2004: 15). Others followed Consedine's maxim 'Guilt has no place in the Treaty debate. The focus is personal responsibility' (Hawke's Bay Treaty educators, in Huygens 2004: 55).

It seems that these facilitation strategies encouraged emotional practices of humility, sadness and shame about ignorance, rather than guilt. Directing guilt into 'support for Māori aspirations – the ally approach' (Rowan Partnership, in Huygens 2004: 59) kept participants' focus on working to restore trust in the Māori–Pākehā relationship and may also have helped to avoid self-centred guilt. Most educators agreed that the hopeful goal ahead was a relationship of trust between Pākehā and Māori, created through responsive actions that honoured the Treaty (or other mutual agreements) and fulfilled Māori aspirations.

Pākehā/Tauwi identity and belonging

References to reconstructing identity, subjectivity and belonging were made by learners and educators, for example 'This [Treaty] workshop has established another dendrite to ... New Zealand and I now feel more attached to this land; a sense of attachment' (Tangata Tiriti – Treaty People programme 2016). Interestingly, as predicted in the aims of Treaty education, learners needed affirmation of their own identity and cultural backgrounds before they could take on new, challenging information and feelings: 'I would have been shattered ... but with my own culture strengthened, I felt I could cope' (Barron and Giddings 2002 [1989]: 16). Bell (2007) has theorised that an avoidance of historical memory and lack of responsiveness in the relationship with Māori creates an 'emptiness' of identity for Pākehā. Māori scholar Bronwyn Campbell (2005), studying Pākehā journeys in bicultural spaces, found that the Treaty offered Pākehā a conscious relational identity with Māori. Her Pākehā participants initially experienced discomfort upon entering a bicultural space, whereas understanding Te Tiriti offered an ethic

276 Ingrid Huygens

of respectful encounter with Māori that allowed Pākehā a safe subjectivity. Similarly, Omura (2014) found that Asian immigrants, as a result of learning about the Treaty, went through a process of redefining their identity in a new country rather than just adjusting to or coping with a different environment. In his view, learning about the Treaty facilitated psychological integration after migrating to New Zealand (Omura 2014).

Conclusions

Research into experiences of Treaty education by learners and educators has shown that Pākehā and other non-Māori in Aotearoa New Zealand report significant emotional responses as they learn about the Treaty and subsequent colonisation. Most participants in Treaty education avoided affective practices of hostility and indifference and instead moved to alternatives of sincere empathy, humble reflection and insightful re-evaluation. Some reported feeling hopeful, inspired, excited or determined about a new relationship between themselves and Māori that reflected the intentions for peace and mutual prosperity expressed by Māori leaders in the Declaration of Independence and in Te Tiriti o Waitangi. The affective–discursive practices of 'using the head and the heart' enabled Pākehā to understand and empathise with the remembered history of Māori, and the ethic of relationships intended in Te Tiriti o Waitangi. Empathy, remorse and humility were new emotional moves for these Pākehā that disallowed indifference, opened up alternative moral views of colonisation as a social order, and brought closer the possibility of a respectful and responsive relationship with Māori.

The findings affirm that the emotional journeys of the coloniser are vital in decolonisation. Indifference, or lack of emotional response towards Indigenous people, is a constructed affective practice in a colonial situation. In Gergen's (1994) terms, the Pākehā learners studied here chose alternative affective practices to meeting anger with anger or defence – instead, an 'awakening' of the heart and mind was stimulated as they understood the causes of the anger, and responded with empathy, humility and remorse. In McConville et al.'s (2014) and Weber and Carter's (2003) terms, the new affective practices contributed to the emotional labour required to restore a relationship of trust and optimism, Clearly, such affective practices are a less restricted repertoire of emotions than those posited by Nandy (1983) and Moane (1999) for the coloniser. Indeed, they are crucial companions to an awakened sense of justice and hope for a future trusting relationship. Since 'trust' is co-constructed, these emotional practices serve to prepare Pākehā for the covenantal relationship understood by Māori leaders signing Te Tiriti. Hearing a sympathetic portrayal of the Māori text of the treaty and a critical portrayal of subsequent colonisation provided possibilities for a mutually intelligible interpretation of the past. The new affective and discursive practices bring closer the possibility of a shared moral order in which uneasy relationships could be repaired and trust built. The new affective practices also serve to build the sense of relational identity with Māori that for Pākehā and other Tauiwi seemed to provide a more secure sense of belonging and identity with Aotearoa New Zealand.

Implications for heritage presentations in museum and commemorative settings

The research reported here endorses the new directions in museology and heritage studies which take account of, and indeed encourage, experiential and emotional engagement.

These research findings extend the argument that heritage should be treated as a cultural, emotional and political resource (Watson 2015: 11) by affirming that emotional responses to contested histories are crucial to achieving new learning. It is a complex challenge to encourage people to engage with a shared history that is forgotten or hidden. Avoidance, or feeling 'on guard', is likely unless there are clear mechanisms to facilitate emotional engagement and support. As Smith and Campbell (2016: 455) point out, people have emotional agency in managing their emotional responses, therefore research in heritage studies must engage with the agency context, and above all the consequences of the affective moment. The findings presented here suggest that, to maximise the impact of engaging emotionally with heritage, it is important to offer viewers a sense of belonging and identity, and a position from which to feel empathy and hope. Useful strategies appear to be strengthening the viewer's own cultural identity, awakening a sense of responsiveness and responsibility rather than guilt, and inspiring hope in the possibility of new relationships in society.

It is exciting to find that, by facilitating emotional engagement, one can open up the possibility of trust between cultural groups involved in reconciliation and decolonisation. Revealing and responding to Aotearoa's two remembered histories with both 'head and heart' will require thoughtful and skilful work in education, museum and heritage settings.

Notes

1 Pākehā, as the original settler group within the larger grouping of Tauiwi (all non-Māori), are foregrounded throughout this article, since their agenda for colonisation was enacted by the government.
2 For discussion of the contemporary focus on interpreting the two treaty texts, see Healy, Huygens and Murphy 2012.
3 Inscribing a list of legislation breaching the Treaty to emphasise its dishonouring was first communicated to the Pākehā public by the Auckland Māori Council in a submission to Parliament (Walker 1990). Māori activist group Waitangi Action Committee (1984, 1985) began publishing such timelines of colonising legislation

278 Ingrid Huygens

and government actions. Treaty educators adopted these, and went on to develop many others for use in health, education, local government and constitutional discussions.

4 See Walker (1990) for a history of Māori struggle, and Huygens (2007: Appendix 1) for timelines of Māori and Pākehā actions side-by-side.

References

Abel, S., 1997. *Shaping the News: Waitangi Day on Television*. Auckland: Auckland University Press.

Ahmed, S., 2004. Declarations of whiteness: The non-performativity of anti-racism. *Borderlands e-journal*, 3(2). Available from www.borderlands.net.au/vol3no2_2004/ahmed_declarations.htm.

Barron, J. and Giddings, L., 2002 [1989]. Perspective shift: Self-reported experiences of six women who attended a two-day anti-racism workshop. In J. Margaret, ed. *Pakeha Treaty Work: Unpublished Material*. Manukau: Manukau Institute of Technology Treaty Unit.

Bell, A., 2007. Becoming Pakeha: Dominance and its costs. Paper presented at *'Sweet As?': Ethnic and Pakeha NZers Talk Identity and Dominance in a Colonised Land*, 9–10 June, Te Whanganui a Tara/Wellington.

Binney, J., 2002. Maori oral narratives, Pakeha written texts: Two forms of telling history. In J. Binney, ed. *The Shaping of History, Essays from the New Zealand Journal of History*. Wellington: Bridget Williams Books, 2–14.

Bolger, J., 2016, 1 May. Interview with Wena Harawira. *Native Affairs*, Māori Television.

Came, H., 2012. *Institutional Racism and the Dynamics of Privilege in Public Health*. PhD Thesis. University of Waikato.

Campbell, B., 2005. *Negotiating Biculturalism: Deconstructing Pakeha Subjectivity*. PhD Thesis. Massey University.

Césaire, A., 1972. *Discourse on Colonialism*. Trans. J. Pinkham. New York and London: Monthly Review Press.

Consedine, R. and Consedine, J., 2005. *Healing Our History: The Challenge of the Treaty of Waitangi*. Auckland: Penguin.

Cooper, E., 2012. Toku reo, toku ngakau: Learning the language of the heart. *Psychology Aotearoa*, 4(2): 97–103.

Fanon, F., 1967. *The Wretched of the Earth*. Ringwood: Penguin.

Gergen, K. J., 1994. *Realities and Relationships: Soundings in Social Construction*. Cambridge: Harvard University Press.

Healy, S., Huygens, I. and Murphy, T, 2012. *Ngāpuhi Speaks: He Wakaputanga and Te Tiriti o Waitangi – Independent Report on Ngāpuhi Nui Tonu Claim*. Whangarei: Te Kawariki and Network Waitangi Whangarei.

Humphries, M. T. and Martin, B. 2005. Diversity ethics: A compass pointing to relationality and reciprocity for navigating turbulent seas. *The International Journal of Knowledge, Culture and Change Management*, 1235–1240.

Huygens, I., ed., 2004. *How Pakeha Change in Response to te Tiriti: Treaty & Decolonisation Educators Speak – Collected Focus Group Records*. Tāmaki Makaurau/Auckland: Treaty Publications Group.

Huygens, I., 2007. *Processes of Pakeha Change in Response to the Treaty of Waitangi.* PhD Thesis. University of Waikato. Available from http://researchcommons.waikato.ac.nz//handle/10289/2589.

Huygens, I., 2011. Developing a decolonisation practice for settler-colonisers: A case study from Aotearoa New Zealand. *Settler Colonial Studies*, 1(2), 53–81.

Huygens, I., 2016. Pākehā and Tauiwi Treaty education: An unrecognised decolonisation movement? *Kōtuitui: New Zealand Journal of Social Sciences*, 11(2), 146–158.

Martin-Baro, I., 1994. *Writings for a Liberation Psychology.* Cambridge: Harvard University Press.

McConville, A., Wetherell, M., McCreanor, T. and Moewaka Barnes, H., 2014. 'Hostility won't deter me, says PM': The print media, the production of affect and Waitangi Day. *Sites New Series*, 11(2), 132–149.

McCreanor, T., Rankine, J., Moewaka Barnes, A., Borell, B., Nairn, R. and McManus, A., 2014. The association of crime stories and Māori in Aotearoa New Zealand print media. *Sites New Series*, 11(1), 121–144.

Memmi, A. A., 1965. *The Colonizer and the Colonized.* Boston: Beacon Press.

Ministry of Social Development, 2010. *The Social Report: Te pūrongo oranga tangata.* Available from http://socialreport.msd.govt.nz [Accessed 4 September 2015].

Moane, G., 1999. *Gender and Colonialism: A Psychological Analysis of Oppression and Liberation.* Houndmills: Macmillan.

Moewaka Barnes, A., Gregory, A., McCreanor, T., Nairn, R., Pega, F. and Rankine, J. M., 2005. *Media and Te Tiriti o Waitangi 2004.* Tāmaki Makaurau/Auckland: Kupu Taea: Media and Te Tiriti Project.

Moewaka Barnes, A., Borell, B., Taiapa, K., Rankine, J., Nairn, R. and McCreanor, T., 2012. Anti-Māori themes in New Zealand Journalism: Toward alternative practice. *Pacific Journalism Review*, 18(1), 195–216.

Morton, A., 2013. *Emotion and Imagination.* Cambridge: Polity.

Nairn, R. and McCreanor, T., 1990. Insensitivity and hypersensitivity: An imbalance in Pakeha accounts of racial conflict. *Journal of Language and Social Psychology*, 9(4), 293–308.

Nairn, R. and McCreanor, T., 1991. Race talk and commonsense: Patterns in Pakeha discourse on Maori/Pakeha relation in New Zealand. *Journal of Language and Social Psychology*, 10(4), 245–262.

Nandy, A., 1983. *The Intimate Enemy: Loss and Recovery of Self under Colonialism.* Delhi: Oxford University Press.

O'Connor, T., 2016, August 30. Land Wars were a civil war. *Waikato Times/stuff. co.nz*, p. 6.

Omura, S., 2016. *The Treaty of Waitangi and Asian Immigrants in Aotearoa: A Reflective Journey.* PhD Thesis. University of Waikato. Available from https://researchcommons.waikato.ac.nz/handle/10289/8833.

Pekarik, A. J., 2002. Feeling or learning? *Curator: The Museum Journal*, 45(4), 262–264.

Reddy, W. M., 2001. *The Navigation of Feeling.* Cambridge: Cambridge University Press.

Reese, A., 2013. *Reconciliation and the Quest for Pakeha Identity in Aotearoa New Zealand.* PhD Thesis. University of Auckland.

Smith, L., 2006. *Uses of Heritage.* London: Routledge.

Smith, L. and Campbell, G., 2016. The elephant in the room: Heritage, affect and emotion. In W. Logan, M. Nic Craith and U. Kockel, eds. *A Companion to Heritage Studies.* Oxford: Wiley Blackwell, 443–460.

Treaty Education for Migrants Group, 2006. *Tangata Tiriti – Treaty People: An Interactive Workbook on the Treaty of Waitangi.* Tāmaki Makaurau/Auckland: Auckland Workers Educational Association.

Tangata Tiriti – Treaty People Inc., 2016. Workshop evaluations 2011–2016. *Tangata Tiriti – Treaty People.* Available from www.treatypeople.org.

Tuffin, K., Praat, A. and Frewin, D. 2004. Analysing a silent discourse: Sovereignty and Tino Rangatiratanga in Aotearoa. *New Zealand Journal of Psychology*, 33(2), 100–108.

Waitangi Action Committee, 1984. *Te Hikoi ki Waitangi 1984.* Tāmaki Makaurau/ Auckland: Waitangi Action Committee.

Waitangi Action Committee, 1985. *Te Hikoi ki Waitangi 1985.* Tāmaki Makaurau/ Auckland: Waitangi Action Committee.

Walker, R., 1990. *Ka whawhai tonu matou: Struggle without End.* Auckland: Penguin.

Watson, S., 2015. Emotions in the history museum. In A. Witcomb and K. Message, eds. *The International Handbooks of Museum Studies. Volume 1: Museum Theory.* Chichester: Wiley Blackwell, 283–301.

Weber, L. R. and Carter, A. I., 2003. *The Social Construction of Trust.* New York: Kluwer Academic/Plenum.

Wetherell, M., 2012. *Affect and Emotion: A New Social Science Understanding.* London: Sage.

Wevers, L., 2002. Being Pakeha: The politics of location. *Journal of New Zealand Studies*, 4(5), 1–9.

Chapter 17

Raw emotion

The *Living Memory* module at three sites of practice

Celmara Pocock, Marion Stell and Geraldine Mate

Introduction

This chapter investigates the effectiveness of emotion as a framing tool for engaging visitors at heritage sites and museums. *Living Memory* is a video recording module that invites a visitor to contribute their personal story through a fixed emotional lens. The selection of an emotive theme for story-telling forces contributors to think about how a story makes them feel, rather than focusing on conventional historical narratives of events and time. This chapter outlines how this module was trialled at three sites of practice. The results suggest that storytelling as affective practice can produce a surprising counter-narrative, even within seemingly safe and conventional topics. Significantly, too, this affective framing of visitor participation promotes meaningful engagement, and facilitates greater inclusiveness of diverse stories in museum and heritage spaces.

Events organised to mark an achievement, milestone or reunion provide opportunities for community members to contribute individual and personal stories to the historic record in a museum, heritage or local setting. In reality, this task can be daunting to the amateur storyteller. How people select and tell their highly personal stories in a public setting can privilege certain groups in society, not least through education, gender, race and socio-economic differences. It can rely heavily on self-confidence while selecting out the shy, the modest and the taciturn. Our aim was to discover whether, if care is taken to frame personal responses around the emotions in the collection of these memories and stories, a different language can begin to be assembled and recorded and whether a wider selection of the community might actively engage.

The *Living Memory* project eschews the traditional life-story approach in favour of a targeted response to emotional stimuli. In practice, there is some resistance to this method, especially among those with a strong chrono-logical narrative agenda, but when a subject connects with an emotion, new perspectives and language about the past can emerge. This chapter discusses the trialling and use of the *Living Memory* module (a portable specialist computer video program that records heritage-related stories filtered through a choice of 10 emotions) at three sites of practice – educational, industrial and community. The 10 emotions or affective themes used encapsulate a range of experiences and triggers, namely Passion, Fear, Loneliness, Separation, Chance, Mystery, Devotion, Hope, Joy and Thrill (Stell 2001). In driving the collection of memories, this affective language has the potential to influence how people view the past and provide them with alternative narrative structures. Our project sought to unite disparate stories across sites by structuring an emotional resonance to representations of the past. We further explore whether emotion might be an effective means through which to represent otherwise marginalised stories. Each of the three Australian sites of practice – Junction Park State School, Brisbane (educational), The Workshops Rail Museum, Ipswich (working-class industrial) and the XII Commonwealth Games Local Community Commemoration, Brisbane (community) – offers examples of how emotion triggered by emotive themes enhances the stories that can be told about the past.

Emotion, narrative and co-produced interpretation

There is now extensive literature on the role and use of emotions in museum and heritage spaces (see for example, Ballantyne 2003; Cameron 2003; Legrenzi and Troilo 2005; Best 2007; Trofanenko 2011; Alelis, Bobrowicz and Ang 2013; Del Chiappa, Andreu and Gallarza 2014). Much has been written concerning the emotive response to exhibitions and places, especially to the now popular 'difficult history' museum topics such as slavery and conflict, and trauma sites. However, emotion can play a role in engagement in a range of interpretive topics, including the mundane and everyday. Emotion is itself a strong force for engagement between the audience and the subject of interpretation (Stell, Pocock and Ballantyne 2006). Smith and Campbell (2016: 445) discuss the ways in which affective responses are triggered in a museum and heritage site setting, suggesting that 'visitors have expressed a range of emotions'. However, they note that these 'do not just happen spontaneously' but rather are contingent on a contextual response and the emotional intelligence of the audience. Our project thus seeks to frame and empower audiences through providing a structured emotional context.

The importance of engagement – the creation of a relationship between display and audience – is exemplified in recent moves towards co-production in museum and heritage interpretation. Co-production can refer to any collaboration between museum employees and external partners or individuals, including volunteers and consultants brought in to work on an exhibition (Davies 2010: 306). To some extent such co-producers can be regarded as having a professional or quasi-professional interest in the exhibition or museum, with many professionals and volunteers hailing from similar socio-economic and educational backgrounds to museum curators, and sharing similar biases and interests with regard to the representation of history. However, an increasingly important form of co-production relates to the inclusion of 'source communities' (Kahn 2000; Peers and Brown 2003; Harrison 2005; Mygind, Hällman and Bentsen 2015). These communities are characterised as the subject of representations in museums, and are commonly from marginal or minority cultural groups. Various factors influence how communities are engaged and how they in turn choose to participate (Kahn 2000; Harrison 2005; Golding and Modest 2013). At least some degree of effectiveness might be attributable to the culture of the institution itself (Harrison 2005), while curators can equally influence the effectiveness of participation (Wilson 2010). Despite the challenges of effective co-production, there is a continuing effort and commitment to more effectively incorporate and represent disempowered, marginalised and minority communities. Significantly, Nightingale (2006: 34–35, 2011) notes that diversity is often interpreted as cultural diversity, whereas in fact diversity exists within every culture and museums have been slow to acknowledge diversity with regard to gender, age, class, sexuality and ability.

Direct personal representations have made a significant and powerful addition to these new forms of heritage and museum interpretation, bringing the personal, often impassioned, voice of marginalised individuals to bear on the past. The use of oral testament in social history brings to light events, people and viewpoints that are unrecognised in official histories and archival documents (Darian-Smith and Hamilton 1994, 2013; Hamilton and Shopes 2008). These stories can be not only illustrative, but also highly evocative and emotionally charged. Consultation with source communities has also ensured new and different approaches to interpretation, and the inclusion of oral testament has been paramount in building an understanding of the social significance of heritage sites to contemporary communities (Byrne, Brayshaw and Ireland 2001; Jones and Leech 2015; Pocock, Collett and Baulch 2015). These personal narratives offer a powerful new perspective, and oral histories have made significant contributions to our understandings of the past, and enhanced our understanding of history and heritage. However, much of the direct and emotional content of such testament can become obscured or even erased in the process of writing history and producing interpretation.

In seeking to validate previously unrecorded histories, the academic process strives for objectivity, and oral testament is commonly transcribed, and then tested against and combined with more traditional archival sources to create new *written* sources. This process, despite being more inclusive than many other histories, can silence the spoken voice and make visual and bodily expression invisible. Even when oral testament is specifically sought out for interpretation, it is largely rewritten and translated by curators into a uniform and standardised museum label (Kahn 2000). Hedlund (1994: 34, cited by Kahn 2000: 62), for example, suggests that 'authorship become[s] blurred as teamwork progresses' and the '[l]ayers of complexity compound through the translative editorial processes of exhibition design, educational programming, and public relations'. This can diminish the immediacy of emotion that characterises direct storytelling.

The ability to directly represent the storyteller through digital video has revolutionised museum interpretation in the same way as oral history revolutionised social history. In contrast to the flattened emotion of transcribed and edited oral testament, the representation of the embodied spoken voice offers a potentially powerful mechanism of engagement. The human voice is imbued with meaning through tone, inflection, volume and cadence, and thus oral testament is a potent conveyer of emotion (Golding 2010; Stanley 2010). However, this meaning is further emphasised by facial expression, posture and movement. Video recording captures both aural and visual feedback. Nevertheless, many videos created for museum spaces are professionally produced; they are scripted, rehearsed and edited before being shared with the public.

One of the challenges of incorporating multiple voices into an exhibition is that there are always more voices than can be represented in a static display. No matter how inclusive the process of consultation, it is never possible to include every facet of a culture or a theme. Consequently, it is quite common for an audience member to feel that their story is absent (Kahn 2000). Providing an opportunity for continuous contributions from the public is thus a potentially powerful mechanism for engagement and more effective representation. It is also potentially powerful if the contributions capture and communicate stories that connect with new audiences through the emotion they convey. It is within this space of collaboration and inclusion through emotional storytelling that the *Living Memory* module makes its contribution.

The *Living Memory* module

While emotion can be an important element of personal testament, it is also something that can be lost in the retelling of a story multiple times, or for an inexperienced individual telling their story publicly for the first time. The *Living Memory* module, rather than relying on the prior storytelling skill or experiences of the visitor, seeks to actively manipulate and semi-prescribe the emotions and so encourage the visitor to reframe their past and current experiences through a fixed emotional lens. This forces the contributor to think about how their story makes them *feel* rather than emphasising a sequence of events. Storytelling thus becomes an affective practice that can add an extra dimension to representations of the past. Such affective practice, as outlined by Wetherell (2015), recognises the centrality of meaning-making that is embodied, social, reflective, mutable, engaged and communicative. Importantly, rather than curating an affective experience, *Living Memory* facilitates affective practice as meaning-making between authorised heritage interpretation and visitors, as both storytellers and listeners. This can create alternative and at times challenging representations of the past within and among seemingly banal topics and in safe spaces. It quietly radicalises the past by providing an individual voice to the under-represented, reticent and reflexive visitor. It actively works against a form of community history that privileges ancestry, longevity, the family and 'first achievers' over the neglected individual and in doing so creates a counter-narrative.

The *Living Memory* module is based on a computer program that supported one of the five foundation exhibitions at the National Museum of Australia in 2001 entitled *Eternity: Stories from the Emotional Heart of Australia*, which was developed by Stell (2001).[1] Visitors to the *Eternity* exhibition, rather than being drawn through Australian history and material culture in a chronological pattern, were encouraged to re-imagine that history conceptualised through 10 affective themes. Using a complex matrix developed by Stell (2001), 10 themes were selected: Chance, Devotion, Fear, Hope, Joy, Loneliness, Mystery, Passion, Separation and Thrill. Thus, the exhibition aimed to facilitate the practical understanding of Australians and their history for local, interstate and, most importantly, international visitors using a more intuitive thematic framework. At the conclusion of the *Eternity* gallery visitors were encouraged to contribute their own story in a module called *Your Story* – a guided one-minute video submission based around one of the 10 themes. The experience was highly popular, with thousands of stories being recorded in the first 10 years of the permanent exhibition's life and replayed on a loop within the exhibition space.

Stell and Pocock subsequently redeveloped the module, now called *Living Memory*, with a set of guidelines for use at independent sites. It consists of a portable touch-screen computer that can be set up quickly in any space. The module takes contributors through a series of steps, inviting them to select one of 10 themes on which to base their account; asking for consent to use their story, providing a count-down display as the story is recorded to limit the account to one minute, and asking them to review and accept or reject the piece. The most critical step in the effectiveness of the module is the selection of an affective term through which to construct a story. A separate study by Stell *et al.* (2006) had sought to extend the success of the *Eternity* exhibition to other forms of heritage interpretation, specifically by developing a more extensive range of affective themes applicable to Australian social history. While the project successfully identified hundreds of themes, it also found that the broad meaning and deliberate ambiguities of the original *Eternity* themes rendered them capable of encompassing and reflecting the overall diversity of historical events, sites and topics. In the interests of simplicity and to enable a direct comparison, the *Eternity* themes were adopted for the *Living Memory* module.

The module has the potential to both record stories and display stories through curated selection. The program has been trialled at a number of sites and the initial results of these trials are discussed below.

Living Memory pop-up trials

The three sites selected for the pop-up trials involved community groups who were celebrating a milestone or reunion either in their original heritage setting or at an associated site. The case studies were principally generated by community groups who invited the research team to use the *Living Memory* module at their events. These provided a good opportunity to trial the module in its new form beyond the well-resourced National Museum of Australia setting with its highly trained staff; carefully designed and controlled space, sound and light; cutting-edge technology; and expert exhibition design. While the module was developed for use at a variety of cultural heritage sites, in responding to and developing an engaged community-driven research approach we were able to test the module at a greater diversity of sites. The mixture of venues included a temporary exhibition at a regional museum as well as site-based and thematically organised events. The case studies revealed a diversity of local community participants, including traditional museum visitors, former industrial workers and labourers, community volunteers and amateur historians. While the selection of case studies was largely serendipitous, the research team on occasion rejected running the module where there was no apparent heritage or historical theme or site on which to focus the event. For example, we declined an invitation to exhibit the module at a general aged care services expo. None of the selected events were controversial in nature, nor were they expected to attract a counter-narrative to the history being celebrated.

The timed one-minute video submissions crystallise moments in history. These run counter to the traditional 'life-story' approach of oral history, where individuals are usually invited to spend at least an hour providing back story, detail and highlights of their life. The one-minute format forces the visitor to get across their affective story quickly and concisely. It is the visitor who decides what to include and what to edit out. At the conclusion, of course, they constitute only one moment in time, and no context is provided. The traditional history narrative is disadvantaged in this format, with little time to establish ancestry, longevity or importance of family connection (as evidenced below). Rather than being curator-led, the stories and memories represent an absolute choice by the visitor to construct their own moment in history. The rawness of the set-up, the quickness of the video and the forced selection of the theme go some way towards discouraging the visitor from reproducing often-told stories about their past, or repeating unnecessary details. The overtelling and repeated rehearsal of stories may lead to an embellished story, but ironically one which loses the original emotive tone and fragility in the telling. This may lead to stories that become unreliable or boring over time. Stories which are retold multiple times are often indicative of what is significant to a society or group. An understanding of common narratives is revealed by stories that are told multiple times, not only by an individual but by many people in a group. However, in interpretive contexts visitors want to hear something new. A story needs to be fresh – in content and in its telling – if it is to engage visitors. While a retold story may reflect actual events, the manner of telling the story may lose its connection with the audience when it fails to convey emotion. As J. M. Coetzee queries, 'What are the qualities of a good (a plausible, even a compelling) story?' (Coetzee and Kurtz 2015: 1). In conversation with psychologist Arabella Kurtz, he asks, 'given the wealth of material I hold in memory, the material of a lifetime, what should or must I leave out, bearing in mind Freud's warning that what I omit without thinking … may be the deepest truth about me?' (Coetzee and Kurtz 2015: 2). The *Living Memory* module helps the visitor to select the most compelling aspects of their story. It entices the visitor to share a memory, retold through an emotion that has the potential to span the 'registers of engagement' (Smith and Campbell 2016: 444).[2]

Taken together, the stories from *Living Memory* trials demonstrate a new diversity in visitor engagement, and a more conscious affective practice in telling their story. Our selection of stories from the trials, presented here, is judged principally on how well the contributor has engaged with the theme. Our critique focuses on their effectiveness for heritage and museum interpretation, and thus focuses on stories that are most engaging and which offer new perspectives on established histories. In transcribing these contributions for discussion in this chapter, we are conscious that the stories are flattened on the page and fall foul of our own critique that oral history transcription loses the embodied and nuanced affect of spoken language (cf. Wetherell 2012). We have therefore attempted to include not just the words but also observations on the manner, tone and context of the telling. In the receiving of a story, the listener and viewer picks up many visual and aural clues, consciously and subconsciously assigning outward socio-economic markers. In the following examples we attempt to capture something of the person, the background and the contextual elements to their story and show how these affect both the telling and the receiving. Time codes are included to demonstrate the use of the 60 seconds to help portray how quickly or confidently each contribution is delivered to camera. Each story delivers at least two affective moments – the first is generated by the teller, but importantly the story also triggers an emotion in the receiver, and these can be different for the listener and viewer, and more emotive for these participants than for the reader. The one-minute story is predicated on engaging with a core of emotion/affect that shuts down the longer context of a conventional narrative and which is superfluous to the interpretive context of fresh telling. So even someone with a highly rehearsed and disengaged story is asked to reconnect with the heart. Technical issues also affect both the telling and receiving of a story, and we have considered lighting, background noise, privacy and movement in our trial and analysis. Of these the latter two, privacy and movement, impact notably on the reception of the story, and our analysis identified four categories of interactions: talking to camera, addressing companions, recollecting or re-imagining the story, and the presence and interactions of background figures.

Junction Park State School 125th Anniversary Fete

The Junction Park State School celebrated its 125th anniversary in April 2013 with a 'Heart and History'-themed fete. This primary school, which was established in the suburb of Annerley in inner-south Brisbane at a meeting point between a middle-class township and a working-class estate, has witnessed generations of the same (often very large families) attending the one school since 1888. The school was the site of one of the rare state school swimming pools and also tennis facilities. School enrolments reached over 1,100 pupils. The fete coincided with the publication of a history of the school (Buch 2015), and included a number of other activities that emphasised school history, such as displays of historical documents and pictorial displays in the school library.

The *Living Memory* module, also set up on site in the school library, and competing with an adjacent slide projection in a darkened space, attracted several video submissions. Visitors – former and current pupils and parents – recorded their stories under eight of the 10 available themes – Chance, Devotion, Fear, Hope, Joy, Loneliness, Passion and Separation. Interestingly, a number of visitors referred to their selected theme within their video, and also to other themes they might not have selected but which they felt were relevant to their stories. These themes have been bolded in the transcripts below.

Fear JPSS-1

My first **fear** at this school was having our injections. We were in the old wooden building which was down the back behind the manual science building and it was one of the original school buildings and we had our injections on the top floor. We were all in a line and we had our shirtsleeves up so we could have it ready; if we cried we were told we would get a smack. This was also the building that I spent my first year of school in. [0:43]

Fear JPSS-2

My first **fear** at this school and only **fear** was when I learnt to swim and I was in Grade 3, in the smaller pool. I couldn't float. We were taught how to swim and each day I was worried about my lesson until the **thrill** of the day when I swam by myself. I still remember that feeling so I owe it all to this school for all the certificates I did here for life saving and followed on at high school and I have loved the water ever since. [0:41]

Fear JPSS-3

In 1959 I was in Grade 3, Miss O'Grady was the Small teacher, she used to send us to the head office to get the cuts for not doing our homework or getting our homework wrong and I'm afraid I was a regular visit to the office. 'Popeye' Irish was the Principal and they used to have a rack of canes, I would say about six or seven racks of canes on the wall. The canes were varying diameters. The larger the diameter was administered to the younger grades and the higher the grade the thinner the cane. If you were really bad you got the cane with the split down the end. What happened as this cane hit your hand it used to open … For large misdemeanours a large cane was administered with a split down the end which used to open on your hand and give you a bit of a blood blister. Of course us kids used to rub our hands with brill cream on our hair (when we had hair) and hold your hand just at a slight angle down so the cane hopefully would deflect off your hand. Of course the headmasters were very much aware of that and they would force your hand up into the horizontal position. Good old corporal punishment. [1:38]

In the first two of the group of stories on fear (Fear JPSS-1 and 2), two middle-aged women sit together in front of the module. Both are in semi-darkness caused by the adjacent slide show, creating a sense of intimacy and privacy. Neither looks directly at the screen, and both can be seen remembering their story while looking into the middle distance. The first weaves a sense of place into her story by including the small detail of the building and the second enlivens her theme with thrill and then passion. Both stories capture the central compelling fears of their story, and unsettle the receiver by beginning with the words 'My first fear', as if more are to come. The women validate their stories by nodding at each other. In the third story of fear, a middle-aged man uses two segments to tell his story (Fear JPSS-3) while addressing the camera directly. His story is replete with hand movements that demonstrate the diameter of the cane, recoiling from the punishment and transferring the brill cream. By using these hand gestures as well as scratching and using a loud and confident tone he presents as an adult taking back control from his schoolboy days. This is affirmed by the light tone that he takes in telling the story as slightly humorous in the present. What also emerges in looking at stories across a theme – as in the case of fear – is the unexpected range and diversity of activities, events and circumstances that could be a source of fear for different individuals. In other words, these stories clearly disrupt the singular narratives that often equate particular experiences with particular emotions.

The stories also indicate that emotions can be reclaimed and overcome, either within the story or within the storytelling. This becomes more apparent in several stories selecting the theme joy. These provide a counterpoint to those on fear, but surprisingly this line becomes blurred. A middle-aged man (Joy JPSS-6) sits comfortably and directly addresses his selected theme while also providing traditional contextual background including coming from a large family and learning to swim. It provides a counterpoint and corroboration of the story in fear (Fear JPPS2), where swimming was initially a trauma but later a thrill. This story reassures the listener that, for the majority, school life has been an enjoyable experience.

Joy JPSS-6

My memory of Junction Park School is the **devotion** of the teachers. It was actually a **joy** to come to school, there was a lot of children here in those days it was a very big school and we were very fortunate, we had a swimming pool which very few schools had and the teachers were quite **devoted** to us, to learning, and also to sports, other activities and my family of six boys and girls all attended the school and I think we all have similar memories. It was a nice school to be in, it was a big school so you always found a group where you fitted in, big classes, and all my brothers and sisters enjoyed it the same, we all became very good swimmers, because of the swimming pool we had here and we all moved on and did well later in life. I'd like to thank the teachers and staff. [1:00]

In contrast, the story from an elderly woman who has also selected joy (Joy JPSS-7) destabilises this story of enjoyment and happiness.

Joy JPSS-7

I used to watch the tennis club and I would have loved to play tennis but the school didn't have tennis racquets in those days so I wouldn't ask my parents to buy me one so I just had to watch. I had a really happy time at Junction Park, it was very, very good. [0:35]

She speaks quietly, confidence drawn from the noisy background, but it is a story about socio-economic disadvantage and the inability to participate in what the school had to offer. The manner in the telling runs counter to the accepted narrative of school as happy and full of opportunity, a narrative even the teller holds to be true, but which her telling belies. Embarrassed, she belatedly addresses the theme joy, stating she had a happy school life, but the listener is left with a sense of regret.

Two stories recorded within the theme of loneliness particularly underline the value of the *Living Memory* module in capturing the counter-narrative. The first woman (Loneliness JPSS-1) approached the recording without hesitation, clearly gave her full name, and spoke softly yet determinedly through the background noise to place her story on record. Not looking at the camera, she speaks to the middle distance, and ends by shaking her head in disbelief at her unkind treatment from both teachers and classmates. It is a moving story, and as a listener it is difficult not to shake one's own head. The sadness in her voice conveys a life overshadowed by discrimination and loneliness.

Loneliness JPSS-1

Hello, my name is L— M— C—. I came to Junction Park State School when I was in Grade 4. I was the only child who had a disability, I was called spastic then, but it's cerebral palsy. I found that teachers and students didn't want to communicate with me or understand that I needed special needs. I just felt **lonely** at times and sat by myself a lot because that's what I had to do to survive school life. I just had to cope and that was the only way. [1:00]

The second middle-aged woman (Loneliness JPSS-3) sits close to the camera, addresses it directly, and relates the difficult parts of her story quickly. In contrast, she slowly explains the importance of her sewing skills.

Loneliness JPSS-3

It was probably 1959 and I was either in Grade 3 or 4, I began here in 1955, and I had not attended a lot of school through illness and family problems, separation and so forth, and I had, I was in sewing class and I had never ever been taught to hand stitch and this was fancy work, and as a result I didn't do very well and the teacher kept a few of us in after school and I was really scared because I had to catch the bus home so I waited until the teacher turned her back and I skipped out of the room and ran all the way. [1:00]

Reading the story one could believe that this was a slightly naughty child, but the nervous laughter of telling about her escape suggests that fear alone drove her to run away. Both these Loneliness stories use the full minute of the recording time but use fewer words than other one-minute stories. The viewer and listener is left with a deep sense of unease and discomfort created by these stories.

Separation JPSS-1

The theme is **separation** because I was the youngest of my family to start school and I didn't want to leave my mother of course. After I had got rid of my elder brother to school we had a lovely time without him and mum took me to school on the first day but you would never believe that she did not come to pick me up. Shirley my eldest sister took me home and

I had to wait an extra half hour because we got out at half past 2 and the big school got out at 3 o'clock. So from that day on mother never took me to school, Shirley and Carol always took me to school and I couldn't believe that today that these mothers today have got to take them in cars and be there every five minutes when I had to suffer coming home from school with my big sister and I never wanted to come home with my big brother because he always got us into trouble on the way home. My early memories of Grade 1 was just lovely because if we did something good we got a boiled lolly and if we did something bad we got punished, but being number four I was always very, very good. [1:03]

Taken together, these compelling stories of hope and passion, and a humorous story on separation, have the ability to expand the historical record away from family lines and teachers, to some deeper personal stories of discrimination, bias, economic hardship, sadistic punishment and ridicule. When stories engage with the affective themes they provide some raw and crystallised moments of memory. Among the events of the day of celebrations, they stand out as undervalued voices about school life, ones that rarely appear in sanctioned school history. They provided a counter-narrative at the fete. In contrast, when a storyteller fails to reframe a story around the affective theme, the stories fail to engage. The following story, delivered by a quietly spoken middle-aged man, failed to address his selected theme of joy (Joy JPSS-9):

Joy JPSS-9

I would just like to record that in a 40-year period from 1950 on there was a Gibb at Junction Park State School, all my parents' family of eight children went to Junction Park and our three children have gone on to Junction Park right up until '86 I think it was. That was my story about Junction Park. [0:34]

It is an example of a story that follows a traditional narrative path, rather than centring emotion in the story or the telling. As such it fails to engage the interest of, or make a connection with, the listener and viewer.

The Workshops Railway Museum, Ipswich (2010)

The Workshops Railway Museum in Ipswich, Queensland, is a working museum and heritage site opened to the public in 2002 with an active heritage group. It is located on the site of the North Ipswich Railway Workshops, the centre for rail construction in Queensland from the 1880s. The Workshops employed more than 3,000 workers at its peak during World War Two, making it the State's largest employer at the time. Many workers retain connections with the site, including through an Annual Workers Reunion Day on site. A number of oral histories of these workers have been conducted over the years.

The *Living Memory* module was trialled at the site during its Annual Workers Reunion Day, in August 2010, in order to capture the stories of those associated with the industrial site, but not necessarily represented by the traditional oral histories. Together they provide an insight into the effect of the industrial site not only on the people employed by the Workshops, but also on those living nearby and in the surrounding towns. The individuals who contributed through the *Living Memory* module recorded their stories under several themes, most particularly Chance, Devotion, Separation and Thrill. The stories were recorded in a darkened section of the exhibition space but with a portable light used to illuminate the participant. All recordings capture visitors walking past the storyteller, stopping and looking, in the background. The noise within the exhibition space spills over into the recording and most people sit close to the screen, creating an intimacy. Most stories recorded at this site used the full minute, with many participants speaking quickly.

Devotion WRM-1

Hello I am Joy —, I used to be Joy —, we lived in Pine Street. I used to meet my father as he was one of the 3,000 men who poured out of the gates, especially at the latter part of the war years, and after that I used to stand up where the pet shop now is on the corner of Down Street and Delacy Street and watch for my father to separate from the crowd of 3,000 men and then I would walk home with him, so we weren't allowed to see what was behind these hallowed grounds in those days so I made sure I was one of the first people to come along when the Railways opened up to outsiders to see where my dad had been cloistered away, and later my husband. [0:54]

Separation WRM-1

Whilst in the railway gang I married a local Jericho girl and I thought I would be able to get quarters in the gang which was halfway between Jericho and Barcaldine at the time, the camp there, there was already a married fella living there with his wife so I thought we would be able to move in there so I went up there every weekend and after work each day clearing the land, raking it and making it nice and even, planted tomatoes, cucumbers, cabbages and all sorts of fruit or vegetables ready for when we got married and moved in. And before we moved in the ganger suddenly decided he wasn't going to have any more married fellows living on the job even though the other fellow was already there, so I done all the work for nothing and we weren't allowed to live there so I resigned and went fencing, dingo barrier fences, after that I took the job in the council offices and worked my way up to shire clerk. [1:00]

Thrill WRM-1

Gidday my name is Sean. One of my greatest **thrills** and memories of the Workshops was selling papers after school, I'd get down here at 3.30 and I'd work for Downer Street News and I'd have a little table set up at the front at the exit gate there. 3.30 the early shift would finish and we'd make a little bit of profit from a few papers sold, but the biggest **thrill** was at five to 4 when the first buzzer goes off and everyone puts tools down and they'd wait under the annex until the 4 o'clock buzzer went off. When that buzzer went off it was like a mad house between 4 and 4.15 there was a stream of people running through the gates and we'd be singing out 'paper' 'Tele', selling the afternoon paper for 40c. Every afternoon we'd make a profit, either $4, $5, $6 because of course the workmen never wanted to wait for their change, they'd just throw the money on the table and go. [1:00]

These stories raise some new themes for the Workshops Rail Museum to represent in its future site exhibitions. The elderly woman relating the Devotion story speaks to the mystery of the industrial site, the gendered nature of the work and the secrecy behind closed doors, the exclusion of wives and daughters both from the site and from the historical narrative. This story, and the Thrill story related by a young Asian-Australian man working at the news agency, reflect the visceral swell of the 3,000 workers exiting the site all at once back into the town. While many stories of the railways – especially at workers' reunions – are about the camaraderie of long-term employment, the Separation story, related by an elderly man, reflects disappointment with the railway gang work and the lack of accommodation for women on gang sites. This story is in contrast to the commonly related narrative of camp life that emphasises the chronological postings of particular employees, and the clichéd stories of mateship and misbehaviour during site work. Instead the man relates a highly individual and personal story that allows the listener to connect intimately with his experience.

The style of stories collected with the *Living Memory* module is in stark contrast to those normally recounted (well-rehearsed, shared stories, normally told by several different informants). The content of the stories also contrasts to usual histories which revolve around workshop activity and mateship, often related to specific events that mostly reflect the community history of railways work. These usual stories may be considered part of the collective organisational memory and experience (Strangleman 1999: 726). The *Living Memory* accounts instead reveal more personal and emotive stories. The capacity to capture individual accounts based on a very specific, self-identified topic, from a range of informants, means that the stories hear the diversity of voices and recognise disparate experiences, in accord with the aim of recent approaches to working-class and industrial heritage (Taksa 2000:8; Strangleman 2001; Smith, Shackel and Campbell 2011: 3). Similarly, the contribution from Sean, in the Thrill story, highlights the homogeneity of dominant representations of the Workshops employees. While Sean was not an employee of the Workshops, his age and ethnicity stand in strong contrast to the audience of older white men who watch on as he relates his story. The video enables the viewer to identify Sean as someone of Asian appearance, but simultaneously recognise his accent, inflection, vocabulary and humour as clearly Australian. As a counter to the more homogeneous (and often nostalgia-laden) discourse, these stories serve to enrich understandings of lived experience related to an industrial workplace and its place in people's lives, using inherent emotional detail (Strangleman 1999: 726; Shackel 2001; High 2013). In providing a means of understanding different experiences and differing events of importance, the accessibility of the *Living Memory* module allows stories of women, ethnic minorities and disenfranchised workers to sit side by side with the more traditional narratives. The former workers did, however, find the non-narrative form of the approach challenging at times, and occasionally struggled with the technology. Despite these issues, the *Living Memory* module opened up the stories of the Workshops to include exactly the kinds of stories that are generally missing from the predominantly industrial story of the site.

XII Commonwealth Games Local Community Commemoration (2012)

The Local Community Commemoration of the Commonwealth Games 30th Anniversary was organised independently by the Sunnybank District History Group and Cooper's Plains Local History Group Inc. and held on Saturday 6 October 2012 at the Sunnybank Library in Brisbane. The Commonwealth Games had been held in Brisbane in 1982, and the main stadium for the Games was built in the suburb of Nathan (now the site of Griffith University). The commemoration attracted members of the local history groups and others who lived in the local community, particularly those who had acted as volunteers for the Games.

In contrast with the School and Workshops, in this instance the *Living Memory* module was installed in the site of commemoration – the local library – rather than on the site of the Games themselves. The library had displays of Commonwealth Games memorabilia, including photograph albums, and encouraged a community sharing of stories.

Here the *Living Memory* module recorded stories primarily under the themes of Joy, Thrill and Chance, as might be anticipated for stories associated with holding the Commonwealth Games and the presence of dignitaries and sporting heroes. Nevertheless, two such stories failed to keep within the one-minute timeframe. Delivered through the themes Thrill and Chance, they told of meeting former athlete Marjorie Jackson (the Lithgow Flash) and of meeting the Queen and the Duke of Edinburgh. Both stories required three one-minute segments to complete the telling – not that they were complex in detail, but perhaps reflecting the life importance that each teller placed on their 'trophy' story. Both stories, we suspected, had been recounted many times since 1982, and it was difficult to judge the level of embellishment that each had been subject to. We witnessed this play out in the Marjorie Jackson story. Before the *Living Memory* module had been set up, the participant recounted her thrill and excitement in brushing so close to one of her sporting idols. By the time she came to record the story, she had reverted to a more formal chronological telling that completely lost the breathlessness of her first account. Wetherell (2012: 115) has described 'social actors operating as jukeboxes':

> Press the right buttons and the affective tunes appropriate to status, position and habitus will blare out. Middle-class competitiveness will burst discordantly into life while for some factions of the working class the only tunes are deference, envy and shame.
>
> (Wetherell 2012: 115)

Taking the jukebox analogy further, we can see how the same recited story ceased to tell us something new, and failed to project the emotion identifiable in a less-rehearsed account. The story had been told in a trying manner that attempted to establish the teller as important. There is a shift from the sharing of excitement at being an ordinary person in close proximity to someone famous, and a downplaying of the emotion in claiming the fame or importance for the self.

Countering this 'brush with famous person narrative' were other stories that hinted at the more mundane aspects of traffic issues and the impact on the local community who saw the need to 'get out of town'.

Joy CG-1

The Commonwealth Games was a pretty exciting time where I lived because I just lived down the hill from where they were putting on the event. I lived in Cooper's Plains with my young family and it was a wonderful thing to see the stadium being built and roads being built and the electric railway going through and having all these people from all over the world come and enjoy the wonderful event. I can still remember the loud cheering when something was going on in the stadium and we would all look at one another and say 'ooh, somebody must have won a medal'. It was pretty exciting, but I didn't go – I don't know why I didn't go, I might have been caught up with family at that time, lots of things to do. [0:50]

Joy CG-3

My name is Angela, I lived in the local area at that time, 1982, and my memory of it was it was a big event and I actually worked for the company that made the medals so it was a big time for the company, a very busy time, and the construction of the stadium and Australia in general, it was an exciting time, I spent most of the time avoiding it because of where I am, but it was exciting to see the activity and everything. [0:47]

In the first of these two stories recorded under the theme Joy (Joy CG-1), a woman in her sixties speaks off to the side, never directly addressing the camera. In the second (Joy CG-3), a woman in her fifties speaks loudly to be heard amidst the background noise and engages with companions who are listening to her. Both women have a sense that it was a joyous occasion but struggle to convey any sense of personal joy, instead expressing some regret at not having attended the Games.

The story in Separation by a man in his late fifties has a more whimsical personal touch while still conveying the inconvenience of the Games infrastructure. To live so close to the Games stadium, and then to drive for several hours only to watch the spectacle on television, conveys a unique disconnect with society.

Separation CG-1

My parents lived on Orange Grove Road about a kilometre from the QE II Stadium at the time, they thought the best thing was to get out of town and get away from the traffic and the crowds, we had never been crowd people, so they went to the North Coast at that time to have a holiday and watch a bit of the Games on TV. I was about 19 so I was able to make my own decisions, but I decided to go with them as I had a girlfriend on the North Coast so I was probably more interested in a love affair than the Games at the time. [0:46]

At such a celebratory event, it was surprising to record this neglected aspect of the legacy of a major sporting event and its impact on the local landscape. There were few mentions of medal tallies, or pride in the Australian sporting performance or individual athletes, or even satisfaction that Brisbane could host such a major international event. The opinions expressed were not strident, but quietly conveyed the impact on the local community, and demonstrate the failure of the Games to ignite deep passions in the local community. It is perhaps a consequence of the event being organised by a local history group that the stories are largely from those who lived in the immediate vicinity, and do not necessarily capture the excitement of spectators who travelled further and did not take the event for granted. In retrospect,

298   Celmara Pocock *et al.*

many locals regretted not making more of an effort to be involved, and this is somewhat ironically reflected in their participation in the commemorative event. The stories are admittedly not life-changing stories, but rather simple reminiscences of fleeting engagement that do not leave a lasting impression. They nevertheless counter the celebratory rhetoric of Games organisers.

Trials, tribulations and conclusion

The three trial sites developed from the serendipitous interactions of working with industry and community groups, and, as a result, the case studies self-selected away from some of the more traditional heritage settings that we had first envisaged for trialling *Living Memory*. While the three case studies may superficially appear homogeneous and perhaps less representative of the kind of ethnic diversity often discussed by the 'inclusive museum', they proved to be inclusive of a great deal of diversity. However, this was somewhat incidental. The participants were not primarily motivated to participate as representatives of a particular identity in terms of ethnicity, gender or class. Furthermore, the focus of the *Living Memory* module away from ideas of who or what is important, in order to foreground how people feel about an event, site or history, proves to be extraordinarily inclusive. By focusing on affective themes participants lose anxiety about how 'important' they are, or how significant their story is. This is a significant shift. Even oral history, which attempts to capture the unrecorded, disempowered and marginal histories of society, tends to seeks out those individuals with a high profile or an existing level of recognition. The *Living Memory* module is more readily able to capture the everyday, the ordinary and the mundane. And within the everyday is a great diversity that renders the collections extraordinary and moving. Much of this is not apparent in the transcripts. Accents, physical appearance and dress, manners of speech show a range of ages, classes, education levels, ethnicities and genders generally poorly represented in heritage and museum interpretation, and more akin to the types of diversity that Nightingale (2006, 2011) has highlighted as significant. The voices convey much: tremulousness belies the bold story; humour masks pain; and sorrow envelops courage; while manner of speech suggests education, ethnicity and class. The significance of the *Living Memory* module is not only that the affective themes engage visitors, but also that the visitor becomes the storyteller in an unfolding spiral of inclusion and engagement.

The contributions through *Living Memory* are in stark contrast to much museum and heritage interpretation that struggles to engage and include those outside the well-educated and middle class. The stories that have been captured through these trials demonstrate that a focus on emotion is an equaliser that allows all people to feel able to contribute. While it is arguable whether emotions are universal (see Wetherell 2015), by centring storytelling as affective practice, a lay person is able to engage with the stories of others, and more importantly make a direct connection with themselves that empowers them to tell their own story – not as a significant event or as an important historical character, but as a person who has experienced joy, fear, thrill, loneliness, separation, mystery, devotion, passion, chance or hope.

These pop-up trials conducted under fairly basic and sometimes compromised recording conditions suggest that, despite these problems, those people with a story to tell engage with both the affective themes and the technology to provide powerful and evocative stories. People are willing to use the technology – regardless of their education, skill or confidence – and are unfazed by the 'rawness' of some of the pop-up recording conditions. In fact, the presence of qualities that could be described as problematic – for example, background noise and people walking by – proved useful in relaxing the visitors, encouraging participation and freeing them to share very personal accounts. When people engage and think about the theme, emotion is foremost in their telling. Those stories that are most effective are the ones where people have embraced the theme – and it is often a feeling or experience they have held for a long time. The force of this feeling can often override the conditions of the telling and the quality of the recording. It is clear (on playback) that the stories are told anew. While the story may have been told before, by asking the storyteller to think about how their story makes them *feel*, we open the possibility of alternative emotional framing for their stories. This disrupts the rehearsed story and re-engages the affective practice to produce fresh telling.

In all over 50 stories were collected during the pop-up trials. While our observations and experiences of the module in operation highlighted a number of issues, an analysis of the recordings suggests that overall the technology and framework were very successful. For instance, while we thought the absence of a museum interpretive framework made it more difficult for people to understand how to use themes, 80 per cent of users addressed the theme. About 20 per cent of users reverted to a traditional narrative without an emotive theme; these individuals tended to be those with a pre-prepared or well-rehearsed story. The most significant contributions come from those individuals who were perhaps least likely to be otherwise engaged. At the anniversary celebrations of Junction Park State School, stories of discrimination, marginalisation, ridicule, class-consciousness, economic hardship and sadistic punishment were told. The stories also tell of empowerment, opportunity, excitement and fulfilment. Overwhelmingly, the most powerful aspect of the *Living Memory* module remains its capacity to provide inclusive and engaging storytelling that imparts and shares knowledge and encourages reflection.

Museums and heritage sites have increasingly recognised the power of emotions and the need to confront, challenge and engage audiences in this way. However, the emotional responses provoked either by exhibition content or by heritage locations are sometimes left without a space being provided for audiences to process or reflect on them. Packer and Bond (2010: 432) have suggested that a more 'restorative experience could also be enhanced by encouraging visitors to take the time to think about what they are seeing, to make personal connections with exhibits, and to exercise their imaginations'. The *Living Memory* module offers one such mechanism in otherwise intense interpretive spaces. In offering the opportunity to record these reflections, the module becomes a contemporary visitors' book that allows people to reflect on their visit, and on their own wider experiences and their relationship to the event, site or exhibition. They choose which emotion to use to frame their story. Despite the often public nature of the recording space, and the potential for dissemination of the recorded stories, the module also acts as a confessional. Furthermore, stories can be told from anywhere and anytime – the themes provide the common framework – and have the potential to be aggregated and shared without the need to retain the original space or site (cf. Wilson 2010).

Perhaps the most significant aspect of the *Living Memory* module is that which cannot be effectively portrayed in analysis or writing, and is therefore absent from this chapter too, namely the affect and feeling of the oral testaments themselves. Reviewing these stories together for analysis, or presenting them during conferences and seminars, has universally moved the audience. The stories are told with passion, humour, pain, anger and, quite often, nervousness. Sometimes the emotion of the telling runs counter to the emotion selected by the storyteller. Regardless of how long ago the events occurred, the experience is brought to the present through the raw emotion of the storyteller's voice, their facial expressions and bodily movements. The poignancy of 'seeing' people looking inwards, reflecting on a story, adds to the power of the spoken word. An important aspect of the *Living Memory* module is that the stories are collected not principally as oral history sources, but as personal testament that can re-interpret and enliven museum and heritage spaces. The confessional and forceful manner in which stories are told makes the emotional telling and receiving genuine. The playback feature of the module allows a selected aggregation of voices to be played back into the space in which they are recorded, producing an ever evolving and increasingly deep and diverse cacophony of voices that enrich our understanding and connection with the past. The *Living Memory* module facilitates affective practice that in operation can introduce a more inclusive counter-narrative to mainstream history in a space where people can express themselves. Thus, the storytelling becomes about the past in the present, and the shaping of futures.

Acknowledgements

We would like to acknowledge the funding from the STCRC and Valley Vision, and the organisations that participated in the trial: The Workshops Railway Museum, Sunnybank Historical Society and Junction Park State School. We are especially grateful for the constructive criticism of the editors who have helped to make this a much stronger chapter.

Notes

1 For the evolution of the *Living Memory* module see Pocock *et al.* (2010).
2 The ethical and intellectual property aspects of the *Living Memory* module are described in the *Living Memory* report (Pocock *et al.* 2010), including the submission process, which enables review before submission, and the copyright process. Many people willingly include their full names in the recording, but these have been redacted in this chapter.

References

Alelis, G., Bobrowicz, A. and Ang, C. S., 2013. Exhibiting emotion: Capturing visitors' emotional responses to museum artefacts. In A. Marcus, ed. *Design, User Experience, and Usability. User Experience in Novel Technological Environments.* Berlin: Springer, 429–438.

Ballantyne, R., 2003. Interpreting apartheid: Visitors' perceptions of the District Six Museum. *Curator: The Museum Journal*, 46 (3), 279–292.

Best, M., 2007. Norfolk Island: Thanatourism, history and visitor emotions. *Shima: The International Journal of Research into Island Cultures*, 1(2), 30–48.

Buch, N. D., 2015. *No Regrets in the Evening of Life: The History of Junction Park State School (1888–2013).* Salisbury: Boolarong.

Byrne, D., Brayshaw, H. and Ireland, T., 2001. *Social Significance: A Discussion Paper.* Sydney: Research Unit, Cultural Heritage Division, NSW National Parks and Wildlife Service.

Cameron, F., 2003. Transcending fear. Engaging emotions and opinions: A case for museums in the 21st century. *Open Museum Journal*, 6, 1–46.

Coetzee, J. M., and Kurtz, A., 2015. *The Good Story: Exchanges on Truth, Fiction and Psychotherapy.* London: Harvill Secker.

Darian-Smith, K. and Hamilton, P., eds., 1994. *Memory and History in Twentieth-Century Australia.* Melbourne: Oxford University Press.

Darian-Smith, K. and Hamilton, P., 2013. Memory and history in twenty-first century Australia: A survey of the field. *Memory Studies*, 6 (3), 370–383.

Davies, S. M., 2010. The co-production of temporary museum exhibitions. *Museum Management and Curatorship*, 25 (3), 305–321.

Del Chiappa, G., Andreu, L. and Gallarza, M. G., 2014. Emotions and visitors' satisfaction at a museum. *International Journal of Culture, Tourism and Hospitality Research*, 8(4), 420–431.

Golding, V., 2010. Dreams and wishes: The multi-sensory museum space. In S. Dudley, ed. *Museum Materialities: Objects, Engagements, Interpretations.* Oxford and New York: Routledge, 224–240.

Golding, V. and Modest, W., eds., 2013. *Museums and Communities: Curators, Collections and Collaboration.* London: Bloomsbury Academic.

Hamilton, P. and Shopes, L., 2008 *Oral History and Public Memories.* Philadelphia: Temple University Press.

Harrison, J., 2005. Shaping collaboration: Considering institutional culture. *Museum Management and Curatorship*, 20(3), 195–212.

Hedlund, A. L., 1991. Speaking for or about others? Evolving ethnological perspectives. *Museum Anthropology*, 18(3), 32–43.

High, S., 2013. 'The wounds of class': A historiographical reflection on the study of deindustrialization, 1973–2013. *History Compass*, 11(11), 994–1007.

Jones, S. and Leech, S., 2015. *Valuing the Historic Environment: A Critical Review of Existing Approaches to Social Value*. Report for the AHRC Cultural Value Project, University of Manchester.

Kahn, M., 2000. Not really Pacific voices: Politics of representation in collaborative museum exhibits. *Museum Anthropology*, 24(1), 57–74.

Legrenzi, L. and Troilo, G., 2005. The impact of exhibit arrangement on visitors' emotions: A study at the Victoria and Albert Museum. Paper presented at the Eighth International Conference on Arts & Cultural Management. Available from http://neumann.hec.ca/aimac2005/PDF_Text/LegrenziL_TroiloG.pdf [Accessed 12 March 2009].

Mygind, L., Hällman, A. K. and Bentsen, P., 2015. Bridging gaps between intentions and realities: A review of participatory exhibition development in museums. *Museum Management and Curatorship*, 30(2), 117–137.

Nightingale, E., 2006. From the margins to the mainstream: Embedding diversity across the V&A. *engage*, 19, 34–41.

Nightingale, E., 2011. From the margins to the core?: Working with culturally diverse communities at the V&A Museum. *International Journal of the Inclusive Museum*, 3(3), 49–64.

Packer, J. and Bond, N., 2010. Museums as restorative environments. *Curator: The Museum Journal*, 53(4), 421–436.

Peers, L. L. and Brown, A. K., eds., 2003. *Museums and Source Communities: A Routledge Reader*. London: Routledge.

Pocock, C., Collett, D. and Baulch, L., 2015. Assessing stories before sites: Identifying the tangible from the intangible. *International Journal of Heritage Studies*, 21(10), 962–982.

Pocock, C., Stell, M., Frost, L., Crozier, J. and Ancher, S., 2010. *Living Memory and the Interpretation of Heritage: Developing a Multimedia Interactive to Record and Store Personal Stories for Use in Heritage Interpretation and Research*. Gold Coast: CRC for Sustainable Tourism.

Shackel, P., 2001. Public memory and the search for power in American historical archaeology. *American Anthropologist*, 103(3), 655–670.

Smith, L. and Campbell, G., 2016. The elephant in the room: Heritage, affect and emotion. In W. Logan, M. Nic Craith and U. Kockel, eds. *A Companion to Heritage Studies*. Oxford: Wiley Blackwell, 443–460.

Smith, L., Shackel, P.A. and Campbell, G., 2011. Introduction: Class still matters. In L. Smith, P. A. Shackel and G. Campbell, eds. *Heritage, Labour and the Working Classes*. Oxford and New York: Routledge, 1–16.

Stanley, M., 2010. 'Queensland speaks': The case for digital listening. *The Oral History Association of Australia Journal*, 32, 24–27.

Stell, M. K., 2001. *Eternity: Stories from the Emotional Heart of Australia*. Canberra: National Museum of Australia.

Stell, M. K., Pocock, C. and Ballantyne, R., 2006. *'Essential Australia': Towards a Thematic Framework for the Interpretation of Cultural Heritage in Tourism*. Project 80082. Gold Coast: Sustainable Tourism Cooperative Research Centre.

Strangleman, T., 1999. The nostalgia of organisations and the organisation of nostalgia: Past and present in the contemporary railway industry. *Sociology*, 33(4), 725–746.

Strangleman, T., 2001. Networks, place and identities in post-industrial mining communities. *International Journal of Urban and Regional Research*, 25(2), 253–267.

Taksa, L., 2000. Like a bicycle, forever teetering between individualism and collectivism: Considering community in relation to labour history. *Labour History*, 78, 7–32.

Trofanenko, B. M., 2011. On difficult history displayed: The pedagogical challenges of interminable learning. *Museum Management and Curatorship*, 26(5), 481–495.

Wetherell, M., 2012. *Affect and Emotion: A New Social Science Understanding*. London and Los Angeles: Sage.

Wetherell, M., 2015. Trends in the turn to affect: A social psychological critique. *Body & Society*, 21(2), 139–166.

Wilson, R., 2010. Rethinking 1807: Museums, knowledge and expertise. *Museum & Society*, 8(3), 165–179.

Index

Aboriginal soldiers 63, 65; *see also* Indigenous Australians
Acid Brass (Deller, 1997) 89, 95, 96
active empathy 15
affect 1–4, 5, 10, 59–60, 75–76, 95–97, 215–216, 217, 226; emotion 8, 16–17, 27, 200–201; learning 213–214, 215, 218, 227
affective economies 165, 167–168, 169, 170
affective learning 215, 227
affective practices 2–7, 8, 10, 16–17, 109, 166–167, 216–218, 284–285; learning 215, 217–218, 225–227
affective responses 11, 12, 16, 59, 75, 97, 149, 282
affective synecdoche 13, 165, 168, 170–171, 174, 175
affect theory 88, 95–96
AHD *see* Authorised Heritage Discourse (AHD)
Ahmed, S. 47, 169, 173, 224; affect 48, 167, 168; affective economies 165, 167–168, 169; emotion 5, 41, 48, 168, 200; guilt 275
Ahonen, S. 204
Alexander, C. 143
Anderson, B. 4, 106, 216
Anderson, M. 257
Anzac Day, Australia 36, 56, 59, 60–61, 67, 68
Aotearoa, New Zealand 265, 266; colonisation 265, 268–270, 276; Māori 265, 266, 268, 269, 270, 275–277; Pākehā 265, 266, 269, 270–274, 275–277; Te Tiriti o Waitangi 266, 268, 275–276; Treaty education 266–267, 269, 270–275, 276; Treaty of Waitangi 15, 266, 268, 269, 270, 275

apartheid, South Africa 15, 230, 231, 233, 241, 242
Archer, M. S. 1, 10
Arendt, H. 207
artefacts 72, *73*, *74*, 75, 77–79, 81–82, 83
Ashton, P. 257
assemblage 4, 216–217
attachments 2, 11, 16, 17, 181, 215
Augoustinos, M. 12
Australia 11, 105, 109, 246; Anzac Day 36, 56, 59, 60–61, 67, 68; *Australia in the Great War* 11, 57, 61–64, 67, 68; colonisation 119, 121, 248, 251; history textbooks 247, 248–249, 251–257, 258–260, 261; *Identity: Yours, Mine, Ours* 213, 219, 223–224, 225, 226; national apologies 108, 110, 111–120, 121; national identity 67, 105–106, 115–120, 121; racism 13, 223–224; reconciliation 246, 249, 250–251, 260; Stolen Generations 12–13, 106, 108, 110, 112–113; war commemorations 11, 56–57, 58, 60, 67; *WWI: Love and Sorrow* 11, 57, 64–65, 66–68; *see also Living Memory* module
Australia in the Great War (Australian War Memorial) 11, 57, 61–64, 67, 68
Australian War Memorial 60–61
Authorised Heritage Discourse (AHD) 7, 9, 10, 87–88, 92–93, 98, 100, 181

Babić, D. 12
Bærenholdt, J. O. 82
Bailey, M. 92–93, 94, 97
Balkans 181, 184
Ballantyne, R. 285
Barbalet, J. 205
Barkan, E. 108

Index

battlefields, Russia 25–27, 29, 30–32, 33–36

Battle of Orgreave, The (Deller, film, 2001) 12, 87, 88, 89–92, 93, 94–95, 96, 97–100

Beatrice (Noni's story) 239–240, 241

Beech, D. 91

Belfast, Northern Ireland 163, 168, 169–170; black cab tours 13, 164, 165–166, 169, 170, 171–174, 175; interface communities 168–169, 171; murals 13, 163, 164, 165–166; mural tourism 164, 166, 167, 170–171, 174–175; mural tours 13, 163, 164, 165, 167, 169–170, 171–174, 175; Troubles 13, 40, 41, 46–47, 51–52, 53, 164–165, 169, 171; Troubles tourism 163–164, 166, 167, 172, 174–175

Bell, A. 275

belonging 12, 16, 29–30

Berlant, L. 47–48, 49, 235

Best, D. 39, 45, 46, 47, 51

Beven, J. 247

Billig, M. 107

Bishop, C. 91, 97

black cab tours, Belfast, Northern Ireland 13, 164, 165–166, 169, 170, 171–174, 175

Blackfoot Nations, Canada 153–154

Blackman, L. 216

Bleiker, R. 208

Bloody Sunday, Northern Ireland 46–47

Boler, M. 231, 232–233, 241, 261

Bond, N. 299–300

bonfires, Northern Ireland 45–46

Bonnel, J. 108

Bonnett, A. 143

Bosnia-Herzegovina 203

Bourdieu, P. 2, 6

Bozalek, V. G. 15, 233

Briscoe, L. 246

Britzman, D. P. 198, 199

Brown, W. 205

Bulgaria 179–181; cultural heritage 180, 187, 189–190; cultural property 183, 185–187; mosques 13–14, 179, 180, 181–187, 189–190; national identity 188–189

Butler, D. 97

Butler, J. 242–243

Callaghan, P. 12

Campbell, B. 275

Campbell, G. 7, 27, 28, 87–88, 125, 199, 268, 277; heritage sites 100, 214, 282

Canada 105, 158; human rights 150–151, 153, 154; museums 13, 150, 151, 152–153, 155–158, 159; national apology 151; *Task Force Report* 151, 152, 155

Canadian Truth and Reconciliation Commission (TRC) 151

Carolissen, R. 233

Carter, A. I. 267, 276

Carter, J. 151

cheap sentimentality 207

Chinese Canadian Military Museum (CCMM), Vancouver, Canada 152, 155, 156–157

Chinese Head Tax and Exclusions Laws, Canada 151

Coetzee, J. M. 287

cognition 1–2, 3, 14, 110

Cole, E. 203

collective emotions 4, 106, 107, 180

collective identity *see* national identity

collective memory 126, 131, 143, 144–146, 183

colonisation: Aotearoa New Zealand 265, 268–270, 276; Australia 119, 121, 248, 251

commemorations 1, 10–12, 26–27, 45–46; *see also* war commemorations

commitments 2, 11, 154, 184

Commonwealth Games Local Community Commemoration, XII, Brisbane, Australia 282, 286, 295–298, 299

compassion 231, 242

contagion 4

contemporary migration 124, 128, 129, 142

contested history 13, 14

Cooper, E. 270

Coplan, A. 126

co-production 282–283

Correia, A. 91–92

Critical Heritage Studies 85, 88, 93, 100, 197

critical social research 2, 6

crowd minds 4

cultural heritage 187, 214; Bulgaria 180, 187, 189–190

Cultural Heritage Act, Bulgaria 186

cultural property, Bulgaria 183, 185–187

Curtin, D. 231, 242

Cvetkovich, A. 41, 51

306 Index

Dahlin, J. 10–11
Dawney, L. 222
Deane, S. 45
de Certeau, M. 170
decolonisation 15, 269–270, 276
Deleuze, G. 215, 216–217
Deller, J. 86–87, 89, 91, 92, 93, 99
Denominations Act, Bulgaria 183
Derry/Londonderry, Northern Ireland
    39, 43–46; Temple art installation
    11, 39, 40–41, 42, 43, 44, 46, 47–48,
    49–51, 52, 53
Destination Tyneside (Discovery
    Museum, Newcastle, UK) 124–125,
    126, 127–131, 131–140, 142, 143, 144
Dicks, B. 9, 13, 125
Dierking, L. D. 60
difficult exhibitions 108, 197, 202
difficult heritage 126, 197, 198, 199, 201,
    202, 204, 208
difficult histories 14, 53, 57, 126, 155,
    197, 204, 282
difficult knowledge 14, 15, 197, 198–199,
    231, 241
digital storytelling 15, 231, 241, 284;
    Noni's story 235–240, 241, 242, 243
Discovery Museum, Newcastle, UK
    124–125, 126, 127–131, 131–140, 142,
    143, 144
Downtown Eastside community,
    Vancouver, Canada 151, 153
Dragojlovica, A. 215
Družetić, I. 72, 77
Dupnitsa, Bulgaria 180, 183–184

Ebrington, Northern Ireland 43–44
education 14–16, 231; emotion 214,
    217, 232
Edwards, D. 109–110, 114
Elaine (*Destination Tyneside*) 132–133,
    135, 140, 140–143
embodied learning 213–214, 218, 226,
    257–260
embodied meaning-making 27, 36, 37
emotion 1–4, 5, 6, 8, 10, 16–17, 109–110,
    200–201; affect 8, 16–17, 27, 200–201;
    education 214, 217, 232
emotional engagement 13–15, 71, 79–81,
    83, 198, 242, 268, 270, 277, 282
emotional landscapes 169, 172
emotional performance 82, 266
emotional practices 256, 266, 267–269, 269
emotional reflexivity 15

emotional regimes 14, 197–198, 201–202,
    204, 205–208, 247–248
emotional responses 8, 13, 17, 71,
    144–146, 149–150, 268, 269, 277,
    299–300
emotional rules, gendered 232
emotional truth 268, 274
emotional vulnerability 150
emotion management 199, 201
emotion–reason rhetoric 108–110,
    120–121
empathetic understanding 202,
    204–205
empathy 13, 15, 28, 126, 145–146,
    206–208, 242, 246–247, 260–261;
    Indigenous Australians 250–251,
    255–256, 257–260; reconciliation 247
empty sentimentality 207
*Eternity: Stories from the Emotional
    Heart of Australia* (National Museum
    of Australia) 285
exclusion 10, 12, 16
exhibitions 59–60, 127, 136, 139, 145,
    145, 149, 151–153, 213
expertise 7, 8, 9

Fabre, D. 181, 190
Falk, J. H. 60
feeling 1; rules of 197, 201, 205, 206,
    208; structures of 6, 14, 208
Figgis, M. 86, 87, 91, 93, 97, 100
Finland 204
First Nations, Canada 151–152,
    153–155, 156
Flam, H. 201, 206
Focus on Australian History
    (history textbook) 257
forced removal of children, Australia
    12–13, 106, 108, 110, 112–113
The Forgotten (Museum of
    Anthropology, Vancouver, Canada)
    152, 154
Foucault, M. 57, 232

Gachago, D. 15
Gair, S. 247
Galani, A. 13
Gergen, K. J. 267, 275, 276
Gilbert, D. 91, 92
Glenbow Museum, Canada 153–154;
    Niitsitapiisinni: Our Way of Life 154;
    *The Spirit Sings: Artistic Traditions of
    Canada's First Peoples* 151, 152

Goldie, P. 126
Grand Mufti's Office, Bulgaria 14, 179, 182, 183, 186, 187, 188, 189
Gregg, M. 95–96
Grianan fort, Northern Ireland 45
Griffiths, B. 247
Grubišić, D. 72, 76–77
Guattari, F. 215, 216–217
guilt 108, 114, 233, 234–235, 241, 275

habitus 6
Hage, G. 107
Haldrup, M. 82
Hall, S. 7
harmonisation 203–204, 206, 207, 208
Hastie, B. 12
Hedlund, A. L. 283–284
Henderson, J. 152
heritage 1, 2, 7–10, 16–17, 180, 181, 182, 185, 191, 277
Heritage, Labour and the Working Classes (Smith, Shackel and Campbell, 2011) 92
heritage practices 39, 42, 45, 51, 53, 202, 208
heritage sites 9, 14, 28, 149, 201–202
heritage studies 2, 3, 5, 7, 8, 17, 85, 149, 199, 247, 277
heritage tourism 7
Herzfeld, M. 180, 183
heterotopias 57–58, 63, 66, 67–68
Heumann Gurian, H. 58, 70
Heynen, H. 58
higher education (HE), South Africa 230, 234, 235
historical narratives 60, 105, 120–121, 247, 281
historic migration 124, 128
History Alive 9 (history textbook) 248, 257
History Alive 10 (history textbook) 248, 251–252, 258, 260
history education 198, 202–203; Australia 246, 249–250; harmonisation 203–204, 206, 207, 208; multiperspectivity 204, 207, 208; separation 203, 206, 208
history textbooks 198, 202, 203, 256; Australia 247, 248–249, 251–256, 258–260, 261; Indigenous Australians 248–249, 251–257
Holocaust 198, 224–225
Hook, D. 200
House (Whiteread, 1993) 88

Howard, J. 105, 108, 120
Howard government (Australia, 1996–2007) 106, 112
human rights, Canada 150–151, 153, 154
Humphries, M. T. 270
Hutchison, E. 208
Huygens, I. 15

Identity: Yours, Mine, Ours (Immigration Museum, Australia) 213, 219, 223–224, 225, 226
immigration *see* migration
Immigration Museum, Melbourne, Australia 218–219; *Identity: Yours, Mine, Ours* 213, 219, 223–224, 225, 226; *Tram Scenario* exhibit 223–224, 225, 226
inclusion 10, 12, 16
Indian Residential Schools (IRS), Canada 151, 153
indifference 15, 269, 276
Indigenous Australians 15, 106, 108, 110, 120, 121, 246, 247, 249; empathy 250–251, 255–256, 257–260; history textbooks 248–249, 251–257; Nelson apology 108, 110, 111, 115–120, 121; reconciliation 246, 249, 250–251, 260; Rudd apology 108, 110, 111–115, 120, 121; soldiers 63, 65; Stolen Generations 12–13, 106, 108, 110, 112–113
Indigenous Canadians *see* First Nations, Canada
indirect knowledge 230–231
intangible heritage 8, 9–10
interface communities 168–169, 171
Islam 185, 186, 188–189

Jackson, A. 100
Janet (*Destination Tyneside*) 132–133, 135–136, 138–139
Jansen, J. 230
Japanese Internment, Canada 151
Jarman, N. 172
John (*Destination Tyneside*) 132–133, 141–143
Juliff, T. 12
Junction Park State School, Brisbane, Australia 282, 286, 288–292, 299

Karakusheva, S. 13
Karlovo, Bulgaria 179, 180, 182–183, 184, 187, 188

308 Index

Katie (*Destination Tyneside*) 132–133, 133–135, 140, 142, 144
Kearsey, B. 65
Keating, P. 249
Keen, S. 256, 259
Keightley, E. 247
Kidd, J. 100
Kirshenblatt-Gimblett, B. 9, 71
knowledge 214; difficult 14, 15, 197, 198–199, 231, 241; indirect 230–231; non-presentational 234
Kohler Riessman, C. 236
Kurtz, A. 287

Lamm, C. 246–247
Landsberg, A. 247
Lauren (Noni's story) 238–239, 241, 242
learning 214–215, 217; affect 213–214, 215, 218, 227; affective practices 215, 217–218, 225–227
legacies 184, 190
Leibowitz, B. 233
Leonard, M. 164
Leys, R. 59
Linda (*Destination Tyneside*) 132–133, 133–135, 140, 142, 144
Lisle, D. 167, 173, 175
Little Lon exhibit, Melbourne Museum, Australia 219–223
Living Memory module, Australia 281–282, 284–285, 286–299, 298–299, 300; Commonwealth Games Community Commemoration 282, 286, 295–298, 299; Junction Park State School 282, 286, 288–292, 299; Workshops Rail Museum 282, 286, 293–295, 299
Lloyd, K. 13
Lord, B. 66
Lowenthal, D. 7
Lugones, M. 240–241
Luke, A. 106

Māori, Aotearoa New Zealand 265, 266, 268, 269, 270, 275–277; Treaty education 271, 272, 273, 274, 275
McConville, A. 269, 276
McCourt, J. 46–47
McCreanor, T. 269, 276
McCully, A. 202, 204
Macdonald, S. 9, 145
McDowell, S. 164, 166, 171
McKernan, A. 11–12

McKernan, M. 64
McLeod, J. 11–12
McLoughlin, M. 98
Markham, K. 13
Marriage, H. 41, 45–46
Martin, B. 270
Mason, R. 13
Massumi, B. 4
Mate, G. 15
Maureen (*Destination Tyneside*) 132–133, 136, 137–139, 139
MBR *see* Museum of Broken Relationships (MBR)
Melbourne Museum, Museum Victoria, Australia 218–223
The Melbourne Story, Melbourne Museum, Australia 219
memory schemata 125, 145
migration 13, 124, 126, 131–132, 140–142, 145–146; contemporary 124, 128, 129, 142; historic 124, 128; *see also Destination Tyneside*
Miklošević, Ž. 12
Miners' Strike (UK, 1984–1985) 12, 85–86, 92, 94, 95
mnemonic communities 125, 143, 144, 146
MOA *see* Museum of Anthropology (MOA)
Moane, G. 269, 276
Moewaka Barnes, H. 269, 276
moral evaluations 267–268
mosques, Bulgaria 13–14, 179, 180, 181–187, 189–190; Dupnitsa 183–184; Karlovo 179, 182–183, 184, 187, 188; Razgrad 187; Stara Zagora 184, 188
Mulcahy, D. 14
multiperspectivity 204, 207, 208
murals, Belfast, Northern Ireland 13, 163, 164, 165–166
mural tourism, Belfast, Northern Ireland 164, 166, 167, 170–171, 174–175
mural tours, Belfast, Northern Ireland 13, 163, 164, 165, 167, 169–170, 171–172, 175
Murphy, C. 50
Murtagh, B. 168–169, 171
museology 7, 8, 152
museum communication 71, 75, 80–81, 82
museum education 15, 202, 207, 208
museumification 184, 187, 188
museum interpretation 82, 283, 287, 298

museum objects 72, *73*, *74*, 75, 77–79, 83
Museum of Anthropology (MOA), Vancouver, Canada 152, 154, 157
Museum of Broken Relationships (MBR), Zagreb, Croatia 12, 70–71, 72–75, 76–82, 83
museum practices 8, 70, 83, 202, 208, 242
museums 1, 7, 8, 9, 13, 14–16, 58–60, 70, 71, 124, 149; Australia 57, 58; Canada 13, 150, 151, 152–153, 155–158, 159
museum sites 201–202
museum studies 2, 3, 5, 7, 8, 199, 214, 247
Museum Victoria, Australia 64, 65–66, 215, 218–219; *WWI: Love and Sorrow* 11, 57, 64–65, 66–68
Muslim Denomination, Bulgaria 13–14, 179, 181–182, 183, 185, 186, 187, 189

narration 82
narrative templates 125, 144
nation 8, 10, 105, 106, 120; Australia 60, 67
national apologies 106, 107, 108, 110, 121; Australia 108, 110, 111–120, 121; Canada 151
national heritage 8, 180–181; Bulgaria 188–189, 190; Ottoman Empire 187–188
national histories 105, 106, 107, 110, 121
national identity 10, 105, 106, 107–108, 180–181; Australia 67, 105–106, 115–120, 121; Bulgaria 188–189
nationalism 1, 7, 8, 106–107, 183
National Museum of Australia 285, 286
national narratives 12–14, 105, 107, 110, 121
Neale, K. 64
Nelson, B. 13, 106, 120; national apologies 108, 110, 111, 115–120, 121
Newton, R. 163–164, 172, 174
New Zealand 105; soldiers 61, 67; *see also* Aotearoa New Zealand
Ng'ambi, D. 15
Nicholls, L. 233
Nightingale, E. 283, 298
Niitsitapiisinni: Our Way of Life (Glenbow Museum, Canada) 154
Noni's story (digital storytelling, South Africa) 235–240, 241, 242, 243
non-presentational knowledge 234
Non-Representational Theory (NRT) 8

Nora, P. 26, 27
Northern Ireland 41–42, 50, 162, 164; *see also* Belfast
nostalgia 7, 8, 143, 145, 145, 149, 183

Omura, S. 276
oral testaments 283–284, 286–288, 298–299, 300
Orange, J. 151
Orgreave (1984) 85–86, 94, 97, 98
Orthodox Christians, Bulgaria 14, 179, 182, 183, 184
Ortner, S. B. 5
Other 60, 202, 205, 206–207, 208, 214
Ottoman Empire 13–14, 180–181, 185, 187–188, 189–190, 191

Packer, J. 299–300
Pākehā New Zealanders 265, 266, 269, 270, 275–277; Treaty education 270–274, 275
passive empathy 15
Paxson, M. 29–30
pedagogy 8, 199; of discomfort 231–233
Pedersen, A. 247
Pedwell, C. 247
performance 82, 85
performance analysis 235, 236
perpetrators 201, 205, 206, 207, 208
phenomenology 2–3
Pickering, M. 247
Pickering, S. 164–165
Pingel, F. 203
place 30–31, 36, 37, 42–43
Pocock, C. 15, 285
political tourism 163, 174
Popple, S. 92–93
post-conflict societies 203, 230
post-traumatic stress disorder (PTSD) 39–40, 51
practice social theories 4–5
'The Price of Victory' album, Russia 32–33
psychobiology 3
Purkis, H. 127

race: Australia 115, 121; South Africa 230
racism 249; Australia 13, 223–224; South Africa 230
Razgrad, Bulgaria 187
reason, appeals to 13
Reckwitz, A. 216, 225

310 Index

reconciliation 206, 207, 208, 247; Australia 246, 249, 250–251, 260
reconciliation efforts 198, 204
reconciliation processes 14, 197, 201, 202–203, 208; harmonisation 203–204, 205, 207, 208; multiperspectivity 204, 207, 208; separation 203, 206, 208
Reddy, W. M. 201, 247–248
Reese, A. 266, 270
refugees 13
Regan, P. 159
religious buildings 188–189, 190–191; mosques 13–14, 179, 180, 181–187, 189–190
remembrance 1, 10–12; *see also* commemorations
resentment 205–206, 207, 208
Residential and Indian Day School Art Research Program (RIDSAR), University of Victoria, Australia 151, 152, 153–154, 155, 157
Reynolds, P. 49
Rice, J. 200–201, 215
Robinson, J. C. 13, 15
Rohleder, P. 233
Rosenwein, B. H. 248
Rudd, K. 12, 106, 120, 249; national apology 108, 110, 111–115, 120, 121
Russia: battlefields 25–27, 29, 30–32, 33–36; soldiers remains 10–11, 25–26, 27, 28–29, 30, 32–33, 34–36, 37; war commemorations 27, 33, 36–37

Salber Phillips, M. 207
Salmon, P. 235
Samuel, R. 7
Sayner, J. 13
Scampton, W. 49, 50–51, 52
Schatzki, T. 5, 150, 216
Scherer, K. R. 3
Scienceworks, Museum Victoria, Australia 218–219
search movement, Russia 27, 28–33, 37; tours 29, 33–36
Seigworth, G. J. 95–96
sentimental history 204, 207
sentimentality 48–49
separation 203, 206, 208
shame 15, 108, 114, 233, 234, 235, 241
Shea, M. 11, 13
Shirlow, P. 168–169, 171
Shotwell, A. 233–234

Shuman, A. 242
Siege of Derry (Northern Ireland, 1689) 43
Silverman, H. 152
Simon, R. I. 108, 198, 199
Singer, T. 246–247
Skinner, J. 164
Smith, L. 7, 13, 26, 27, 28, 87–88, 125, 151–152, 199, 224–225, 268, 277; heritage sites 9, 100, 214, 282
social actors 4, 5, 6
social history 6, 64, 87, 88, 92, 283
social justice 124, 215, 223, 227, 232, 268
social practices 5, 6
social research 2–3, 5
soldiers remains, Russia 10–11, 25–26, 27, 28–29, 30, 32–33, 34–36, 37
source communities 283
South Africa 204, 230, 241; apartheid 15, 230, 231, 233, 241, 242; digital storytelling 15, 231, 235–240, 241, 242, 243, 284; higher education 230, 234, 235; Noni's story 235–240, 241, 242, 243; racism 230
The Spirit Sings: Artistic Traditions of Canada's First Peoples (Glenbow Museum, Canada) 151, 152
Stara Zagora, Bulgaria 180, 184, 188
Stastny, A. 15
Stell, M. 15, 285
Stewart, K. 50
stickiness 169, 173, 174
Stolen Generations, Australia 12–13, 106, 108, 110, 112–113
storytelling 231, 236, 281, 283–284, 198–299; digital 15, 231, 235–240, 241, 242, 243, 284; *Living Memory* module 281, 284–285, 286–288, 300; Noni's story 235–240, 241, 242, 243
Strahilov, I. 13
subjectivity 126, 127
sufferings 201, 204–205, 207, 208
Sullivan, S. 96
Swartz, L. 233
Switzer, C. 171

Tamboukou, M. 57–58, 66, 67
Task Force Report on Museums and First Peoples (Assembly of First Nations and Canadian Museum Association, 1992) 151, 152, 155
Temple, G. 47

Temple art installation, Derry/ Londonderry, Northern Ireland 11, 39, 40–41, 42, 43, 44, 46, 47–48, 49–51, 52, 53
terror tourism 163
Te Tiriti o Waitangi (Aotearoa New Zealand, 1840) 266, 268, 275–276
Thrift, N. 4, 215
Todorova, M. 180
Torres Strait Islanders 246, 249
Tout-Smith, D. 64, 66
Tram Scenario exhibit (Immigration Museum, Australia) 223–224, 225, 226
TRC *see* Canadian Truth and Reconciliation Commission (TRC)
Treaty education, Aotearoa New Zealand 266–267, 269, 270–275, 276
Treaty of Waitangi (Aotearoa New Zealand, 1840) 15, 266, 268, 269, 270, 275
Trofanenko, B. M. 59
Troubles, Belfast, Northern Ireland 13, 40, 41, 46–47, 51–52, 53, 164–165, 169, 170
Troubles tourism, Northern Ireland 163–164, 166, 167, 172, 174–175

Veracini, L. 250
victims 201, 203–204, 205, 206, 207, 208; sufferings 202, 204–205, 207, 208
Vištica, O. 72, 76–77, 79

Wakeham, P. 151
Walker, I. 247
Wallworth, L. 213
Walsh, A. 153, 154–155, 159
war commemorations 36–37, 68; Australia 11, 56–57, 58, 60, 67;

Australia in the Great War 11, 57, 61–64, 67, 68; Russia 27, 33, 36–37; *WWI: Love and Sorrow* 11, 57, 64–65, 66–68
Waterton, E. 8
Watson, S. 8
Weber, L. R. 267, 276
Welcome Wall, Immigration Museum, Australia 213
Wertsch, J. 144, 145
Wetherell, M. 8, 27, 56, 59, 109, 173, 267, 269, 276; affect 75, 167, 215; affective economies 166–167; affective practices 109, 165, 166–167, 216, 217, 224, 225–226, 284
Wevers, L. 270
white guilt 15, 234, 235
Whitehead, C. 82
Whiteread, R. 88
Wiedenhoft-Murphy, W. A. 164, 171
Williams, R. 6
Wilson, R. 149
Witcomb, A. 14, 59–60, 127, 197
witnessing 231, 242
The Workshops Rail Museum, Ipswich, Australia 292–293; *Living Memory* module 282, 286, 293–295, 299
World History and Citizenship (history textbook) 257, 259
WWI: Love and Sorrow (Museum Victoria, Australia) 11, 57, 64–65, 66–68

Young, I. M. 234–235

Zembylas, M. 14, 230, 232–233, 247
Zerubavel, E. 144